THE BHĀGAVATA PURĀṆA

THE BHĀGAVATA PURĀṆA

Selected Readings

Ravi M. Gupta and Kenneth R. Valpey

COLUMBIA UNIVERSITY PRESS
New York

Columbia University Press
Publishers Since 1893
New York   Chichester, West Sussex
cup.columbia.edu
Copyright © 2017 Columbia University Press
All rights reserved

Library of Congress Cataloging-in-Publication Data
Names: Gupta, Ravi M. (Ravi Mohan), 1982– editor. | Valpey, Kenneth Russell, 1950– editor.
Title: The Bhāgavata Purāṇa : selected translations / Edited by Ravi M. Gupta and Kenneth R. Valpey.
Description: New York : Columbia University Press, 2016. | Includes bibliographical references and index. | Translated from Sanskrit.
Identifiers: LCCN 2016000353 (print) | LCCN 2016040118 (ebook) |
ISBN 9780231169004 (cloth : alk. paper) | ISBN 9780231169011 (pbk.) |
ISBN 9780231542340 (electronic)
Classification: LCC BL1140.4.B434 E5 2016 (print) | LCC BL1140.4.B434 (ebook) |
DDC 294.5/925—dc23
LC record available at https://lccn.loc.gov/2016000353

Columbia University Press books are printed on permanent
and durable acid-free paper.
Printed in the United States of America

COVER DESIGN: Noah Arlow

COVER IMAGE AND FRONTISPIECE: Detail from "Krishna Welcoming Sudama, from a Bhagavata Purana Manuscript." Color and gold on paper, c. 1700, Pahari School. Freer Gallery of Art and Arthur M. Sackler Gallery, Smithsonian Institution: Purchase—Charles Lang Freer Endowment, F1930.25

To Shaunaka and Keshava,
and all our friends at the Oxford Centre for Hindu Studies

satāṁ prasaṅgān mama vīrya-saṁvido
bhavanti hṛt-karṇa-rasāyanāḥ kathāḥ
taj-joṣaṇād āśv apavarga-vartmani
śraddhā ratir bhaktir anukramiṣyati

In the company of good souls,
discourses about my prowess
become the elixir narratives for ear and heart.
By delighting in them,
confidence, attraction, and devotion will quickly follow
for one on the path of freedom.

—Bhāgavata Purāṇa 3.25.25 (Kapila to Devahūti)

CONTENTS

FOREWORD

C. Mackenzie Brown,
Jennie Farris Railey King Professor of Religion, Trinity University

The Bhāgavata Purāṇa is perhaps the most popular of all the great Hindu Purāṇas—sacred dialogic narratives revealing ancient happenings that, for their followers, are relevant for today's living. Until very recent times, the Purāṇas have not been as well known in the West as the four Vedas and their affiliated Upaniṣads, but the Purāṇas surpass the latter two revelatory texts in terms of their everyday impact on religious practice. The various Purāṇas are embraced by one or another school of Hinduism, such as the Śaivas, Śāktas, and Vaiṣṇavas. They provide the spiritual seekers in these schools with answers to what is real, what is false, and in light of what is real, what ideals to follow.

The Purāṇas themselves at times make the claim that they are the equivalent of the Vedas, or a "fifth Veda," but, unlike the Vedas, they are, in the strictest sense, open to all regardless of class, caste, or gender. The Bhāgavata Purāṇa makes precisely such a claim and promises to offer everyone the means for liberation from the suffering-infused round of birth and death. This ongoing round is the fundamental predicament of humankind assumed by the text and its followers. By reading and listening to the text, with its many stories of the cosmic and terrestrial exploits of Krishna, one can attain the liberating state of Krishna consciousness.

The Bhāgavata Purāṇa is one of the foremost sacred texts of the Gauḍīya Vaiṣṇavas, founded by Caitanya Mahāprabhu, the great sixteenth-century Bengali saint. An important contemporary branch of this group is the International Society of Krishna Consciousness (ISKCON), founded by Swami Bhaktivedanta Prabhupāda in 1966 in New York. For these followers, what is real is Krishna, and the highest goal is to reflect and meditate constantly on Krishna and to perform his service—that is, to develop total devotion, or bhakti, to Krishna.

The present volume by Ravi M. Gupta and Kenneth R. Valpey provides a useful introduction to the Bhāgavata, discussing its relation to older sacred literature, especially the Vedas, Brahmasūtra, and Mahābhārata, its assimilation of various philosophical schools of thought such as the Sāṁkhya, Vedānta, and Yoga, its rhetorical style and structure, and its major devotional themes. The heart of the volume is a translation of selected passages constituting approximately fifteen hundred of the Bhāgavata's more than fourteen thousand verse couplets, with explanatory endnotes that often incorporate the interpretive insights of numerous commentators. The authors connect these translated passages with succinct summaries, offering a sense of the Bhāgavata as a whole. Further, the volume provides four "commentarial excursions" that give a taste of the rich and complex commentarial tradition and its various, alternative interpretations of the text, drawing from the famous Advaitic commentary of Śrīdhara Svāmī and other, more dualistic commentaries of the Vaiṣṇava theologians. A glossary assists the reader unfamiliar with basic Sanskrit terms.

It should be noted that there is a companion volume, a set of scholarly essays on the Bhāgavata, edited by Gupta and Valpey, that provide in-depth analysis of significant issues in the Bhāgavata that are of universal relevance, such as the problem of suffering and God's alleged impartiality. This question, for instance, is raised in Book One, 8:28–29, for which explanatory notes are provided that give, among other things, Swami Bhaktivedanta's interpretive resolution of the theodical problem by saying God's grace is like the sun that shines on all, but some people prefer darkness—those who oppose service to Krishna. The notes make reference to an essay in the companion volume that deals more extensively with the Bhāgavata's theodicy and concludes that Krishna sometimes, to favor his devotees, showers them with misfortune to turn their hearts toward him and away from the world. While the Bhāgavata's perspective may not convince those who do not look forward to an afterlife, this volume and its companion make the text come alive, with issues that inspire reflection, if not always agreement.

The volume is clearly a work of scholarly dedication. Gupta and Valpey set for themselves the task of rendering "an accessible yet academically sound translation," surely a difficult task for a work as expansive and complex as the Bhāgavata Purāṇa. The authors were well equipped to handle the task, both having received a doctoral degree from Oxford University in religious studies and completed their dissertations on aspects of Gauḍīya Vaiṣṇavism. Gupta holds the Charles Redd Chair of Religious Studies at Utah State University, Logan. Valpey is a permanent research fellow for the Oxford Centre for Hindu Studies. So we may now ask, how well did they succeed in their scholarly and pedagogical tasks?

Before answering this query, let me raise certain questions I tell my own students they need to ask, as critical readers, whenever they approach a text: what is the background of the author or authors, who is their audience, and what are their assumptions and purpose? With this book, I and my students would note the academic background of the authors. We would also recognize that aside from their scholarly and pedagogical aspirations in composing this book, the authors are motivated by various spiritual aspirations.

The subtle nuancing of ethical and theological issues throughout the text from a Krishnaite perspective reflects the authors' existential concerns with the right way to lead a life. They acknowledge that they hope to inspire others to undertake "a lifelong exploration of the Bhāgavata that goes much beyond the pages of this book." This is a natural objective for Valpey and Gupta, active members of ISKCON. Valpey has been a student of the Bhāgavata for forty years and is a Gaudiya Vaishnava theologian. Gupta has served on ISKCON's Interfaith Commission and on the executive board for the Ministry of Educational Development.

The relevance of the scholarly and religious backgrounds of our authors becomes clear with one further question I raise with my students: who best speaks for a religious tradition, scholars, religious leaders, or lay practitioners? Clearly, Gupta and Valpey attempt to combine the roles of scholar and religious leader. But what exactly is involved in these roles? The late scholar of Chinese religions and ritual, Catherine Bell, in an insightful lecture on "Who Owns Religion? Religion and the Messiness of History," notes the three general approaches to engaging with a religious tradition just mentioned—of scholars, of religious leaders, and of practitioners. Bell cautions us that these are not exclusive categories. I concentrate here on the first two approaches, the most relevant to our understanding of this volume and its authors.

Bell focuses on the scholar of religion as a historian. Religion scholars today, unlike the Western historians of the eighteenth and nineteenth centuries, are no longer dismissive of non-Western traditions and tend rather "to see themselves as champions of the tradition" (Bell 2001, 5).

Religious leaders, on the other hand, perhaps in part as a reaction to the legacy of eighteenth- and nineteenth-century historians, have tended "to see scholars as trying to undermine religion" (ibid.).

But even today, historians of religion raise questions that may discomfort the devotee. The historian often questions, or even denies, that there is some timeless, eternal truth revealed in a tradition, applying a radical historicizing method that emphasizes dissent, fracture, and change within traditions. Religious leaders have a different task and method. They "have the task of formulating a religious persuasion based on revelation, unique insight, or a sacred story." They approach the task in two ways. First, "they present a body of doctrines and beliefs as a timeless and coherent whole." And second, they "take pains to show that this holism is tightly tied to the key sacred events of the past." In this manner, history becomes less important, while leaders take great pains to present "a set of ideas . . . as a timeless body of 'truths' relevant today and as nothing less than 'the truth' revealed in the past" (6).

These features are frequently reflected in the volume at hand, as Gupta and Valpey nicely argue for the relevance today of the truths revealed by Krishna in the past. Thus the concerns of lay devotees and practitioners are well met. At the same time, scholars will find the fine introductory essay, notes, and commentarial excursions helpful and insightful. And non-Hindu students who are willing to invest intellectual energy to overcome the hurdle—so common in many Sanskritic narrative texts—of strange and lengthy Sanskrit names will find in this one volume, as promised by the authors, a delightful taste of the Bhāgavata as a whole, with the translated sections very readable and contemporary. As a non-Hindu Purāṇic scholar and teacher of the Hindu tradition on the undergraduate level, I find the present volume to be an academically inspiring and insightful work that promises to be a valuable text to use in the classroom.

As Bell concludes, by appreciating the different approaches that scholars, religious leaders, and practitioners take toward a tradition, or a revelatory text, scholars and religious leaders can learn not to talk past one another but to see more clearly the various goals and aspirations of each. Echoing Bell's conclusion, Gupta himself declared in a 2014 lecture at Princeton, "Clearly, both the practitioner's and the scholar's perspectives are useful—no, *necessary*—for understanding a religious tradition." Those outside the tradition can learn to see the lived and living nature of a tradition, and those within better how to configure their tradition within the global context. The interaction between traditions, at its best, helps us to share what is common, to influence one another, and where there are genuine differences, the historical record can play a mediating role, as it stands on relatively neutral ground and provides a needed corrective to isolated traditions. In this volume, we see the beginnings of such an endeavor of mutual understanding on the part of the scholar-devotees responsible for it.

PREFACE

Sacred texts lie at the very heart of human history, where they are much more than pieces of paper bound between covers. Sacred texts are dynamic literary creations, possessing extraordinary beauty and power that can be applied for a variety of purposes. The Bhagavata Purāṇa, in particular, has been recited orally for generations, copied in hundreds of manuscripts, retold in dozens of languages, performed onstage, painted on canvas, debated in public assemblies, employed in daily worship, and venerated as an object of worship. The Bhāgavata has been used to incite action and facilitate meditation, to establish religious institutions and inspire devotional fervor. Most importantly, the text has given meaning and direction in the lives of countless individuals—philosophers and singers; religious leaders and laypersons; men, women, and children.

The Bhāgavata Purāṇa can rightly be called a classic—a text that emerged out of India but belongs to the world. Professor David Tracy, a theologian at the University of Chicago, has described what it means to be a classic:

> To understand the concrete we always need good examples. Among good examples, some stand out as paradigmatic. Among good examples of written texts, the truly exemplary ones are named classics. The classics, therefore, are exemplary examples. . . . In their production there is also the following paradox: though highly particular in origin and expression, classics have the possibility of being universal in their effect. . . . We can drift half-asleep through nonclassic period pieces. We cannot with the classics. Indeed, the temptation to domesticate

> all reality is a temptation that any classic text will resist. The classics resist our engrained laziness and self-satisfaction. Their claim to attention must be heeded if understanding is not to slide into either domesticating similarity or mere sameness. . . . Classics, whether texts, symbols, events, persons, or rituals, command our attention. (Tracy 1994, 12, 15)

Indeed, the book you hold in your hands is evidence of the Bhāgavata's continuing ability to "command our attention" and speak to us across cultural and linguistic boundaries. In recent years we have seen growing interest in the Bhāgavata Purāṇa, evident in the steady stream of books, articles, public recitations, and even television serials that draw from, or respond to, the text. In the present work, we have sought to render an accessible yet academically sound translation that includes important passages from all twelve books of the Bhāgavata. We hope that these "selected readings" will provide readers with an informed sense of the work as a whole. We encourage our readers to give careful consideration to the introduction, where we explain the various facets of this translation and how best to make use of them.

The idea for this book came as something of a surprise, for we did not set out to translate the Bhāgavata. Rather, our intent was to bring together some fine, recent scholarship on the Bhāgavata and thus revitalize academic interest in this sacred classic. We wanted to create a "companion" to the Bhāgavata Purāṇa, and this effort resulted in a volume published in 2013 by Columbia University Press called *The Bhāgavata Purāṇa: Sacred Text and Living Tradition*. It was our editor at Columbia, Wendy Lochner, who came to us and asked, "You are creating a 'companion' book, but what exactly would this be a companion *to*? Is there a manageable, academic translation of the Bhāgavata Purāṇa out there that is accessible to students and scholars?" And so the idea for this book was born, and we remain ever grateful to Wendy and her outstanding team at Columbia for their continuous encouragement, patience, and support as our translations took shape. The two books together form a happy (and, we hope, useful) pair of primary- and secondary-source readings.

As with our first volume, this book has been a collaborative effort between the two of us, with significant input from others. We explain some of the dynamics of translation as a collaborative process in the introduction; but here we want to register our heartfelt appreciation for each other's expertise, thoughtfulness, patience, and cheerful companionship that made the process of writing this book a joyous affair. Regular online meetings were complemented by monthlong intensive retreats, where we could work together in person to review each other's translations. Our only regret now is that this work has come to an end, at least for the time being. We hope that something of the book's richness as a product of our collaboration will be experienced by our readers.

The publication of our two books with Columbia University Press represents the completion of the first phase of the Bhāgavata Purāṇa Research Project of the Oxford Centre for Hindu Studies. Indeed, we have dedicated this book to our friends at the Oxford Centre for Hindu Studies, not least to its director, Shaunaka Rishi Das, and to his dear wife, the late Keshava Kiernan. We wish to underline our sense of gratitude to the Oxford Centre for Hindu Studies for providing the academic home for this project—one that has been and continues to be a home in a strong sense of the term.

In fact, the story of this book begins—much before either of us translated our first verse—with those who introduced us to the beauty and challenge of the Sanskrit language. Our teachers over the years include Dr. James Benson, Professors Sally and Robert Goldman, Dr. Nandini Iyer, Professor M. Narasimhachary, Dr. Howard Resnick, and Mr. Gary Thomas.

We are grateful for our institutional support: the College of William and Mary and Utah State University provided summer research funds and office support; and the Chinese University of Hong Kong, Department of Cultural and Religious Studies, also facilitated our work.

Several individuals provided invaluable editorial help: The late Professor M. Narasimhachary (University of Madras), who offered corrections and suggestions for difficult Bhāgavata passages, is deeply missed. Dr. Rembert Lutjeharms, of the Oxford Centre for Hindu Studies, helped with Sanskrit commentary on challenging verses, and Professor Shrikant Bahulkar (Bhandarkar Oriental Research Institute, University of Pune) provided guidance on translating Sanskrit technical terms. Giriraja Swami, Keshava Kiernen, and Chaitanya Charan Das read through parts of our translation and suggested many improvements. Nina Cavazos did the painstaking work of cataloguing variant readings of our selected verses, reformatting the chapters, and making suggestions to improve the clarity of our prose.

Our gratitude goes to several others who have assisted in important ways: Andriy Panasyuk helped us select commentarial passages for translation. Professor Graham M. Schweig (Christopher Newport University) advised us on preparing the book proposal and made valuable suggestions for our treatment of Book Ten. Dr. Neeraja Poddar and Nina Cavazos helped us procure beautiful Bhāgavata-related images from their respective museums. Lior Shlomo facilitated our work with the Bhāgavata critical edition by digitally scanning relevant portions, and Maja Vrieling gave ever-ready managerial assistance.

Our thanks also go to the anonymous peer reviewers for their carefully considered suggestions. And our deep gratitude extends to Professor C. Mackenzie Brown (Trinity University) for contributing his thoughtful foreword.

We also wish to convey heartfelt thanks to the Gupta family for their endless patience and support throughout this project, and to others who hosted us and invited us to home-cooked meals during our collaborative retreats: the Koć family and friends, including Marta Turowska, Andrzej Turowski, and Marcin Krawczyk, in Łubno, Poland; Miroslav Perčun and friends in Površje, Slovenia; and several friends in Pula, Croatia, including Mirjana and Neven Marinelić, Adisa and Dino Muhović, Marija and Emir Komić, and Iva Milovan Delić and Velibor Delić.

To all those who have supported us on this journey, we offer our deepest gratitude.

RAVI M. GUPTA AND KENNETH R. VALPEY

THE BHĀGAVATA PURĀṆA

INTRODUCTION

nigama-kalpa-taror galitaṁ phalaṁ
śuka-mukhād amṛta-drava-saṁyutam
pibata bhāgavatam rasam ālayaṁ
muhur aho rasikā bhuvi bhāvukāḥ

The fruit of the Vedic desire tree, containing ambrosial juice, has issued from the mouth of Śuka. O knowers of *rasa* and people of taste in the world! Drink again and again this reservoir of *rasa*—the Bhāgavata.
(Bhāgavata Purāṇa 1.1.3)

THE FRUIT OF THE VEDIC DESIRE TREE

With these words, the Bhāgavata Purāṇa proclaims its position as the best and most relishable of the complex collection of texts known as, or associated by extension with, the Veda—the canonical literature of brahmanical cultures in the South Asian subcontinent since several centuries before the Common Era. What is it about the Bhāgavata Purāṇa that inspires such vigorous confidence in itself? Why does it offer such an eager invitation for its listeners and readers, even dismissing alternatives (in the prior verse) with the rhetorical flourish "What is the use of other books?" And how has the Bhāgavata come to enjoy a popularity rivaling that of the Rāmāyaṇa to the present day?[1] Addressing these questions will help us appreciate the place of this text both in Indian literary history and in wider contemporary cultures of bhakti—devotional practices dedicated to a supreme being or supreme divinity.

The Bhāgavata's self-confidence, reverberating throughout its twelve books of more than fourteen thousand verse couplets, is in large part rooted in its sense of urgency to effectively convey its message of bhakti, a message that has been carefully passed down over time—as ripe mangoes are harvested with care, brought hand to hand from tree to ground. In Book Two, the sage Śaunaka urges Sūta (Ugraśravās) to speak the Bhāgavata as he had previously heard it from the preeminent sage Śuka.[2] His plea is insistent: "With every rising and setting of the sun our lives are becoming shorter. Not so, as long as our time is engaged with narrations about him whose glory is supreme" (Bhāgavata Purāṇa 2.3.17). All the varied life-forms, Śaunaka continues, cannot be compared to human life, which alone affords the unique opportunity and capacity to become absorbed in the Bhāgavata's higher-order vision of reality. To miss this chance is to live like dull trees, breathe like blacksmith's bellows, eat and procreate like beasts, and to voice praises of unworthy persons (2.3.18–19).

Completely opposite to such unfortunate persons are the "knowers of *rasa* and people of taste"—connoisseurs of the aesthetically pleasing and world-transcending relationships between Bhagavān (the adorable Lord)[3] and his devotees, the *bhaktas* or *bhāgavatas*.[4] And while at first glance the Bhāgavata Purāṇa's appeal may appear exclusivistic in tenor, its potential for reaching any and all persons—far beyond the standard brahmanical scope of qualification—is frequently suggested throughout the text. Anyone and everyone, the Bhāgavata assures, can learn to become a *bhāgavata* of the highest order simply by hearing (or reading) the Bhāgavata.

Presenting itself as the "fruit of the Vedic desire tree," the Bhāgavata authenticates itself through its organic connection with the Vedic corpus (various elements of which it will echo and rework into its own message—more on this later); at the same time, it claims preeminence as the Veda's culmination. As the most desirable and therefore interesting and useful "fruit" of the Vedic "desire tree," it contains within it the "seed" of that corpus, promising for its hearers or readers reproduction and fruition of the Vedas' deepest import, which affords the complete removal, or "uprooting" (1.1.2), of all misfortune. Just how the Bhāgavata proposes to realize its lofty claim is indicated in the second chapter of Book One (1.2.17): "Hearing and speaking about Krishna is virtuous. Indeed, he is the well-wisher of good persons who listen to his narratives, and, abiding deep in their hearts, he drives away what is inauspicious."

Clearly the Bhāgavata's main attraction—over the centuries and currently—is its representation of the life, character, and adventures of Krishna. Catching the imagination of countless generations by his mischievous and attractive charms and triumphs, young Krishna, darling of his foster parents, Nanda and Yaśodā, shines forth as God himself, the very embodiment of ultimacy from whom all existence has its being and upon whom all beings depend. This is the divine slayer of demons sent by the evil Kaṁsa, the famed lifter of Mount Govardhana, and, most especially, the beloved flute player and artful dancer with the young cowherdesses (*gopīs* or *gopikās*) in the nocturnal *rasa* dance. The details of these activities are elaborated most fully in Book Ten. And, importantly, to bring Krishna into the sharpest possible focus, the Bhāgavata's remaining eleven books carefully build a rich frame of interlocking narratives, eulogies, and didactic passages, each successively expanding on prior portions, to make the tenth book the center of a grand textual *maṇḍala*—a circular graphic figure that facilitates meditation.

Strangely, but significantly, while the Bhāgavata's center of attraction and meditation is Krishna, as the primordial and quintessential form of Bhagavān, the text's outermost narrative frame, beginning in Book One, takes as its point of departure Krishna's *absence* from the world, prompting Sūta to reassure his audience (1.3.43), "Now that Krishna has gone to his own realm along with dharma, knowledge, and the like, this Purāṇa is the sun for those whose vision has been lost in this dark age."[5]

Thus the Bhāgavata Purāṇa, having initially identified itself with the authority of the Vedic canon, here identifies itself explicitly with the canonical Purāṇas. In so doing, it presents itself as collective memory, recovering and making sense of all that its compilers considered worthy of preservation for future generations of its community.[6] Like other Purāṇas, the Bhāgavata draws together into a cosmic vision of history narratives of world creation and its successive development, acts of patriarchs, accounts of cosmic progenitors (Manus), and records of royal dynasties, along with a variety of instructional and eulogistic passages dedicated to a particular sacred place or deity.[7] Yet one of the Bhāgavata's special features as a Purāṇa is its sustained attention to accounts of the several *avatāras* of Vishnu or Krishna—divine descents who break into the temporal world from beyond it to perform special salvific acts. Each *avatāra*'s story serves to enrich one's sense of Bhagavān's greatness, and each story serves to point "inward" to the *maṇḍala*'s center, Krishna, reminding one of their source.

Most typically, the Bhāgavata's narrators of *avatāras*' stories are sages and ascetics who, in their efforts to enlighten one or another king, articulate the Bhāgavata's theological and philosophical reflections. Drawing on the classical schools of thought (*darśanas*), the Bhāgavata reweaves them into its own tapestry of propositional expositions. In particular, the schools of Sāṁkhya, Vedānta, and Yoga are strongly represented and infused with its bhakti vision; but also, to lesser degrees, one can find allusions to Nyāya, Vaiśeṣika, and Mīmāṁsā traditions, as well as to the "heterodox" schools of Jain, Buddhist, and Ājīvika thought.

It may well be the Bhāgavata's "catholic" perspective, combined with its finely tuned inclusion and summary of Purāṇic themes, integrated into its longing vision for the singularly beloved, absent deity Krishna, that has earned for it such a high status among sacred texts across India. Indeed, the uncertainty of claims regarding the Bhāgavata's geographical provenance (Bryant 2002) and the wide variety of scripts represented in Bhāgavata manuscripts are indicative of its wide distribution throughout the Indian subcontinent, at least by the twelfth century. These factors may have, in turn, contributed to the raising of the Bhāgavata's status from being one among several Purāṇas to being seen as authenticating the otherwise most revered scripture, the Veda. Indeed, as Christopher Minkowski argues, by the time of Nīlakaṇṭha, the well-known seventeenth-century commentator on the Mahābhārata, the Bhāgavata Purāṇa had attained such authority that it was used to support and justify statements in the Ṛgveda. This was quite the reverse of Purāṇas' traditional position as requiring the support of Vedic texts (*śruti*—that which is heard or revealed) to be recognized as proper tradition (*smṛti*—that which is remembered) (Minkowski 2005; see also Holdrege 2006).

THE BHĀGAVATA'S COMMENTARIES

As noted, a distinctive feature of the Bhāgavata Purāṇa's reception history is the remarkable attention it has received by commentators. Being indicative of the authority enjoyed by the Bhāgavata, commentarial treatment (usually structured as "running commentary"—verse by verse) has lent additional authority for particular bhakti schools, especially as each commentator's explanatory remarks tend to reflect his own school affiliation. In the present volume, we refer to a small group of prominent commentators (whose commentaries, except for the final one immediately following, are accessible to us in printed form through the Bhāgavata edition of Kṛṣṇaśaṅkara Śāstrī; the commentary of Bhaktivedanta is from his English translation and commentary of the Bhāgavata Purāṇa; see Bhaktivedanta and Goswami 1993). These commentators are Śrīdhara Svāmī (probably fourteenth century; referred to henceforth as Śrīdhara); Vīrarāghava Ācārya (probably fourteenth century; henceforth Vīrarāghava); Vijayadhvaja Tīrtha (early fifteenth century; henceforth

Vijayadhvaja); Vallabhācārya (late fifteenth to early sixteenth centuries; henceforth Vallabha); Jīva Gosvāmī (mid to late sixteenth century; henceforth Jīva); Viśvanātha Cakravartī (early eighteenth century; henceforth Viśvanātha); Giridharalāla (early nineteenth century; henceforth Giridhara); Vaṁśīdhara (late nineteenth century); and A. C. Bhaktivedanta Swami Prabhupāda (1896–1977; henceforth Bhaktivedanta).

Śrīdhara is, by far, the most widely known, respected, and quoted commentator on the Bhāgavata, inspiring others to write subcommentaries on his work, the *Bhāvārtha-dīpikā* (Little lamp on the straightforward meaning). Apparently a follower of Śaṅkara's Advaita school of Vedānta, Śrīdhara typically wrote relatively succinct comments, offering straightforward clarification of difficult Sanskrit words and passages, on nearly all verses of the entire twelve books of the Bhāgavata. Despite his Advaita affiliation, his commentary is largely devotional in character, such that many subsequent Vaiṣṇava commentators (who have been more or less opposed to Śaṅkara's Advaita philosophy) have honored Śrīdhara's work, presenting their commentaries as dependent on or following after his. Vaṁśīdhara's work, the *Bhāvārtha-dīpikā Prakāśa* (Elucidation on the *Bhāvārtha-dīpikā*) is, in particular, explicitly titled as a subcommentary on Śrīdhara's commentary, although Vaṁśīdhara is known to also refer to others' commentaries, in particular the commentary of Viśvanātha.

Vīrarāghava and Vijayadhvaja are, respectively, affiliated with the Śrīvaiṣṇava school founded by Rāmānuja (eleventh century) and the (Vaiṣṇava) Mādhva or Tattvavāda school, founded by Madhva (thirteenth century). The marked differences in their Vedāntic viewpoints (Viśiṣṭādvaita and Dvaita, respectively) are occasionally apparent in their commentaries. Vīrarāghava's commentary is titled *Bhāgavata-candra Candrikā* (Moonlight on the moonlike Bhāgavata), and that of Vijayadhvaja is *Pada-ratnāvalī* (The jeweled necklace of verses). In his *Subodhinī* (Right understanding) commentary, Vallabha, founder of the Śuddhādvaita school of Vaiṣṇava Vedānta and a major tradition of bhakti centered in Vṛndāvana, generally provides comparatively lengthy (and often quite complex) explanations of those portions of the text on which he wrote (namely, Books One, Two, Three, Ten, and part of Eleven). Vallabha's follower, Giridhara, provides a simplified subcommentary to Vallabha's in his *Bāla-prabodhinī* (Simplified understanding) and also comments on the entire Bhāgavata.

Jīva, Viśvanātha, and Bhaktivedanta all belonged to the Gauḍīya (or Caitanya) Vaiṣṇava tradition founded by Śrī Caitanya (1486–1534). Since

Jīva concentrated his attention on a systematic theology based on the Bhāgavata Purāṇa in his six-part treatise the *Bhāgavata-sandarbha*, his running commentary (called the *Krama-sandarbha*—"Running treatise") tends to be very brief. Viśvanātha, largely following both Śrīdhara and Jīva, offers useful and interesting insights in his work the *Sārārtha Darśinī* (Revealer of essential meaning) that we, as translators, often found relevant and enriching for our understanding. Finally, the most recent commentator we consulted and occasionally refer to in this volume is Bhaktivedanta. His English running commentary (which he referred to as his "elaborate purports") holds prominence in the story of the Bhāgavata's "migration" to the West (see chapter 12 in Gupta and Valpey 2013). It was written to be accessible to non-Indian readers, covering the first nine books and the first thirteen chapters of Book Ten.

In addition, there are commentaries that deal exclusively with Book Ten. In the present volume we have occasion to refer to those of Sanātana Gosvāmī (sixteenth century; the *Bṛhad-vaiṣṇava Toṣanī* [The greater satisfaction of the Vaiṣṇavas]) and of Baladeva Vidyābhūṣana (eighteenth century; the *Vaiṣṇava-nandinī* [The pleaser of the Vaiṣṇavas])—both theologians of the Gauḍīya Vaiṣṇava school. Sanātana, a contemporary follower of Caitanya, was Jīva's uncle. Baladeva, a disciple of Viśvanātha, is especially known for his full commentary on the Brahmasūtra.

The few commentators mentioned here are the most prominent among those who have composed Sanskrit commentaries on the Bhāgavata Purāṇa. There are said to be many more Sanskrit commentaries (Rocher 1986, 149, citing Tagare), plus several Sanskrit summaries; further, there are the translations and adaptations of the Bhāgavata in Indian vernacular languages and a veritable host of commentaries also in Indian vernacular languages. But also important for us to note is the fully alive and vibrant oral tradition of Bhāgavata recitation and commentary taking place today in India and, since recent decades, worldwide. These recitations and discourses take place in all scales of assembly, from a few Indian villagers sitting under a tree, to a modest gathering in a temple courtyard, to thousands gathered before a well-known reciter-narrator (*kathākār*) in a massive tent (see chapter 11 in Gupta and Valpey 2013). In the course of these events, typically speakers are given relatively free reign to expound, amplify, and embellish the Bhāgavata text as they see fit, often weaving into their presentations extemporaneous commentary on current events or critiquing what they regard as improper views and practices in light of the Bhāgavata's teachings. And all such oral performance points to and reiterates the Purāṇic character of the written text—its dialogical structure and its own commentarial feature, whereby earlier texts as well as what might be called common human experience receive attention in the Bhāgavata's explications of its devotional perspective.

THE BHĀGAVATA'S COMPLEX STRUCTURE

We have alluded to the Bhāgavata's identity as a Purāṇa, an important feature of which is its multilevel dialogical structure. For readers new to this genre, and to the Bhāgavata in particular, it will be helpful to look briefly at how this structure works, after which we should take other structural features into account, to more easily navigate through the text.

Potentially confusing is the layered arrangement of dialogues, in which a speaker (typically Śuka, the main reciter, addressing his interlocutor, King Parīkṣit) quotes an "earlier" speaker (for example, Nārada, addressing King Yudhiṣṭhira, Parīkṣit's uncle, in a dialogue understood to have taken place earlier and elsewhere), who may in turn quote yet another speaker. Two to three such layers are typically operative simultaneously, but there is one instance, in Book Seven, chapters 1 and 2, in which Śuka, responding to a question by Parīkṣit, quotes Nārada, who quotes the demon Hiraṇyakaśipu, who, in turn, quotes the lord of death, Yamarāja (appearing as a young boy), as he instructs the relatives of a recently deceased king, Suyajña. And, finally, to illustrate his point to Suyajña's relatives about mortality, to which all living beings are subjected, Yamarāja "quotes" a male *kuliṅga* bird as it had lamented the loss of its mate. The cumulative effect of these layered discourses is twofold. First, the compounding of voices serves to strengthen the message delivered; and second, one is left with the sense that one cannot, and indeed need not, trace out the origin of the message. Moving from outer to inner frames of speech and narrative, the listener or reader is drawn backward in time, always pointed toward time before time, or to absolute atemporality (see chapter 2 in Gupta and Valpey 2013).

Another structurally related element to be aware of in navigating the text, already mentioned, is the spatial metaphor of the *maṇḍala*, or circular pattern of narrative content. Although it is not until the tenth of the Bhāgavata's twelve books that the "center" of the circle is reached, the sheer length of Book Ten, constituting more than one-third of the entire text, attests to its importance. Moreover, it is in Book Ten that the most celebrated portion, what later tradition refers to as Krishna's *rāsa-līlā*, takes place (chapters 29–33). In this episode, Krishna meets and dances in a circle formation with his several cowherdess beloveds, the *gopīs*. When he plays upon his flute, the *gopīs* abandon their homes and family duties, risking public censure to answer Krishna's call.

Along with occasional brief allusions to the *maṇḍala* motif elsewhere in the Bhāgavata, circularity is also prominent in temporal terms, as repeating cycles of variously extending periods.[8] Book One's concern with the onset of the Kali age—the present, most degenerated of four cosmic periods understood to cycle through the life of the universe—returns in Book Twelve to describe the Kali age in detail. And there are further "layers" of time's movement in lesser and greater scales, resonant with the layered character of the text's dialogues: on the microcosmic scale is the steady expending of Parīkṣit's life span as he listens to Śuka's recitation over his seven remaining days; on a "mesocosmic" scale is the sense of time's passage through several lives (typically of royal dynasties) and the ritual marking of time's passage in elaborate fire rituals (*yajñas*); and there are the vastly longer, macrocosmic lives of the Manus, fourteen of whom are said to live successively during a single "day" of the demiurge Brahmā (whose "day" is said to extend over 4.3 billion earth years, and whose life duration is said to be one hundred "years" of 365 such "days"). From Book Four, the Bhāgavata can be read as "a day in the life" of Brahmā in which, one after another, the Manus and their descendants appear. And as particular *avatāras* or *bhāgavatas* appear—typically as descendants of one or another Manu—the Bhāgavata reciter pauses his dynastic chronology to elaborate on their stories.

Indeed, the sense of circular form and cyclical temporal motion discernible in the Bhāgavata is complicated by elements of linearity and progression. Individual lives progress from childhood to maturity; Vedic rituals are performed beginning to end (or sometimes they are interrupted, as in the story of Dakṣa's *yajña* in Book Four). Another helpful image would be that of a spiral form, in which themes that are introduced briefly in the Bhāgavata's early chapters are revisited later, with increasing degrees of dilation. This motif is especially apparent in the presentation of *avatāras*: whereas Book One, chapter 3, lists *avatāras* with the briefest possible description of them, Book Two, chapter 7, again lists the *avatāras*, but with somewhat more description. Books Three through Nine extend these descriptions and narrations considerably (for some, not all, of the previously mentioned *avatāras*), ending with the full account of Krishna in the tenth and eleventh books.

Again, the procession of *avatāras* points to another sort of progression: On the one hand, all the cyclical temporal units discussed in the Bhāgavata remind listeners or readers of life's repetitions in the mundane sphere, repetitions that largely involve personal or collective tribulations. On the other hand, the *avatāras'* appearances are also understood to be cyclically repeated, over immense periods; and since the *avatāras* provide mortals with the opportunity to permanently end the cycle of repeated births and deaths, they open one to the supertemporal cadences—the divinely musical rhythms—of Krishna's acts with his ever-liberated friends, culminating in the exhilarating rhythms of Krishna's perpetual *rasa* dance. Yet the Bhāgavata suggests, in its final verses of the twelfth book, a listener or reader may choose to return back to the very beginning of Book One. Becoming a "knower of *rasa* and person of taste," one might choose to simply continue to "drink again and again this reservoir of *rasa*" that is the Bhāgavata.

THE BHĀGAVATA'S MAJOR THEMES

The very name "Bhāgavata" indicates that this Purāṇa is about Bhagavān—the glorious Lord. The Bhāgavata leaves little doubt that the supreme divinity is a person—namely, Krishna, who assumes multiple forms, *avatāras*, to address the needs of the world and engage with his devotees, as previously discussed. At the same time, this supreme person is the origin of the world, ever present in all things and in all beings. He is perceived by the accomplished yogi through meditation, by the learned sage through contemplation, and by the righteous worker through the performance of ritual and social duties. Nevertheless, it is the loving devotee whom the Bhāgavata regards as the highest exemplar, for devotion (bhakti) has the power to intimately connect the human being with God.

The Reversing Power of Bhakti

In the Bhāgavata Purāṇa, bhakti for Bhagavān is both the means and goal trumping all others. This message is directly stated at regular intervals by Sūta or Śuka or by devotees as they offer encomia to Vishnu. But the point comes across far more powerfully through the Purāṇa's narratives than it ever could through theological statements alone. Indeed, the text seems to set up each narrative with the express purpose of making this point clear to the reader.[9]

Two well-studied examples are the stories of Vṛtra, the devoted demon, and Nṛsiṁha, the man-lion *avatāra*. The former account tells of how Indra, in a fit of rage, kills his teacher, Viśvarūpa. Viśvarūpa's father then creates a demon to kill Indra and avenge his son's death. That demon is Vṛtra, but he comes with a twist: despite being intent on slaying Indra, Vṛtra is in fact a devotee of Vishnu at heart. When Indra becomes demoralized during battle, Vṛtra encourages him to continue fighting by teaching him about his dharma and destiny. Vṛtra even pauses before his own death to praise Vishnu, to whose abode, the Bhāgavata says, Vṛtra finally returns. After Vṛtra's death, Indra is saddled with the sin of killing a *brāhmaṇa*, and he desperately seeks some means of shedding this sin.

The story of Vṛtra has roots in the Veda and is retold (several times) in the Mahābhārata and in several Purāṇas. The Bhāgavata's version, however, is unique in at least two ways. While the transformation of Vṛtra from wicked to wise demon is already complete in the *śānti-parva* of the Mahābhārata, where Vṛtra teaches Indra about the temporality of the body, the Bhāgavata turns Vṛtra into the consummate devotee. His exemplary devotion to Vishnu is displayed in a way that makes the point clearly—even a demon is capable of attaining the highest end through the power of bhakti, while the meritorious Indra remains bound to worldly aspirations.

But it is what transpires after the killing of Vṛtra that is most telling. For the Mahābhārata and the Viṣṇu Purāṇa, the lesson of the story is the awful effect of killing a *brāhmaṇa*; indeed, the sin of killing Viśvarūpa pursues Indra throughout heaven and earth. But in what C. Mackenzie Brown calls "an astonishing turnabout from the epic [Mahābhārata]," the Bhāgavata proclaims that by praising the Lord (*kīrtana*), even the murderer of a *brāhmaṇa* or an outcaste can be purified. Brown puts it well:

> The *Bhāgavata* is hardly endorsing Brahmanicide, yet the whole tone is obviously quite different from the epic's stress on the heinous and sinful nature of the act. In the epic versions of the aftermath, the basic point is that violating a Brahman—or even worse, two Brahmans—has severe consequences, which in turn requires the service of Brahmans (as performers of the horse-sacrifice) to absolve. For the *Bhāgavata*, the message is that even the worst of sinners and the ritually impure, including outcastes and Brahman-slayers, can be sanctified and redeemed through devotion to the Lord. (1990, 60)

A similar development can be traced in the Bhāgavata's version of the Nṛsiṁha story, as Deborah Soifer argues in her study of Nṛsiṁha across the Purāṇas. In the Bhāgavata, Prahlāda is the hero of the story, and an unlikely hero, for he is both a child and son of a demon. Yet Prahlāda's bhakti has the ability to overcome these liabilities while also helping to restore dharma in the world by evoking the appearance of the *avatāra* Nṛsiṁha.[10] "The *Bhāgavata* myth is, in this frame, richer, multivalent, and portrays bhakti at perhaps its fullest expression. . . . Bhakti triumphs here and takes its place at the top of a universe that it transcends yet still pervades" (Soifer 1991, 98–99).

One finds these role reversals throughout the Bhāgavata. Kings exert power over *brāhmaṇas*, as in the account of King Ambarīṣa and the sage Durvāsā; animals invoke the Lord's appearance, as in the story of Gajendra the elephant; demons demonstrate the highest devotion, as in the demon king Bali's self-surrender to Vāmana *avatāra*; and an unchaste woman like Piṅgalā becomes a wise teacher. Perhaps the most often-cited example is the *gopīs*—the cowherdesses of Vraja—whom the Purāṇa holds up as exemplars of bhakti as they steal away from their homes and husbands to dance with Krishna. And yet there is another narrative in the tenth book that makes the point just as well—the wives of the *brāhmaṇas* who bring Krishna food. The story is relatively brief, comprising just fifty-two verses in an otherwise vast tenth book, and yet its brevity, seeming redundancy, and minimal plotline make the overarching point even clearer.

Krishna is tending the cows on the shores of the Yamunā when his friends complain of being hungry. Krishna sends them to a settlement of *brāhmaṇas* nearby to ask for food in his name. But the boys return empty-handed; the *brāhmaṇas* are performing Vedic sacrifices and take no heed of the request. Krishna sends his friends back to the settlement, but this time with instructions to ask the *brāhmaṇas*' wives for food. The wives are overjoyed to hear that Krishna is nearby, and they run from their homes carrying all manner of food for Krishna to eat. The structure of the story here precisely parallels the famous *rāsa-līlā* narrative (of the *gopīs* dancing with Krishna) that appears later in Book Ten. The *brāhmāṇas*' wives (i.e., *brāhmaṇīs*) run to meet Krishna, despite their husbands' attempts to hold them back. As he does with the *gopīs*, Krishna asks the *brāhmaṇīs* why they have come to the forest and tells them to return home, explaining that he is present in their meditation. The *brāhmaṇīs* complain of Krishna's cruelty and insist that they are ready to sacrifice everything for him. As in the *rāsa-līlā* account, one of the wives is held back by her husband, and she gives up her body in yogic meditation. Krishna enjoys the delicious food brought by the *brāhmaṇīs*, even as he enjoys the *rāsa* dance with the *gopīs*.

But this structural similarity gives way to a final, important difference: the *brāhmaṇīs* are soon reintegrated into dharmic society, receiving the approval and esteem of their families. Krishna promises the *brāhmaṇīs* that their husbands, fathers, brothers, and children will not vilify them upon their return home, and "even the gods will approve" (10.23.31). Indeed, when the wives return home, the *brāhmaṇas* praise their wives' "otherworldly" bhakti for Krishna, feel deep remorse for their own indifference, and proceed to condemn their caste status, vows, and ritual performances, for these markers of merit have turned them away from Krishna (10.23.39–40). Their wives, on the other hand, despite being women—and here the *brāhmaṇas* enumerate their disqualifications—have achieved the final goal that their husbands can only dream of (10.23.43–44). Even at this point, the *brāhmaṇas* wish to follow in their wives' footsteps and go to the forest, but they are too afraid of Kaṁsa, the evil demon and illegitimate king of Mathurā, to risk a meeting with Krishna (10.23.52).

This narrative of the *brāhmaṇas'* wives seems hardly "necessary" in the tenth book; nearly every element of it is found in the *rāsa-līlā* chapters. Yet this apparent redundancy, together with the only significant difference, betrays the overall purpose of the story—to demonstrate the reversing power of bhakti. Indeed, this lesson emerges more clearly in this account than it does in the *rāsa-līlā* because the plot is thinner and the stakes are higher. By serving food to cowherds, the *brāhmaṇas'* wives are transgressing and reversing caste roles in ways that the *gopīs* did not need to. Gender roles are also in sharp focus, for the *brāhmāṇīs* are shown in an upper-caste domestic context—while their husbands perform the fire rituals required of *brāhmaṇas*, the *brāhmāṇīs* are busy in the home, decorated with the signs of auspicious marriage. The wives are of course risking censure from their husbands by going into the forest to meet a man they love passionately. But the risk of censure is also collective; unlike in the *rāsa-līlā* account, where each *gopī* was unaware of the others' journey to the forest, here the *brāhmaṇīs* are placed in a highly visible social context. It is daytime, not the dead of night; the *brāhmaṇīs* are seated together while their husbands perform a public ritual; the *brāhmaṇīs* are invited to the forest by Krishna's cowherd messengers, not by the solitary sound of Krishna's flute; the *brāhmaṇīs* head to the forest as a group, and when they see Krishna, he is strolling along the Yamunā with his friends. The story of the *brāhmaṇa* wives, it seems, repeats the *rāsa-līlā* with the express purpose of placing a perennial theme of the Bhāgavata in sharp focus: bhakti has the ability to transcend all caste, gender, and social boundaries. At the same time, such pure bhakti can coexist with social order and relationships (dharma), as seen by the final reconciliation between the *brāhmaṇīs*, their husbands, and their community.

Kings, Avatāras, and the Need for Social Order

The narrative of the *brāhmaṇīs* makes it clear that the Bhāgavata does not subscribe to categorical notions of dharma—that is, social duty, morality, or ritual.[11] Dharma always depends on context, and when the demands of dharma conflict with those of bhakti, then bhakti always triumphs. Indeed, as the Bhāgavata emphasizes in a famous verse from Book One, "The highest dharma is that which gives rise to bhakti for the transcendent Lord" (1.2.6).

Nevertheless, dharma does not conflict with bhakti under ordinary circumstances; rather, the two support and foster each other. The preservation of dharma is a key reason for the Lord to descend to earth as an *avatāra*, and thus it is an important theme of the Bhāgavata.

We see this concern right from the beginning of the Bhāgavata, in its outermost frame story. Long ago, the Purāṇa tells us, a group of sages gathered in the forest of Naimiṣāraṇya to find a solution to this problem: Bhagavān Krishna has left the world, and dharma has departed with him. The terrible Kali age—a protracted period of human degradation—is soon to begin. What hope is there for the people of the world? The answer, says the sage Sūta, can be found in the Bhāgavata Purāṇa, which gives light to those who have lost their sight because of the darkness of the age. Sūta reassures the sages that Krishna descends repeatedly, in a variety of forms, to reestablish order and preserve dharma.

A significant element of preserving dharma is establishing and maintaining proper state leadership. Indeed, the anxiety over loss of enlightened monarchy is one of the most recurrent themes in the Bhāgavata. Whether it is the gods who have lost their posts in heaven, or human kings who terrorize their subjects, or natural disasters that threaten to destroy the world's leadership, the loss of royal order is a perpetual problem that

Krishna must solve. At different times he appears in the world to destroy corrupt kings, or to protect righteous kings, or to become a king himself and demonstrate ideal leadership.

While the Bhāgavata places special emphasis on the need for enlightened rulers (*kṣatriyas*), it does not ignore the duties of the other three social classes constituting the classical *varṇa* system—the *brāhmaṇa* priests, the *vaiṣya* farmers and merchants, and the *śūdra* workers. Numerous sections of the Bhāgavata are devoted to discussing the organization of society, either through narratives or through direct teaching. The *brāhmaṇas*, in particular, are an important counterweight to *kṣatriya* power. In the story of the evil king Veṇa (Book Four), for example, the *brāhmaṇas* are at first hesitant to intervene in political matters, but when Veṇa's misdeeds become unbearable for the people, the *brāhmaṇas* use their priestly power to kill him and install a new king.

The Bhāgavata's Special Secret—the Play of God

Reestablishing dharma is surely a serious business for Vishnu and his several *avatāras*; and yet the Bhāgavata (unlike any other Purāṇa) identifies Vishnu's *avatāras* collectively as *līlā avatāras*, or "divine descents of play" (12.12.46). To show just how divine acts can be comprehended as play seems to be one of the primary aims of the Bhāgavata. The idea of *līlā* is hinted at in earlier Sanskrit works (including the Ṛgveda and Chandogya Upaniṣad), but the Bhāgavata brings it into focus and explicitly identifies several *avatāras*' activities as *līlā*. Most importantly, the Bhāgavata expands previous accounts of Krishna's playfulness, particularly as a child.[12]

Indeed, in the Bhāgavata Purāṇa, Krishna's *līlās* of childhood and youthful mischief, heroism, and romance are definitive of what divinity is all about in its most exalted form. When, for example, the child Krishna provokes his foster mother, Yaśodā, by stealthily plundering her stores of butter and curd (in Book Ten, chapter 9), readers delight in the paradox that, although he is the supreme Bhagavān, he enjoys the pretense of acting as an ordinary child, becoming so absorbed in this conceit that he becomes genuinely fearful of Yaśodā's attempts to punish him. In the delight of this paradox, readers are invited to participate vicariously in Krishna's *līlā*, thereby enabling them to transcend time's limitations and—the Bhāgavata assures—enter Krishna's atemporal abode, where *līlā* takes place perpetually.

Hearing and Speaking About God's Līlā

As we have already seen in the discussion of the Bhāgavata's layer-cake dialogical structure, there is an immense premium placed on speaking and hearing about the ultimate being and his divine acts. "Thus, with single mind one should forever hear about, praise, meditate upon, and worship Bhagavān, Lord of the Sātvatas" (1.2.14). This is the gist of the Bhāgavata's advice to its readers and listeners, which Śuka elaborates upon in the course of his seven-day Bhāgavata recitation to King Parīkṣit, whose death is imminent. Certainly hearing and reciting or glorifying Bhagavān and his divine names, forms, qualities, and activities are the core activities for the cultivation of bhakti, according to the Bhāgavata and as exemplified by its reciters such as Sūta and Śuka. Yet we also find other sorts of practices exemplified and praised. In Book Seven (chapter 5) the child devotee Prahlāda lists nine types of devotional activity: along with hearing and glorifying the supreme (*śravaṇa* and *kīrtana*, respectively), there is remembrance of Vishnu (*smaraṇa*); rendering services to him (*pāda-sevana*); performing ritual worship (*arcana*); submitting prayers (*vandana*); regarding oneself as the Lord's servant (*dāsya*); acting as the Lord's friend (*sakhya*); and submitting oneself to him entirely and exclusively (*ātma-nivedana*). Each type of bhakti practice has its exemplars in the Bhāgavata, along with elaboration on its method of practice.[13] So, for example, Queen Kuntī's prayers in Book One (chapter 8) exemplify *vandana*; a detailed meditation on Vishnu's form in the yogi's heart (Book Three, chapter 28) demonstrates the practice of *smaraṇa*; and Krishna's lesson to Uddhava on formal worship (Book Eleven, chapter 27) details the Bhāgavata's recommendations for the practice of *arcana*. What is crucial in all practices of bhakti is the cultivation of friendship with other bhakti practitioners and the cultivation of a relationship with Bhagavān.

The Bhāgavata revels in its explorations of the varieties that such relationships can take. Aside from the more formal expressions of bhakti found in the sense of being the Lord's servant, we encounter Krishna's intimate friends, the cowherds (*gopas*) of Vraja, who joke and have mock fights with him; we meet his foster mother, absorbed in regarding Krishna as her son and punishing him when he is naughty (as in Book Ten, chapters 8 and 9); and, most famously, we become privy to the pinnacle of devotional intensity in the romantic relationships between Krishna and his girlfriends in Vraja, the *gopīs* as they meet together secretly in the forest and when they suffer pangs of separation (especially in Book Ten, chapters 29–33, and chapter 47).

In all the Bhāgavata's accounts of bhakti practices, it is divine favor (*prasāda, kṛpā, anugraha*) freely bestowed that completes the circles of reciprocation. Yet one is reminded that Bhagavān is "equal to all beings" (hence not showing favoritism, an important theme in most of Book Seven) and, on the other hand, that his favor is "causeless," much as the adept *bhakta*'s devotional practice is "free from motivation." As a practitioner ponders the mystery of Bhagavān's attributes and deeds, she is led into ever deeper layers of the very same practices, especially of devotional hearing and speaking.

The Bhāgavata's Promise of Perfection

Like nearly all classical religio-philosophical works of India, the Bhāgavata Purāṇa acknowledges the pursuit of liberation (*mokṣa*) as an ultimate aim for human beings—final release from the cycle of death and rebirth. And yet, with bhakti consistently celebrated as the Bhāgavata's highest value, it shuns any conception of liberation that could interfere with bhakti. In addition to "oneness" (*ekatva*) or union with the supreme, the Bhāgavata says that the Lord's devotees refuse to accept all types of liberation including the rewards of divine form, divine opulence, or direct proximity to Bhagavān if, by gaining any of these, they would be denied the opportunity to serve him (3.29.13). As bhakti is the practice, so bhakti is the eternal perfection that devotees seek. Likewise, the eternal perfection that the Lord grants his devotees is joyful devotion, which constitutes the highest form of enlightenment. Indeed, the Bhāgavata is concerned to show that, sooner or later, the Lord grants perpetual devotion even to persons who, because of human weakness, fall temporarily away from the bhakti path (such as Dakṣa in Book Four, Bharata in Book Five, and Ajāmila in Book Six). And to provide a clear and detailed picture of what such perpetual devotion looks like, the Bhāgavata lingers (in Book Ten) on the intensely devotional attitudes and activities of Krishna's associates in Vraja—those of the cowherd men, women, young boys, and young girls.

TRANSLATION AS TEACHING: THOUGHTS ON METHOD

It is well known among Sanskritists, both in India and beyond, that translating the Bhāgavata Purāṇa is no easy task. The Sanskrit text hardly sticks to the expected forms of Purāṇic verse—easy cadences, straightforward grammar, minimal use of compound words, and well-known vocabulary that make the Purāṇas amenable to sight-reading. Indeed, in Sanskrit examinations, "reading from the *ākāśa-purāṇa* [the Purāṇa in the sky]" can be a euphemism for composing verse extempore. Translating the Bhāgavata, on the other hand, serves as the examination itself—a test of skill in the language. The Bhāgavata freely mixes Vedic and Classical grammar, frequently switches into longer meters, and revels in archaic word forms.[14] It is not an uncommon experience for the translator to encounter an unknown word and look it up in Sanskrit dictionaries, only to find that the only known usage of that word is found in the Bhagavata Purāṇa.[15]

This treacherous landscape has led English-language translators of the Bhāgavata Purāṇa to employ one of two time-honored techniques. The first is to keep rigorously to a literal reconstruction of the original, adhering as closely as possible to dictionary meanings, Sanskrit sentence structure, and verbal moods and tenses. This leads to a replication of the original that is useful to the researcher and maybe the philosopher, but it misses much of the literary nuance that makes the Bhāgavata fine literature. The second is to choose a favorite commentator and incorporate his reading into the translation to clarify difficulties. The most frequent choice has been the revered Śrīdhara, whose commentary is shorter than that of others, clearly structured, and always conscious of a verse's context in the narrative. Śrīdhara's reliance on conservative, contextual interpretation, while resisting the overly creative, makes him a safe basis upon whom translators and other commentators can layer their own exegetical insights.

Translation is often thought of as a balancing act, a delicate dance on a tightrope stretched between opposing forces—the literal versus the metaphorical, formal versus colloquial, grammatical structure versus poetic fluidity, meanings driven by scholarship versus meanings driven by tradition, the needs of the audience versus fidelity to the text. No doubt these are the polar forces that make a translator's work headache inducing. We, too, have spent inordinately long periods debating the merits of one choice of word over another. We have struggled to convey double meanings and implications embedded in the Sanskrit without making the translation cumbersome or providing a lengthy endnote (though there are, of course, many in our translation).

However, at some point we realized that by approaching translation as a balancing act, we were reducing both the text and our work to a linear process (a tightrope is, after all, two-dimensional). Why not adopt a translation method tailored to the Bhāgavata's distinctive characteristics? Why not seek to employ methods embedded in the text itself and thus create a bespoke translation? And so we gradually moved beyond the literary tightrope and turned instead to another useful metaphor—translation as an act of teaching.

Teaching is translation in the best sense, and a teacher is forever a translator. A teacher is a learner, one who makes knowledge her own even as she finds ways of delivering it to her audience. Every act of teaching is an act of translation, for if no translation were necessary, then the static language of the textbook would suffice in place of the classroom. The translator-teacher is caught in a polarity, too, but unlike the literal versus metaphorical tightrope, this is a dichotomy of practice—between what has been learned or understood by the teacher and what can be taught to the student. This polarity is dynamic, because both the teacher's understanding and the students' needs are constantly changing. The marker of success here is not to *get it right* but to *get it across*—that is, to be effective and not merely correct.

And this, indeed, is the primary concern of the Bhāgavata itself. Like any Purāṇa, the Bhāgavata aims to teach. The text consists of a series of nested conversations between teacher and student, with each teacher recalling a prior conversation between teacher and student that the teacher witnessed. The outermost frame of the text consists of the sage Śaunaka questioning Sūta, and Sūta begins his answer with a verse that captures the teacher-translator's dichotomy. "When the brilliant sage Śuka recited the Bhāgavata, I was present there, and I understood it by his blessing. That is what I will teach you—as I have learned it, and as I understand it" (1.3.44). The phrase *yathādhītaṁ yathā matiḥ* captures well the teacher-translator's dual obligations of fidelity to source and sensitivity to audience.

The fact that the Purāṇas are didactic texts should come as no surprise to someone with even a cursory knowledge of the genre. And yet to say that the Bhāgavata is didactic is to say something about the heart of the text that goes much beyond conversations between sages and kings. Through and through, the Bhāgavata sees itself as a teacher, not simply in the Purāṇic sense of the bard and his audience but in a manner that is distinctly Upaniṣadic.

The Bhāgavata Purāṇa's close connection to the Upaniṣads is apparent even in its first verse, which consists of a complex series of references to the Vedāntic tradition. The second *sūtra* of the Vedāntasūtra is quoted, the exegetical method of *anvaya* and *vyatireka* is referenced, creation is described as a process of threefold transformation (*trivṛt-karaṇa*), and so on. Śrīdhara Svāmī quotes from both the Taittirīya Upaniṣad and the Vedāntasūtra in his commentary on the first verse, while Madhva recalls a phrase attributed to the Garuḍa Purāṇa—*artho 'yam brahmasūtrāṇām*, "this [Bhāgavata Purāṇa] is the meaning of the Vedāntasūtra." Allusions to the Upaniṣads and Bhagavad Gītā are ubiquitous in the Bhāgavata, which holds in large part to an Upaniṣadic theology. Indeed, as the Bhāgavata aligns itself with the Vedāntic tradition—starting with its first verse—generations of scholars have sought, and found, Vedāntic ideas in its text.

We would argue, however, that the Vedāntic connection goes beyond ideas and terminology; the connection is as much about *method* as it is about content. The Bhāgavata employs an internal method that has much in common with those quintessential teaching texts, the Upaniṣads. Brian Black, for example, has identified several distinctive markers of the Upaniṣads' teaching methods, the first of which is their dialogical structure (2007, 15–23). The Upaniṣadic dialogues offer a fresh approach to teaching that is—like all good teaching—personal, student driven, and collaborative. Teaching in the Upaniṣads is nearly always prompted by the student interlocutor, and, as Jacqueline Hirst has pointed out, it is so unusual for a teacher to ask questions of the pupil that when it happens, Śaṁkara feels obligated to justify the reversal (2005, 71).

So effective is the dialogical method that we soon find it percolating through much of Sanskrit *śāstra*. And while all the Purāṇic bards are prompted by their interlocutors, the Bhāgavata's dialogues are far more carefully structured, student driven, and—well—genuinely dialogical. Here, the student's question serves not merely as a prompt that sends the speaker on a long, winding journey. Rather, each question leads to a carefully circumscribed response, after which the speaker returns to his student, reaffirms the latter's question, and requests confirmation that the answer has been satisfactory. Even when the answer requires narrating a multichapter story, rarely does the speaker get carried away in the kind of digressions that are common in, say, the Mahābhārata or the Skanda Purāṇa.

Another reason for the Bhāgavata's tightly woven structure is, perhaps, its need to be portable. Like Śaṁkara and other Vedānta teachers, this "famously itinerant scripture" (Venkatkrishnan 2013) has traveled across the subcontinent with *kathākārs*, poets, and founders of sectarian traditions. Dozens of Bhāgavata-inspired works appear throughout the subcontinent beginning in the thirteenth century, and the *Bhāgavata Māhātmya* (seventeenth century?) makes it apparent that travel is a perceived trademark of the Purāṇa. But unlike the Mahābhārata, where portability has led to endless fluidity of the text itself, the Bhāgavata has traveled like a teacher would—with great care for the integrity of the content and tools of instruction. The Bhāgavata has received a level of verse-by-verse scrutiny that is rare for texts of this size, leading to a robust practice of text criticism and a Sanskrit manuscript tradition that has remained relatively stable after Śrīdhara Svāmī. And so we find here—as in the Upaniṣads—a clear structure, mostly coherent content, and a focused objective.

Take, for example, the initial dialogue between King Parīkṣit and the eternally itinerant sage Śuka. This is the most important framing dialogue of the Bhāgavata, for it provides the text's raison d'être. The king, who has been cursed to die after seven days have passed, asks several questions of Śuka at the beginning of Book One. The first question encompasses the others—what is the path to perfection for one who is about to die? Śuka's answer constitutes the first two chapters of Book Two, but even at the beginning of the discourse, he states his conclusion: "A person's greatest accomplishment in life, through *sāṁkhya*, yoga, or dedication to one's dharma, is to remember Nārāyaṇa [Vishnu] at the end. Therefore, one who wants fearlessness should hear about, remember, and praise Bhagavān Hari" (2.1.5–6). Śuka then proceeds to explain yogic methods of meditating on Vishnu and preparing for death, as well as the perfected soul's journey after death. He then returns to his original exhortation—hear about, remember, and glorify Vishnu, at all times and in all circumstances—with a promise that one who does this will never return to this world but achieve Bhagavān's divine abode (2.2.36–37). Finally, Śuka turns to Parīkṣit and says, "Thus I have answered the questions you asked me" (2.3.1). The teaching is complete in a neat, two-chapter package, and the teacher seems almost ready to depart, until Parīkṣit asks him to describe how Vishnu creates the world. Indeed, so neatly packaged is Śuka's first teaching that one might argue that the Bhāgavata is complete at this point, since the practical imperative is clear. The sixteenth-century commentator Jīva Gosvāmī, for example, regards the final verse in this teaching—where Śuka promises that the sincere listener will ascend to Vishnu's abode—as the *phala-śruti* for the entire Bhāgavata—that is, the expected result for reading the Bhāgavata

(Gupta 2007, 101). *Phala-śrutis* are nearly always found at the end of a book; for Jīva Gosvamī to locate it at the end of the first major teaching is a significant statement about the Bhāgavata's clean, dialogical structure.

Before we apply these insights to the task of translation, there is a third and final observation that needs to be made about the Bhāgavata's teaching style—its relentlessly focused message. Both the dialogical method and careful structure serve to usher the student into realizing a message that resonates throughout the text—namely, that bhakti for Krishna is the highest goal, one that trumps the limitations of dharma, overcomes human weakness, and leads to liberation from suffering. We have discussed this at length in the preceding and so here only remind our readers about this overarching theme of the Bhāgavata.

What, then, are we to make of all this as translators of the Bhāgavata? How should these observations about the text's dialogical method, tightly woven structure, and focused message guide our translation methods? As we have seen, the Bhāgavata is at heart an argument and exhortation to hear and speak about Krishna as a means to develop bhakti. The text provides the *content* for listening and speaking—namely, Krishna's *līlā*—but, equally important, it provides *models* for effective listening and speaking: Śuka and Parīkṣit, Sūta and Śaunaka, Maitreya and Vidura, and numerous others. How might the methods demonstrated by the text guide our own method as translators?

Here we might take a page from Hirst's decision to model her study of Śaṁkara on Śaṁkara's own methods as a teacher, and the important caveats that she offers about her decision:

> Indeed, this book itself seeks to model the processes of understanding involved, as the outline of its stages above is intended to convey. . . . The modelling I propose is not to be misunderstood as a substitute for sitting at the feet of an Advaitin teacher, nor is its goal the realization that is the proper end of such study alone. But I do hold that, in a strong sense, an engagement with the texts of Advaita is a prerequisite for even an intellectual understanding of Śaṁkara's aims and, in that sense, familiarity with the process as well as with content is not only an appropriate but also a necessary aspect of academic study. (2005, 6)

For us as translators, the shift from tightrope walking to modeling (quite some career change!) created a change in perspective and translation style that is difficult to capture in words. Our translation became less tense and more fluid; instead of fighting the text, we found ourselves running with it. We became more aware of macro elements beyond the grammar of the verse at hand: connections and repetition across chapters, themes emerging within a particular narrative, variations in methods of storytelling, and the role of the implicit listener. We began to notice humor in the text and became convinced that humor is integral to the Bhāgavata's method. When we noticed that a particular passage was hammering away at a specific theme, we made sure that the theme emerged clearly in our translation—by using more forthright or colloquial language or by resisting the temptation to use multiple English synonyms when the Sanskrit repeats a word four times in the same passage.

The practice of treating the Bhāgavata as teacher, along with the dialogical method that it embodies, continues in the teaching tradition of commentaries, many of which were written for particular communities of student listeners. One major task of commentaries is to translate the text into language that is comprehensible and relevant to their contemporary audience. And so we often selected two commentators who were bound to be poles apart—Vallabha and Viśvanātha, for example, or Vaṁśīdhara and Vijayadhvaja—and traced the themes that they elicited from a passage or the linguistic concerns that they addressed. In Book Three (chapters 15 and 16), for example, Vishnu's gatekeepers are cursed by four child sages for blocking their entrance to Vaikuṇṭha, Vishnu's divine abode. As a result of the curse, the gatekeepers fall from Vaikuṇṭha and undergo birth as demons on earth. Here, the commentators show sustained concern about who is to be blamed for the gatekeepers' fall from grace. Śrīdhara stays closest to the Bhāgavata's own explicit attribution of guilt—the gatekeepers have offended *brāhmaṇas* who are dear to Vishnu. But other attributions of guilt are implicit in the narrative, and by the end of the story, all parties involved—the gatekeepers, the sages, and even Vishnu—have expressed readiness to take blame (and any consequent punishment) upon themselves. Vallabha prefers to place the blame squarely on the four sages for their unreasonable anger, while other commentators distribute the blame among the parties involved. Often these commentarial debates stretch across multiple chapters, resurfacing when the context calls for it. We soon realized that it was important to give our readers a taste of the commentarial concerns that informed our translation. And so to augment the fragmental insights included in endnotes, we decided to include four extended essays where we help our audience read the commentaries with us, following the thread of a debate or argument.

The most significant addition to the project came as we tried to cope with the tightly woven structure of the Bhāgavata. Indeed, extracting a few dozen verses from a chapter, or even a full chapter from a narrative that extends across two books, felt as if we were committing violence to the text. How do we convey the thread of conversation or the line of argument that ties one narrative to another and one chapter to another? We decided then to write the thread ourselves, by connecting each of our selected translations with summaries of the intervening content. These summaries offer not only highlights of the plot but also—keeping with our understanding of the Bhāgavata as teacher—the questions that prompted the narratives and the concerns that they attempt to address. The story of the Nṛsiṁha *avatāra*, for example, addresses Parīkṣit's concern that God behaves in an unjust and partial way when he helps the gods and kills the demons. The story of King Citraketu is prompted by Parīkṣit's query about how a demon like Vṛtra could be so firmly devoted to Krishna when even the gods struggle to cultivate bhakti. The *rāsa-līlā* narrative in Book Ten prompts Parīkṣit to ask how the *gopīs* could have achieved liberation when they knew Krishna only as their beloved and not as God. In response, Śuka reminds Parīkṣit that he already answered this question when he explained (in Book Seven) how Śiṣupāla attained liberation despite his hatred toward Krishna.

Perhaps our most useful means of modeling the Bhāgavata's methods was through collaborative translation. Collaboration brought with it many benefits—it kept us motivated, focused, and cheerful. With a text as multivalent as the Bhāgavata, working collaboratively meant that we could draw on each other's areas of expertise to work through sections dealing with philosophy, ritual, or descriptions of natural scenery. But most of all, collaborative translation meant that, as we recited our translations to each other, raised doubts about meaning, and highlighted areas of confusion, we could in some sense re-create the tradition of teaching that is embedded in the text and its reception history. After all, the Bhāgavata Purāṇa itself constitutes a continuous process of translation—from Vyāsa to Śuka to Sūta to Śaunaka, from commentators to learned readers, from gurus to disciples, from *kathākārs* to their devoted audiences. Indeed, we hope that this book will serve as an invitation for our readers to enter the world of the Bhāgavata and participate in that legacy of translation.

USING THIS BOOK

This volume consists of four components that, when taken together, will serve to introduce the reader to the multifaceted world of the Bhāgavata.

1. At the heart of this reader are, of course, the translations of verses from the Bhāgavata Purāṇa. In selecting passages to translate, we have attempted to offer a representative sampling of the many kinds of narratives, philosophical ideas, and literary styles found in the Purāṇa. Too often translations and studies of the Bhāgavata focus exclusively on Book Ten, which in many ways is quite different from the rest of the Purāṇa. Here we have translated approximately fifteen hundred verses across some fifty chapters and all twelve books of the Bhāgavata. You can tell where you are in any given chapter by noting the verse numbers that are provided in the body of the translation. The word "chapter" always refers to chapters in the Bhāgavata and never to sections in this volume.

2. Another consideration that guided our selection was the importance of a particular narrative for the Bhāgavata's readers through history, as evidenced by the commentarial attention it has received or by its role in the religious practice of communities that regard the Bhāgavata as scripture. We make our readers aware of this reception history in two ways: First, we provide endnotes that explain difficult concepts found in the text and offer nuggets of insight drawn from a variety of commentators. These endnotes keep closely to the verse at hand, not allowing for the extended debates that are often found in commentaries. Second, to experience the richness of commentarial discussion, readers should turn to the final section of the book, where we choose four narratives and provide "guided tours" of the robust commentarial debate that those narratives have engendered.

3. The Bhāgavata Purāṇa is a vast literature, and we have translated no more than 10 percent of the text. But in order to avoid the disjointed feel that can result from selective translation, we have summarized—ever so briefly—whatever material we have not translated. Thus we hope a reader will be able to move smoothly from one passage to another and, in effect, read the entire Bhāgavata Purāṇa, either as a direct translation or as a summary. Because of the Bhāgavata's narrative structure, readers will gain the most by reading the Bhāgavata in order from Book One to Twelve, instead of choosing passages piecemeal.

4. Finally, each chapter provides avenues for further study with a list of suggested readings that explore the themes found in that chapter. Some of these readings are drawn from our earlier book, *The Bhāgavata Purāṇa: Sacred Text and Living Tradition*, which is a collection of essays on the Bhāgavata's many spheres of influence in Indian history, philosophy, and performance. The two books are meant to be studied together as a primary-secondary source pair, and many of the narratives translated in this reader are discussed in the other volume. Our suggested readings also include scholarly books, journal articles, as well as other translations of the Bhāgavata. Indeed, we hope that this reader will inspire a lifelong exploration of the Bhāgavata that goes much beyond the pages of this book.

For this translation, we have consistently used the Sanskrit text of the Bhāgavata as edited by Kṛṣṇaśaṅkara Śāstrī. Although the Śāstrī edition is out of print, it is frequently used by students, scholars, and contemporary publishers, for its readings are attested by numerous commentaries that are provided alongside the main text. Nevertheless, we are aware of the presence of variant readings, as attested to by the Ahmadabad critical edition (Bhāgavata Purāṇa 1996–1998) and occasionally by individual commentators. Given its size, age, and wide geographic distribution, the Bhāgavata Purāṇa has a remarkably stable manuscript tradition. For every verse that we translated, we compared Śāstrī's reading with the critical edition and found only around a half dozen variant readings of one word or longer per chapter. Even among these variants, the great majority were straightforward substitutions of one synonymous word for another. However, whenever we did encounter a variant reading of greater significance or length (and there were one or two in each book), we duly note them in our endnotes.

Finally, we ought to mention some editorial conventions that we follow in our translation. Whenever we find the need to add a clarifying word or phrase of our own, we place that material in parentheses. Sanskrit verse frequently includes pronouns whose antecedent is clear from context or grammar, but the referent is not explicitly named in the verse. Such pronouns with faraway antecedents are considered bad form in English, and so we often resupply the antecedent in our translation. For purposes of smooth reading, we do not place such replacements in parentheses, except when there is genuine ambiguity of reference.

In English, an adjective usually modifies a noun or pronoun, but no such requirement exists in Sanskrit. Thus, "they bowed down to the beautiful" sounds incomplete in English, and so we take the liberty of providing the appropriate pronoun or proper noun to such homeless adjectives: "They bowed down to the beautiful Lakṣmī." Our choice of noun or pronoun is usually explicitly mentioned elsewhere in the same verse or in an adjacent verse.

Sanskrit also has the ability to put long compound words in the vocative (or some other case), which are impossible or unpleasant to translate as such into English. So at times we convert such lengthy words into complete sentences. For example, instead of "Śambhu! Drinker of poison produced from ocean churning!" we write, "Śambhu! You drank the poison produced from churning the ocean." Similarly, Sanskrit participles often need to be translated as verbs in English, and passive sentences are better converted into the active. Sanskrit creates long relative-correlative constructions with ease, whereas in English long dependent clauses can become unwieldy. And so we often break up such relative constructions into multiple sentences, repeating the proper noun or pronoun in each sentence to indicate that the subject remains the same throughout. These grammatical adjustments, we believe, are necessary in order to craft a translation that is not only accurate but also good literature.

In keeping with standard South Asian scholarship, we follow the established system of diacritics for Sanskrit transliteration. There are a few names and terms that appear frequently in our translation and that have become common in English prose; consequently, we don't render them with diacritics—for example, Vishnu and Krishna. To pronounce Sanskrit words, the most important elements to keep in mind are as follows:

c is pronounced much like *ch* in "chat"
ś and *ṣ* are pronounced much like *sh* in "ship"
vowels with a macron are pronounced twice as long—for example, *ā* should be pronounced like the *a* in "father"

Other letters with diacritics (including *ṭ*, *ḍ*, *ṅ*, *ṇ*, *ñ*, *ṁ*, and *ḥ*) are sufficiently approximated when pronounced as the same letters in English without the marks.

BOOK ONE

Introducing the Bhāgavata's Subject
Queen Kuntī Praises Krishna
Bhīṣma Shares His Wisdom
King Parīkṣit and Sage Śuka Meet

Book One serves as an extended introduction and framing narrative for the Bhāgavata Purāṇa as a whole, opening with richly philosophical invocatory verses and closing with the meeting of the text's central interlocutors, King Parīkṣit and the sage Śuka. The work's central theme—bhakti (devotion) to a supreme deity, Bhagavān (variously named throughout the text as Vāsudeva, Nārāyaṇa, Vishnu, Hari, or Krishna)—is initially set out; thereafter a narrative commences that echoes and extends the epic Mahābhārata, representing and refocusing the latter's central characters as *bhaktas*—devotees—and as *bhāgavatas*—persons dedicated to Bhagavān.

This narrative tells of departures—of thc hero Bhīṣma from the world of the living to the atemporal divine abode; of Krishna from the city of the Mahābhārata's heroes, the five Pāndava brothers, to his island city Dvārakā; of the epic's villains' father, Dhṛtarāṣṭra, from home to prepare for death (and liberation); of Krishna from the world to his transcendent realm (narrated again, in greater detail, in Book Eleven); and of the Pāṇḍavas to the Himalayas to end their days. All these departures serve to clear the stage for the appearance of Parīkṣit, the sole survivor of the Mahābhārata's dynastic struggle, even as these departures set up the Bhāgavata's devotional landscape as one of pained yet impassioned remembrance of persons departed. And Parīkṣit, as righteous world emperor, carries with him the central remembrance tethered to intense longing: having glimpsed Lord Krishna as his protector while attacked in his mother's womb by a rival of the family, his inner life is defined by his tireless wish to see his master again. This will indeed take place, but not in a way that the king might have anticipated, and not before the destructive Kali age is ushered in despite Parīkṣit's effort to prevent it.

The first passage from Book One consists in the opening invocatory verses of the first chapter, continuing in the same chapter with the description of a Bhāgavata recitation scene conducted by the learned Sūta (Ugraśravās) to a large assembly of sages, headed by the inquisitive Śaunaka. This scene functions as an important dialogue frame that will appear from time to time throughout the Bhāgavata, punctuating the central dialogue frame—the discussion between the world sovereign Parīkṣit and the master sage Śuka—that begins in Book Two and continues to the end of the Bhāgavata. In this section (which continues into the beginning of chapter two) we are introduced to a central concern of the Bhāgavata—namely, to instill in its audience a sense of urgency for nourishing the spirit. Such nourishment is meant to come from the resolute hearing of the Bhāgavata's narratives. As a result of such attentive listening, the Bhāgavata promises release from the pernicious effects of worldly existence and the debilitations of the current dark age of Kali.

INTRODUCING THE BHĀGAVATA'S SUBJECT

Chapters 1 and 2

Oṁ! Obeisance to Bhagavān Vāsudeva.[1]

From him this (world) is born, etc. (upon him it rests, and in him it dissolves). That cognizant and self-luminous one is (known) by meanings inferred from positive and negative reasoning. He is the one who revealed the Veda through the heart to the first seer, but the gods are confused about him. In him the threefold creation—such as the interplay of fire, water, and earth—is not false, for he has removed all deception by his own power. Upon that supreme truth let us meditate. (1.1)[2] The highest dharma of good persons who are without envy—dharma that is free from deceit—is found here in the Śrīmad Bhāgavata, which was composed by the great sage (Vyāsa). The matter to be known here is genuine—it grants well-being and destroys the three miseries. Those virtuous people who desire to hear this Bhāgavata Purāṇa immediately and at once capture the Lord in the heart! What is the use of other books? (2)[3] The fruit of the Vedic desire tree, containing ambrosial juice, has issued from the mouth of Śuka. O knowers of *rasa* and people of taste in the world! Drink again and again this reservoir of *rasa*—the Bhāgavata. (3)[4]

The remainder of chapter 1 (vv. 4–23) sets the scene for the Bhāgavata's outermost frame of dialogue. Assembled in the sacred forest called Naimiṣāraṇya, sages resolve to perform a thousand-year sacrificial rite. While this rite is being executed, the sage Śaunaka requests a *sūta*, a Puranic reciter named Ugraśravās, son of Romaharṣana, to expound on six topics. These topics are the basis for the remainder of the Bhāgavata Purāṇa: (1) what is most beneficial for humanity; (2) what is the essence of all scriptures; (3) the purpose of Krishna's appearance as the son of Devakī; (4) the activities (*līlā*) of Krishna; (5) the narrations about the *avatāras* of Vishnu; and (6) the shelter for dharma, now that Krishna has departed from the world. Chapter 2 marks the beginning of Sūta's response to these questions.

Vyāsa said: Delighted by the questions of the sages, Raumaharṣani (Sūta) commended them for their inquiry and began to reply. (2.1)

Sūta said: As Śuka was departing home, unschooled and free of obligations, his father, Dvaipāyana (Vyāsa), called out, "Son!," afraid of losing him. But only the trees echoed in return, for they were absorbed in the same feelings. I offer obeisance to that seer who is within the hearts of all beings. (2)[5] Out of compassion, Śuka spoke what he realized himself—the essence of all the Vedas, the secret among the Purāṇas, and the only spiritual torchlight for persons caught in the cycle of rebirth who want to overcome the blinding darkness. I submit myself to that teacher of seers, the son of Vyāsa. (3) After offering homage to Nārāyaṇa, to Nara, the best of men, to Goddess Sarasvatī, and to Vyāsa, one can rise toward victory. (4)

You have questioned me very well, sages! Your inquiry about Krishna is beneficial for all people, for such questions fully satisfy the self. (5) Indeed, the highest dharma for human beings is that through which one attains unmotivated and unceasing bhakti for the transcendent Lord. Such bhakti fully satisfies the self. (6) Bhakti yoga, performed for Bhagavān Vāsudeva (Krishna), quickly and effortlessly generates knowledge and detachment. (7) People's careful practice of dharma is useless toil—indeed, nothing more!—if it does not lead them to delight in the stories of Viśvaksena (Vishnu). (8) The purpose of dharma should be liberation, not wealth. Desire for wealth is meant to be solely for dharma, not personal gain. (9) There can be no satisfaction of the senses by (trying to fulfill one's) desires. One should satisfy the senses only as much as one needs to live. Life's true wealth is inquiry into the truth, not what is gained in this world by selfish action. (10) Knowers of reality declare that reality to be nondual consciousness, called *brahman*, Paramātma, and Bhagavān. (11)[6] Faithful sages, endowed with knowledge and detachment, see that self within the self, by bhakti that is received through aural tradition. (12)[7] Therefore, O best of the twice-born, the complete success of dharma—carefully practiced by people according to the divisions of social orders and life stages—is pleasing Hari. (13)[8] Thus, with single mind one should forever hear about, praise, meditate upon, and worship Bhagavān, Lord of the Sātvatas. (14)[9] Using meditation on Bhagavān as their sword, the wise cut through the knotted fetters of action. Who therefore would not delight in narrations about him? (15)

Learned sages! The faithful and eager listener can gain affinity for narratives about Vāsudeva by service to the great souls and through devoted service to the abodes of virtue. (16)[10] Hearing and speaking about Krishna is virtuous. Indeed, he is the well-wisher of good persons who listen to his narratives, and, abiding deep in their hearts, he drives away what is inauspicious. (17) Through continuous service to devotees of Bhagavān, anything inauspicious is almost fully destroyed, and bhakti for the most-celebrated Bhagavān becomes steady. (18)[11] The mind then becomes satisfied, abiding in illumination (*sattva*) and undisturbed by the effects of passion (*rajas*) and darkness (*tamas*), such as desire and avarice. (19)[12] One who is thus free of attachment, and whose mind is satisfied through bhakti yoga for Bhagavān, comes to understand the true nature of Bhagavān. (20) When one perceives the Lord, the self, all doubts are shattered, the knot in the heart is untangled, and one's actions are terminated. (21)[13] Indeed this is why, with great delight and forever, the wise perform bhakti for Bhagavān Vāsudeva, satisfying the self. (22)

The remainder of chapter 2 (vv. 23–34) highlights the transcendent nature of Vishnu, his being the exclusive object of worship for persons desiring liberation, and (very briefly) how Vishnu creates the cosmos while remaining aloof from it. Chapters 3 through 6 expand on the theme of devoted hearing (*śravaṇa*) and the powerfully transformative results of such hearing. First comes a briefly descriptive list of the several descents (*avatāras*) of Vishnu, the activities of whom are to be the object of such hearing (1.3); then we are introduced to the sage Nārada (who will be an important interlocutor in later portions of the Bhāgavata) as he chides and advises his student Vyāsa, the revered traditional author of the epic Mahābhārata. Urging Vyāsa to surpass himself by writing a work that will deal exclusively with matters of spiritual concern, Nārada prompts Vyāsa to discover within himself by meditation the higher vision that he should then expound in his rendering that becomes the Bhāgavata Purāṇa. Nārada also narrates to Vyāsa his own story of becoming enlightened—momentarily meeting Krishna—in his previous life after serving and being instructed by sages as a child, subsequently becoming orphaned, and then practicing meditation as he had learned from the sages (1.4–6).

In order to lead into the story of King Parīkṣit's meeting with the sage Śuka, the scene shifts to events narrated in the Mahābhārata in the aftermath of the devastating fratricidal war that is the central story of that epic, with a focus on the devotional qualities of the hero, Arjuna, and his wife, Draupadī, and of Kuntī, the mother of Arjuna and his brothers, the Pāṇḍavas (1.7–8). The following passage highlights the devotional tenor of the Bhāgavata's remembrance of the Mahābhārata in Kuntī's address to Krishna as he prepares to depart for his home after the war.

QUEEN KUNTĪ PRAISES KRISHNA

Chapter 8

Kuntī said: "I shall bow down to you, the primordial supreme person, master of material nature. You exist within and outside all beings, and yet they do not recognize you. (8.18)[14] Like an actor wearing a costume, you are covered by the veil of *māyā*, imperceptible to the ignorant. You are unchanging, and yet you are not recognized by the foolish observer. (19)[15] Your purpose is to teach bhakti yoga to the most excellent ascetics and sages with flawless character. How then can we women see you? (20)[16] Obeisance to Krishna, son of Vasudeva and Devakī. Obeisance to Govinda, the boy of Nanda and the cowherds (of Vṛndāvana village). (21)[17] Obeisance to the Lord with a lotus navel! Obeisance to him who wears a lotus garland! Obeisance to the one with lotus eyes! And obeisance to you whose feet are like lotuses! (22)[18] Lord of the senses!

"You liberated (your mother) Devakī, who had been imprisoned for a long time by the cruel King Kaṁsa. Likewise, omnipresent Lord, it was you who saved me and my children from constant danger. (23) You saved us from poison, the great fire, the uncivilized assembly, from meeting with cannibals and from the travails of life in the forest. Again and again, Hari, you saved us from the weapons of many great warriors on the battlefield. And (now), you saved us from the weapon of Aśvatthāmā, son of Droṇa. (24)[19] Teacher of the world! Let those dangers come again and again, for in every instance we saw you. And seeing you means that we will not see birth and death again. (25) A person who is obsessed with improving social status, wealth, erudition, or physical appearance cannot approach you, for you are accessible only to the dispassionate. (26) You are the wealth of the destitute—obeisance! You are the Lord of liberation, indifferent to the workings of the *guṇas*, self-satisfied and tranquil—obeisance! (27)

"I regard you as eternal time, the ruler without beginning or end. You behave equally toward everyone, but people create discord among themselves. (28)[20] Bhagavān! No one knows the plan you have in mind, for you act like the common people. They think that you are partial, but you have neither favorite nor foe. (29)[21] O self of the universe! You, the unborn and nonacting self, take birth and act among animals, humans, sages, and aquatics—this is very confusing! (30) When you misbehaved (as a child), the cowherdess Yaśodā took a rope (to tie you), and you stood there fearfully, with your face lowered, your eyes brimming with tears, and your mascara in disarray. Your condition is bewildering to me, for even Fear itself is afraid of you! (31)

"Some say that the unborn takes birth in order to glorify the virtuous King Yadu, who is dear to him. He is born in that dynasty like sandalwood grows in Malaya. (32)[22] Others say that you, the unborn, took birth to kill the enemies of the gods and thus give relief to (your parents) Devakī and Vasudeva, who had beseeched you (to become their son). (33) And others say that you were born at Brahmā's request to remove the burden of the Earth, who was sinking in despair like a boat overloaded at sea. (34) Some say that those who are suffering in this world because their actions are driven by desire and ignorance—the Lord takes birth to get them to hear, meditate, and worship. (35) Only those persons who hear, sing about, proclaim, continuously meditate upon, and rejoice in your activities will swiftly see your lotus feet, which put an end to the river of rebirth. (36)

"Now that you have accomplished all that you desired, O Lord, are you planning to leave us—your friends, your dependents? We gave trouble to the kings (in battle), and now we have no refuge other than your lotus feet. (37) Who are we—the Pāṇḍavas and the Yadus, with our reputation and stature—if we do not see you? We will be like the senses without their ruler (the mind). (38) This land will no longer look beautiful, as it does now. Krishna, wielder of the club! At present, this land shines with your footprints, which are distinguishable by their characteristic markings. (39)[23] The realm is prosperous, plants and herbs are flavorful, and these forests, rivers, hills, and seas are flourishing—all because they are seen by you. (40) Lord of the universe! Soul of the universe! Form of the universe! Now please sever my strong bond of affection for my kin—the Pāṇḍus and the Vṛṣṇis. (41)[24] Lord of the Madhus! As the Ganges hastens toward the sea, let my heart transport my love to you, and to no one else. (42) Śrī Krishna, friend of Arjuna, best of the Vṛṣṇis, destroyer of ruling dynasties who abuse the earth! O Govinda, lord of limitless valor, you descend to relieve the suffering of the cows, *brāhmaṇas*, and gods. Master of yoga, teacher of all! O Bhagavān, obeisance to you!" (43)

The semidivine Bhīṣma plays a pivotal role in Vyāsa's Mahābhārata. Though himself childless, Bhīṣma acts as grandfather to both rival parties, the five sons of Pāṇḍu (the Pāṇḍavas), and their cousins, the iniquitous Kauravas. As the Mahābhārata narrates, and as the Bhāgavata summarizes in the following passage, Bhīṣma's death is delayed several weeks after he is mortally wounded in the epic's great war, giving him time to speak extensively on dharma, the duties of human beings in various contexts of social life. In this passage, the Bhāgavata's summary (narrated by Sūta), Bhīṣma reflects on ultimate causes and expends his final breaths in offering words of praise to Krishna as the truly ultimate cause, personally present to hear him.

BHĪṢMA SHARES HIS WISDOM

Chapter 9

Sūta said: Thus anxious for having killed (so many) people, and wanting to know all about dharma, King Yudhiṣṭhira went to the scene of the destruction, the battlefield of Kurukṣetra, where Devavrata (Bhīṣma) had fallen. (9.1) Then all the brothers followed on chariots drawn by fine horses decked in gold. The *brāhmaṇas*, such as Vyāsa and Dhaumya, also went. (2) Sage among *brāhmaṇas*! Even Bhagavān (Krishna) went there on a chariot with Dhanañjaya (Arjuna). Accompanied by all of them, King Yudhiṣṭhira shone like Kuvera, god of wealth, with his attendant Guhyakas. (3) Seeing Bhīṣma lying on the ground, like a god fallen from heaven, the Pāṇḍavas bowed before him, as did their companions and Krishna who carries a disk. (4) Most virtuous one! The *brāhmaṇa* sages, royal sages, and celestial sages were present there to see the hero of the Bharatas. (5) O *brāhmaṇa*! Parvata, Nārada, Dhaumya, the blessed Lord Bādarāyaṇa, Bṛhadaśva, Bharadvāja, Paraśurāma, the son of Reṇukā, with his disciples, Vasiṣṭha, Indrapramada, Trita, Gṛtsamada, Asita, Kakṣīvān, Gautama, Atri, Kauśika, Sudarśana, and other pure ascetics, such as Brahmarāta (Śuka), Kaśyapa, and Aṅgirasā, all arrived there accompanied by their disciples. (6–8) The best of Vasus (Bhīṣma) received and honored the assembled illustrious sages, for he knew dharma and its application according to time and place. (9) Seated there was Krishna, Lord of creation, who abides in the heart and manifests his form through his divine power (*māyā*). Bhīṣma knew of his glory and so he worshipped him. (10)[25] The sons of Pāṇḍu sat nearby, having gathered in love and respect. Bhīṣma gazed at them with eyes blinded by tears of affection. (11)

"Oh what hardship! What injustice! You sons of dharma would not have survived such distress, but you were protected by the *brāhmaṇas*, dharma, and the infallible Lord. (12)[26] When the general Pāṇḍu died, his wife, Pṛthā (Kuntī), was left with young children. Again and again, your mother endured many difficulties for your sake. (13) I believe all these unwelcome events were the work of Time, which controls the world and its rulers, like the wind pushes a cloud bank. (14) (Otherwise) where there is King Yudhiṣṭhira, the son of Dharma; the voracious Bhīma, who wields a club; the dark-hued archer Arjuna, with his bow Gāṇḍiva; and his friend Krishna—how could there be adversity? (15)[27] Indeed, O king, one can never know Krishna's plan. Philosophers try to ascertain it, but even they are thoroughly confused. (16)[28] Best of the Bharatas! Lord and protector! You should therefore accept this as divine arrangement, Krishna's plan, and look after the citizens, who have no protector. (17)

"This person is indeed Bhagavān himself, the original Nārāyaṇa. He bewilders the world by his elusive power and walks unrecognized among the Vṛṣṇis. (18) His most confidential nature, O monarch, is known to Bhagavān Shiva, the royal sage Nārada, and Kapila, who is directly

Bhagavān. (19) You regard him as your maternal cousin, beloved friend, and greatest well-wisher. Out of affection, you made him your counselor, messenger, and now your charioteer. (20) Krishna's actions are never motivated by favoritism, for he is the self of all beings and he sees all equally. He is blameless, one without a second, and yet free of self-conceit. (21) Even then, O king, see how compassionate he is toward those who are exclusively devoted to him! Indeed, Krishna has come directly before my eyes as I give up my life. (22) With mind absorbed in Krishna through bhakti, and with speech repeating his name, the yogi gives up his body and is freed from the karma of selfish desires. (23)[29] May that God of gods, Bhagavān, wait here as I abandon this body! The pathway of (my) meditation leads to his four-armed form and delightful lotus face, with reddish eyes and bright laughter." (24)

Sūta said: Upon hearing those words, Yudhiṣṭhira asked Bhīṣma, who lay on a bed of arrows, about various kinds of dharma, and the sages listened closely. (25) O seer! Bhīṣma, who knew the truth, described the dharmas prescribed according to a person's nature, social order, and stage of life; the characteristics of both the attachment and detachment perspectives, as taught in scripture; the dharmas concerning philanthropy; the dharmas of a king; the categories of dharmas concerning liberation; the dharmas of women; the dharmas in relation to Bhagavān, in overview and in detail; and (the four aims of human life—namely,) dharma, wealth, pleasure, and liberation, along with the means for attaining them, as exemplified in various histories and narratives. (26–28) As Bhīṣma was speaking about dharma, the sun's course ran into the northern hemisphere. Indeed, that time is desired by a yogi who can die at will. (29) Then Bhīṣma, leader of thousands, concluded his speech and, with wide-open eyes, focused his mind, free of all attachment, on the original person, Krishna, who was standing before him with four arms and brilliant yellow clothes. (30)[30]

At this point, Bhīṣma offers his final prayers to Krishna, remembering the Lord's beautiful form as he saw it on the Kurukṣetra battlefield. Focusing his mind and vision on Krishna, Bhīṣma breathes his last. Overcome with grief, all the gathered family and sages fall silent, "like birds at the end of the day."After Bhīṣma's demise, Sūta narrates Krishna's departure from the city of the Pāṇḍavas, Hastināpura, and return to his own city, Dvārakā (1.10–11). The reunion of Krishna with his devoted citizens prefigures later meetings of Bhagavān with his devotees, and in particular it prefigures the longing of Parīkṣit to meet his Lord. The cause of Parīkṣit's longing is narrated in the dramatic story of his being protected by Bhagavān in his mother's womb (chapter 12), followed by a sketch of his life as a righteous sovereign resolved to uphold dharmic principles in his realm. In chapters 16 and 17, Parīkṣit confronts the personification of the Kali age, who, threatened by Parīkṣit with death for harassing a cow and a bull (personifications of Earth and Dharma), begs the king for clemency. Since Kali displays submissiveness, Parīkṣit considers himself duty bound to grant him amnesty. With Kali henceforth residing within his kingdom, the present age of decadence and conflict is thus ushered in.

Our last passage in Book One consists of chapters 18 and 19, with which the book concludes. Chapter 18 tells of the crucial turning point in Parīkṣit's life when, in his prime, he is cursed by a *brāhmaṇa* child to die after the passing of seven days for having insulted the child's father (who, absorbed in meditation, had failed to receive the thirsty king while hunting). In this chapter, the portrayal of conflicting perceptions of reality and propriety set the stage for the Bhāgavata's extended explorations of these topics in later books.

In chapter 19 Parīkṣit, having thus been cursed to die, abandons all worldly duties to prepare for his imminent death. He soon meets Śuka, who will recite the Bhāgavata Purāṇa to the king without interruption during the king's remaining seven days and nights. It is this recitation that constitutes the primary dialogical frame of the Bhāgavata text as a whole, and which will commence in Book Two.

Here Sūta continues to speak to the assembly of sages at Naimiṣāraṇya, a sacred forest in present-day northern India. In the beginning verses of chapter 18 (here excluded) the sages have urged Sūta to expound on the activities of the "Unlimited" (*ananta*), as he had heard them previously when Śuka had spoken with Parīkṣit. We begin with Sūta's initial response, which is to narrate the circumstances leading to Parīkṣit's seeking sagely counsel in preparation for death. Parīkṣit then encounters Śuka and requests him to recite the Bhāgavata Purāṇa.

KING PARĪKṢIT AND SAGE ŚUKA MEET

Chapters 18 and 19

(Sūta said:) Sunlike sages! Questioned by you, I will expound to the extent of my own understanding. As birds soar in the sky as high as their ability allows, so the wise traverse along the path to Vishnu. (18.23) Once, taking up his bow and wandering in the forest in pursuit of deer, Parīkṣit became greatly fatigued, hungry, and thirsty. Searching for water, he happened upon a hermitage. There he beheld an ascetic seated peacefully, his eyes closed. (24–25) With restrained senses, breath, mind, and intelligence, the sage was in complete repose. He had reached unchanging existence in *brahman*, beyond the three states (wakefulness, dreaming, and dreamless sleep). (26)[31] His head was covered with scattered, matted locks, and he was seated on the skin of a *ruru* antelope. (27)

His palate parched with thirst, the king asked the sage for water. Yet the king received neither a straw mat to sit on, nor ceremonial water, nor even welcoming words. And so he grew irritated, considering himself disrespected. (28)[32] O *brāhmaṇas*! Suddenly afflicted by hunger and thirst, for the first time ever the king became envious and angry toward a *brāhmaṇa*. (29) Indeed, on departing, he spitefully draped a dead snake over the *brāhmaṇa* sage's shoulder with the tip of his bow; then he returned to the city. (30) (The king then considered) whether the sage's senses had been genuinely stilled or whether he had merely closed his eyes in feigned trance because of his thinking, "Why bother with these so-called *kṣatriyas*!" (31)

The sage's son, though a young boy, possessed great brahmanical power. While playing with other children, the boy heard about the king's offense to his father and immediately declared, (32)[33] "Alas, like fat crows that eat ritual remnants, or like (unfaithful) watchdogs, the transgression of kings is that of servants who sin against their master. (33)[34] It is clearly determined by *brāhmaṇas* that a mere *kṣatriya* is but a doorkeeper; how can a doorkeeper be allowed to eat from the master's plate in the master's home? (34) Gone is Lord Krishna, the subduer of the wayward! The boundaries of propriety have been laid asunder, so today *I* shall subdue them. Behold my power!" (35)[35]

Having announced this to his friends, the copper-eyed son of the seer touched the water of the Kauśiki River and released a thunderbolt of words. (36)[36] "Impelled by my curse, in seven days Takṣaka (the snake king) will surely bite this destroyer of his own dynasty, enemy of my father, for his transgression of social order." (37)[37] The boy then returned to the hermitage and saw the snake carcass on his father's neck. Infuriated, he wailed without restraint. (38) O *brāhmaṇa* (Śaunaka), the descendant of Aṅgirā heard his son's crying, and, gradually opening his eyes, he also saw the dead snake on his shoulder. (39)[38] Throwing the snake aside, he asked, "Son, why are you crying? By whom have you been troubled?" Then the boy explained. (40)

The *brāhmaṇa* heard of the undeserved curse upon the king and had no praise for his son. "Alas, today you have caused great trouble! For a slight wrong you have imposed an excessive penalty. (41) You, of unripe intelligence, have no right to equate this god among men—recognized as superior—with ordinary people. The citizens have been prosperous and free from anxiety under the protection of this king's incomparable prowess. (42) This emblem of sovereignty represents Vishnu, wielder of the disk. When he is gone, the world, left suddenly unprotected as if without shelter, will be plundered by hordes of thieves. (43) From today incomparable evil approaches us. Because the monarchy is destroyed, for the sake of plundering one another's wealth, the barbaric people will revile and kill one another, taking animals, women, and goods. (44) Then the dharma of honorable people, consisting of rules from the three Vedas for the *varṇas* and *āśramas*, shall be lost; henceforth the *varṇas* shall become intermingled, and, just like dogs and monkeys, people will be overcome with lust and greed. (45) Not only is this king the protector of dharma; he is highly regarded as emperor, as a great devotee of the Lord, and as a king-sage, having performed the horse sacrifice. To curse him was unwarranted, for he was overcome with hunger, thirst, and fatigue. (46)[39] A sin has been committed against innocent dependents of the king by a child of immature intelligence. May the blessed Lord, the self of all beings, pardon him! (47) Whether reviled, cheated, cursed, cast out, or beaten, the Lord's devotees, though they are powerful, never seek revenge." (48)

Thus the great sage regretted his son's misdeed, considering as unimportant the king's offense against himself. (49) Because their refuge is the self, beyond mundane qualities, saints engaged by others in the dualities of the world are generally neither agitated nor exultant. (50)

Sūta continued: Meanwhile on returning home, King Parīkṣit pondered the contemptible deed he had done. Deeply vexed he cried, "Alas, what a low, ignoble act I have committed against a faultless and powerful *brāhmaṇa*! (19.1) Surely, therefore, for my neglect of divine order, an unavoidable disaster is not far off. But my resolve is to let events take their course, that I may become free of sin; thus I shall never commit such a mistake again. (2) Today let my kingdom, youth, and abundant wealth be burned in the fire of the *brāhmaṇas*' anger, so that my sinful attitude may never again disturb the twice-born, gods, and cows." (3)[40]

While thus contemplating, the king heard that the sage's son had cursed him to die by the lethal and imminent snakebite of Takṣaka.

Parīkṣit welcomed this news as the perfect way to achieve detachment, for one clinging to this world. (4) And so, from the beginning, Parīkṣit resolved to reject both this and the next world as negligible. Considering service to Krishna's feet as the highest engagement, he sat down near the river of immortality to end his life, fasting. (5)[41]

"Who, destined to die, could fail to resort to this river bearing the most excellent, rippling waters, mixed with dust from Krishna's feet and blessed *tulasī* leaves? She purifies both worlds, and their rulers." (6)[42] So resolving to fast and await death by the river that emanates from Vishnu's foot, this descendant of the Pāṇḍavas, avowed to silence and freed from all mundane association, dedicated himself exclusively to the feet of Mukunda (Vishnu). (7) Whereupon greatly wise sages whose presence purifies the whole world arrived with their disciples on pretexts of making pilgrimage to sacred places, though actually such saints themselves purify the sacred places. (8)[43] (Prominent among the arriving sages were) Atri, Cyavana, Śaradvān, Ariṣṭanemi, Bhṛgu, Vasiṣṭha, Parāśara, Viśvāmitra, Aṅgirā, Paraśurāma, Utathya, Indrapramada, Idhmavāhu, Medhātithi, Devala, Ārṣṭiṣena, Bāradvāja, Gautama, Pippalāda, Maitreya, Aurva, Kavaṣa, Kumbhayoni, Dvaipāyana, and the blessed Nārada. (9–10)[44]

In verses 11–23 Parīkṣit explains that he has been cursed to die after the passing of seven days, and he announces his intention to remain fasting until that moment. The sages approve his plan, promising to remain with him until his demise. In the remainder of the chapter Parīkṣit asks the sages a crucial question; the most honorable sage Śuka arrives in their midst; and Parīkṣit praises him and begins to inquire of him about ultimate matters.

"Experienced *brāhmaṇas*, with confidence I therefore ask you that which must be asked: among the various duties for all beings, especially those soon to die, what is the right thing to do? Please deliberate!" (24)

Just then the blessed son of Vyāsa (Śuka) happened to arrive there while indifferently roaming the earth. He was without visible signs of *āśrama*, self-satisfied, surrounded by children, and negligently dressed. (25)[45] At sixteen years of age, his body had delicate feet, hands, thighs, arms, shoulders, and forehead. His charming face had wide eyes, a high-bridged nose, equally fine ears, and beautiful eyebrows. His neck was like a well-formed conch. (26) His collarbone was flush with his broad, raised chest; he had a swirled navel and rippled stomach. He was clothed by the directions (naked), with curly, scattered hair, long arms, and skin the hue of the highest of gods (Krishna). (27) With his darkish complexion, exceptional features, and winning smile Śuka was attractive to women's minds. Although his splendor was concealed, all the assembled sages, being able to read character from outward appearance, rose from their seats. (28) Parīkṣit, whose life was granted by Vishnu, showed reverence to Śuka with bowed head, receiving him as a welcome guest. The ignorant women and children disbanded, and the respected Śuka was invited to take a raised seat. (29)[46] There he was surrounded by an assembly of the greatest seers—*brāhmaṇa*, royal, and celestial—as the resplendent moon is surrounded by a multitude of planets, constellations, and stars. (30)[47] The devotee king respectfully approached the intelligent sage, who sat there peacefully. Offering obeisance with bowed head and joined palms, he questioned him in earnest tones. (31)

Parīkṣit said: "O *brāhmaṇa*! How wonderful it is that today we lowly *kṣatriyas* may serve the saints! By kindly appearing as an unexpected guest you have made us into a place of pilgrimage. (32)[48] Indeed, any residence is quickly sanctified merely by the remembrance of such persons as yourself, not to mention seeing and touching you, cleansing your feet, or offering you a seat. (33) Great yogi! By your presence even the worst evils are instantly vanquished, just as demons are vanquished in Vishnu's presence. (34) To please his cousins, Lord Krishna, who is dear to the sons of Pāṇḍu, accepted me, their grandson, as his kin. (35)[49] Otherwise why would you, who were previously unseen, now become visible for us? It is the complete munificence of a perfected being upon those of us who are about to die. (36)[50] And so I ask you, the best teacher of yogis, by all means to tell me what is the ideal practice for a person preparing to die? (37) Master, kindly inform me what is to be heard, chanted, performed, remembered, and shared by human beings, and what should be avoided. (38)[51] O *brāhmaṇa*! Your blessed presence at the homes of pious householders is rarely to be seen, except possibly when the cows are being milked." (39)

Sūta said: Thus expressly questioned by the king with gentle voice, the blessed son of Vyāsa, knower of dharma, proceeded to reply. (40)

SUGGESTIONS FOR FURTHER READING

Biardeau, Madeleine. 1999. *Hinduism: The Anthropology of a Civilization*. New Delhi: Oxford University Press.
Discusses classical Hindu concepts of kingship and of the ideal *brāhmaṇa* (relevant especially to chapters 18 and 19); see in particular pp. 53–63.

Doniger, Wendy. 1993. "Echoes of the *Mahabharata*: Why Is a Parrot the Narrator of the *Bhagavata Purana* and the *Devibhagavata Purana*?" In *Purana Perennis*, edited by Wendy Doniger, 31–57. Albany: SUNY Press.
Explores three versions of Śuka's story, comparing and contrasting Śuka with Kāmadeva, Cupid (relevant to chapter 19).

Gupta, Gopal K. 2013. "Ethics: 'May Calamities Befall Us at Every Step': The Bhāgavata's Response to the Problem of Evil." In *The Bhāgavata Purāṇa: Sacred Text and Living Tradition*, edited by Ravi M. Gupta and Kenneth R. Valpey, 63–75. New York: Columbia University Press.
Refers to and elaborates on the discussion about causality in chapter 9.

Gupta, Ravi M. 2007. *The Caitanya Vaiṣṇava Vedānta of Jīva Gosvāmī: When Knowledge Meets Devotion*. New York: Routledge.
Pp. 105–12 provide an analysis of Vedānta as represented in the first verse of the Bhāgavata Purāṇa.

Haberman, David L. 2002. *The Bhaktirasāmṛtasindhu of Rūpa Gosvāmin*. Delhi: Motilal Banarsidass.
The introduction provides a helpful presentation of the Indian aesthetic notion of *rasa* (taste, relish, relationality); relevant specifically to Bhāgavata Purāṇa 1.1.3. and generally to the entire Bhāgavata Purāṇa.

Valpey, Kenneth R. 2009. "The *Bhāgavata Purāṇa* as a *Mahabharata* Reflection." In *Parallels and Comparisons: Proceedings of the Dubrovnik International Conference on the Sanskrit Epics and Puranas, September 2005*. Zagreb: Croatian Academy of Sciences and Arts.
This article calls attention to important Bhāgavata Purāṇa passages, especially in Book One, that function as reflections on the epic Mahābhārata.

BOOK TWO

The Sage Śuka Begins His Answer
Vishnu's Descents: An Overview
The Bhāgavata in a Nutshell

With the final chapter of Book One, the setting of the scene for the remainder of the Bhāgavata Purāṇa's core narrative is complete. Now in Book Two begins the interlocution between the questioning King Parīkṣit and the responding sage Śuka. What might be termed the beginning proper of the text is what constitutes Book Two, or one could designate it grand opening number two, acknowledging the importance of Book One as an equally significant, if more broadly circumscribed, introduction to the Bhāgavata.

In stark contrast to the Bhāgavata Purāṇa's longest book, Book Ten (with its ninety chapters), Book Two is the shortest, with ten chapters. Yet Book Two serves important purposes in setting out a cosmic-transcosmic interrelationship that makes possible and purposeful devotional practice—bhakti—directed toward the one absolute being, Bhagavān, identified as Nārāyaṇa, Vishnu, Hari, Vāsudeva, or Krishna. Parīkṣit's interest in this subject is focused entirely by his acute awareness of his imminent death, and Śuka exhibits a full sense of the situation's gravity and of his own critical role in the proper exposition of the Bhāgavata's manifold theme.

Our first passage in Book Two constitutes the book's beginning, in which Śuka praises Parīkṣit's profound and urgent question (1.19.37–38), and then, after denouncing the mentality of persons too preoccupied with worldly pleasures to ask such questions, he offers his initial answer. At the end of this passage (vv. 2.1.16–21), Śuka gives a brief description of yoga practice reminiscent of classical eightfold yoga that, however, calls explicit attention to Vishnu as the object upon which the yogi is recommended to direct the mind.

THE SAGE ŚUKA BEGINS HIS ANSWER

Chapter 1

Oṁ! Obeisance unto Vāsudeva, who is Bhagavān!

The blessed Śuka spoke: O king, your inquiry is most excellent, for it benefits the world. Knowers of the self agree that among subjects of human discourse, this is the best. (1.1)[1] Best of kings, there are thousands of subjects for discussion among humans who, blind to self-knowledge, pursue domestic happiness. (2)[2] O king, their lives are spent at night with sleep, their vigor is robbed by sexual intercourse, and their days are depleted by moneymaking or family maintenance. (3) And so they are lost amid their own soldiers—body, children, wife, and whatnot—although these are transitory. Though seeing their end, one sees not. (4) Descendant of Bharata, the self of all, the adorable Lord Hari, is therefore to be heard about, praised, and remembered by one desiring peace. (5)[3] The highest reward of a human birth, by practices such as *sāṁkhya*, yoga, and complete dedication to one's dharma, is remembrance of Nārāyaṇa at the end of life. (6) King, most sages indifferent to rules and prohibitions, and situated beyond worldly qualities, still rejoice in accounts of Hari's qualities. (7)

This Purāṇa named Bhāgavata is equivalent to the Veda. When the Dvāpara age began I learned it from my father, Dvaipāyana. (8)[4] Sage among kings! Although I was thoroughly situated beyond worldly qualities, my mind was captivated by the pastimes of the best praised Lord. That is the account I studied. (9) That same Bhāgavata Purāṇa I shall recite to you, a devotee of the supreme person. Thus your faithful attitude shall soon abide in Mukunda (Krishna). (10) O king, for those despairing, for those desiring, and for the disciplined, ongoing recitation of Hari's names is the assurance of complete fearlessness. (11) What use are a hedonist's countless unconscious years in this world when it is known that one moment spent pursuing the highest excellence is better? (12) The sage-king Khaṭvāṅga, having become aware that his remaining life span was short, instantly renounced everything and resorted to Hari, who is fearlessness itself. (13)

Kaurava! You similarly have but seven days of life remaining, during which you must prepare everything for passage to the next life. (14) When the end-time (death) arrives, a person must be free of fear. With the weapon of nonattachment one must cut off longing for one's body and what is related to it. (15)[5] A resolute person should depart from home, bathe in the water of a sacred place, and sit on a clean, solitary, properly prepared seat. (16) One should practice mentally reciting the pure and sublime three-part syllable (*a-u-m*); with breath controlled, not forgetting the seed of the Veda (*auṁ*, or *oṁ*), one should subdue the mind. (17)[6] With the intellect as guide, a person should withdraw the senses from their objects with the mind. The mind, ever distracted by previous actions, should then be set intently upon realizing felicity. (18)[7] Finally, with undistracted consciousness, one can meditate on the Lord's bodily limbs, one by one, while the mind, yoked off from sensuality, ought not recall any sense objects. That most excellent form of Vishnu is where the mind can be completely pleased. (19) One's mind is distracted by passion and fooled by darkness. The wise must endeavor with such concentration as removes the impurity caused by them. (20)[8] Yogis who thus maintain concentration soon attain yoga steeped in devotion such that they behold the auspicious shelter (Vishnu). (21)

In the remainder of chapter one (vv. 22–39) Śuka instructs Parīkṣit in a meditational practice whereby various specific features of the cosmos are identified as particular parts of Bhagavān's bodily form. For example, various realms (or "planets"—*loka*), from lowest to highest, are his feet, legs, hips, chest, neck, and head; various celestial beings are his bodily sense organs; rivers are his veins, trees are his body hair, and the air is his breathing; clouds are his head hair, and the moon is his mind.

Śuka advises further meditational practice in chapter two, directed inward, to Bhagavān situated in one's own heart in a form described in some detail—as being charmingly dressed and ornamented and as sporting a winning smile and glancing eyes (see Book Three, chapter 28, for a more detailed description of such meditation). This description is followed by a brief account of how the yogi prepares for death by a process of cosmic devolution—the reverse of cosmic creation. Depending on one's aim there are various possible destinations after death, and the next chapter lists several gods to be worshipped, each for the fulfillment of a specific desire. Śuka contrasts such pursuit of desires with that of one "whose intelligence is noble" (2.3.10), who directs all attention to Bhagavān, the supreme person.

Sūta reports to Śaunaka that Parīkṣit had taken these preliminary instructions of Śuka to heart, resolving to abandon all lingering bonds to temporal life. Parīkṣit then proceeds in earnest to ask Śuka about Bhagavān, starting with inquiry about the supreme divinity's relation to the manifest world. The remainder of Book Two consists of Śuka's responses to these questions, which he provides in the form of a dialogue between the cosmic demiurge, Brahmā, and his son, the sage Nārada. Brahmā sketches a picture of cosmic order that unfolds by the power and direction of the supreme being, Bhagavān, or Vishnu, who, in turn, is identified bodily with various features of the world (elaborating on Śuka's earlier description of the cosmic divine form). In the next passage (chapter seven), Brahmā describes the "pastime descents" (*līlā avatāras*) of Vishnu, suggesting that their various activities in the world for the restoration of dharma dramatically illustrate how the supreme divinity actively relates with the world.

VISHNU'S DESCENTS: AN OVERVIEW

Chapter 7

Brahmā said: When the infinite Lord in his boarlike form constituted of all sacrifices undertook to raise the earth, with his tusk he dashed asunder the first demon who had come forth like a mountain from within the Great Ocean, just as Indra smashed mountains with his thunderbolt. (7.1)[9]

Suyajña, born to Prajāpati Ruci and his wife, Ākūti, fathered the deathless gods headed by Suyama with his wife, Dakṣiṇā. Since Suyajña removed (*hara*) great distress from the three worlds, Svāyambhuva Manu then called him Hari. (2)

O twice-born! Thereafter Kapila, along with nine sisters, was born to Prajāpati Kardama and his wife, Devahūti. He spoke to his mother on the self's sojourn by which she achieved Kapila's refuge, having been cleansed of the self's impurity—the mud from contact with the *guṇas*. (3)[10]

Satisfied with Atri, who prayed for offspring, the Lord promised, "I shall be given (*datta*) by me." Hence that "given" one is the Lord. Yadu, Haihaya, and others, whose bodies were purified by the dust of Datta's lotus feet, gained both yogic perfection and worldly prosperity. (4)[11]

In the beginning, I undertook austerity with the desire to manifest the manifold realms. As a result of my austerity, the ancient Lord initially became the four Sanas (Sanatkumāra, Sanaka, Sanandana, and Sanātana). Self-knowledge had been destroyed by the previous cosmic inundation, and yet once again it became thoroughly manifest, so that sages could again see the self. (5)[12]

Mūrti, Dharma's wife and Dakṣa's daughter, gave birth to the twins Nara-Nārāyaṇa. Seeing those Lords' power of austerity, Anaṅga's *apsarā* minions were unable to undermine Nara-Nārāyaṇa's practices of self-restraint. (6)[13] Adepts burn up lust by their wrathful glance, yet they cannot burn up their own burning, unrestrained wrath. But lust dares not enter the Lord's heart, not to mention his mind. (7)

Though a mere child, Dhruva entered forests to practice austerity, having been pierced by the sharp words of the king's co-wife. Pleased, the Lord bestowed upon him the coveted position of *dhruva* (the pole-star), to which celestial sages from above and below offer praise. (8)[14]

King Vena was falling toward hell, his power and influence destroyed by the twice-borns' searing words for straying from the righteous path. Pṛthu, who had been prayed for (by the twice-born), saved Vena from hell and gained the position of heir apparent on earth. He then milked the earth for all kinds of produce. (9)[15]

The Lord as Ṛṣabha, the son of Nābhi and Sudevī, performed the yoga of inertness, gaining the vision of sameness that seers celebrate as the *paramahaṁsa* state. Ṛṣabha was self-situated, with senses entirely calm, fully liberated from worldly contact. (10)[16]

Then the Lord, horse-headed Hayaśirāḥ, appeared as a golden-hued personification of sacrifice in my *satra* rite. Constituted of Vedic hymn and ritual, he is the very self of all the gods. Sublime words came forth from his breathing through the nostrils. (11)[17]

When the aeon was ending, Matsya appeared to Manu as the earthlike shelter for the aggregate of all beings. When the Vedic teachings slipped out of my mouth into the fearsome flooding waters, he picked them up and happily frolicked. (12)[18]

When the best of gods and demons were churning the Milk Ocean to gain the elixir of immortality, the primeval Lord appeared in the form of a turtle. He held up a mountain on his back, and as that rotating peak scratched his itch, he dozed. (13)[19]

He then adopted the form of a man-lion with terrible maul and teeth and rolling eyebrows, dispelling the gods' great fear. In no time he set the club-flailing and trembling demon king upon his thighs and ripped him asunder with his claws. (14)[20]

The leader of a herd (of elephants), while in a lake, was grasped on the foot by a powerful crocodile. Distressed, his trunk grasping a lotus, the elephant exclaimed, "O primordial person, Lord of unlimited realms, you are celebrated as a sacred crossing place, the hearing of whose names is auspicious!" (15) The immeasurable Hari perceived him as one in need of refuge. Seated on the wings of Garuḍa, king of birds, and armed with his disk, the Lord split the crocodile's mouth with his disk. Taking hold of the elephant's trunk, with compassion the Lord freed him. (16)[21]

Then he who is the principle of sacrifice strode upon these worlds. Though the youngest of Aditi's sons, in virtues he prevails: by a three-step ruse as a dwarf he gained the earth. Even lords cannot depose (a king) who follows the path of dharma, except by begging (from the king). (17)[22] Bali's bearing upon his head the water that had washed the feet of Urukrama rendered meaningless for him the superintendence of the gods. Indeed, dear Nārada, even without his promise, he had no other intention than to dedicate himself to Hari. (18)[23]

And unto you, noble Nārada, with deep affection the ingratiated Lord expounded yoga and knowledge of God, which is the lamp for the truth of the self. Only those whose shelter is Vāsudeva truly know this. (19)[24]

Then, among the succession of Manus, one descendant of the Manu dynasty bears the disk, his own power. Undeterred in the ten directions, the disk subjugates evil kings, spreading its shining fame by its exploits among all the three worlds. (20)

The blessed Lord Dhanvantari is fame personified. By invocation of his name he rapidly removes disease from the sickly human beings. He recovers (from the demons) the elixir of immortality that was his share in the sacrifice. Appearing in the world he instructs the knowledge of preserving life. (21)[25]

The military order, which abandoned the right path in its longing to suffer hell and which was hostile to the *brāhmaṇas*, was destined to die. The great one, the ferocious hero Paraśurāma, plucks out twenty-one times that oppressive thorn with his keen ax. (22)[26]

Appearing in Ikṣvāku's dynasty with his expansions in order to please us, the Lord of all powers, Rāma, remains within the forest on his father's order, together with his wife, Sītā, and younger brother Lakṣmaṇa. Opposing him, the ten-headed Rāvaṇa meets destruction. (23) Like Shiva, Rāma had desired to raze the enemy's city. The ocean, teaming with sea beasts (*makara*), snakes, and crocodiles, all boiling from Rāma's crimson glance that was stirred with anger for the sake of his beloved, in fear and trembling had hastily given passage to him. (24)[27] With the tusks of Indra's vehicle elephant shattered by the encounter with Rāvaṇa's chest, the hearty laughter of the abductor of Rāma's wife will mock all directions. Then suddenly Rāma will break forth with the thunderous twanging sounds of his bow from amid the armies and remove Rāvaṇa along with his vital airs. (25)

Along with his counterpart (Balarāma), he of glossy black hair (Krishna) appears to reduce the earth's anguish caused by oppression from the armies opposed to the gods. He whose way is uninferable by common folk will also perform acts demonstrating his own greatness. (26)[28] As an infant he will suckle the life from the giant-bodied Pūtana, and as a three-month-old baby with his foot he will overturn a cart; or as a toddler crawling between two sky-scraping *arjuna* trees he will uproot them. No other could ever perform such deeds. (27)[29] Indeed, with the shower of his merciful glance he will bring to life the pasture animals and herders of Vraja who all will have drunk poisonous water. Sporting in that water (of the Yamunā), to purify it he will then eradicate the snake whose rolling tongue exudes deadly poison. (28)[30] At night as the denizens of Vraja rest, the dry forest will burst into blazing flame. As their time of death becomes imminent, Krishna, whose prowess is incomprehensible, along with Balarāma, will have them close their eyes and free them from the fire. His acts are indeed divine. (29) Whatever rope his mother gathers for binding her son will not be long enough. Her mind made apprehensive by seeing all the worlds in his wide-open mouth, that cowherdess will be awakened. (30)[31] Further, Krishna will free Nanda (his foster father) from fear (of the python) and from Varuṇa's noose. He will also free the cowherds who will be arrested in caves by the son of Maya (Vyoma). Verily, Krishna will take the residents of Gokula, who are busy working hard during the day and so sleep soundly at night, to the Vaikuṇṭha realm. (31) The celestial lord Indra sends forth heavy rain to inundate Vraja when his sacrifice is neglected by the cowherd men. Mercifully desiring to protect the animals, as if picking a mushroom the seven-year-old Krishna playfully raises aloft Govardhana hill with one hand for seven days. (32) Krishna, intent upon *rāsa*, sports in the forest at night in the moon's splendorous light, accompanied by beautiful songs and extended melodies of the Vraja men's wives, whose pangs of passion are inflamed. He will then sever the head of Kuvera's attendant, Śaṅkhacūḍa, an abductor. (33)[32] There are also Pralamba, Khara (Dhenuka), Dardura (Baka), Keśī, Ariṣṭa, the wrestlers, the elephant (Kuvalayāpīḍa), Kaṁsa, Kālayavana, and the likes of Pauṇḍraka and the ape (Dvivida); and others, led by Śālva, Kuja (Naraka), Balvala, Dantavakra, the seven bulls, Śambara, Vidūratha, and Rukmi; and Kāmboja, Matsya, Kuru, Sṛñjaya, Kaikaya, and others brave in battle, armed with bows and arrows. Although deserving simply to vanish, they will be dispatched to his own abode by Lord Hari, sometimes acting under the assumed names of Bala (Balarāma), Pārtha (Arjuna), or Bhīma. (34–35)[33]

Pondering the lost understanding and shortened life span of human beings by the passage of time and the difficulty for persons to comprehend his own Veda, the Lord will appear as Satyavatī's son (Vyāsa). In accord with the age he will surely divide the Veda tree into several branches. (36)

Those inimical to the gods will become well positioned in the Vedic way and destroy the worlds with darting invisible cities created by Maya. Contriving an alluring disguise that unsettles their conviction, the Lord (as Buddha) will expound various subdharmic principles. (37)[34]

At the end of the Kali age, when there are no discourses on Hari even in the sanctuaries of saints, when the twice-born become heretics and the lower classes become human gods (kings), and when the utterances *svāhā*, *svadhā*, *vaṣaṭ* are not heard anywhere, then the Lord will appear as the divine punisher Kalki. (38)[35]

During cosmic generation there are austerity, myself (Brahmā), and the nine progenitor sages; during cosmic sustenance there are dharma, sacrifice, the Manus, the gods, and the protective lords; but during cosmic demise there is adharma, Hara (Shiva), demons and other such entities ruled by anger. All these wondrous beings share in the Lord's immense power. (39)

Who in this world is able to enumerate the powers of Vishnu, who measured the three worlds by his strides? That genius supported the three worlds, which violently quaked because of his swift, unhindered movement from the resort of the triple equilibrium (*pradhāna*) to the highest abode. (40)[36] Neither I nor these sages older than you, much less those who are junior, know the extent of the supreme person's wondrous power (*māyā*). To this day the thousand-headed primal lord Śeṣa sings his virtues but can reach no end. (41)[37] To those sincere ones whose entire shelter is the Lord's feet, this unlimited Lord invariably bestows mercy, and they cross beyond the Lord's insurmountable illusion (*māyā*). Not so for those who have an "I-mine" mentality absorbed in the body, which will become food for dogs and jackals. (42)

Truly, I know the supreme's wondrous opulence (*yoga-māyā*), as do you and the blessed lord Shiva, as also the best of Daityas (Prahlāda), Manu's wife (Śatarūpā), Manu, their progeny (two sons and three daughters), Prācīnabarhi, Ṛbhu, Aṅga (Purūrava), and Dhruva; also Ikṣvāku, Aila, Mucukunda, Videha (Janaka), Gādhi, Raghu, Ambarīṣa, Sagara, Gaya, Nāhuṣa (Yayāti), and so on; further, Māndhātā, Alarka, Śatadhanu, Anu, Rantideva, Devavrata (Bhīṣma), Bali, Amūrttaraya, Dilīpa, Saubhari, Utaṅka, Śibi, Devala, Pippalāda, Sārasvata, Uddhava, Parāśara, and Bhūriṣena; so also the eminences Vibhīṣaṇa, Hanumān, Upendradatta (Śuka), Pārtha (Arjuna), Arṣṭiṣeṇa, and Śrutadeva. (43–45) Indeed all these persons comprehend and overcome the Lord's illusion (*māyā*). So also do women, *śūdras*, Hūnas, Śabaras, and even unfortunate beings when they are guided by the behavior of those who resort to Vishnu of marvelous strides. Even animals can do this; what then need be said of those who are learned? (46)[38]

What the wise person calls *brahman*—unlimited happiness; free from sorrow; eternal; at peace; fearless; constituted of faultless knowledge; pure; equipoised; the supreme self (*paramātmā*) of all existence, manifest and unmanifest; sacred sound; the great performer of acts who has nothing to gain from action—that indeed is an aspect of the supreme person Bhagavān. *Māyā* shyly retreats from his presence. (47)[39] Ascetics give up the method to achieve nondifference when their minds are controlled, just as the self-sufficient Indra does not require a spade used to dig a well. (48)[40] The Lord is also the master of rewards, as (he ensures) the accomplishment of a felicitous action bestowed according to position and disposition (of the actor). And when the body is disintegrating, departing from its own constituents, the person, being unborn, never disintegrates, like the sky. (49)[41]

Dear son, I have told you briefly about this Lord, creator of the world. (This world, consisting of) cause and effect, is not different from Hari, and yet he is different from it. (50) This Bhāgavata, which the Lord spoke to me, is a summary of his glories. You may elaborate upon it. (51) Describe this with resolve, in such a way that among people bhakti shall arise for Lord Hari, the self of all and support of everything. (52) When the enchanting ways (*māyā*) of this Lord are described, relished, and heard regularly with faith, one is not perplexed by illusion (*māyā*). (53)[42]

Leading into the remainder of Book Two and much of Book Three, Parīkṣit urges Śuka to continue relating what Nārada had spoken to his audience, having heard from his father, Brahmā. Parīkṣit reiterates the beneficial effects of hearing the Bhāgavata (especially cleansing the heart of worldly tendencies) and then proceeds to ask several detailed questions about the nature of the self in relation to the body, the nature of Bhagavān's body, the relationship of Bhagavān to his energies, the nature of time, action (karma), social structure, and more about the cosmic form of the Lord.

Chapter nine tells the birth story of Brahmā, the demiurge responsible for creating the world using the preexisting great elements (earth, water, fire, air, sky). Brahmā was born from a lotus growing from Vishnu's navel, but when Brahmā first opens his eyes, he knows nothing about his own origin or purpose. While seeking the source of the lotus, Brahmā hears two syllables—*ta-pa*—which together make up a command in Sanskrit: perform austerity! Unable to ascertain the source of the sound, Brahmā decides to follow the command. After a thousand celestial years, Vishnu reveals himself and his world, Vaikuṇṭha. (For a description of Vaikuṇṭha, see Book Three, chapter 15.) Pleased with Brahmā's austerity, he shakes his hand and wishes him good luck in creation. When Brahmā asks to learn about Vishnu's nature and how he generates the cosmos, Vishnu speaks several verses that have come to be regarded as the "essential Bhāgavata." This wisdom is later taught by Brahmā to his son Nārada, and by Nārada to Vyāsa, who then composes the Purāṇa in a more elaborated form.

Most commentators regard four of the seven verses spoken by Vishnu as especially significant, from 33 to 36. These short and yet difficult verses receive extensive attention from commentators, leading to diverse interpretations.

THE BHĀGAVATA IN A NUTSHELL

Chapter 9

Śrī Bhagavān said: Knowledge of me is the greatest mystery. Receive it (now), as spoken by me, along with its application, secrets, and supplements. (9.31)[43] All that I am—my nature, form, qualities, and activities: may you comprehend that truth, by my grace. (32) I alone existed in the beginning, and nothing else that is beyond cause and effect existed. All of this after (creation) is me, and what remains (in the end)—I am also that! (33)[44] Know my *māyā* as that which may appear to be without substance and may appear unrelated to me, like a reflection, like darkness. (34)[45] The primary elements have entered each of the various living beings but have also not entered them. Similarly, I am in all beings and yet I am not in them. (35)[46] One who wishes to know the truth about me should investigate in this way: "It exists in all places and at all times because of its connectedness and separateness." (36)[47] Remain intent on this goal with utmost concentration and you will not be confused during or between creations. (37)

Śrī Śuka said: Thus Hari, who moves all people, thoroughly instructed the highest Brahmā. Then as Brahmā watched, Hari concealed his own form. (38) Brahmā folded his hands in reverence for Hari, the goal of the senses, who had become invisible. Then he (Brahmā), who contains all beings, created this universe as it was before. (39)[48]

The tenth and final chapter of the second book begins with a list of ten topics that are identified as the defining characteristics of the Bhāgavata. The standard list of characteristics for a Purāṇa consists of only five topics: creation, dissolution, genealogies, the periods of Manus, and the histories of kings. The Bhāgavata's list includes these five, while adding five of its own. Each listing includes (in parentheses) a brief explanation of each characteristic:

1. *sarga*—creation (of the primary elements and senses)
2. *visarga*—secondary creation (of varieties of beings by Brahmā)
3. *sthāna*—continuance (preservation by Vishnu)
4. *poṣaṇa*—nourishing (Vishnu's mercy toward his devotees)
5. *manvantara*—the periods of the Manus (the right dharma)
6. *ūti*—impetus (the living entities' desires for action)
7. *īśānukathā*—narrations of the Lord (activities of Vishnu and his devotees during the Lord's various descents)
8. *nirodha*—circumscribing (while sleeping, Vishnu breathes in the creation)
9. *mukti*—liberation (returning to one's constitutional position)
10. *āśraya*—refuge (the Supreme Truth, refuge of all)

The Bhāgavata makes it clear that the tenth topic is the most important and the first nine are meant to highlight the tenth. Commentators have suggested various ways of correlating each topic with one of the twelve books of the Bhāgavata. Śrīdhara, for example, states that beginning with Book One each book discusses one topic, in order, so that the greatest topic (*āśraya*) is elaborated in Book Ten, which narrates the activities of Krishna.

Upon completing this general description of the Bhāgavata's contents, chapter 10 launches immediately into the first topic, creation. The history of creation is told several times and in various ways throughout the Bhāgavata Purāṇa. This chapter picks up on a favored cosmogonic theme of the Bhāgavata—creation of the primary elements from the body of the cosmic person (*puruṣa*). Here the various aspects of the universe are correlated with the limbs and faculties of the cosmic body. (Chapter 1 of Book Two discusses a similar theme.) For example, when the Cosmic Person has a desire to see, all the requisite elements are manifested—light, the eyes, the power of vision, and the objects of sight. Creation usually moves from the subtle to the more tangible, and desire is always the impetus behind each step. Śuka ends this description by making a rather surprising statement: the wise do not accept this cosmic body as a genuine form of Bhagavān, for it is a product of matter. Rather, they know the Lord's body to be transcendent and unaffected by the work of creation.

SUGGESTIONS FOR FURTHER READING

Edelmann, Jonathan B. 2013. "Dialogues on Natural Theology: The Bhāgavata Purāṇa's Cosmology as Religious Practice." In *The Bhāgavata Purāṇa: Sacred Text and Living Tradition*, edited Ravi M. Gupta and Kenneth R. Valpey, 48–62 New York: Columbia University Press.
This chapter (relevant to the end of chapter 1) offers an overview of three ways in which the Bhāgavata presents cosmography and cosmology as objects of yogic meditation. It is also relevant for Book Three and Book Five.

Holdrege, Barbara A. 2006. "From Purāṇa-Veda to Kārṣṇa-Veda: The Bhāgavata Purāṇa as Consummate Smṛti and Śruti Incarnate." *Journal of Vaishnava Studies* 15, no. 1 (fall): 31–70.
This article discusses ways in which the Bhāgavata has been regarded in relation to the Veda (relevant to verse 2.1.8).

Joshi, Rasik Vihari. 1974. "Catuḥślokī or Saptaślokī Bhāgavata: A Critical Study." *Purāṇa* 16, no. 1:26–46.
An overview of the debates surrounding the length and interpretation of the "essential Bhāgavata," spoken by Vishnu to Brahmā (in chapter 9).

BOOK THREE

Brahmā's Creation and the Measures of Time
Four Sages Curse the Gatekeepers of Heaven
The Nature of Temporal Nature
Yogic Meditation on the Form of Vishnu

Book Three opens with the Pāṇḍavas' uncle Vidura, while wandering in exile, meeting Uddhava, a close friend of Krishna. As an instance of the Bhāgavata's structural feature comparable to a widening spiral (see the introduction), readers are here brought back to the subject of Krishna's passing from the world (introduced in Book One). With deep emotion Uddhava recollects highlights of Krishna's life; then he advises Vidura to approach the sage Maitreya for spiritual instruction (3.4). Vidura encounters Maitreya at Haridvara (Hardwar), where they converse on a wide variety of topics (covering the remainder of Book Three—chapters 5–33). Maitreya initially speaks (in chapter 8) of cosmic creation, beginning with a description of Brahmā's appearance on a lotus that sprouts from the navel of Vishnu as he reclines in a state of semislumber on a couch formed by the cosmic king of serpents (Ananta). Only after long meditation is Brahmā able to see Vishnu, the source of his own existence, and only then (in chapter 9), after offering praises to Vishnu, is he able to hear Vishnu's command to re-create the universe and to receive his blessings to properly accomplish the task; thereafter Vishnu disappears from Brahmā's sight. In chapter 10, Maitreya discourses on basic categories of cosmic creation set into motion by time and the high divinity Brahmā. In chapter 11 Maitreya elaborates on the nature of time, both gross and subtle, providing a breakdown of time divisions of increasing length, leading eventually to the topic he promises (in the final verse of chapter 10) to discuss—namely, the ages of the Manus (major progenitors and earth sovereigns). Although the following selection can be challenging reading, it serves well as representative of the Bhāgavata's concern for detail regarding cosmogony and time.

BRAHMĀ'S CREATION AND THE MEASURES OF TIME

Chapters 10 and 11

Vidura questioned: After the Lord's disappearance, how many sorts of corporeal and mental progeny did Brahmā, the mighty grandfather of the worlds, bring into being? (10.1)[1] Blessed one, best knower of many things, explain to me, in proper order, these subjects I have asked you about, and destroy all my doubts! (2)

Sūta said: Bhārgava (Śaunaka)! Thus urged by Vidura, the sage Kauṣāravi (Maitreya) was pleased and responded to those heartfelt questions. (3)

Maitreya said: Just as the birthless Bhagavān advised, Viriñca (Brahmā) practiced austerity for one hundred celestial years, directing himself toward the self. (4)[2] Brahmā noticed that the lotus from which he was born and on which he sat, as well as the (surrounding) waters, trembled in devastating wind blowing at that time. (5) He whose power and understanding had matured by redoubled austerity and self-knowledge drank up both the wind and the water. (6)[3] Seeing spread throughout the sky the lotus on which he was situated, Brahma thought, "I will create the worlds that have been absorbed in this lotus!" (7) Brahma then entered the calyx of the lotus and, impelled by Bhagavān's (initial creative) action, divided the lotus's unity into a multiplicity, making a threefold and then a fourteenfold division. (8)[4] This lotus was arranged according to the differences in nature among living beings. Brahmā is surely the greatest among them, for he is mature in the selfless performance of dharma. (9)[5]

Vidura said: Excellent *brāhmaṇa*, since you have mentioned that which is called time, kindly describe for us this feature of Hari, the wonderful actor having many forms. (10)[6]

Maitreya said: Formless and unlimited, the supreme person (as time) is the very form of the *guṇas*' interactions. By divine play he manifested himself as the material cause of the world. (11) Indeed, the world is merely this *brahman* (because) it is formed by Vishnu's energy (*māyā*). It is circumscribed by the Lord through his unmanifest form of time. (12)[7] As the universe is in the present, so it was in the beginning; and so shall it be hereafter. (13)[8] The universe's creation is of nine types, categorized as elemental and derivative creations. The universe's dissolution is of three kinds, affected by time, matter, and the qualities (*guṇa*). (14)[9]

The first creation consists of the diversification of the *guṇas* out of the self's great primal substance (*mahat-tattva*). Second is ego (*ahaṁkāra*), from which arise materiality, knowledge (sensory awareness), and activity. (15) Third is the creation of elements—five subtle principles of perception that energize material objects. Fourth is the creation of senses—knowledge senses and action senses. (16)[10] The fifth creation consists of the principal gods and the mind. And sixth is the creation of darkness, by which a master (of one's body) is rendered ignorant. (17) These six creations are primary products of nature (*prakṛti*).

Now also hear from me of the secondary creations (*vaikṛti*). This is the wonder work of the blessed lord Brahmā, who is imbued with passion and (yet) understanding of Hari. (18)[11] Fruit-bearing trees without flowers, trees bearing both fruits and flowers, medicinal herbs, creepers, self-supported plants, and tubular plants—these six types of stationary life-forms make up the seventh creation, the first (of the secondary creations). They draw nourishment upward (from the ground), are nearly unconscious, but have internal sensation, and are of manifold variety. (19–20)

The eighth creation, considered to be of twenty-eight types, is of animals that are ignorant, deep in darkness, perceiving by odor, and without purposefulness of heart. (21)[12] Venerable Vidura! Cow, goat, bull, antelope, boar, gayal, deer, sheep, and camel—these are the split-hoofed animals. The donkey, horse, mule, gaur, *śarabha* deer, yak—these have single hooves. Hear of five-clawed animals: they are the dog, jackal, wolf, tiger, cat, rabbit, porcupine, lion, monkey, elephant, tortoise, lizard, and such animals as the *makara*. (22–24)[13] Birds include the demoiselle crane, vulture, heron, hawk, *bhāsa* (a carnivorous bird), the *bhallūka*, peacock, swan (or goose), sarus crane, ruddy shelduck, crow, and owl. (25)

Vidura! The ninth creation has a single category, consisting of human beings, whose passage of food is downward. They have a predominance of passion and are preoccupied with work, thinking they are happy amid misery. (26) Venerable one, these last three, as well as the (lesser) gods, are exclusively secondary (*vaikṛta*) creations. But the principal gods (are primary creations), as previously mentioned. Furthermore, the Kumāras are both primary and secondary creations. (27)

And the (tenth) creation of (lesser) gods has eight types—namely, *vibudhas* (gods); *pitris* (forefathers); *asuras* (antigods); *gandharvas* (male angelic singers) and *apsarās* (female celestial dancers); *yakṣas* (attendants of Kuvera) and *rākṣasas* (ogres); *siddhas* (perfected semidivine beings), *cāraṇas* (wandering celestial singers), and *vidyādharas* (wizards or knowers of spells); also *bhūtas* (ghosts), *pretas* (transitional beings), and *piśācas* (ghouls); and such beings as *kinnaras* (celestial musicians).

These are called the ten creations, Vidura; they are made by the cosmic creators (the supreme Lord and Brahmā). (28–29) Now I shall tell of dynasties and the ages of the Manus. The self-existent Hari, his resolve unfailing, as the creator infused with passion (Brahmā), creates through different cycles of time such as the *kalpa*. In this way the self alone manifests the self by means of the self. (30)

The ultimate irreducible part of any created thing is the *paramāṇu*, the microatom. One should always know the *paramāṇu* as countless in number despite human beings' mistaken sense of uniformity. (11.1)[14] On the other hand, when a created material object is (seen as) situated in its own form—in its wholeness as always a unity—it is the *parama-mahān*, the ultimate macrocosm. (2) Venerable one, time is similarly known by (an object's) movement through various spaces, both great and small. Time is Bhagavān, the unmanifest, the pervader of the manifest, the great. (3) Indeed, that period in which (the sun) moves through the space of a microatom is microatomic time (*paramāṇu-kāla*), the shortest instant of time. On the other hand, that period in which (the sun) moves through the total creation is macrocosmic time (*parama-mahān-kāla*), the largest unit of time. (4)[15]

Two microatoms (*paramāṇus*) become an atom (*aṇu*); a triple *aṇu* is called an atom of dust (*trasareṇu*). These dust particles are seen only in the air, floating in rays of the sun passing through a lattice. (5)[16] The time it takes (the sun) to traverse a triple *trasareṇu* is called a *truṭi*. One hundred times a *truṭi* constitutes a *vedha*, three of which make a *lava*. (6)[17] Three *lavas* are known to be a *nimeṣa* (an eye wink), three of which are called a *kṣaṇa* (an instant). Five *kṣaṇas* are known to be a *kāṣṭhā* (about four seconds), and fifteen of these are a *laghu*. (7)[18] Further, fifteen *laghus* are said to constitute exactly one *nāḍikā*, two of which make a *muhūrta*. In human terms, six or seven *nāḍikās* make a *prahara* (stroke) or *yāma* (a watch, a quarter day or night). (8)[19] (A *nāḍika* is) the time it takes to sink into a *prastha* of water a six-*pala* vessel that has been bored by a gold (needle) weighing four *māṣas* and measuring four fingers in length. (9)[20] Giver of praise (Vidura)! There are eight *yāmas* in a human day and night cycle. The bright and dark lunar fortnights each consist of fifteen days and nights. (10) The combination of these two fortnights is one month—a day and night cycle of the ancestors (*pitris*). Two months are one season, and six months constitute the sun's southern or northern course through the firmament. (11) And it is said that the sun's six-month course is one day (of the gods). Twelve months are known to be one year, while a full hundred years is determined to be the ideal life span of human beings. (12)[21]

The mighty unblinking deity (the sun) moves around the universe through the orbits of planets, lunar mansions, and stars, in terms of time, from the microatomic moment up to the solar year. (13) Vidura! (The durations of these various completed orbits) are named thus: *saṁvatsara*, *parivatsara*, *iḍā-vatsara*, *anuvatsara*, and *vatsara*. (14)[22] (As the sun, it is the Lord) who makes visible the different living beings and elements. He courses through the sky to end the human being's aimless wanderings, while prodigiously charging the energy of all that grows with his own energy. He manifests the fruit of ritual actions in his aspect of time. Tribute should be rendered unto him, the source of the five types of annual cycles (*vatsara*). (15)

Vidura said: This (reckoning) represents the ideal life span of ancestors, gods, and humans. Do explain the fate of superior, enlightened beings who may live longer than an aeon (*kalpa*). (16)[23] Clearly the blessed one (Maitreya) knows the way of the blessed Lord as time, for the wise see the universe with vision perfected by yoga. (17)[24]

Maitreya said: The four ages—the Tetrad (*kṛta*), the Triad (*tretā*), the Pair (*dvāpara*), and the Single (*kali*)—along with their intervening periods are understood to comprise twelve (thousand) celestial years. (18)[25] (The lengths of each of the four ages:) the Tetrad, and so on, are sequentially calculated thus: a thousand years is multiplied by four, three, two, or one, adding two hundred (multiplied by four, three, two, or one). (19)[26] Learned astronomers call an age (*yuga*) proper the time between its before and after junctures (*sandhyā*). The duration of these junctures is determined by factors of one hundred. It is during the ages proper that prescribed duties (dharma) are performed. (20)[27] In the Kṛta age, human beings follow prescribed duties comprehensively. In subsequent ages dharma invariably diminishes by one-quarter increments with irreligion's increase. (21)[28]

Beyond the three worlds, up to and including Brahmā's abode, one thousand four-age cycles equals one day. Dear Vidura, the night has the same duration, during which the cosmic creator sleeps. (22) Commencing from the night's end, the cosmic aeon of the (triple) world follows. Fourteen Manus thrive during this period, Brahmā's day. (23) Each Manu thrives for a period of time slightly longer than seventy-one (cycles of four ages). The (successive) Manus appear simultaneously at the end of (previous) Manu periods, along with their dynasties, the seers, gods, Indras, and their followers. (24) This is Brahmā's day-by-day creation during which the three worlds revolve and wherein appear animals, humans, ancestors, and gods, with (reference to their previous) actions. (25) Throughout the periods of the Manus, the preeminently potent Bhagavān retains pure (independent) existence while governing this world by his own forms as Manu and other *avatāras*. (26)

At the end of Brahmā's day, Bhagavān remains silent, accepting a trace of darkness (*tamas*) and suspending his power, all beings becoming absorbed in him by the influence of time. (27) And then the three worlds—Bhūḥ, Bhūvaḥ, and Svaḥ—become hidden, deprived of sun and moon in the night's succeeding duration. (28) As those three worlds are incinerated by powerful fire from Saṅkarṣaṇa, Bhṛgu and others afflicted by the heat traverse from Maharloka (up) to Janaloka. (29)[29] Then, at the end of Brahmā's day, the swollen seas, their gigantic tossing waves stirred by violent winds, inundate the three worlds. (30) Reposing on Ananta in that water is the Lord, Hari. While hymned by the denizens of Janaloka, his eyes are shut in meditative sleep. (31) Even Brahmā's superior life span of one hundred years is depleted by such procession of days and nights marked by the march of time. (32) One-half of his life span is called a *parārdha*. The initial *parārdha* (of the current Brahmā's life) is passed, and the latter half is just commencing. (33)

In the beginning of the first half of Brahmā's life, the great aeon, called Brāhma-kalpa, occurred when Brahmā first appeared. The wise know this to be when the Veda became knowable. (34) Following Brāhma-kalpa occurred Pādma-kalpa, during which the cosmic lotus (*padma*) emerged from the pool that is the navel of Hari. (35) Descendant of Bharata! Similarly this (present) aeon of the previously mentioned second half of Brahmā's life is called Vārāha-kalpa, in which Śūkara Hari (the Lord as a boar *avatāra*) has appeared. (36) This time span known as a *dvi-parārdha* (the life span of Brahmā) is but an eye wink of the beginningless, endless, and changeless Lord of the universe. (37) Time—from the microatomic moment to the life span of Brahma—is the controller. It is the controller of all beings who identify their bodies as themselves. Yet time is not the controlling master of ultimate totality. (38)

This universe has an outer diameter of five hundred million *yojanas*. It is filled with (eight) particular elements and (sixteen) integrated transformations. (39) The universe, appearing like a microatom, is covered by layers of each element, each layer ten times the thickness of the previous layer. And multitudes of such universes are clustered together. (40)[30] That (totality of creation) is said to be the imperishable supreme *brahman*, the cause of every cause, the very body of the great person Vishnu. (41)[31]

Whereas chapters 10 and 11 describe Brahmā's cosmic creation in quite abstract terms, the next chapter focuses on the creation of specific prominent beings. Brahmā's initial creative efforts are fraught with difficulties, leading him to make a second attempt. This time he is frustrated by the refusal of four of his sons—Sanaka, Sananda, Sanātana, and Sanat-kumāra—to obey his command to become progenitors. Brahmā's consequent anger produces Rudra, who in turn produces progeny who begin to devour the universe. Subduing Rudra by ordering him to practice penance, Brahmā can finally proceed with creation of the ten principal cosmic sages. But trouble persists: these sages—Brahmā's sons—find it necessary to appeal to their father to give up his sexual attraction to his own daughter, Vāk (speech). Ashamed and remorseful, Brahmā abandons his lustful body, after which, with the help of the Vedas, he is able to properly accomplish the work of creation, culminating in the manifestation, from his body, of Svāyambhuva Manu and Śatarūpā, who then unite as the first of cosmic progenitors by sexual reproduction.

Yet again there are complications: the planet earth, which is to be the realm of Svāyambhuva Manu and his wife, Śatarūpā, must first be retrieved from the ocean's depths. This task is accomplished by Bhagavān, appearing as a cosmic boar, who then secures the earth's position by fighting and killing the demon Hiraṇyākṣa (golden eye), after which he accepts encomia by the cosmic sages. Beginning with chapter 14, Maitreya then narrates the background story of how Hiraṇyākṣa—together with his brother Hiraṇyakaśipu (golden cushion)—were produced from the ill-timed union of Diti and Kaśyapa. In turn, this account leads to an explanation, in the next section, of how these two brothers had been cursed to be born as demons.

FOUR SAGES CURSE THE GATEKEEPERS OF HEAVEN

Chapters 15 and 16

Brahma said: My sons, Sanaka and the others (Sanātana, Sanandana, and Sanat) were born from my mind and are your older brothers. Free of desire, they wander the worlds through the sky and among people. (15.12) One day those pure souls went to that place worshipped by all people—Vaikuṇṭha, the residence of the blessed Lord Vaikuṇṭha (Vishnu). (13)[32] All the people who live there have Vaikuṇṭha bodies, and they worship Hari by virtuous acts that are not motivated by any aspiration. (14)[33] And there dwells Bhagavān, the original person, who is understood through scripture. The virtuous Lord is situated in goodness that is free of passion, and he delights us, his own people. (15)

The forest called Naiḥśreyas sparkles there with wish-fulfilling trees that possess the beauty of all seasons. Indeed, this forest is like the very form of absolute bliss. (16) The residents of Vaikuṇṭha travel with their wives in aerial cars, continuously singing about the Lord's activities, which destroy sin. They ridicule the breeze that carries the fragrance of sweet *mādhavī* flowers, blossoming in the water, because it breaks their meditation. (17) The tumult of pigeons, cuckoos, sarus cranes, shelducks, gallinules, swans, parrots, partridges, and peacocks briefly stops when the chief black bee hums loudly, as if singing the stories of Hari (Vishnu). (18) Flowering plants in Vaikuṇṭha—Indian coral tree, star jasmine, *Barleria*, blue water lily, champac magnolia, teak, Alexandrian laurel, rose chestnut, bulletwood, lotus, and *pārijāta*—greatly honor the austerities of *tulasī* (holy basil), for her fragrance is privileged by Vishnu, who decorates himself with *tulasī* leaves. (19)[34] Vaikuṇṭha is crowded with aerial cars made of *vaidurya* gems, emeralds, and gold, which can be gained simply by bowing to Hari's feet. In Vaikuṇṭha, the ladies, with their lovely smiling faces and large hips, do not incite passion by their smiles and feminine gestures in those whose minds are fixed on Krishna. (20)[35] The beautiful and faultless Śrī (Lakṣmī), for whose grace others exert themselves, seems to be dusting the gold-lined, crystal walls in Hari's house with her play lotus, (the anklets on) her lotuslike feet tinkling. (21) Attended by her handmaidens, Śrī was worshipping the Lord in her garden with *tulasī* leaves. There she saw her face, with its beautiful locks of hair and prominent nose, in crystal clear ponds that had coral banks and nectarlike water, and thought, "My face was kissed by the blessed Lord!" (22)

Those who listen to useless discussion on topics other than accounts of Hari's creative acts do not approach Vaikuṇṭha. Such discussion is devoid of substance, it destroys good judgment, and it is heard by unfortunate persons who are thrown into dark worlds without refuge. (23)[36] Even we gods ask for a human birth, wherein both dharma and knowledge of the truth are obtainable. Alas! Those who have attained human birth but do not worship that blessed Lord are bewildered by extensive *māyā*. (24) Those who are devoted to the most excellent among the gods (Vishnu) leave far away the punishments of hell and go instead to Vaikuṇṭha, which is beyond even us (the gods). Indeed, we desire their virtuous qualities. While describing their master's glorious fame to one another they become overwhelmed with love, their voices falter because of tears, and their bodies become thrilled with joy. (25)[37] In all the worlds, Vaikuṇṭha alone is praiseworthy. That extraordinary, divine place is ruled by the universal teacher and illumined by wonderful aerial cars carrying the best of the wise.

Now that the (four) sages had arrived in Vaikuṇṭha by the strength of their yogic power, they felt the highest happiness. (26) Here the sages passed through six gates without lingering, but at the seventh they saw two celestial beings holding clubs. Both were of equal age, and they were beautifully dressed with the most excellent crowns, earrings, and armlets. (27)[38] The gatekeepers were each adorned with a garland of forest flowers—placed between their four dark-blue arms—that attracted intoxicated bumblebees. Their faces appeared slightly agitated, with reddish eyes, arched eyebrows, and flared nostrils. (28) As the gatekeepers looked on, the sages entered the door without asking, just as they had entered the preceding gold-and-diamond-encrusted doors. These sages wander everywhere, fearless and unobstructed, for they see all places equally. (29)[39] Seeing the four boys—clothed by the wind, ancient but (appearing only) five years old, knowers of the truth of the self—the gatekeepers laughed at their boldness and blocked them with maces. The gatekeepers' conduct was displeasing to the Lord, for the boys did not deserve such treatment. (30)[40] As (other) divinities looked on, those two gatekeepers of Hari forbade the sages from entering, although the sages were certainly most worthy. When their desire to see the best of friends (Vishnu) was frustrated, their eyes suddenly became agitated with a little anger, and they spoke thus. (31)[41]

The sages said: "How is it that both of you have achieved this distinguished service to Bhagavān in Vaikuṇṭha, amid residents who possess qualities like the Lord, and yet you possess a troublesome nature? Indeed, why fear for that peaceful Lord, who is without opposition? The (only) persons you should fear are imposters like yourselves. (32) In Vaikuṇṭha, the wise see the self in the self, like the sky in the sky. They see no differences within Bhagavān. The Lord holds everything in his belly, so what is this fear that has caused both of you—posing as gods—to see class distinctions here? (33)[42] Therefore, let us consider how to do good for you dim-witted (servants) of the supreme master of Vaikuṇṭha. Leave this place and go with your exclusionary vision to the worlds where a sinful person has these three enemies (lust, anger, and greed)." (34)[43]

When the sages uttered these terrible words, the gatekeepers realized that this was a *brāhmaṇa*'s curse, which cannot be counteracted by any number of weapons. The servants of Hari became very fearful and immediately fell to the ground, grasping the sages' feet in desperation. (35)[44] (They said:) "The punishment given to a sinner by holy persons—let it happen! Indeed, may that punishment remove (our offense) of disrespecting godly persons. But please be a little compassionate toward us, and do not let illusion destroy our remembrance of Bhagavān as we descend lower and lower in these worlds." (36)[45]

When Bhagavān learned of his own servants' offense toward the saints, he immediately proceeded to that place with Śrī (Lakṣmī). The Lord, who is cherished by noble people, and from whose navel grows a lotus, walked with those very feet that are sought by great sages and ascetics of the highest order. (37)[46] The child sages saw that the goal of their deep meditation was (now) directly visible to them. The Lord arrived with his own men, who brought along various accoutrements. The whisks (used to fan the Lord) were beautiful like swans, and in their gentle breeze swayed the strings of pearls on the radiant parasol, like drops of nectar falling from the moon. (38)[47] His beautiful face full of grace, that most desirable person touched the heart with artful, loving glances. With the lovely Śrī upon his dark, broad chest, it was as if the Lord were beautifying his own abode, which is the crest jewel of all celestial worlds. (39) His full hips were clothed in fine yellow garments and adorned by a glittering girdle. He wore a garland of forest flowers humming with bees, and he had lovely bracelets upon his wrists. One hand rested on the shoulder of Vinatā's son (Garuḍa), and with the other he twirled a lotus. (40)[48] They saw his countenance—he had a distinguished nose, and his cheeks were befittingly decorated with *makara* earrings that mocked lightning. His crown was encrusted with gems and the Kaustubha jewel adorned his neck. A captivating, incomparable necklace was visible between his many strong arms. (41) The Lord's servants thought in this way: "The Lord is so very beautiful that he defeats the pride of even Indirā (Lakṣmī)." Indeed, he reveals this form to me (Brahmā), Shiva, and all of you. After gazing upon him with unsatiated eyes, the sages bowed their heads. (42) A breeze carried (the fragrance) of nectar from *tulasī* flowers mixed with the filaments of the lotus feet of the lotus-eyed Lord. Although the sages were devoted to the Imperishable, when that breeze entered their nostrils, it shook their bodies and minds. (43)[49] Their gaze moved upward—his smiling face was like the whorl of a dark-blue lotus and his lips were lovelier than jasmine flowers. Then again they looked down—the toenails on his feet appeared like rubies. Indeed, the sages meditated upon the Lord intently. (44)[50] For those who seek progress in this world by means of yoga, he is the esteemed object of meditation. He possesses the eight pleasures, which cannot be acquired by others but are inherent to him. Showing the sages his human form, he delights their eyes.[51]

Together they praised him: (45) "Limitless one! You remain hidden, although you are situated even in the hearts of wicked people. Indeed, you entered the cave of our hearts through the openings of the ears when our father told us about your mystery. Today, by appearing here, you have become the direct object of our vision. (46) The supreme soul, the ultimate reality—we know this is you, O Blessed Lord! By your very nature, you evoke love in these (residents of Vaikuṇṭha). Those sages who are without passion or possession also experience this love in their hearts by endeavoring with steadfast devotion, learned through repentance. (47)[52] Verily, those who have found refuge at your feet are connoisseurs of *rasa*; they relish narrations about you, which are glorious, sacred, and worthy of recitation. Such persons disregard even the gift of liberation, not to mention other perils that you can give simply by raising your eyebrows. (48)[53] We do not mind birth in hell because of our sinful ways, so long as our hearts can delight like bees at your feet, our words are blessed like *tulasī* leaves at your feet, and our ears are filled with your many good qualities. (49) Lord! We have found great delight in seeing the widely praised form that you have shown here. Bhagavān is rarely visible to those who are not self-realized, and yet he is manifest to us. Indeed, let us offer obeisance to him, Bhagavān." (50)

Brahmā said: The omnipresent Lord, who lives in Vaikuṇṭha, graciously accepted the praise offered by the ascetic yogis, and spoke thus. (16.1)

Śrī Bhagavān said: "These two—Jaya and Vijaya—are my attendants. By disregarding me, they have committed a serious transgression against you. (2) Sages! I approve of the punishment you, my devotees, have given these two because of their contempt for *brāhmaṇas.* (3) Thus, now I seek your forgiveness. The *brāhmaṇa* is the highest deity for me. Since you were wronged by my men, I feel that I did it myself. (4) When a servant commits a crime, people criticize the person whose name comes to mind (namely, the master's), and it's *his* reputation that is ruined, just as leprosy ruins (all) the skin. (5) All people, including an outcaste, are purified by submerging themselves in hearing about the unblemished, immortal glory of Vaikuṇṭha (Vishnu). I am that very Vaikuṇṭha, and my unbounded fame is due to you. Indeed, I would cut off my arm if it were adverse to you!" (6)[54]

In the intervening verses, Vishnu states that he considers the *brāhmaṇas* to be like his own self and thus worthy of worship. Vishnu acknowledges the gatekeepers' transgression and requests leniency from the Kumāras: "Let these two attendants of mine, who were unable to ascertain their master's intention, immediately reap the result of their transgression toward you. But then let them return close to me. Please arrange my servants' exile to be short—that would be a great favor to me" (v. 12). The Kumāras in turn express their own unworthiness and subservience to Vishnu and their willingness to accept whatever Vishnu decides for them and the gatekeepers.

(The sages said:) "Master! Whether you decide to punish or pardon these two, we will readily accept that. Indeed, we will accept whatever punishment you consider appropriate for us, for we have implicated two innocent persons." (25)

Śrī Bhagavān said: "*Brāhmaṇas!* You should know that I alone ordained this curse. These two will now become demons, but through intense yogic concentration born of anger, they will soon return close to me." (26)[55]

Brahmā said: Thus, after seeing Lord Vaikuṇṭha, who brings joy to the eyes, and his self-luminous abode, Vaikuṇṭha, the sages requested permission to leave. They circumambulated Bhagavān, fell down at his feet in reverence, and then returned home, praising Vishnu's glory. (27–28)

Bhagavān said to his attendants: "Go, but do not fear! Good fortune to you! Although I am capable of nullifying a *brāhmaṇa*'s power, I do not desire to do so, for I hold it in high regard. (29) This (curse) was foretold by Ramā (Lakṣmī) a long time ago. She was angry, for she was turned away at the door while I was sleeping. (30)[56] Through the yoga of anger directed toward me, you will atone for insulting a *brāhmaṇa*. In a very short time, you will come back again, close to me." (31)

After advising the doorkeepers, Bhagavān returned to his abode, which is decorated with many aerial gondolas and endowed with riches surpassing all. (32) Because of the invincible curse of a *brāhmaṇa*, those two best of gods fell from Hari's abode, having lost their splendor and their smiles. (33) My children! Then, as they fell from Vaikuṇṭha's world, a great cry arose from the celestials seated on fine aerial cars. (34) Those very doorkeepers, most excellent among Hari's attendants, have now entered Kaśyapa's powerful semen, which has entered Diti's womb. (35) Today, your power has been overcome by the power of those twin demons. At present, Bhagavān wants it this way! (36) The first person, the cause of the birth, sustenance, and dissolution of the universe, whose yogic power is impossible to overcome even by the masters of yoga—that very Bhagavān, ruler of the three worlds, will look after our safety. What, then, is the point of our deliberations on this matter? (37)

The narrative continues in the next chapter with Jaya and Vijaya's descent as two powerful demons, Hiraṇyakaśipu and Hiraṇyākṣa. Their birth is accompanied by a slew of ill omens, and they soon begin terrorizing the worlds with unprovoked acts of aggression. The younger brother, Hiraṇyākṣa, seeks to fight Vishnu, whom he regards as a worthy adversary, and finds him in the depths of the cosmic ocean. Vishnu has taken the form of a boar (Varāha) in order to rescue the earth, which he lifts with his tusks from the bottom of the ocean. Hiraṇyākṣa attacks the Lord with abusive words and then with his club. The two engage in a fierce battle, while Brahmā and other gods arrive to watch. The Lord playfully fights with the demon, receiving his blows "like an elephant struck by a wreath of flowers." When Varāha drops his club after a particularly forceful strike from the demon, the gods beg the Lord to play with the demon no longer. Soon, Varāha dispatches Hiraṇyākṣa with a slap to his face. Brahmā marvels at the demon's fortunate death by the hand of Vishnu.

In chapter 20, we return to the conversation between Maitreya and Vidura and to the larger concern of Book Three—namely, the creation of the world. Now that the earth is reinstated in its proper orbit, Vidura asks about how it was populated with creatures. Maitreya describes the birth of Brahmā from Vishnu and then Brahmā's work of creating the gods, demons, and sages. As Brahmā creates each class of beings, he repeatedly sheds his body, and these bodies also become constituents of creation.

Continuing the account of creation, in chapter 21 Vidura asks about Brahmā's son, Svayambhūva Manu, and his descendants, beginning with Manu's daughter, Devahūti. The narrative about Devahūti, her husband, Kardama, and their son, Kapila, the speaker of Sāṁkhya philosophy, will take us to the end of Book Three. The stories of Manu's other children will lead us all the way to the beginning of Book Five.

The sage Kardama was commanded by Brahmā to beget children and help populate the earth, and so Kardama meditates upon Vishnu through long ascetic practice. Vishnu appears before the sage and promises that he will soon receive Devahūti's hand in marriage and that eventually Vishnu himself will be born as their son, Kapila. The events transpire just as Vishnu had foretold, and after Kardama and Devahūti enjoy a prolonged period of celestial pleasure, they conceive nine daughters and a son. After his daughters are married and his son has grown up, Kardama leaves home for a life as an itinerant mendicant. Devahūti meanwhile develops her own determination for spiritual pursuit and, knowing her son to be the Lord himself, requests him to show her the path to liberation. Kapila begins his teaching in chapter 25 with an eloquent exposition on bhakti: "The *bhāgavatas* (devotees of Bhagavān Vishnu) never wish for oneness with me, for they delight in service to my feet. Seeking me, they gather with one another to celebrate my valorous deeds" (v. 34).

The conversation between Kapila and Devahūti constitutes one of the most complex philosophical sections of the Bhāgavata. Beginning in chapter 26, the Purāṇa presents a system of Sāṁkhya dualism that explains the material creation as a product of two realities: the unchanging conscious self (*puruṣa*) and the forever-changing material nature (*prakṛti*). Despite its many similarities with classical Sāṁkhya, the Bhāgavata's theistic Sāṁkhya asserts the unitary origin of all things in Vishnu as the supreme *puruṣa*, with bhakti as the most effective means of attaining him. The following chapter begins the discussion of Sāṁkhya by explaining the transformation of *prakṛti* into all the constituent elements of the material world—from subtle to gross—including intellect, ego, mind, the senses, and the five gross elements.

THE NATURE OF TEMPORAL NATURE

Chapter 26

Devahūti said: O Supreme Puruṣa! Please describe the characteristics of *puruṣa* (the conscious self) and *prakṛti* (material nature)—the causes of this world, which constitute both what is eternal and what is temporal. (26.9)[57]

Śrī Bhagavān said: The undifferentiated, eternal, unmanifest combination of the three *guṇas* is called *pradhāna*, which constitutes both what is eternal and what is temporal. The differentiated manifestation is called *prakṛti* (material nature). (10) This aggregate *brahman*, consisting of twenty-four items—(categorized in groups of) five, five, four, and ten—is called *pradhāna.* (11) The five gross elements (*mahā-bhūtas*) are earth, water, fire, air, and sky. There are as many subtle elements (*tan-mātras*), which I regard as fragrance, taste, form, touch, and sound. (12) The senses are identified as ten—ears, skin, eyes, tongue, nose, (the organ of) speech, hands, feet, genitals, and anus, the tenth. (13) The mind, intellect, ego, and consciousness constitute the internal (organs). This fourfold distinction is perceived according to their characteristic functions. (14)

Indeed, thus far I have enumerated the composition of *brahman* with qualities. Time is considered the twenty-fifth item. (15) Some say that time is the *puruṣa*'s power that causes fear in the agent (living being) who is deluded by ego, having associated with *prakṛti.* (16) Daughter of Manu! It has been indicated that time is Bhagavān, because of whom there is movement in the undifferentiated equilibrium of *prakṛti*'s *guṇas.* (17) This very Bhagavān, by his own *māyā*, abides within all beings as the *puruṣa* and outside as time. (18)

The Supreme Puruṣa placed his seed into his own womb (*prakṛti*)—whose equilibrium had been disturbed according to destiny—and begot the golden *mahat-tattva* ("the great element," the first transformation of *prakṛti*). (19)[58] By its own brilliance, the unchanging sprout of the universe, which manifests everything within itself, swallowed the dense darkness that was keeping it asleep. (20) The clear, serene, *sattvic* consciousness called Vāsudeva, which is the mark of Bhagavān, became part of the *mahat-tattva.* (21) Like the pristine nature of water, the characteristics of consciousness are described by its modes—clarity, serenity, and being unchanging. (22) The evolving *mahat-tattva*, born from Bhagavān's seed, produced the ego, which is the energy of activity. The ego is threefold—modified (*vaikārika*), energetic (*taijasa*), and dim (*tāmasa*)—from which arose the mind, senses, and gross elements (*mahā-bhūtas*). (23–24) The ego, consisting of the mind, senses, and gross elements, is the *puruṣa* called Saṅkarṣana, who is known to be none other than the thousand-headed Ananta. (25) The ego is characterized as the agent of activity, the instrument of activity, and the effect. It may also be characterized as serene, passionate, or dull. (26)

From the transformation of modified ego (*vaikārika*) was born the element of mind. The mind's alternating ideas give rise to desire. (27) The mind is known by the name of Aniruddha, the great ruler of the senses. He has a dark complexion like the autumnal blue lotus, and he is achieved gradually by yogis. (28) Virtuous lady! The transformation of energetic ego (*taijasa*) gave rise to the element of intellect (*buddhi*), which discerns objects when they come into view and assists the senses. (29) Now, the characteristics of the intellect, according to its different functions, are said to be doubt, repudiation, conviction, memory, and sleep. (30) The senses, born from energetic ego (*taijasa*), are classified (in two categories): the senses of action and the senses of knowledge. The energy of action belongs to the vital breath and the energy of knowledge belongs to the intellect. (31)

The transformation of dim ego (*tāmasa*)—moved by Bhagavān's virility—gave rise to the subtle element sound, and from sound came sky as well as the ears, which perceive sound. (32) Sound conveys meaning, indicates (the presence of) the seer, and constitutes the subtle element (*tan-mātra*) of sky. Philosophers know these as the characteristics of sound. (33) The characteristic function of sky is to provide interior and exterior space for living beings, for sky is the abode of the vital breath, the senses, and the self. (34)

By the force of time, tactility evolved from sky and the subtle element sound. The tactile was followed by air and skin, which perceives the tactile. (35) Softness, hardness, cold, and heat are the defining characteristics of the tactile, which is the subtle element in air. (36) Moving, displacing, encompassing, carrying sounds and substances—these are the characteristic actions of air, which is the essence of all the senses. (37)[59]

Propelled by destiny, form came about from air and the tactile subtle element. Then arose fire and the eyes, which perceive form. (38) Saintly mother! The characteristics of the subtle element form are substantive volume, distinctive shape, qualities, and the light in fire. (39) Illuminating, cooking, eating, drinking, destroying cold, drying, as well as (creating) hunger and thirst—these are the functions of fire. (40)[60]

Propelled by destiny, the subtle element flavor evolved from fire and the form element. From flavor, there arose water and the tongue, which perceives flavor. (41) Flavor is one, but it separates into many—sour, pungent, bitter, sweet, and astringent—due to the modification of (various) substances. (42) Moistening, coagulating, (causing) satisfaction, giving life, swelling, dissipating heat, and flowing abundantly—these indeed are the functions of water. (43)

Propelled by destiny, the subtle element odor evolved from water and the flavor element. From odor arose earth and the nose, which perceives odor. (44) Odor, although one, is differentiated according to the proportions of (various) substances. For example, odors can be mixed, fetid, fragrant, mild, acrid, or acidic. (45) Constructing (forms of) *brahman*, (providing) location, holding (substances), possessing distinguishing attributes, and displaying the qualities of all the elements are the characteristic functions of earth. (46)[61]

The sense whose object of perception is the distinguishing quality of sky (i.e., sound) is called hearing. The sense whose object of perception is the distinguishing quality of air (i.e., tangibility) is known as touch. (47) The sense whose object of perception is the distinguishing quality of fire (i.e., form) is called sight. The sense whose object of perception is the distinguishing quality of water (i.e., flavor) is known as taste. The sense whose object of perception is the distinguishing quality of earth (i.e., odor) is called smell. (48) The nature of the prior (element) can certainly be seen in the following one. Thus the distinguishing attributes of (all) substances can be observed in earth. (49) When these seven items—the *mahat-tattva* and the others—were still unmixed, the origin of the universe (Bhagavān) entered them, accompanied by time, karma, and the *guṇas*. (50)

The remainder of chapter 26 describes the universe as Vishnu's body (*virāṭ puruṣa*) and creation as a process of constructing his body (recalling the *puruṣa-sūkta* hymn of the Ṛgveda). Each natural element, along with the associated deity, appears in the appropriate part of the cosmic body. In chapter 27, Kapila explains how the self (*puruṣa*) becomes bound to matter (*prakṛti*) and thus suffers through this world, claiming ownership of activity that is in fact performed by *prakṛti*. When Devahūti asks how the *puruṣa* could possibly exist without *prakṛti* and all its transformations (mind, senses, body, etc.), Kapila replies that such freedom is possible through bhakti, just as one can wake up from a dream and realize one's independent identity.

The following section continues Kapila's extended discourse with his mother, Devahūti. Here Kapila offers an overview of "object-meditational" yoga practice (*sabīja-yoga*), where the object to be meditated upon is the form of Vishnu as a whole and as so many particular features of his bodily form. The emphasis here is on visualization of divine form and hence divine personhood; but in the concluding verses the theme of yogic practice aiming at yogic perfection suggests, with some ambiguity, a leaning toward "impersonal" realization of ultimate reality as formless. Still, the chapter returns to an ultimate distinction between the individual self and the supreme self.

YOGIC MEDITATION ON THE FORM OF VISHNU

Chapter 28

The venerable Kapila said: Descendant of royalty (Devahūti), I shall explain the features of yoga, along with its object of meditation. By following this method the mind surely progresses along the joyful path of spirit. (28.1)[62] Being fully alert, the life airs (*prāṇa*) regulated, one should gradually engage the mind—hitherto corrupted and distracted—by means of the intellect. (This process is supported by) performing one's own duties as far as possible; avoiding wrongful acts; being satisfied with what is obtained by providence; worshipping the feet of those who know the self; avoiding vulgar conduct and delighting in conduct conducive to liberation; always eating appropriate foods in moderation; resorting to peace and solitude; observing harmlessness, truthfulness, not stealing, chastity, austerity, and cleanliness; minimizing possessions; studying the Veda; worshipping the Lord; observing silence and gradually mastering yogic postures and breath; maintaining steadiness and, by means of the mind, withdrawing the senses from objects and turning attention to the heart; concentrating the mind on the breath in a single place amid the body's energy vortices (chakras); and then meditating on divine pastimes. In this way one attains complete mental absorption (*samādhi*). (2–7)[63]

Having mastered yogic posture in *svastikāsana* (toes placed in the hollow of opposite knees, or on the thighs), upper body upright, one should practice (regulating the breath) on a seat arranged in a sanctified place. (8)[64] One should clear the passage of life air by inhaling, retaining, and then exhaling, or by the reverse (sequence), such that the mind, fluctuation abandoned, is stilled. (9)[65] As surely as metal smelted by air and fire releases dross, so does the mind of a yogi whose breathing is mastered quickly become free from impurity. (10) One can burn away bodily deficiencies by controlled breathing (*prāṇāyāma*); sensual attachment by sense withdrawal (*pratyāhāra*); offensive acts by concentration (*dhāraṇā*); and unruly tendencies by meditation (*dhyāna*). (11)[66] Once the mind is freed from its own impurity and is thoroughly concentrated by yoga practices, one should meditate on the Lord's exquisite form while keeping the tip of the nose in sight. (12)[67]

One should meditate on the entire form of the Lord until the mind is no longer distracted. The Lord has a gracious, lotuslike countenance and reddish eyes like the calyx of a lotus, with a complexion that is dark, like blue lotus petals. He bears conch, disk, and club (in three of his four hands), the mark of Śrī on his chest, and the Kaustubha jewel about his neck. He is dressed in shining silk the yellow color of lotus filaments, and his hips are wrapped in an excellent glistening sash. He is wreathed with a garland of forest flowers around which hover maddened bumblebees, and he bears a crown, priceless pearl necklaces, bracelets, upper-arm ornaments, and anklets. He is in the prime of youth, peacefully seated on the heart's lotus as the perpetually handsome cynosure of all eyes and minds. He is keen to bless his devotees, and it is he who confers glory on the renowned. He is honored by all the worlds, his well-deserved glory calling for praise. (13–18)[68] With a pure condition of consciousness one should meditate on the attractive, beloved Lord as he stands, walks, sits, or reclines in the deep recesses of the heart. (19)[69]

When the consciousness has become fixed in the Lord, comprehending all his limbs together, the sage should then focus on each of the Lord's limbs individually: (20) one should meditate on the Lord's lotuslike feet, which are adorned with the marks of a thunderbolt, elephant goad, flag, and lotus. The heart's dense gloom is ousted by the gleaming moonlike beams from their arched crimson toenail orbs. (21)[70] Shiva became *śiva* (auspicious) by receiving upon his head the sacred Ganges water that washes and comes forth from those feet (that act as) a thunderbolt hurled against the mountain of vices in the meditator's mind. One should meditate on the lotuslike feet of the Lord for a long time. (22) The lotus-eyed Lakṣmī, mother of the cosmic creator, Brahmā, who is extolled by the gods, places the transcendent Lord's lower legs and knees on her thighs and massages them with her delicate, radiant fingers. One should compose this image in the heart. (23)[71]

One should envision in the heart the Lord's splendid, powerful thighs, blue like flax flowers, as he sits upon the shoulders of Garuḍa. Those thighs are clothed in long, fine yellow cloth tied with an ornamented sash around the Lord's well-formed hips. (24)[72] One should meditate on the Lord's lakelike navel, situated as a cave in his belly and as the shelter for the worlds from which the cosmic lotus, Brahmā's abode, has sprung forth. Then one should meditate on the Lord's two precious emerald-like nipples that reflect the luster from his dazzling white pearl necklace. (25) One should fix within the mind the chest of the supreme Lord, who is venerated by all the worlds. His chest is the resting place of Lakṣmī, and it renders delight to human beings' minds and eyes. One should also meditate on the Lord's neck, which serves to embellish the Kaustubha gem. (26)[73] Then one should contemplate the Lord's arms—guardians of the worlds—the ornaments of which are burnished by the rotating action of Mount Mandara. With these arms he bears the thousand-spoked disk of insuperable resplendence as well as the conch, appearing as the best of swans in his lotuslike hand. (27)[74] One should remember the Lord's beloved mace, Kaumodakī, which is smeared with stains of blood from inimical combatants; and the flower garland that reverberates with the hum of a honeybee swarm; and the pure Kaustubha gem on the Lord's neck—an emblem of the individual self. (28)[75]

One should contemplate the lotuslike face of the Lord, who assumes forms in this world out of compassion for his devotees. The mind completely identifies with his face, which is framed by a mass of curly hair and features an aristocratic nose and crystal-like cheeks lit up by the to-and-fro dance of his glittering *makara* earrings. One should attentively meditate upon the Lord's lotuslike eyes and trembling eyebrows, which, by their intrinsic excellence, taunt a lotus attended by bees and sheltering a pair of fish. (29–30) For a long time and with abundant feeling one should ponder within the heart the Lord's exceptional, richly gracious glance. That glance, cast with tenderness from his eyes and augmented by his affectionate smile, mitigates the exceedingly dreadful threefold torments. (31)[76] The Lord's gentle smile dries up the ocean of tears arising from the severe suffering of all humble folk. By his own contrivance his curved eyebrows are so positioned to thoroughly stupefy Makara-dhvaja (Kāmadeva, Cupid), thus favoring the sages. (32)[77]

An object of effortless meditation is the Lord's laughter, revealing a row of fine jasminelike teeth, reddened by his full, lustrous lips. Desiring to see nothing else, with mind offered in deep devotion, one should meditate on the laughter of Vishnu, who resides in the core of the heart. (33)

By thus meditating one gains deep feeling for Bhagavān Hari, the heart flowing with devotion and horripilation arising out of great joy. Being suddenly overwhelmed by tearful, incoherent expressions of longing, even the hooklike mind then gradually withdraws from that (object of meditation), soon to become like a steady flame—liberated, unattached to any object, dispassionate, and pacified. Thus freed from the stream of (temporal) qualities, one comprehends the self as an unfragmented unity. (34–35)[78] Furthermore, with this final quietude of the mind, one is lifted to the exalted state entirely beyond the limitations of happiness and misery. Indeed, the yogi no longer falsely regards himself to be the cause of happiness and misery, having realized the perfect, supreme self. (36)[79] Because a perfected yogi has discovered his own intrinsic identity, he has no awareness of his final body—whether active or stationary, by destiny obtained and then by destiny's imperative lost—much as one blinded by the intoxication of liquor is unaware if or how he is dressed. (37)[80] The yogi's (final) body, with its life breath, surely continues to function by destiny's imperative, in accordance with his own instigated actions. But he never again undergoes that phenomenal dream (of bodily existence), for his yogic meditational perfection is accomplished, his essential being awakened. (38)

As a mortal is surely different from his son and his wealth, although out of affection he regards them as himself, similarly a person is different from his body and whatever is associated with it. (39) Fire is distinct from its own fiery products—ember, spark, and smoke—although these are regarded as fire's very self. Similarly the supreme self, the witness—what is known as *brahman*—is distinct from what is known as the living being, primordial nature, physical elements, senses, and the inner faculty (the mind). (40–41) With single-mindedness one should see the supreme self in all beings and as the self of all beings, as one sees in all products their basic substance. (42) As one fire appears variously in different types of fuel, similarly the self, situated in temporal nature, appears variously due to the *guṇas*' diversity of bodies. (43) Therefore, having surmounted this insurmountable temporal nature, which is the Lord's own and which consists of cause and effect, the yogi abides in his intrinsic identity. (44)

The remaining five chapters of Book Three recommend the path of bhakti and offer a stern warning about the alternative—namely, continued suffering in the cycle of rebirth. In chapter 29, Kapila delineates the practice of bhakti—hearing about the Lord, singing his name, worshipping his image, and seeing his presence in all beings. In the following chapter, Kapila describes the inexorable power of time to humiliate a man who remains attached to home, family, and wealth. Such attachment leads to a painful separation at death, a miserable journey through hell, and rebirth in another body. Kapila then describes a child's month-by-month development in the mother's womb and the child's prayers to the Lord for release from its painful confinement. The child grows into a young man, unaware of life's purpose, and finds anew the cause of his attachment—namely, an attractive woman. A woman is the cause of bondage and the very form of God's illusive *māyā*. Similarly, for a woman, says Kapila, her husband, children, and home are forms of *māyā* that lead the unsuspecting woman to eventual death, as a hunter's song lures a deer.

Nevertheless, Kapila ends his teaching on a positive note, encouraging his mother to seek refuge in the supreme Lord and to cultivate selfless love for him. In chapter 33, Devahūti marvels at how the supreme Lord took birth from her womb, giving her the privilege of seeing him directly. Even an outcaste becomes venerable, she affirms, if that person even once hears or chants Bhagavān's name.

Maitreya concludes his account of Devahūti by describing how she took her son's instruction to heart, gave up worldly attachments, focused her thoughts upon Vishnu, and returned to his everlasting abode.

SUGGESTIONS FOR FURTHER READING

Hamilton, Sue. 2001. *Indian Philosophy: A Very Short Introduction.* Oxford: Oxford University Press.
Chapter 7 provides a clear summary of classical Sāṁkhya and yoga in less than a dozen pages (relevant to chapters 26 and 28).

Larson, Gerald James. 1979. *Classical Sāṁkhya: An Interpretation of Its History and Meaning*. 2nd ed. Delhi: Motilal Banarsidass.
Relevant to chapter 26, Larson provides a thorough study of classical Sāṁkhya and its historical development, including a translation of Īśvarakṛṣṇa's *Sāṅkhyakārikā*. In appendix D, Larson argues that the theistic Sāṁkhya of the Purāṇas preserves elements of an early Sāṁkhya tradition, found also in the Mahābhārata, that had a different set of goals and audience than the later, more technical system of classical Sāṁkhya.

O'Flaherty, Wendy Doniger. 1980. *The Origins of Evil in Hindu Mythology.* 2nd ed. Berkeley: University of California Press.
With chapters on themes such as "The Fall of Man," "The Necessity of Evil," and "The Good Demon," this is a wide-ranging study of evil in the Purāṇas. However, the theory of karma (as a theodicy) is better treated in O'Flaherty's *Karma and Rebirth in Classical Indian Traditions* (1980), where she revises her views on the topic.

BOOK FOUR

Confrontation and Death at Dakṣa's Sacrifice
King Pṛthu's Competition with Indra

Book Four continues from Book Three the genealogical account of progeny originating with Brahmā, concentrating on key members of the fourth generation after him and highlighting dramatic episodes, foundational figures, and didactic exchanges occurring within that generation. This book is constituted entirely of a dialogue between Vidura and Maitreya that commenced early in Book Three (chapter 5), continuing Maitreya's elaboration on Vāsudeva and the cosmic creation.

Kapila's teachings at the end of Book Three were framed largely in terms of theistic Sāṁkhya (see the explanation in the previous book). Here, in Book Four, there is a shift in philosophical thrust, with a focus on the futility of action (karma—especially ritual action centered in the performance of Vedic sacrificial rites) as an endeavor for worldly gain. Narratively, Book Four can be characterized as a series of accounts describing excessive pursuits by members of royalty, leading to sagely correctives—reforms of thought and behavior conducive to the development of bhakti. Dakṣa, Dhruva, Pṛthu, and Prācīnabarhiṣat are kings who each receive instruction—some brief and others quite extensive—to correct or secure them in the bhakti path. Dakṣa is humbled and corrected by the gods Shiva and Brahmā for his inflated self-perception; Dhruva is directed by his mother and by the sage Nārada to worship Vāsudeva in order to fulfill his ambitious desire for a kingdom; then later, he is corrected by his grandfather Svayambhuva Manu for his excessive exercise of vengeance against the Yakṣas, one of whom had slain his brother; Pṛthu is persuaded not to insist on completing his one hundredth horse sacrifice, and he is pacified by Goddess Earth from his anger at her, then instructed by the four Kumāra sages in proper governance; and Prācīnabarhiṣat is sobered by Nārada about the dire effects of his worldly pursuit of kingly piety through excessive rituals involving animal sacrifice.

After an initial chapter of genealogical information describing the next two generations after Brahmā, Dakṣa (dexterous in sacrifice), one of Brahmā's ten sons, is introduced as a cosmic progenitor whose strained relations with his divine, ascetic son-in-law Shiva leads to the death of Dakṣa's daughter Satī ("faithful wife," appearing in her next life as Parvatī). In this narrative an important theme in the Bhāgavata is introduced—namely, the problematic nature of ritual sacrifice. While the Bhāgavata subscribes to the brahmanical assumption that such rites are essential for maintaining cosmic order, it also calls attention to the dangers of malpractice—through excesses of either royal sponsors or of *brāhmaṇa* ritual specialists. Dakṣa, a member of the royal order, is proud of his competence in executing ritual sacrifices. In the altercation that ensues, he is decapitated, later to receive in substitution the head of a goat. Opposing Dakṣa and his *brāhmaṇa* followers are the followers of Shiva, the object of Dakṣa's ire. Shiva's followers bear the brunt of curses ensuring their exclusion from the brahmanical social sphere because of degradation and rejection of Vedic authority. Here the Bhāgavata distinguishes between Shiva's followers, seen as more or less heretical, and Shiva himself, whom the text repeatedly exalts as second only to Vishnu. Satī is also clearly affirmed in this passage as the exemplar of wifely sacrifice for the reputation of her husband, despite her act of disobedience in attending her father's sacrifice against Shiva's advice.

Chapters 2 and 4—translated here—narrate this dramatic confrontation between Dakṣa and his son-in-law, the powerful god Shiva, followed by the self-immolation of Satī in the presence of her father. In chapter 2 the stage is set and the trouble begins with cursing and countercursing between Dakṣa and followers of Shiva, sparked by Dakṣa's perceiving Shiva's yogic trance as intentional disrespect.

CONFRONTATION AND DEATH AT DAKṢA'S SACRIFICE

Chapters 2 and 4

Vidura said: Why did Dakṣa, so affectionate toward his daughters, display contempt for that best among the virtuous, Shiva, while disregarding his own daughter Satī? (2.1) How could anyone abhor that guru of moving and nonmoving beings, amicable embodiment of peace, the great cosmic divinity who is pleased within himself? (2) O *brāhmaṇa*, tell me this: due to what ill will between son-in-law and father-in-law did Satī abandon her vital breath, which is so difficult to abandon? (3)

Maitreya replied: During a previous *satra* rite of the cosmic creators, great seers were assembled, along with all the undying gods, fire gods, and sages, as well as their followers. (4) There the seers witnessed Dakṣa enter that great assembly, shining with a luster like the sun, dispelling darkness. (5) Except Brahmā and Shiva, all those assembled, including the fire gods, rose from their positions, their minds struck by his brilliance. (6) The blessed Dakṣa was well received by the leaders of the assembly. He bowed to Brahmā, the unborn teacher of the worlds, and with his permission turned to sit down. (7)

Seeing Shiva already seated and not receiving any honor from him, Dakṣa became indignant. Looking at him disdainfully with burning eyes, he said, (8) "*Brāhmaṇa* sages, along with gods and fires, hear me! I speak about the conduct of the cultured neither out of ignorance nor envy. (9) This impudent Shiva destroyed the reputation of the world protectors. This dullard has polluted the path pursued by the righteous. (10) This Shiva became my subordinate because, like a cultured man, he accepted the hand of my daughter, who is like Sāvitrī, before *brāhmaṇas* and fire. (11)[1] This monkey-eyed Shiva took the hand of my fawn-eyed Satī (yet) did not honor me by rising, or even by words, although I am worthy of being honored in this way. (12) Though not wishing to, I gave the girl to one whose practice of daily ritual is lost; who is unclean, haughty, and who has broken the bounds of propriety. It was like imparting sacred speech (Veda) to a *śūdra*. (13) Amid the terrible haunts of the dead he is surrounded by ghosts and spirits. He wanders naked, hair scattered, laughing and crying—like a madman. (14)[2] He bathes with funerary ashes, is garlanded with skulls, and is ornamented with human bones. Though touted as "Shiva," he is *aśiva* (inauspicious). Being mad, he is dear to the mad rabble and is the master of the lords of the fiends (*pramathas*), whose nature consists entirely of darkness. (15) Alas, pressured by the superior god Brahmā, I bestowed this respectable girl upon that unclean and wicked lord of the insane. (16)[3]

Maitreya said: Thus reviling the mountain-dwelling Shiva, who remained nonadversarial, angry Dakṣa then prepared to curse, touching water: (17)[4] "This entity, worst of gods, shall not receive a share in sacrifice for the gods, as received by Indra, Upendra, and other gods." (18)[5] Kauravya (Vidura)! Despite the assembled chiefs' protestations, Dakṣa, boiling with rage, spewed out this curse upon Shiva, the protector of mountains, and then left for his own residence. (19) Shiva's principal follower, Nandīśvara, heeding the curse and overcome with passionate anger, let fly a terrible (counter)curse on Dakṣa and on those *brāhmaṇas* who had enjoyed his rant: (20) "An ignorant person who has differential vision with regard to this mortal body bears malice toward the nonmalicious lord (Shiva). May such a one be bereft of the truth! (21)[6] Persons whose good sense is deranged by Vedic pronouncements perform elaborate rituals. Because of their desire for domestic pleasures they are ensconced in households governed by pretense. (22)[7] One who has forgotten the goal of the self, with the intelligence given over to what is other (than the self), is an animal. (Therefore) Dakṣa, whose lust for women is excessive, will soon have a goat's head. (23) That stupid one regards ignorance consisting of ritual as knowledge. Those who follow him in disrespecting Śarva (Shiva) shall continue to transmigrate in this world. (24) The enemies of Hara (Shiva), agitated by the enchanting heady aroma of flowery Vedic hymns, shall remain profoundly bewildered. (25) Those *brāhmaṇas* shall wander this world as beggars eating anything and everything, pursuing knowledge, austerity, and vows only for business—enjoying wealth, body, and senses." (26)

When Bhṛgu heard Nandīśvara's curse pronounced upon the *brāhmaṇa* clan, he also countered with a curse—the insurmountable punishment by a *brāhmaṇa*. (27) "Those who keep vows for Bhava (Shiva) will become heretics along with their followers, opposing true scriptures. (28)[8] Unclean and dull witted, wearing matted hair, ashes, and bones, they shall take to Shiva initiation, wherein wine and liquor are (considered) sacred. (29) The Veda and *brāhmaṇas* whom you blaspheme are the only bridge sustaining human beings; you have therefore taken to heresy. (30) This (bridge) alone is the eternal auspicious (*śiva*) path for all people. It is established on the authority of Janārdana (Vishnu) and has been followed since ancient times. (31) That Veda is the supremely pure, eternal path of saints. Blaspheming the Veda and regarding the master of ghosts (Shiva) as your lord, you shall become heretics." (32)[9]

Maitreya said: Thus Bhṛgu pronounced his curse; then the blessed Bhava, somewhat saddened, departed with his followers. (33) O great archer (Vidura), nevertheless for one thousand years those cosmic creators executed the *satra* rite, wherein the most excellent Hari is to be worshipped. (34) Everyone performed postsacrificial ablutions where the rivers Ganges and Yamunā meet; then with pacified mind they went to their respective abodes. (35)

The fusillade of curses and countercurses during Dakṣa's sacrificial rite prompts Shiva to depart the arena in silence. Sometime later (in chapter 3) Shiva's wife, Satī, hears that her father will again be conducting a grand sacrifice. Satī voices her wish to attend her father's event and there socialize with her relatives. Shiva, having no intention to attend the rite himself, advises Satī against her going, warning that under the present circumstances of strained relations her presence there would surely lead to disaster. In chapter 4 Shiva's prediction proves true beyond his worst fears.

Maitreya said: After saying this much, Śaṅkara (Shiva) fell silent, worried that his wife could die in either case. Desiring to see her relatives yet apprehensive of Bhava (Shiva), Satī was torn between going out and staying home. (4.1)[10] Upset over being prevented from seeing her relatives, crying out of affection, overwhelmed with tears, and trembling with anger, Bhavāni (Satī) glared at the peerless Bhava (Shiva), as if to burn him. (2)[11] Breathing heavily, Satī then left him who is dear to saints and who had given her half his own body because of affection. Her heart pained with grief and anger and her mind perplexed by her womanly nature, she went to her father's household. (3)[12] Satī had departed swiftly alone; but then thousands of the three-eyed Shiva's followers and associate *yakṣas* headed by Maniman and Mada unhesitatingly speeded after her, led by the king of bulls (Nandī). (4) Shiva's followers had Satī ascend Nandī, and then they all proceeded, accompanied by singers, drums, conchs, and flutes. They were equipped with her pet parrot, ball, mirror, lotus flower, white umbrella, chowries, garland, and other accessories. (5) They all arrived at the place of sacrifice, where the imposing Vedic chants for sacrificial killing resounded. Everywhere were stationed *brāhmaṇas* and seers, as well as the gods. There were specially made implements of clay, wood, iron, gold, *darbha* grass, and skins. (6) Out of fear of the sacrificer, Dakṣa, no one received Satī when she arrived. Although she was slighted, her caring sisters and mother, their voices choked by tears of love, joyfully embraced her. (7) She was duly questioned and updated by her sisters, mother, and maternal aunts and attended well with a seat, worship, and gifts; yet Satī rejected (everything), having not been welcomed by her father. (8) She saw that the sacrifice did not include a share for Rudra (Shiva), and (thus) her father had disrespected the great god Shiva. Slighted in the sacrificial assembly, Princess Satī was infuriated. It was as if she would incinerate all the worlds with her wrath. (9) Restraining her own battle-ready associates by her command, with voice choked in anger Satī denounced Shiva's foe, whose exertions in ritual gave rise to vanity. The goddess was heard by all. (10)[13]

The goddess (Satī) said: "No one excels Shiva, to whom none is dear nor detestable. He is loved by all creatures. Except for you, what person would oppose that soul of all who is free of enmity? (11) Twice-born Dakṣa! The likes of you see only faults. Saints notice no faults among others' virtues; and the greatest saints magnify any trace of virtues. Yet you saw a fault among those greatest of saints. (12)[14] Malicious derision of the great is always (heard) among lowly persons who say that the dead body is the self. This is no surprise; indeed it is as it should be, for their prominence is eclipsed by the dust of the feet of those great souls. (13)[15] Shiva's two-syllable name, even if audibly pronounced once by human beings, immediately eliminates evil. His fame is pure; his rule is inviolable. But alas, you hate Shiva, being quite his opposite! (14)[16] Exalted ones serve his lotus feet with their minds, like bees pursuing the nectarean bliss of *brahman*, while ordinary supplicants are showered by him with their desired objects. And yet you are hostile unto this friend of the universe! (15)[17] Don't you know that no one but you thinks that 'Shiva' is *aśiva* (inauspicious)? Accompanied by fiends, with scattered, matted hair, he lives in cremation grounds from where he obtains his garland, ashes, and human skull. Yet Brahmā and others bear on their heads whatever falls from his feet. (16)[18]

"When the dharma-protecting Lord is blasphemed by unbridled brutes, if one is unable (to counter the blasphemy), one should block the ears and go away. But if able, one should forcibly cut out the vilifying evil tongue and then give up one's own life. That is dharma! (17)[19] So I will no longer sustain this body born of you who abuse the blue-throated Shiva, for if abhorrent food has been eaten by mistake, the prescribed method of purification is vomiting. (18)[20] Just as the way of gods is distinct from that of humans, so the mind of a great sage may not follow the injunctions of the Veda, for he delights in his own realm. He who is committed to his own dharma should not revile the other. (19)[21] Engaged and disengaged action are both appropriate, and their symptoms are distinguished in the Veda. It is incompatible for both to be present simultaneously in one actor; thus action does not apply to one situated in *brahman*. (20)[22]

"Father! The traits (of the fiery path) are present in Shiva and me, but they do not belong to you! These unseen characteristics are cherished by *avadhūtas*, but they are not at all appreciated by those who follow the smoky path. Such people are content with the ritual food offerings made in sacrificial arenas. (21)[23] Enough with this contemptible birth! Enough with this body born from the body of an offender of Hara (Shiva)! I have become ashamed of my relationship to an evil man. Condemned is this birth from one who reviles the exalted! (22) Whenever Bhagavān (Shiva), whose emblem is the bull Nandī, calls me 'Dākṣāyanī' because of my relationship to you, I become deeply depressed and my humor and smile vanish. So I will relinquish this corpse born of you." (23)

Maitreya said: Vidura, destroyer of enemies! After speaking thus to Dakṣa in that place of sacrifice Satī sat in silence on the ground facing north. Wrapped in fine yellow cloth, she touched water, closed her eyes, and deeply entered the yoga pathway. (24) The blameless Satī, fixed in posture and balancing the life airs (*prāṇa* and *apāna*), then gradually raised the upward moving air (*udāna*) from the navel chakra into the heart and established it by means of the intellect in the upper chest; she then drew it from the throat to the middle of her eyebrows. (25)[24] Out of anger against Dakṣa she was resolved to abandon the very same body that Shiva, the greatest of the great, often placed caringly upon his lap. Thus the resolute Satī directed her concentration on the air and fire within all her limbs. (26) Finally, Satī meditated on the nectar of the lotus feet of her husband, the universal guru, and she envisioned none other. With her body's impurities removed, she suddenly blazed with the fire born of complete trance. (27)[25] From those on the earth and in the heavens who had witnessed this great wonder a terrific roar of exclamations arose:

"Alas, the goddess who is the beloved of the greatest of the gods has given up her life! By whom was Satī so angered? (28) Intelligent Satī, who was born of a man who despised her, always deserves respect. Alas, witness this excessive disregard of kin by Dakṣa, the progenitor of all living beings, because of which Satī gave up her life. (29) This hard-hearted hater of Shiva, enemy of the Supreme, will obtain great infamy in the world, for he did not stop his own daughter as she prepared for death because of his insult." (30)[26]

As the people who had witnessed Satī's astonishing death were speaking like this, Shiva's attendants rose with upraised weapons to slay Dakṣa.

(31) But then the powerful Bhṛgu saw the threat of those assailants, so he offered an oblation into the southern fire with a Yajurveda hymn to destroy those who would destroy the sacrifice. (32) When the Yajurveda priest Bhṛgu offered this oblation, thousands of gods named Ṛbhus, who had received *soma* by austerity, burst forth forcefully. (33)[27] Attacked by those gods carrying flaming firebrand weapons, the fiends (*pramathas*) and trolls (*guhyakas*) scattered in all directions by the force of (Bhṛgu's) brahmanical power. (34)

The next three chapters (5–7) narrate Shiva's violent reaction to the news of his wife's death and the subsequent mediation of Brahmā. From one of his hairs that he dashes on the ground, Shiva creates Vīrabhadra (auspicious valor), who, with other followers of Shiva, desecrates Dakṣa's sacrificial arena. Vīrabhadra then beheads Dakṣa on the sacrificial stake. The survivors approach Brahmā, who advises them to submissively beg Shiva for pardon, and together they go to meet Shiva at his idyllic abode on Mount Kailāsa. Brahmā beseeches Shiva to show compassion toward those bewildered by worldly pursuits, returning life to Dakṣa and putting right all the disorder wreaked by Shiva's followers. This Shiva does, but on his order Dakṣa is given the head of a goat. Dakṣa, now revived, is remorseful and repentant, and he prays to Shiva for pardon, which, being granted, makes possible the peaceful resumption of Dakṣa's sacrifice.

Maitreya then proceeds (in chapter 8) to narrate about the child Dhruva (constancy), son of Uttānapāda and grandson of Svāyambhuva Manu. Having been denied a position equal to that of his stepbrother by his stepmother, Surūci, Dhruva becomes resolved to acquire a kingdom that surpasses even that of his great-grandfather, Brahmā. Like Dakṣa, Dhruva pursues reputation, but unlike the former, Dhruva readily undertakes extreme ascetic practices while worshipping Vāsudeva (Vishnu)—with a mantra received from Nārada—to gain his goal. After five months of extreme ascetic efforts that threaten cosmic suffocation, Dhruva is rewarded with the appearance of Vāsudeva, who grants him perpetual lordship over the polestar (*dhruva-loka*). Despite having received these divine blessings as a child, Dhruva later gives vent to unrestrained rage over his stepbrother's death at the hands of a *guhyaka* (a troll attendant of the god Kuvera), leading him to vengefully attempt to exterminate the entire class of such beings until Svāyambhuva Manu intervenes. The account of Dhruva concludes with his ascension to the atemporal realm, Vaikuṇṭha, after "stepping over the head of death," accompanied by his mother, Sunīti.

Book Four dedicates a further nine chapters (15–23) to an account of King Pṛthu, an *avatāra* of Vishnu celebrated as an ideal monarch who reigns over the earth in the Tretā-yuga (see also 2.7.9). As an ideal king, Pṛthu sponsors extensive Vedic sacrifices; but like Dhruva, he displays excessive ambition, aspiring to perform one hundred times the great horse sacrifice (*aśvamedha*) to demonstrate his unrivaled sovereignty. In the following excerpt from chapter 19 Pṛthu's efforts to complete the final sacrifice are undermined by Indra, whose preeminent position among the gods is based on his having himself performed one hundred such sacrifices. Should Pṛthu succeed in completing his hundredth rite, Indra could lose his post.

In the next passage, we begin with verse 7 of chapter 19, after the scene of the sacrifice has been set: In Brahmāvarta, where the river Sarasvatī turns east, in the presence of Brahmā, Vishnu, and Shiva, Pṛthu is performing his horse sacrifices, and the increasing number of them has alarmed Indra. Well-known sages, such as Nārada, Kapila, Dattātreya, and the four Kumāras, are also present to witness Pṛthu's ritual accomplishments. The sage Maitreya continues to speak to Vidura.

KING PṚTHU'S COMPETITION WITH INDRA

Chapter 19

O descendant of Bharata, Goddess Earth, who yields dharma and all desires, was present (at the sacrifice) and yielded the sacrificial sponsor's desired aims. (19.7) The rivers flowed with milk, yogurt, clarified butter, and all juices; the mighty trees bore fruit and streamed with honey. (8)[28] The seas yielded masses of jewels, and the hills supplied the four kinds of food. All peoples, with their guardians, rendered presentations (to the king, Pṛthu). (9)[29] And yet Bhagavān Indra, envious of the great fortune of him whose Lord is Adhokṣaja (Vishnu), created an obstacle: (10) Just as the son of Vena was sacrificing to the Lord of Sacrifice with the final Aśvamedha, rivalrous Indra stealthily carried off the horse to be sacrificed. (11)

The venerable sage Atri spotted him hastening through the sky dressed as a heretic who was confusing dharma with what is not dharma. (12)[30] Urged by Atri to kill him, Pṛthu's heroic son angrily gave chase, commanding, "Stop! Stop!" (13) But seeing Indra appearing as he was, besmeared with ashes and bearing matted hair, Pṛthu's son thought Indra to be dharma personified, and so he did not release his arrow. (14)[31]

Again Atri urged him who had refrained from killing to kill: "Young man, go slay that destroyer of sacrifice, big shot Indra, vilest of the gods!" (15) So ordered, the son of Venu's son again angrily coursed through the sky just as the king of vultures chased Rāvaṇa. (16)[32] Self-ruling Indra then abandoned both horse and disguise and became invisible to that hero, who returned to his father's sacrifice bringing the animal. (17) Master Vidura! The great sages saw his wonderful deed, so they gave him the name Horse Winner (Vijitāśva). (18) Then the powerful thief Indra created dense darkness. So covered, he again stole the horse that had been bound with a golden tether to the sacrificial post. (19) Atri again exposed Indra, now disguised as one who bears a skull-topped staff, coursing quickly through the sky. The hero Vijitāśva again did not kill him. (20)[33] But incited by Atri, angry Vijitāśva placed an arrow to his bow. Indra, again abandoning horse and disguise, reassumed invisibility. (21) The hero once more took the horse and proceeded to the sacrifice of his father.

Since that time weak-minded persons have imitated Indra's blameworthy disguise. (22) All the forms Indra adopted to steal the horse are the aggregate (*khaṇḍa*) of evil (*pāpa*). Here the word *khaṇḍa* is taken in the sense of "sign" (hence *pākhaṇḍa* can also mean "a sign of evil"). (23)[34] Thus when Indra stole the horse in order to stop Pṛthu's sacrifice, accepting and abandoning *pākhaṇḍas* (heretical guises), people thought, "This is dharma!" and became committed to the subdharmic heretics. Those clever smooth talkers were often naked, clad in red, or otherwise strangely dressed. (24–25)[35] The powerful, valorous Pṛthu comprehended all this. Indignant toward Indra, he took up bow and arrow. (26) Terrible to behold, he dashed forth unconstrained. But the sacrificial priests saw his intention to kill Indra and forbade him:

"Whoa! High-minded one! It is not right for you to kill others here, for it is so decreed. (27)[36] King, *we* shall call Indra, lord of storm gods and spoiler of your sacrificial purpose, whose splendor is eclipsed by your glory. With fresh sacrificial mantras we shall hurl your enemy into the fire this very instant!" (28)

Vidura! So advising the master of sacrifice, with ritual ladles in hand the priests furiously set about making the invocation, when self-born Brahmā forbade them. (29) "Indra is not to be killed by you, for he is Yajña, whose body is the Lord, and the gods are the worshipped bodies of he whom you wish to kill by sacrifice (*yajña*). (30) Twice-born *brāhmaṇas*! Behold this great transgression of dharma! The king's sacrificial action affects naught but Indra's further disruptive tricks. (31) So let Pṛthu be famed as he who performed ninety-nine sacrifices. And you (Pṛthu) who know the dharma for liberation, the sacrifices you have already done so well are quite enough. (32) Being situated in the self alone, you need not bring enmity against great Indra. Indeed let there be good fortune for both of you, who are both forms of him who is praised with superb verses. (33) Great king, think no longer on this matter and take my words to heart, for brooding over what providence has undone is to make the enraged mind enter dense darkness. (34) Let this sacrifice, which is but a bad show among the gods, be put to rest. Where this goes on there is only violation of dharma with the heresies engendered by Indra. (35)

"Look! The people are being charmed by these captivating evils brought forth by Indra, that sacrifice-spoiling horse thief! (36) Son of Vena! You have descended into this world to deliver people's dharma befitting the times, currently suppressed by Vena's wickedness. Indeed, you are a portion of Vishnu appearing from Vena's body. (37) Protector of the people! Master! Considering this state of affairs, you are to preserve this creation's purpose and eradicate these vicious heretics' illusory path, the mother of irreligion created by Indra." (38)

Maitreya continued: Thus the guru of the worlds, Brahmā, advised the world protector Pṛthu, who then showed friendliness toward bountiful Indra, with whom he resolved his differences. (39) The gods, givers of blessings, having been satisfied in those sacrifices, gave blessings to Pṛthu of mighty deeds, who had completed the postsacrificial ablutions. (40) Vidura! Honored *brāhmaṇas* who bestow viable benedictions, pleased by receiving sacrificial fees respectfully given, blessed that first of kings, Pṛthu: (41) "Summoned by you of mighty arms, all the ancestors, gods, sages, and humans have been appropriately worshipped with wealth and honor." (42)[37]

In chapters 20 through 23 Maitreya continues to tell about Pṛthu as the ideal king of the entire earthly realm: As a pious ruler, he instructs his citizens in the social and life-stage principles of *varṇāśrama-dharma*, and he is in turn instructed by the sage Sanāt Kumāra on spiritual matters. Finally, after making arrangements for the rule of the kingdom by his sons and attending to his citizens' welfare, Pṛthu retires with his wife, Arci, to the forest to practice bhakti and penances in preparation for death. Upon his death in a state of yogic transfixion, Arci cremates her husband's body and, to the great astonishment and admiration of the wives of the gods, she herself enters that fire, achieving the same exalted destination as her husband.

After a brief account of Pṛthu's descendants, most of the remainder of Book Four (chapters 25–29) tells of Prācīnabarhiṣat, Pṛthu's great-grandson, and the lessons he receives from Nārada about the futility of ritual sacrifices for worldly gain. Nārada delivers these lessons in the form of an extended allegory: A certain King Purāñjana (embodied person) settles in a city of nine gates (the body, with its orifices), seeking happiness but meeting only troubles. Nearing death in his old age, because of his overattachment to his wife, Purāñjana subsequently becomes Vaidarbhī, a woman, in his next life. Vaidarbhī, in turn, becomes attached to her husband, whose death causes her to grieve deeply. Finally, a certain *brāhmaṇa* "friend" (representing the Lord) instructs Vaidarbhī with a city-as-body allegory that echoes and reiterates Nārada's extended allegory within which the *brāhmaṇa*'s allegory is embedded.

Book Four ends with an account of Prācīnbarhiṣat's (or Prācīnabarhi's) ten sons, the Pracetas, who observe ten thousand years of austerity within water to please Vishnu and qualify themselves to become cosmic progenitors (in chapter 30). After receiving Vishnu's benedictions and offering him prayers, they emerge from the sea, only to find that the earth is covered with trees, obstructing human activity such as agriculture. It is with Brahmā's intervention that they are dissuaded from burning down the entire planet's forest. Under Brahmā's direction, the Pracetas accept Māriṣā as their wife, and by them they collectively father Dakṣa (who had to be reborn after having previously offended Shiva). Finally, in chapter 31, the Pracetas retire to practice meditative yoga; the sage Nārada then meets them and reminds them of the goal of their yoga practices—namely, to please Hari, the Lord. The Lord is pleased by one who shows mercy to all beings, who is satisfied in all conditions, and who is able to control the senses.

The end of Book Four completes the dialogue between Vidura and Maitreya, after which Vidura returns to Hastināpura to meet those of his relatives who had survived the Kurukṣetra war (as elaborated in the Mahābhārata, Parvan 11–15).

SUGGESTIONS FOR FURTHER READING

Goodall, Dominic. 1996. *Hindu Scriptures.* Berkeley: University of California Press.
With respect to Book Four's references to Vedic sacrificial practices, the first section, "From the Ṛg-Veda" (pp. 1–17), provides translations of a few important hymns associated with the sacrifice. Of these, "The Sacrifice of Primal Man" (p. 13) is especially well known (and is alluded to in Bhāgavata Purāṇa Book Two, chapter 6).

Hudson, D. Dennis. 2008. *The Body of God: An Emperor's Palace for Krishna in Eighth-Century Kanchipuram.* New York: Oxford University Press.
Appendix 3, "The People's Indra" (pp. 515–27), is a useful elaboration on the story of King Pṛthu, represented in the particular temple, of which this book is a detailed study. The author highlights how the story of Pṛthu is positioned as a parallel to the story of the Pallava king who commissioned the temple's construction.

Kinsley, David. 1988. *Hindu Goddesses: Visions of the Divine Feminine in the Hindu Religious Tradition.* Berkeley: University of California Press.
Chapter 3, "Parvatī" (pp. 35–54), provides a brief overview of sources and variations on the mythology of Satī, who is generally identified as the initial form of Shiva's consort, later appearing as Parvatī.

Klostermaier, Klaus K. 2007. *A Survey of Hinduism.* 3rd ed. Albany: SUNY Press.
Chapter 16, "Śiva: The Grace and Terror of God" (pp. 116–31), offers a useful overview of Hindu traditions of Shiva and his worship, including their textual sources, Śaiva orders and schools, and Śaiva saints and singers.

BOOK FIVE

Ṛṣabha Counsels His Hundred Sons
Bharata Becomes a Deer
Description of Jaṃbūdvīpa

The dialogical frame of Book Five returns—after an interlude consisting of a talk between Vidura and Maitreya that includes most of Books Three and Four—to the discussion of King Parīkṣit and the sage Śuka. The first two chapters resume the genealogy recounted in the previous two books. Priyavrata, the powerful and duty-conscious brother of Uttānapāda (whose son Dhruva appears in Book Four), is featured in chapter 1, and his son, the passionate Āgnīdhra, with his wife, the celestial nymph Pūrvacitti, is the focus of chapter 2. Among their nine sons, Nābhi becomes prominent as the father of Ṛṣabha, whose birth, virtues, teachings, renunciation, and death are recounted in chapters 3 through 6. The next eight chapters relate the story of Bharata, the eldest son of Ṛṣabha, highlighting his initial failure in yoga practice, followed by glorious yogic-devotional success in his subsequent life as an apparent dullard. Following further genealogical details in chapter 15, the remainder of Book Five (chapters 16–26) consists of wondrous cosmographic description that includes delineations of the several "islands" of the earthly realm, Bhū-maṇḍala; the sun's path through the heavens; subterranean heavenly realms; and the torments of hellish realms.

In the next selection, as King Ṛṣabha prepares to renounce home and kingdom, he exhorts his sons to pursue self-knowledge rather than self-indulgence and to guide their dependents by the same principle. After concluding by praising the *brāhmaṇas*, Ṛṣabha leaves everything to wander as a seemingly mad ascetic, indifferent to abuse and to the powers he gains through yogic accomplishment.

ṚṢABHA COUNSELS HIS HUNDRED SONS

Chapter 5

Ṛṣabha said: "Dear sons, among all life-forms, this mortal body in the human realm is not meant for pursuing the lowly pleasures of dogs and pigs. Rather, it is meant for practicing divine penance, by which one may purify one's existence, yielding endless joyfulness in *brahman.* (5.1) It is said that service to exalted souls is liberation's gateway; association with men given over to women is the gateway to darkness. Exalted are those whose minds are equipoised, who are at peace, free from anger, kind-hearted, and upright—those whose aim is to cultivate affection for me, the Lord. These exalted souls are disinclined to mix with common people absorbed in bodily maintenance and the domestic charms of wife and children. They attend only to the bare necessities of life in this world. (2–3)[1] Indeed, a mad person commits forbidden acts that are undertaken for pleasing the senses. I consider this unwise, for although the body is temporary, it is the source of misery for the self. (4) As long as one does not seek knowledge of the self, one remains a defeated dullard; indeed, as long as the mind pursues (self-centered) action (karma), a mundane mentality persists—the cause of corporeal bondage. (5)

"Thus when the self is engulfed by ignorance, the mind is brought under the subjection of action (karma); as long as one has no love for me, Vāsudeva, one will not be free from the body's yoke. (6) When a learned person fails to see that pursuit of temporal pleasure is inappropriate for one's own good, he or she soon becomes mad. With memory (of wise instruction) gone, such an ignorant person is ensconced in sexuality's domain, where one is subjected to afflictions. (7) It is said that this sexual penchant of man and woman is their shared knot in the heart, tying them thenceforth to house, land, children, relatives, and wealth, of which they foolishly claim, 'This is I!' and 'This is mine!' (8)[2] Should one's tight knot of the mind and heart—the bondage of karma—be unraveled, then one eschews it (sexual gratification). Escaping the cause of bondage, one is liberated and proceeds to the supreme. (9) Dear sons! An able person who firmly pursues purity can remove all trace of pretension by devotedly following me as the spiritual preceptor; by freedom from desire; by tolerating temporal dualities; by comprehending the plight of creatures everywhere; by inquisitiveness (about ultimate truth); by austerity; by abstaining from worldly activity; by regularly acting for me and speaking about me; by performing the praise of my qualities in the company of my respected devotees; by tranquility arising from equanimity and non-enmity; by longing to abandon the attitude that one's body and home are oneself; by transpersonal yoga performed in seclusion, effectively controlling breath, senses, and self; by having faith in the truth and by constant observance of continence; by sober and restrained speech; by a clear-sighted sense of my omnipresence; and by self-discipline infused with knowledge and with wisdom seasoned by resolve, perseverance, and prudence. (10–13) Having practiced this discipline as instructed, having completely removed the stock of karma—the heart's knot of bondage, which comes about through ignorance—a careful person should then give up preoccupation with the discipline. (14) A king or guru who seeks my mercy, longing for my abode, should instruct sons and students who are ignorant of this practice. One should not enlist in mundane actions persons deluded by karma. What gain is won by so employing persons whose vision is lost, surely causing them to fall into the depths? (15)[3] Steeped in hostility among its members, a pleasure-seeking society, blind to its own benefit, foolishly pursues the gains of momentary happiness and cannot fathom its (impending resultant) perpetual misery. (16) Seeing a fool absorbed in his own ignorance, what wise, compassionate person who knows the truth would prompt him to again keep away from the path (of elevation), like a blind person? (17) One should not presume to be a lord, a guru, a guardian, a father, a mother, or a husband who cannot foster the liberation of a dependent whose death is certain. (18) This body of mine defies comprehension. Pure spirit is my heart, where dharma is situated, whereas adharma is distant, situated behind me. Therefore noble persons call me Ṛṣabha (the best). (19) Therefore with unflagging resolve, all you sons, born of my heart, should render supportive service to the best of your brothers, Bharata, in his guardianship of the citizens. (20)

"Among living beings, reptiles are superior to plants; higher than reptiles are beings that rely on intelligence; then there are human beings, followed by *pramathas*, *gandharvas*, *siddhas*, and attendants to the gods. (21)[4] Superior to (such) gods and demons are the gods whose chief is the munificent Indra. Superior to them are the sons of Brahmā beginning with Dakṣa, and Bhava (Shiva) is superior to them. In turn, Brahmā, who fathers Shiva, is superior to him. Brahmā regards me as superior; and I am the lord who regards the *brāhmaṇas* as his lords. (22) Dear *brāhmaṇas*! I see no being equal—not to mention superior—to *brāhmaṇas*, to whom people faithfully offer sacrificial food. I do not relish oblations in ritual fires as

I relish these offerings (to *brāhmaṇas*). (23)[5] The ancient lore (Veda), which is my body, is maintained by *brāhmaṇas*, in whom exist superlative pure illumination, equanimity, self-restraint, truthfulness, mercy, austerity, forbearance, and understanding. (24) Those possessionless (*brāhmaṇas*) who are devoted to me seek nothing from me, although I am unlimited, above the greatest, the sovereign of the celestial and mortal realms. What, then, would they seek from others? (25) O sons! In every circumstance you are to regard all moving and stationary beings as my dwelling place. Indeed, your worship of me shall consist in sustaining such judicious vision. (26)[6] Only by the direct employment of mind, words, vision, and senses is my worship accomplished, without which a person, due to great delusion, is unable to be freed from fate's fetters." (27)[7]

Śuka said: Thus, for the sake of guiding the people, the greatly dignified Lord appearing as the sublime benefactor Ṛṣabha personally instructed his sons, although they were (already) educated. He taught the dharma for the best adepts, the great ascetics whose disposition is tranquil, having retired from (selfish) action. That dharma has the characteristics of devotion, knowledge, and renunciation. Then, for ruling the earth, he consecrated Bharata, the eldest of his hundred sons, regarding him as a perfect *bhāgavata*, or one who is dedicated to the Lord and the Lord's votaries. All that Ṛṣabha kept for himself at home was his own body. Finally, placing the sacred fire within himself, he wandered forth from Brahmāvarta like a madman, with naked body and wild hair. (28)[8] Adopting the appearance of an *avadhūta*—like a ghostly madman who is dull witted, blind, dumb, and deaf—Ṛṣabha remained silent, sustaining a vow to refrain from speaking, even if people addressed him. (29) Here and there along the way among cities, towns, mines, farms, mountain settlements, gardens, military camps, pastures, cowherd settlements, caravans, hills, forests, hermitages, and so on, he would be surrounded by roving rabble, like a wild elephant surrounded by flies.

Disregarding their abusive words, threats, beatings, their urinating and spitting upon him, and their throwing of dust, stones, feces, or passing of foul air on him, he was undisturbed in mind amid the unreal condition known as the body that is considered real, because he did not accept the conceptions of "I" and "mine." With innate understanding of the real and the unreal, Ṛṣabha roamed alone in the world, situated in his own glory. (30) His bodily limbs were well proportioned, with full chest and shoulders, long arms and neck; and he had exceptionally fine hands, feet, and facial features. His bright face bore the natural smile of a winning disposition.

His sparkling eyes, reddish like the rising sun, with cooling irises, were broad like the petals of a young lotus. Equally lovely were his forehead, ears, neck, and nose. Due to the grand festival of his modestly smiling face surrounded by a great mass of curly, matted, reddish-brown hair, desire arose in the minds of the city women. By the appearance of his neglected, filthy body, he seemed ghostly haunted. (31) Indeed, when he, Bhagavān, saw the people's utter opposition to his yoga practice, he abhorred retaliatory action. Instead he vowed to behave like a boa snake; he would eat, drink, chew, urinate, and defecate, all while lying (on the ground). Rolling about in (his own) excrement, he became smeared with it. (32) Even so, the air, sweetly perfumed by his excrement, made the entire area fragrant within a radius of ten *yojanas.* (33) In like manner (as with the snake vow), assuming the behavior of a cow, deer, or crow, when walking, standing, sitting, or reclining, he acted like a crow, deer, or cow as they drink, eat, or urinate. (34)[9] Thus Bhagavān Ṛṣabha, master of detachment, performed various yoga practices. O king! He was indifferent to all the yogic powers that he gratuitously gained in full, such as flying with the swiftness of the mind, becoming invisible, entering another's body, and perceiving remote objects. With expressions of incessant and unrestrained tears he apprehended the uninterrupted ultimate transcendent bliss—that of the self's presence in Bhagavān Vāsudeva, who is within all living beings. (35)

Śuka continues to eulogize Ṛṣabha in the subsequent chapter. As a teacher of yoga, Ṛṣabha demonstrates how to face the death of one's body with indifference by peacefully allowing his body to be consumed in a forest fire. Śuka then levels criticism against a certain King Arhat for "imitating" Ṛṣabha, thereby condemning Jain principles as heretical. In contrast, Ṛṣabha's eldest son, Bharata, is a genuine follower of his father who, after dividing his kingdom among his five sons, withdraws to a hermitage to absorb himself in devotional meditation on Vāsudeva. In the next reading, we see how he became distracted from this task.

BHARATA BECOMES A DEER

Chapter 8

The glorious Śuka said: Then it so happened that once, having done his obligatory religious ablutions in the Great River (Gaṇḍakī), Bharata sat at the water's edge, pronouncing the *brahman* syllable (*oṁ*) for three moments. (8.1)[10] King Parīkṣit! There approached at that time one thirsty doe at the water source. (2) Just as the doe was intently drinking water, there resounded at close quarters the world-frightening roar of a lion. (3) Its thirst yet unslaked, upon hearing that sound the naturally skittish she-deer, looking to and fro in alarm, out of anxiety immediately leapt forth, its heart overtaken by excessive fear of the lion. (4) The doe had been pregnant, and as it sprang up in terror the fetus was expelled from the womb and fell into the river's current. (5) Exhausted from its frightened flight and (consequent) giving birth, separated from its herd, in a cave the black doe collapsed and died. (6) The sage-king Bharata noticed the wretched, cast-off fawn carried along by the river's current. (Thinking) "Its mother has died," like a friend, he compassionately took it and brought it to his hermitage. (7)

And then, day by day, as a result of his excessive attentions toward the fawn, which he came to regard as his own child—feeding, protecting, cuddling, and indulging it—he neglected one by one his self-regulations, disciplines, and services to the Lord, and, within but a few days, all these practices ceased entirely. (8) (Bharata thought) "Alas, this wretched fawn, through the rapid rotation of the Lord's chariot's wheel (time), has lost its own kind—friends and relations—and has resorted to my shelter. It knows no other than me as its mother, father, brothers, kinsfolk, and comrade. And so I, who am without envy and who know the fault of neglecting one who has taken refuge, must feed, protect, indulge, and cuddle this one for whom I am the only refuge. (9) Quite certainly in such condition of need, honorable saintly persons whose conduct is tranquil and who are kindhearted to the helpless neglect even their own pressing needs." (10)

And so, when sitting, lying down, walking, bathing, eating, and so on with the fawn, Bharata became attached, his heart bound by affection. (11) Intending to gather *kuśa* grass, flowers, firewood, leaves, fruit, roots, and water, when he would enter the forest, (he did so) with the fawn, being anxious over the danger from wolves, dogs, and the like. (12) Bharata would carry the fawn on his shoulder while roaming along the (forest) paths, his mind so engrossed by its charming innocence and his heart bearing affection because of its helplessness. He would also keep the fawn on his lap or chest, finding great delight in cuddling it. (13)[11] Even in the midst of performing his routine daily rituals, the lord of the realm (Bharata) would get up repeatedly when he wished to see the fawn. With his mind pacified, he would bestow blessings: "My little darling, let there be all well-being for you!" (14)[12] At other times, with greatly disturbed mind, like one made wretched by destitution, with excessive craving, his heart burning with compassionate anxiety in the fawn's absence, constantly fretting over it, he was seized by deep dejection, saying, (15) "Alas, I am devoid of piety, my mind ignoble and uncivilized! Will this poor orphaned fawn that is fully trustful of me come back, overlooking all my faults, like a cultured person? (16) Will I (again) see this ward of the gods safely grazing on the fresh grass in the hermitage grove? (17) Or could it be that some wolf, dog, pack-ranging boar, or alone-roving tiger devours it? (18) Already the mighty sun, who sustains the well-being of the whole world, whose very self is the threefold Veda, is setting. Still, my charge, abandoned by the doe, does not return! (19) Could it be that upon returning, removing the anxiety of its kin, the little deer prince will bring joy to me who am devoid of piety, by displaying its various charming antics as a fawn? (20) Upon returning, because of anxious affection, in its playfulness it ever so cautiously prods me—who feigns being in a trance with eyes closed—with its soft antlers that feel pleasing like drops of water. (21) When I scold it for having polluted the ritual offerings that had been set out on sacrificial grass, it suddenly stops its play and timidly sits like a sage's son, all its senses subdued. (22) Oho! What austerity has this ascetic earth performed, by which this ground, with a trail of beautiful, most auspicious soft hoofprints of the gentle little black deer fawn, shows the way to wealth for me who am wretched, bereaved by destitution? With these hoofprints, the earth has decorated herself and has become a place of sacrifice to the gods for the twice-born *brāhmaṇas* who desire heaven or liberation. (23)[13] Could it be that, because of the danger of a lion, the glorious lord of constellations (the moon), who is kind to pitiable persons, with compassion protects the motherless fawn, estranged from its own hermitage? (24) Or could it be that, having sheltered this fawn, my roselike heart being afflicted by the blazing flames of the forest fire of separation from my own son, I am being relieved by the rays of the moon—ambrosia-like waters from the moon's mouth—rich with cool and unwavering affection?" (25)

Thus he whose heart was agitated by confused longings fell away from his yogic pursuits, disciplined austerity, and practice of worshipping the Lord because of his own action prompted by a baby deer. How else could the sage-king Bharata, who had previously renounced what is difficult to give up—his beloved sons—have such strong attachment for a young fawn—a different species—and have such utter scorn for life's ultimate aim, allowing this obstacle to disrupt his yoga practice? So much was he feeding, protecting, indulging, and cuddling the fawn that by this constant preoccupation he neglected his own soul. As a serpent (enters) a mouse hole, the dreadful, insurmountable power that is time fell upon him. (26)[14] Even then, noticing the fawn remaining by his side, lamenting as if it were his own son, Bharata's mind was absorbed in the deer alone. While giving up this world and the deer, his body expired. Thereafter he obtained the body of a deer; but unlike others, his memory of his previous life was not destroyed. (27) Indeed, even then he remembered why he had become a deer, and with a feeling of longing to worship the Lord, he deeply repented, saying, (28) "Alas, I am fallen from the way of the self-possessed—I, for whom all (mundane) association was ended, whose shelter was a secluded sacred forest, who was self-possessed, whose mind was entirely concentrated, thoroughly absorbed, at all times occupied by practices of repeated hearing, reflecting on, praising, worshipping, and contemplating the mighty Vāsudeva, the self of all selves. But my foolish mind, following from a distance the fawn, became deranged." (29) In this mood of remorseful detachment he abandoned his deer mother at Kālañjara, resorting instead to the hermitage of Pulastya and Pulaha at Śālagrāma, a place of the Lord beloved by sages of tranquil character. (30)[15] There he waited expectantly for the time of death, with the (supreme) self as his sole companion, ever fearful of other association. Anticipating only the termination of his condition of being a deer, living on dry leaves, grass, and herbs, bathing in sacred water, he gave up the deer body. (31)[16]

The next six chapters (9–14) narrate Bharata's life as the apparently deaf and dumb Jaḍa Bharata. In his determination to perfect his yoga practice after the detour into the body of a deer, the *brāhmaṇa* Jaḍa Bharata avoids all social interaction by acting as if deaf and dumb. His deception serves its function but also requires him to tolerate the abuse of family and neighbors and to endure being abducted by worshippers of the goddess Kālī to serve as a sacrificial victim. After a Kālī image "comes alive" and slays his captors, the young man is then employed as a palanquin carrier for the local ruler, Rahūgaṇa. Jaḍa Bharata's irregular pace (caused by his effort to avoid stepping on ants) angers the king, leading to an extensive discussion: Jaḍa Bharata (now setting aside his "deafness") wins the king's respect and expounds for him on the nature of the self and the necessity to avoid becoming lost in the "forest" of illusory, worldly existence.

Chapter 15 resumes the genealogical account that begins Book Five, naming several descendants of Bharata—all devotees of Vishnu. Then, in the beginning of chapter 16, King Parīkṣit requests Śuka to elaborate on what he had only briefly mentioned in chapter 1—namely, that once, when following behind the sun in his chariot, Priyavrata had created seven oceans from the chariot's wheel tracks. Here begins Śuka's detailed description of the universe, at the center of which is a horizontal, target-shaped expanse of ringlike "islands" interspersed with "oceans." In the center of this expanse is Jambūdvīpa island.

DESCRIPTION OF JAMBŪDVĪPA

Chapter 16

The seer (Śuka) said: Emperor! Even with the life span of a god, no person is capable of fully comprehending or describing the splendors of Bhagavān's *māyā*, which consists of the *guṇas*. Therefore, I will explain only the most important, defining features of the earth sphere, including names, forms, measurements, and characteristics. (16.4)[17] This island (Jambūdvīpa, where we reside) is the innermost area of the earth, which resembles the whorl of a lotus flower. Jambūdvīpa is one hundred thousand *yojanas* in diameter and uniformly circular, like the leaf of a lotus plant. (5)[18] The island consists of nine regions (*varṣas*), each nine thousand *yojanas* long, which are clearly separated and demarcated by eight mountain ranges. (6)[19] In the center of these regions is located the region called Ilāvṛta, and at its center is the solid-gold Mount Meru, the best of preeminent mountains. Meru's height equals the diameter of the island. As the pericarp of the lotus-shaped earth, Meru is thirty-two thousand *yojanas* wide at its peak and sixteen thousand *yojanas* wide at its base, and it extends sixteen thousand *yojanas* below the surface of the earth. (7)[20] Successively northward from Ilāvṛta are the regions called Ramyaka, Hiraṇmaya, and Kuru, which are bounded, respectively, by the three mountains Nīla, Śveta, and Śṛṅgavān. These mountains are each two thousand *yojanas* wide, running lengthwise east and west to the saltwater ocean. Going northward, each mountain is ten percent shorter in length than the previous one. (8) Similarly, on the southern side of Ilāvṛta, there are (from north to south) the regions called Hari, Kimpuruṣa, and Bhārata, which are bounded by the mountains Niṣadha, Hemakūṭa, and Himālaya, respectively. (9) Like Nīla and the other northern mountains, these mountains also extend east to west and are ten thousand *yojanas* high. Similarly, on the western and eastern sides (of Meru) stand, respectively, Mount Mālyavān and Mount Gandhamādana. They are each two thousand *yojanas* high, extending (north to south) toward Mount Nīla and Mount Niṣadha and marking the boundaries of Ketumāla and Bhadrāśva. (10)

The mountains Mandara, Merumandara, Supārśva, and Kumuda form a barrier on all four sides of Meru. They are ten thousand *yojanas* wide and high. (11) Four magnificent trees—mango, rose apple, kadamba, and banyan—stand like flagstaffs on these four mountains. They are each over one thousand *yojanas* tall, and their branches spread the same distance. The circumference (of their trunks) is one hundred *yojanas*. (12)[21] Best of the Bharatas! There are four lakes, containing milk, honey, sugarcane juice, and pure water (respectively). The hosts of demigods, who possess innate yogic powers, frequent these lakes. (13) There are also four celestial gardens, known as Nandana, Caitraratha, Vaibhrājaka, and Sarvatobhadra. (14) The powerful gods, husbands of many celestial beauties, frolic in those gardens as their glories are sung by the hosts of demigods. (15) Ambrosial fruits, the size of mountain peaks, fall from the top of a celestial mango tree—eleven hundred *yojanas* tall—that stands on the slopes of Mount Mandara. (16) The pleasing juice from those broken fruits—very sweet, richly fragrant, reddish, and abundant—becomes the river called Aruṇodā, which cascades down from Mount Mandara's peak and irrigates Ilāvṛta's eastern side. (17) Bhavānī's attendants, wives of pious men, enjoy that river, and so the breeze becomes fragrant when it touches their limbs. That breeze perfumes an area within a radius of ten *yojanas*. (18)[22] Similarly, the rose apple fruits, which are the size of elephants yet have very small seeds, break when they fall from a great height, and their juice forms a river called Jambū. The river falls from Mount Merumandara's peak—ten thousand *yojanas* high—to the surface of the earth and flows across southern Ilāvṛta. (19) The earth on both banks of the river Jambū becomes saturated with rose apple juice, and with contact from the sun and wind, this mixture turns into gold called Jambūnada, which always adorns the denizens of heaven. (20)

Chapter 16 ends with further details about the mountains, trees, and rivers of Jambūdvīpa, concluding by noting that on the plateau atop the central mountain, Meru, rests the city of the Self-born (Brahmā), surrounded by eight cities of the principal celestial divinities. A description of the river Ganges follows in the next chapter: after descending down through the universe onto the top of Mount Meru, where it flows through Brahmāpurī, it divides into four streams, one of which is the river known by this name "Ganges" in Bhāratavarṣa (the land usually identified as present-day India). The regions (*varṣas*) of Jambūdvīpa are the subject of further discussion, with attention to how particular forms of Vishnu are worshipped in each region. The text highlights Bhārata-varṣa as of special note as the region where the residents are particularly privileged to worship Vishnu while upholding the social system of *varṇāśrama-dharma*—regulations of occupation and life stage.

Moving outward from the central island, Jambūdvīpa, we read of the six concentric circles of oceans (each containing different types of liquid) and islands that make up the remainder of the horizontal plane called Bhū-maṇḍala. At the periphery of this vast area is Lokāloka, a mountain (or mountain range) that limits the reach of the sun's illumination to within the inhabited terrain of the universe. The sun's motion is next described (in chapter 21), as it rotates on the sun god's chariot, the single wheel of which is the wheel of time, called Saṁvatsara (year). This chariot is said to be drawn by seven horses, each of which is one of the important poetic meters of the Veda. Still further from Jambūdvīpa is the moon, the waxing and waning of which governs day and night in the celestial realms. Beyond the moon are the several planets, noted for their positive and negative influences on living beings. Then, beyond Saturn, are the seven sages, who circumambulate Dhruvaloka (the North Star). There is also the dolphin-shaped, luminous mass of stars we know as the Milky Way, called Śiśumāra (literally, "child killer," the Gangetic dolphin or porpoise). Like the seven sages, Śiśumāra is identified as an external, temporal form of Bhagavān, Vishnu. At the end of chapter 23 is a meditative and submissive prayer to this form of Vishnu.

From the top of the universe, or outer space, Śuka now turns to intermediate space, where he locates various realms above the earth, named Siddhaloka, Cāraṇaloka, and Vidyādharaloka. Below these reside various more or less malignant beings—Yakṣas, Rākṣasas, Piśacas, ghosts, and the like. Further down, below the earth, is Bila-svarga—"pit heaven"—where demonic and serpent beings enjoy all varieties of illusory charms. Several other types of beings live in seven lower realms, and among them is the devotee-king Bali (whose adventures are described in Book Eight). Below the lowest of these realms, Pātāla, resides the divine, multihooded serpent

Ananta (unlimited), also known as Saṅkarṣaṇa (drawing together). It is upon his countless hoods that all the worlds are sustained, and it is by his direction that Shiva executes the periodic cosmic annihilation. Finally, Book Five ends with Śuka's description of twenty-eight lower realms of punishment, where the correction of persons who, in their previous lives, have acted contrary to dharma is accomplished.

SUGGESTIONS FOR FURTHER READING

Broo, Måns. 2013. "Heresy and Heretics in the Bhāgavata Purāṇa." In *The Bhāgavata Purāṇa: Sacred Text and Living Tradition*, edited by Ravi M. Gupta and Kenneth R. Valpey, 145–61. New York: Columbia University Press.
This is relevant to chapter 5, as it calls attention to how the Bhāgavata criticizes various groups, including Jains, Buddhists, and Śaivas.

Minkowski, Christopher Z. 2001. "The Paṇḍit as Public Intellectual: The Controversy over Virodha or Inconsistency in the Astronomical Sciences." In *The Pandit: Traditional Scholarship in India*, edited by Axel Michaels, 79–96. New Delhi: Manohar.
This is relevant to chapter 16, as it shows that sixteenth-century Indian astronomers were concerned about inconsistencies between such Puranic cosmologies as the Bhāgavata Purāṇa presents and their own astronomical knowledge.

Theodor, Ithamar. 2010. *Exploring the Bhagavad Gītā: Philosophy, Structure, and Meaning.* Farnham, U.K.: Ashgate.
Chapter 8, "Quitting One's Body, the Ephemeral and Eternal Worlds," is relevant to chapter 8, as it summarizes the notion of preparation for death and determination of postdeath destination that is generally accepted in the Bhāgavata Purāṇa.

Thompson, Richard L. 1996. *Vedic Cosmography and Astronomy.* Los Angeles: Bhaktivedanta Book Trust.
Chapter 3, "Vedic Cosmography," is relevant to chapter 16; though titled "Vedic" cosmography, Thompson deals with the Bhāgavata's Puranic account, exploring how it might be interpreted in modern astronomical terms.

BOOK SIX

Ajāmila's Near-Death Lesson
Indra's Grave Mistake
Indra Slays Viśvarūpa
Indra Slays Vṛtra
Indra's Lament
Citraketu Cursed to Become Vṛtra

Traditional Bhāgavata commentators generally associated Book Six with the Bhāgavata's fourth of ten topics—namely, "nourishing" (*poṣaṇa*), or "Vishnu's mercy toward his devotees" (see 2.10.1). Viśvanātha calls attention to three figures in this book as recipients of Vishnu's mercy despite their various transgressions: Ajāmila (described in the first three chapters), Indra (in chapters 7–13), and Citraketu (in chapters 14–17). Here we include excerpts from the episodes involving these figures. Book Six also resumes the description from Book Four of Dakṣa's endeavors as cosmic progenitor and concludes—after listing descendants of Aditi and Diti, wives of the progenitor Kaśyapa—with an account of Diti's failed attempt at revenge against Indra for his complicity in the death of her sons Hiraṇyākṣa (3.19) and Hiraṇyakaśipu (7.8). Book Six concludes with details of the ritual Diti performs under Kaśyapa's guidance.

At the end of Book Five, the main reciter, Śuka, had described various realms where, after death, punishments are inflicted on persons for specific transgressions committed by them in their preceding lives. Now Parīkṣit asks Śuka to expound on the means by which a human being may be freed from having to undergo such terrible ordeals. Śuka proceeds initially to suggest self-disciplinary practices of atonement; but Parīkṣit rejects these suggestions as insufficient means for thoroughly purging the heart. To counteract bad actions with good actions is to remain bound by the desire for gains won by one's own efforts. Nor, admits Śuka, can penance and austerity sufficiently purify the heart. Rather, what is needed is to adopt the practice of pure bhakti dedicated to Vāsudeva (Krishna). Bhakti alone has the power to completely destroy the heart's impurities, just as the sun alone can disperse dense fog.

To illustrate the matchless detergent power of bhakti, Śuka relates the following story. Ajāmila, despite leading a deplorably sinful life in negligence of his brahmanical culture and upbringing, gains deliverance to Vaikuṇṭha (the divine realm) by virtue of inadvertently, in desperation, resorting to Lord Nārāyaṇa by calling out for his own son, incidentally named Nārāyaṇa, with his dying breath.

AJĀMILA'S NEAR-DEATH LESSON

Chapters 1, 2, and 3

In Kānyakubja lived a *brāhmaṇa* named Ajāmila who married a maidservant. In her company his good character was destroyed. (1.21)[1] This corrupt fellow's lifestyle was degraded; he maintained his family by kidnapping, cheating, thieving, and otherwise harassing people. (22) Much time passed in this way, O king, with Ajāmila indulging his sons and wife up into his eighty-eighth year. (23) Of the old man's ten sons, the youngest, named Nārāyaṇa, was most dear to both father and mother. (24) The old man, his heart captured by the small child and his babbling talk, was filled with delight seeing him play. (25) Caught up in his affection for the boy, while eating, drinking, chewing, and feeding his son, the fool was unaware of death's arrival. (26)[2] And so, as the time of death drew near, that ignorant Ajāmila absorbed his mind in his young son named Nārāyaṇa. (27)[3] Seeing three fearsome men approaching with twisted faces and bristling hair, carrying ropes to drag him off, in confusion he tearfully called out to his son Nārāyaṇa, who was intently playing at a distance. (28–29) Great king! On hearing the name of their master, Hari, from the mouth of the dying man, Vishnu's messengers suddenly arrived. (30) The messengers of Yama were dragging Ajāmila, the maidservant's husband, (from his body), out of his inner heart. But Vishnu's messengers emphatically forbade them from doing so. (31)

Thus obstructed, the attendants of Yama, son of Vivasvān, enquired: "Who are you, opposing the rule of the King of Dharma (Yama)? (32) Whose servants are you? From where have you come? Why do you forbid this man's arrest? Are you gods, minor gods, or most perfected beings? (33) You all have eyes like lotus petals, yellow silk garments, crowns, ear ornaments, and radiant lotus garlands. (34) You are all in the prime of youth, all with four splendid arms bearing (variously) bow, arrow quiver, sword, club, conch, and lotus. (35) By your powerful radiance you illuminate all directions. Why do you obstruct us, the agents of dharma's protector?" (36)

Śrī Śuka said: Thus addressed by the attendants of Yama, Vāsudeva's (Vishnu's) servants smiled and gave this reply, their voices resounding like thunderclouds. (37) Vishnu's messengers said: "If you are really the executors of the Dharma King's orders, then explain for us the true character of dharma and its opposite, adharma. (38) How is the rod of punishment to be wielded, or what is its intended application? Are all performers of action to be punished or only some?" (39) Yama's messengers replied: "Dharma is enjoined in the Veda, and adharma is dharma's opposite. We have heard, 'The Veda is directly the self-born Nārāyaṇa (Vishnu).' (40)

"All these states of being, consisting of activity, illumination, or inertia, with their various qualities, names, actions, and forms, are manifest fittingly by him (Vishnu), who remains in his own realm. (41)[4] The sun, fire, sky, wind, cows, the moon, twilight, night and day, the directions, water, earth, and Dharma himself: all these are witnesses of the embodied being. (42) By these witnesses, adharma is identified and punishment appropriately applied. All those who act deserve punishment in accordance with their actions. (43) O sinless ones! Favorable and unfavorable situations will surely arise because of the contact of actors with the mundane qualities (*guṇas*); an embodied being cannot possibly be a nonactor. (44)[5] Indeed, precisely in the manner and to the extent one pursues adharma or dharma in this life determines one's manner and extent of suffering or pleasure in the next life. (45) Best of gods! As the three kinds of effects accrue in this world according to the diversity of the *guṇas* among living beings, so the same variety can be inferred to exist in the other world. (46)[6] As the present time indicates the qualities of past and future, so this life indicates the dharma and adharma of past and future lives. (47) Situated in his abode, the blessed, unborn lord mentally discerns the previous state of a person; he accordingly deliberates on that person's next state. (48)[7] As an ignorant, sleeping person inhabits a dream body unaware of his previous or future condition, so also one knows neither previous nor future lives, having lost memory at birth. (49) The one (living being) enjoys the three (types of experience) with sixteen (constituents): with five (motor organs) he pursues his aims and with five (senses of perception, along with the mind) he comprehends five (types of sense objects). He himself is the seventeenth. (50)[8] This sixteen-constituent body consisting of the three powerful forces (*guṇas*) subjects the living being to repeated transmigration, which gives jubilation, lamentation, fear, and pain. (51) The ignorant, embodied being, whose five senses and mind are unsubdued, is impelled to perform actions even without desiring them. Like a silkworm, the self, covered by its own actions, is bewildered. (52) At no time—not even for a moment—does anyone cease to act. Indeed, action is performed without one's willing, by the force of one's inherent *guṇas*. (53)[9] Accruing unseen causality by force of one's own disposition, a gross and subtle body comes about according to a mother's womb and a father's seed. (54) A person's misfortune occurs because of contact with material nature; yet such misfortune is quickly dissolved by contact with the Lord. (55)

"This Ajāmila had been well versed in the Veda and was a reservoir of good character, conduct, and qualities; he had been firm in his vows, mild mannered, self-controlled, truthful, pure, and well versed in the knowledge of mantras. (56) He was ever attentive to the guru, the ritual fire, guests, and the elderly, and was prideless—a friend to all beings, honorable, measured in speech, and without envy. (57) Once, on the order of his father, this *brāhmaṇa* Ajāmila went to the forest to gather fruit, flowers, fuel, and *kuśa* grass. (58)[10] While returning home he saw a lustful *śūdra* man together with a servant girl. Her eyes rolled drunkenly from the honey liquor she had consumed. (59) This degraded and shameless *śūdra* sang, laughed, and flirted intimately with the besotted girl, while her dress became loosened. (60) Seeing her embraced passionately by the *śūdra*, immediately Ajāmila became bewildered, succumbing to dormant desire in his heart. (61) Curbing himself by his will as best he could according to what he had been taught, Ajāmila nevertheless could not steady his mind, being agitated by the god of love, Madana. (62) Distracted by her, grasped by the stealthy crocodile of concupiscence, meditating on her exclusively, he abandoned his own dharma. (63) He then sought to satisfy her as far as possible with his father's wealth and with such worldly goods as would please her mind. (64) His mind deranged by the woman's glances, the sinful Ajāmila soon rejected his own young and high-class *brāhmaṇa* wife. (65) And whether by honest or ill-gotten means this obtuse Ajāmila maintained the woman's family of many children. (66) Therefore Ajāmila was in violation of scripture, irresponsible, and thoroughly contemptible. Because of his moral flaws, he passed his life as a sinner for a long time. (67) Hence we shall bring this unrepentant evildoer before Daṇḍapāṇi, Yama, where he will be purified by the rod of chastisement." (68)

The revered Bādarāyaṇi (son of Vyāsa, Śuka) spoke: O king, thus the Lord's messengers, learned in proper conduct, heard the appeal of Yama's messengers and then replied to them. (2.1)

The blessed messengers of Vishnu spoke: "Alas, what a scandal it is that adharma has touched an assembly of those who see dharma. They are wrongly punishing those who are sinless and undeserving of punishment! (2) The rulers of the citizens are meant to be saintly, equal-minded administrators of law. If they become unjust, where shall the citizens go for shelter? (3) Whatever superiors do, that is what others pursue. People follow whatever standard a superior sets. (4)[11] They sleep with their heads faithfully on the lap of their master, like an animal that, on its own, knows neither its dharma nor adharma. (5) How could a compassionate leader, who should inspire faith in everyone, exploit a vulnerable refugee who has placed trust in him? (6) This Ajāmila has done penance sufficient to counter sins committed in millions of lives because in desperation he called out the name of Hari (Vishnu), which is the means of good fortune. (7) When the sinful Ajāmila called out, 'Come, Nārāyaṇa,' he pronounced the four-syllable name of Hari. By this act alone, his sins would have been nullified. (8) A thief, a drunkard, the betrayer of a friend, the murderer of a *brāhmaṇa*, one who has sexual intercourse with his guru's wife, the killer of a woman, ruler, father, or cow—(9)[12] such sinners as these and any others can all be freed from sin simply by thus calling out Vishnu's name, by which one attracts the attention of Vishnu. (10) A sinful person is not purified nearly as much by any rites of atonement prescribed by the sages as by pronouncing the syllables of Hari's names. These names evoke the divine qualities of him who is most highly praised. (11) Even if one carefully performs atonement, the mind does not become steady but repeatedly courses down the wrong path. Rather, for those desiring complete removal of karma, it is the persistent chanting of Hari's qualities that brings about purity. (12)

"So do not take away him who has atoned for endless sins by thoroughly embracing the Lord's name while dying. (13) The learned know that the chanting of Vaikuṇṭha's name removes unlimited sins, whether done to signify something else, as a joke, as musical entertainment, or carelessly. (14)[13] Even if one falls, slips, has bones broken, is bitten, has fever, or is mortally wounded, by accidentally chanting Hari's name one need not feel tormented. (15) Distinguishing heavy and light sins, the great seers have prescribed heavy and light procedures for atonement. (16)[14] By acts of atonement such as austerity, charity, vows, and the like, sins are eradicated but not the heart's opposition to dharma; rather, this is accomplished by service to the feet of the Lord. (17) As fire burns fuel, so the name of the most renowned Lord shall burn away sin, whether chanted in ignorance or in knowledge. (18) As a powerful medicine will act by its own potency even if ingested inadvertently and unknowingly, similarly a mantra will act when pronounced (even in ignorance of its power)." (19)

In the remainder of chapter 2, Ajāmila laments his years of waywardness from brahmanical propriety, and he reflects on his good fortune at having seen and been protected by Vishnu's messengers. He then resolves to reform himself by practicing self-control, rejecting identification with his physical body, and directing his attention to the praise and worship of Vishnu. Eventually, after performing ascetic and devotional practices at Haridvāra (present-day Hardwar), Ajāmila dies and is then fetched to Vishnu's transcendent abode by the same deputies of Vishnu who had protected him previously from those of Yama. The chapter ends with a reminder that Ajāmila's good fortune came to him as a result of having pronounced Vishnu's (Nārāyaṇa's) name, and thus readers are exhorted to chant with faith such divine names. In the next chapter, the king of death, Yama, speaks to his confused messengers on the power of chanting divine names; he also expounds on the divine virtues of Vishnu's devotees.

King Parīkṣit enquired: Having heard a detailed report from his servants, how did the King of Dharma, Lord Yama, answer them? This person (Ajāmila) is under his rule, yet his order was foiled by the messengers of Murāri (Vishnu)! (3.1)[15] O seer! Never before has it been heard that Lord Yama's punishment was subverted. Sage! I am sure that no one but you can destroy the doubts people could have about this. (2)[16]

The blessed Śuka said: O king, the messengers of Vishnu foiled the efforts of Yama's messengers, who then informed their master, the lord of the city Saṁyamanī. (3)

Yama's messengers asked: "Master, how many rulers *are* there who actually award the results of people's three types of action? (4)[17] If in this world there are multiple rulers who administer punishment, who will suffer hell and who will not? Who will enjoy heaven and who will not? (5)[18] But if there are many rulers of many workers, then rulership would amount to mere bureaucracy, as is the case with local administrators. (6) Thus surely you are that one overlord of living beings and their rulers, the bearer of the rod of chastisement, and the superintendent who decides what is good and bad among human beings. (7) Yet now your ordained rule has become ineffective in this world; your command has been undermined by those four sublime, supernatural beings. (8) On your order we dragged the sinful Ajāmila toward the punishment chambers; but they forcefully released him, cutting the ropes. (9) If you think us fit, we wish to understand those beings who, when the name 'Nārāyaṇa' was uttered, swiftly arrived saying, 'Do not fear!' " (10)

The revered Bādarāyaṇi spoke: Thus addressed, the deity Yama, regulator of the populace, was delighted. He replied to his messengers while remembering the lotus feet of Hari. (11)[19]

Yama spoke: "There is one other than me, superior to all moving and nonmoving beings, in whom this universe exists, woven like the warp and woof of a cloth. From a mere portion of him arise cosmic creation, sustenance, and destruction. This world is under his control, as a bull is controlled by a rope in the nose. (12) As one binds several cows to a rope using (smaller) cords, so he binds people to his rope of (Vedic) language using names. Bound by the fetters of names and actions, they all timidly submit offerings to him. (13)[20] Myself, Indra, Nirṛti, Varuṇa, Soma, Agni, Shiva, Vāyu, Brahma, Āditya, Viśva-vasu, the Sādhyas, the Maruts, the Rudras, the Siddhas, additional cosmic progenitors and undying lords, as well as sages like Bhṛgu, are untouched by passion and darkness. When those who are grounded in goodness know not the Lord's desire, what then can be said of others who are touched by *māyā* (consisting of passion and darkness)? (14–15)

"As the limbs of one's body do not perceive one's eyes, which are superior to the limbs, living beings do not perceive the self of selves within the heart—neither with their senses, mind, breath, heart, nor words. (16) The great self is the independent master of *māyā*. The messengers of that Lord Hari are most enchanting, for they roam mainly in this world with bodily features, qualities, and temperament just like his. (17) Vishnu's most wonderful agents, their forms difficult to see, are worshipped by the gods. They protect mortals who have devotion for him—from me, from enemies, and from every adverse condition. (18)[21] In fact dharma is established directly by the Lord; neither seers nor gods, nor the best of *siddhas* comprehend it, much less the demons, humans, *vidyādharas*, *cāraṇas*, or others. (19)[22] O servants! The self-born Brahmā, Nārada, Shiva, the Kumāras, Kapila, Manu, Prahlāda, Janaka, Bhīṣma, Bali, Śuka, and myself—we twelve know well this dharma established by the Lord. It is esoteric, pure, and difficult to comprehend, but one who understands it enjoys immortality. (20–21)[23]

"Thus the highest dharma for human beings in this world is deemed to be the yoga of devotion to Bhagavān, beginning with invoking his names. (22)[24] My sons! Just see the greatness of pronouncing Hari's name! By this means even Ajāmila was freed from the rope of death. (23) When the sinful, dying Ajāmila cried out for his son, 'Nārāyaṇa!' even *he* achieved liberation. Thus, just this much glorification of Bhagavān's virtues, acts, or names is enough to remove the sins of human beings. (24)[25] Alas, a great authority in Vedic ritual usually does not know this power of the divine names, his mind utterly bewildered by the goddess Māyā. With his mind dulled by the sweet and flowery three Vedas, such a person engages in grandiose sacrificial ritual. (25) Yet those with good discrimination, reflecting on the infinite Lord, surely adopt the yoga of devotion with their entire being. They do not deserve my punishment even if they might have committed some sin; they remove such sin by the praise of he who makes wide strides. (26)[26] Such saints of equal vision, being surrendered to the Lord, are celebrated in sacred song by gods and perfected beings. Do not approach them, who are well guarded by Hari's mace. Neither we nor time itself have the power to punish them. (27) Instead, always fetch only those contemptible beings who reject the sweet taste of Mukunda's (Vishnu's) lotus feet that is relished by saints who are free from worldly possessions and attachments. Those captured by thirst for home comforts are on the path to hell. (28)[27] Whose tongue does not voice the Lord's qualities and names, whose heart does not remember his lotus feet, and whose head does not bow to Krishna even once—bring *such* contemptible beings who have not performed service to Vishnu! (29) May the blessed Lord Nārāyaṇa, the primeval person, forgive the wrongdoings of my men. How forgiving is the great Lord toward his ignorant people whose hands are joined in supplication! Obeisance to that bountiful person." (30)[28]

Śuka spoke: Descendant of Kuru (Parīkṣit), know therefore that glorification of Vishnu affords complete atonement even for the greatest of sins. Such praise benefits the whole universe. (31) Purification of the self inevitably occurs for those who repeatedly hear and chant the boundless, heroic acts of Hari with sincere bhakti, not by observance of vows and the like. (32) One who licks the honey of Krishna's lotus feet no longer enjoys the rejected worldly qualities of *māyā*, which bear misery. Others who are smitten by lust perform ritual to cleanse the dust from the heart, yet subsequently that dust is sure to return. (33) O king, having thus been told of the Lord's greatness by their master, Yama's astonished servants remembered well his order. From that time forth they fear to approach or even look upon any person who has taken shelter of Acyuta (Vishnu). (34) The powerful son of Kumbha narrated this esoteric account while residing in the Malaya hills and worshipping Hari. (35)[29]

Book Six now resumes (in chapters 4–6) the account from Book Four of Dakṣa's expanding the world's population. Dakṣa, finding his efforts hampered, retires to Vindhya Mountain to practice penance and submit several prayers (containing noteworthy metaphysical reflections) to Vishnu. Thereupon Vishnu, pleased by Dakṣa's eulogy, appears before him, blessing him to complete his task by bestowing upon him a wife, Asiknī, the daughter of Pañcajana. Among his progeny from Asiknī are two groups—namely, ten thousand sons known as Haryaśvas, followed by one thousand sons called Savalāśvas, all of whom are commanded by their father to further increase the world population. However, the sage Nārada convinces them all to become renunciants instead, prompting a curse from Dakṣa: Nārada shall henceforth be a wanderer without residence. Dakṣa then fathers sixty daughters who eventually become the mothers of a wide variety of superhuman, human, and nonhuman beings.

Prompted by Parīkṣit, Śuka now explains the background to an incident he had alluded to in the previous chapter regarding the priest Viśvarūpa. The scene shifts to the throne hall of Indra, king of the gods. Indra, one day distracted by the royal pleasures afforded by his office, fails to notice the entry of his guru, Bṛhaspati, into the assembly. Thus disrespected, Bṛhaspati soon departs silently and Indra, realizing the gravity of his mistake, is remorseful.

Indra and the gods search in vain for Bṛhaspati, who has made himself invisible. Taking advantage of the gods' weakened position, the demons conquered them. The gods then approach Brahmā for help. Brahmā reprimands the gods for disrespecting their guru, contrasting them with the demons, who have become powerful as a result of properly respecting *their* guru, Śukra. Brahmā then advises the gods to approach the young *brāhmaṇa* Viśvarūpa, son of Tvaṣṭā, to act as their priest. After hearing their petition, Viśvarūpa replies to the gods.

INDRA'S GRAVE MISTAKE

Chapter 7

The revered Viśvarūpa said: "O masters, (acting as a priest is) prohibited by those who follow dharma, for it undermines brahmanical preeminence. But being requested by the celestials, how can one such as I—your subordinate—refuse? Compliance is said to be in one's self-interest. (7.35) (However), great lords, the gleaning of neglected grains is the only proper means of livelihood for those who have chosen the path of poverty. So how shall I be gladdened by the practice of lowly priesthood, by which one becomes mean-spirited? (36)[30] Nonetheless, let not whatever little is requested by gurus be refused! I shall fulfill your every wish with all my wealth and strength." (37)

Śrī Śuka said: Thus assuring them, the great ascetic Viśvarūpa, commissioned as their priest, executed rituals with great concentration. (38) With a Vishnu mantra the great (Viśvarūpa) snatched away the power of the gods' enemies despite their being protected by Śukra's magical technology. (39)[31] Noble-minded Viśvarūpa uttered that mantra for protection unto the great, thousand-eyed Indra, who then defeated the demon's army. (40)

Śuka then relates (in chapter 8) Viśvarūpa's instruction to Indra on how to recite a Vishnu mantra known as the Nārāyaṇa-kavaca (Shield of Nārāyaṇa), which is constituted largely of prayers to Vishnu in his many forms, each of whom is requested to protect the supplicant in a particular type of circumstance or at a certain portion of the day. Thus, for example, Varāha (the cosmic boar *avatāra*) is invoked to protect one during journeys; Paraśurāma (the ax-wielding *avatāra*) is invoked to protect one on mountaintops; and Rāma, together with his brother Lakṣmaṇa, is invoked to protect one in foreign lands.

With the help of Viśvarūpa as priest, Indra has successfully recovered the celestials' power over the demons. But now (in chapter 9) Indra slays Viśvarūpa upon discovering his secret loyalties for the adversary. As Indra performs penance for killing a *brāhmaṇa*, Tvaṣṭā seeks revenge for his son's death by creating, out of a sacrificial rite, enemies of Indra. However, the opposite of what Tvaṣṭā intends occurs because of a slight mistake in the rite's performance. Instead of manifesting a being who could kill Indra, the sacrificial fire brings forth a monstrous demon named Vṛtra (coverer) whom Indra will slay. Upon Vṛtra's appearance, he answers to the gods' initial attack by devouring them. These celestials manage to regroup and offer several prayers to the supreme Lord, as situated within their hearts. This same Lord then appears before the gods externally, and they proceed to offer further prayers of praise and obeisance, articulating his transcendent character, the difficulty of comprehending him, and his position as ultimate cause of the world. A few of these prayers are as follows.

INDRA SLAYS VIŚVARŪPA

Chapter 9

"There is certainly no contradiction in your—Bhagavān's—twofold character. Your attributes are without measure, (so) your glory cannot be grasped. You are not accessible to the argumentation of obstinate disputants whose shelter is the mind, which is confused by scriptures and inclined toward guesswork, dubious reasoning, deliberation, and non-substantive proofs. From you all illusion is withdrawn; although pure spirit, you place your own magical power amid this world. Indeed, what aim can you not accomplish, since your constitutional form is absolute? (9.36) You are not opposed to the opinion of those whose understanding is either right or wrong; (in either case) the opinion is like considering a piece of rope to be a snake. (37) Again, you alone are the real substance in all substances, the Lord of all, the original cause of all universes. Because you are the inner self of all, you alone remain when the insubstantiality of all matter is perceived. (38)

"How wonderful! Because of the incessant flow of joy within their minds afforded by a mere drop of the ambrosial *rasa* ocean of your glories, the exalted *bhāgavatas* forget all trace of happiness in sense objects seen or heard. Their minds ever tranquil, they are completely devoted exclusively to you, the dear friend of every being, situated within the self of all. O Destroyer of Madhu, how indeed could such saints—dear friends of the self, for whom the good is their only interest—abandon service to your lotus feet, where there is no return to mundane existence? (39)[32] O Lord, whose home is the threefold world, who took three strides, who has three eyes (or who leads the three worlds), who charms the minds of all in the three worlds! Though Diti's sons and other demons are also your features of power, if you think, 'This is not their time for domination,' please kill Tvaṣṭā, in the same way that you punish transgressors by assuming the forms of gods, humans, animals, mixed forms, or aquatics, by your own *māyā*." (40)[33]

After the gods complete their prayers and appeals for Vishnu's help, the latter responds (much as Brahmā had done previously) first with a mildly elliptical reprimand for approaching him with a mundane desire. He then advises them to approach a certain powerful and generous sage Dadhīci to request from him his body, out of which a potent weapon to kill Vṛtra might be fashioned.

Dadhīci playfully refuses the gods' request, but then he agrees and proceeds to shed his body by entering yogic trance. Indra then takes up the thunderbolt weapon fashioned from Dadhīci's bones and prepares to face his enemy, Vṛtra.

In the ensuing battle, the demons, because they lack devotion to Lord Krishna, find that their weapons (including hurled trees and mountains) have no effect on the gods and their soldiers. Out of fear they then flee, abandoning their leader, Vṛtra, who pleads for them to remain and fight, accepting a glorious death. But the demon soldiers will not listen. Vṛtra then scolds the gods for pursuing the fleeing demons and challenges them to face him in battle. As Vṛtra then tramples the gods underfoot, Vṛtra and Indra prepare to face off. Vṛtra hurls insults and taunts at Indra, and he reassures Indra that his (Indra's) thunderbolt weapon will be effective, reminding him that it has been imbued with the power of Vishnu and of Dadhīci's austerities. Vṛtra then expresses eagerness to be slain by Indra, affording him release from mortal existence. He then addresses prayers to the Lord, declaring his longing to see him and to have friendship with the Lord's devotees.

INDRA SLAYS VṚTRA

Chapter 12

The venerable seer (Śuka) said: Vṛtra took up his trident and attacked the lord of the gods, as Kaiṭabha attacked the great Lord in the water. O king, eager to relinquish his body in combat, Vṛtra regarded death as superior to victory. (12.1)[34] Then Vṛtra, that heroic lord of the demons, whirling his trident with its searing tongues of flame from the fire of cosmic devastation, let it fly at Indra, furiously roaring, "Sinful wretch, you are dead!" (2) Seeing that terrible, spinning trident approach like a comet out of the sky, the fearless Indra sundered it with his hundred-limbed thunderbolt and also severed one of Vṛtra's arms, which was like the coiled king of serpents. (3) Having lost one arm, Vṛtra, enraged, lunged toward Indra and with an iron bludgeon struck him on the jaw and struck his elephant, causing Indra to drop his thunderbolt. (4) The gods, demons, *siddhas* (perfected beings) and *cāraṇas* (celestial singers) applauded Vṛtra's extraordinary feat; but seeing Indra's peril they cried frantically, "Alas, alas!" (5) Ashamed, Indra would not again take up the thunderbolt that had fallen from his hand in his enemy's presence. Vṛtra urged him: "Hari (Indra), now is no time for sulking. Take the thunderbolt and kill your enemy!" (6)

In the remainder of this chapter, Vṛtra continues to urge Indra to take heart and resume the fight, lecturing him on his ultimate dependence on the will of the supreme Lord, and on his own (Vṛtra's) imminent defeat. Indra recovers his courage and, again taking up his thunderbolt, praises Vṛtra, recognizing him to be the Lord's devotee (*bhakta*). After discussing together about bhakti, they resume the fight, and with his thunderbolt Indra destroys Vṛtra's mace and severs his remaining arm. In that condition Vṛtra assumes a giant form and swallows both Indra and his elephant; but Indra is unhurt, protected as he is by the mantra shield he had received from Viśvarūpa, and with his thunderbolt he slices his way out of Vṛtra's body. It then takes Indra an entire year to sever Vṛtra's head from his body, at which moment Vṛtra, as the nonmaterial and effulgent *ātmā*, attains the eternal realm.

Indra had not wanted to kill Vṛtra because the latter was a *brāhmaṇa*, and he feared the severe sinful reaction accruing to killing a *brāhmaṇa*. But the gods had persuaded him that any reaction would be counteracted by their performance of a certain ritual, a horse sacrifice, on his behalf. Indra had then agreed to kill Vṛtra, but now he laments his action.

INDRA'S LAMENT

Chapter 13

Śrī Śuka said: Thus encouraged by the *brāhmaṇas*, Indra slew his enemy; when Vṛtra was killed, Vṛṣākapi (Indra) was burdened by the sin of killing a *brāhmaṇa*. (13.10) So for that action Indra endured torment; joy found no place in him. Even virtues give no happiness for one who has acquired shame and infamy. (11) He saw that sin stalking him in the form of an outcaste woman, calling, "Wait, wait!" Consumptive and trembling with old age, her dress bloodied and her gray hair scattered, she polluted the road with her breath's fishy odor. (12–13)[35] O king, Thousand-eyed Indra fled to the sky, then to all directions; hastening to the northeast, he entered the Mānasa lake. (14)[36] He dwelled for one thousand years, unseen, amid the network of lotus fibers in the lake and without food supplies, even from his messenger, the fire god. Remaining deeply remorseful, Indra was freed from the sin of killing a *brāhmaṇa*. (15) During that time Nahuṣa—possessor of knowledge, austerity, self-discipline, and strength—ruled heaven. His discrimination blinded by the madness of wealth and power, he was led to the destination of snakes by (his attraction to) Indra's wife. (16)[37] Indra's sinful reaction, impeded by his meditation on Vishnu, was removed, and then he was summoned by the call of the *brāhmaṇas*. The strength of that sin, having been undone by Rudra, lord of the northeast direction, could not overcome him, who was protected by Vishnu's wife, Lakṣmī. (17)[38] Descendant of Bharata! The *brāhmaṇa* seers approached him and initiated him properly, so that he could worship the Lord by means of a horse sacrifice. (18) O king, the great Indra worshipped the Lord, the self of all the gods, in the horse sacrifice performed by the *brāhmaṇas*; just by this act, even the great sin of killing Tvaṣṭā's son was annulled, as fog is dispelled by the sun. (19–20) As recounted, the great Indra became cleansed of sin, having worshipped the primeval person, the Lord of Sacrifice, by performing a horse sacrifice with Marīci and other sages. (21) Wise persons should always read and recite this great narrative of Indra's victory and liberation, which purifies countless sins, eulogizes him whose feet are places of pilgrimage (Vishnu), celebrates bhakti, and describes *bhaktas*. Hearing this account on festival days is the way of auspiciousness, affording (sharpened) senses, wealth, fame, freedom from all sin, victory over opponents, and long life. (22–23)

Chapter 14 opens with King Parīkṣit voicing a doubt: considering the rarity of pure devotion to Vishnu, how is that Vṛtra, ostensibly a demon, proved to be in fact a great devotee? Śuka's answer spans four chapters, telling the adventures of King Citraketu. Childless, Citraketu is blessed with a son by sages Nārada and Aṅgirā, only to lose it soon after birth. In his deep sense of loss, the two sages return to enlighten Citraketu with spiritual wisdom. Taking their words to heart, Citraketu becomes devoted to Vishnu and is eventually awarded a direct vision of Vishnu in his form as Saṅkarṣaṇa. In this enlightened state he once ventures out and happens upon a garden region where he sees Shiva and his consort, Parvatī, surrounded by sages. Then trouble begins: Citraketu laughs loudly at Shiva and Parvatī, astonished to see such exalted beings embracing in public. Parvatī, incensed by Citraketu's blunt disrespect, curses him to be born as a demon monster. Citraketu graciously accepts the curse, thus showing his equanimity toward his own misfortune, and then Shiva praises Citraketu for his heroic indifference, demonstrating his qualification as a *bhāgavata* devotee of Vishnu.

CITRAKETU CURSED TO BECOME VṚTRA

Chapter 17

The venerable Rudra (Shiva) said: "O Parvatī of charming hips! You are witnessing the greatness of great desireless souls, the servants of the servants of Hari, whose deeds are wondrous. (17.27) No one devoted to Nārāyaṇa fears any condition but sees liberation, heaven, and even hell as equal. (28) Being lodged in a physical body, mortals are—by the Lord's arrangement—subjected to the dualities of happiness and distress, birth and death, blessing and cursing. (29) The person of poor judgment sees distinctions of value and of qualities and faults in the self, as one may try to determine the identity of a curled-up object. (30)[39] There is no shelter in any thing (of this world) for those who, energized by knowledge and dispassion, are driven by devotion for Bhagavān Vāsudeva. (31) Being parts of his parts, (yet) regarding ourselves as separate lords, neither myself, nor Brahmā, nor the Kumāras nor Nārada, nor (other) sons of Brahmā—sages who are masters of the gods—know the identity and ways of the Lord. (32) No one is either dear or not dear to him, nor is anyone considered either kin or stranger. Hari is dear to all beings, as the very self of all beings. (33) And this greatly blessed, beloved servant of the Lord, Citraketu, is peaceful, having equal vision in all circumstances. I am also dear to Acyuta (Vishnu). (34) So one need not be astonished about great souls, devotees of the supreme person. Such persons are peaceful, having equal vision." (35)[40]

Śrī Śuka said: King! Having heard this address by the blessed Shiva, the goddess Umā (Parvatī) became peaceful in mind, her perplexity removed. (36) Thus, although he was quite capable of countercursing the goddess, Citraketu accepted her curse upon his head. Such is the characteristic of a *sādhu*. (37) Born of Tvaṣṭā in the southern (ritual) fire, appearing as a demon, Citraketu, well endowed with knowledge and wisdom, became renowned as Vṛtra (coverer). (38) I have explained everything you have asked—why Vṛtra, although born as a demon, was yet dedicated to the Lord. (39) Hearing this glorious, pious account of Citraketu, a great soul among Vishnu's devotees, one will be freed from (worldly) bondage. (40) With restrained speech, one who reads this account with faith upon rising in the morning may, remembering the Lord, go to the supreme destination. (41)

Book Six ends (chapters 18–19) with further genealogical details, listing the sons of Aditi, who would be in opposition to the sons of Aditi's sister Diti (both wives of the sage Kaśyapa). Diti, meanwhile, seeks to avenge the death of her two sons Hiraṇyākṣa (recounted in Book Three) and Hiraṇyakaśipu (to be recounted in Book Seven) by producing a child to kill Indra (the ally of Vishnu, the killer of her two sons, and indirect cause of their death). Her scheme is, however, foiled by Indra: catching Diti in a moment of slight ritual negligence, he is able to enter her womb and divide the embryo into forty-nine beings, who become the forty-nine Maruts. The recollection of this story of the Maruts' birth becomes, in Book Six's final chapter, a component of the Puṁsāvana vow, a ritual practice for producing a male child. The Bhāgavata here provides details of how this vow is to be observed.

SUGGESTIONS FOR FURTHER READING

Jarow, E. H. Rick. 2003. *Tales for the Dying: The Death Narrative of the "Bhāgavata-Purāṇa."* Albany: SUNY Press.
With reference to the voluntary death of Dadhīci (6.10.12) and of Vṛtra (6.12.1–6), *Tales* elaborates on the several ways in which the Bhāgavata Purāṇa treats the subject of death.

Klostermeier, Klaus K. 1994. "Calling God Names: Reflections on the Divine Names in Hindu and Biblical Traditions." *Journal of Vaiṣṇava Studies* 2, no. 2: 59–69.
With a comparative component to biblical traditions, this article provides a useful overview of Hindu theologies of divine names, referring also to the Ajāmila episode of the Bhāgavata, Book Six (relevant to chapters 1–3).
Tull, Herman W. 2004. "Karma." In *The Hindu World*, edited by Sushil Mittal and Gene Thursby, 309–31. London: Routledge.
Tull provides a general overview of the concept of karma, which is relevant to Book Six's treatment of potential or actual reactions to the nondharmic actions of Ajāmila and Indra.

BOOK SEVEN

Hiraṇyakaśipu Seeks Immortality
The Demon King Conquers the World
Hiraṇyakaśipu Torments His Son Prahlāda
Prahlāda Teaches His Friends
Nṛsiṁha Slays Hiraṇyakaśipu

Much of Book Six dealt with the fortunes and misfortunes of the celestial king Indra. The supreme Lord Vishnu is often perceived as being partial to Indra, who, as king of the gods, is perpetually in competition with the gods' counterparts, the demons; yet Vishnu is also celebrated for being entirely aloof, and hence impartial, in relation to all beings. The first ten chapters of Book Seven serve as an extended treatment of this apparent contradiction in Vishnu's character, through an account of how his *avatāra* as Nṛsiṁha—in the form of half man and half lion—appears to protect his votary, the young *bhāgavata* Prahlāda, from the latter's demon father, Hiraṇyakaśipu. The book's remaining chapters elaborate on traditional regulations (dharma) for persons in various categories of responsibility (*varṇa*) and life stages (*āśrama*).

In the first chapter of Book Seven, Śuka responds to a question submitted to him by King Parīkṣit regarding Vishnu's apparent partiality. Śuka initially explains Vishnu's position above the three *guṇas* (illumination, passion, and darkness), which both facilitate and control the activities of living beings. From another perspective, when Vishnu kills a demonic person who has taken the position of Vishnu's enemy, that person is instantly liberated from recurring death. To illustrate, Śuka cites the case of Śiśupāla, the archenemy of Krishna. As is narrated in Book Ten (chapter 74), when, after hurling an incessant volley of provocative insults at Krishna, Śiśupāla was slain by Krishna's disk weapon, Sudarśana, all present witnessed Śiśupāla's soul entering into Krishna's body. Śiśupāla's qualification for receiving this reward of liberation was his constant, albeit inimical, concentration on Krishna.

But the instance of Śiśupāla raises further questions: How could Śiśupāla, previously situated in the Lord's realm, Vaikuṇṭha, have been cursed to be born as a demon? And how could it have happened that Hiraṇyakaśipu, a prior appearance of the same person, could become so inimical to his son, Prahlāda, that he tries to kill him? Here the dialogue shifts to King Yudhiṣṭhira, the eldest of the Pāṇḍava brothers, inquiring from Nārada, taking place just after Śiśupāla's death. Nārada's extensive response to these questions takes us initially to a brief reiteration of events occurring in Book Three (chapters 14–15)—namely, the curse of the Vaikuṇṭha doorkeepers, Jaya and Vijaya, to take birth three times in the temporal world as demons.

In their first birth, Jaya and Vijaya appear as Hiraṇyākṣa and Hiraṇyakaśipu. Hiraṇyākṣa dies in a battle with Vishnu (in his *avatāra* as the cosmic boar Varāha, described in Book Three), leaving Hiraṇyakaśipu to nurture vengeance against Vishnu. After pacifying Hiraṇyākṣa's surviving family with words of wisdom about the ephemeral nature of this world (chapter 2), Hiraṇyakaśipu commences with the practice of extreme austerities to gain power, eventually forcing Brahmā to grant him a series of guarantees that—so Hiraṇyakaśipu believes—will make him immortal. The story continues in this next reading.

HIRAṆYAKAŚIPU SEEKS IMMORTALITY

Chapter 3

Śrī Nārada said: King! Hiraṇyakaśipu wanted to make himself invincible, without rival, the only king, free of old age, and immortal. (3.1) In the Mandara valley, he performed extreme austerity—hands upraised, standing on his big toes, staring at the sky. (2) The beams of light from his matted hair shone like rays from the sun at the time of cosmic dissolution. While he smoldered in austerity, the gods returned to their posts. (3)[1] The fire of austerity, along with smoke, arose from his head and spread upward, downward, and to the sides, burning all directions. (4) The rivers and oceans churned, and the earth, with its islands and mountains, shook. The stars and planets fell, and the ten directions burned. (5)

Scorched by that fire, the gods left heaven and went to Brahmā's world. They told the creator: "God of gods! Master of the universe! Burned by the austerity of the Daitya king, we are unable to remain in heaven. (6)

Abundant one! Superior lord! If you think it right, stop this fire, so that all those who pay homage to you do not perish. (7) There is nothing unknown to you, and yet we tell you. Please listen! Hiraṇyakaśipu, who is doing what is so difficult to do, surely has the following plan: (8)

"'The supreme being, Brahmā, created the animate and inanimate universe through complete absorption in the practice of austerity. He now dwells in his own abode, beyond all other realms. (9) Both the self and time are eternal, and so by increasing my absorption in the practice of austerity (for as long as it takes), I will win the same position for myself. (10) By my power, I will make this universe the opposite of what it should be, and what it was before. What need is there for others like the Vaiṣṇavas, who are destroyed by time at the end of creation?' (11)[2]

"So we have heard: Hiraṇyakaśipu tenaciously continues his extreme austerity. Lord of the three worlds! Do what you think is appropriate, without delay. (12) Master of the universe! Your supreme position is for the well-being, happiness, good fortune, safety, and victory of the *brāhmaṇas* and cows." (13)

King! Thus informed by the gods, the self-born, blessed lord Brahmā, went to the hermitage of the Daitya king, accompanied by Bhṛgu, Dakṣa, and others. (14) Brahmā did not see Hiraṇyakaśipu, for he was covered by anthills, grass, and bamboo. Ants had eaten his fat, skin, flesh, and blood. (15) Hiraṇyakaśipu burned the worlds by his austerity, appearing like the sun concealed by clouds. When Brahmā, who rides a swan, spotted Hiraṇyakaśipu, he was amazed and he spoke to the king with a smile: (16)

Śrī Brahmā said: "Get up! Get up, son of Kaśyapa! Good fortune to you! You have succeeded in austerity, and I, who grants wishes, have arrived. Please ask for your desired wish. (17) I have observed this great, extraordinary endurance of yours. Your body has been eaten by insects, and so your life breath clings only to the bones. (18) No sage in the past has performed this kind of austerity, nor will they perform it in the future. Indeed, who can survive without water for a hundred celestial years? (19) Such strenuous exertion is difficult even for the wise. Your resolute austerity has conquered me, son of Diti! (20) Therefore, I give you all blessings, hero among demons! You are certainly mortal, but your audience with me, an immortal, will not be fruitless." (21)[3]

Śrī Nārada said: After saying this, the firstborn Lord sprinkled the demon, whose body had been eaten by ants, with water from his water pot—divine water that never fails to grant one's wishes. (22) Then Hiraṇyakaśipu arose from the anthill and bamboo thicket like fire arises from fuel. He was possessed of all his limbs, endowed with strength, vigor, and power, solid as a thunderbolt, youthful, and with a complexion of molten gold. (23) Seeing that the god Brahmā was present in the sky, riding on his swan, Hiraṇyakaśipu bowed with his head on the ground, overjoyed to see the lord. (24) Hiraṇyakaśipu got up and folded his hands in humility. Seeing the mighty lord before him, the king cried tears of joy and his hair stood on end. With a faltering voice, he praised Brahmā: (25)

Śri Hiraṇyakaśipu said: "I bow down to the abode of illumination, passion, and darkness, the highest, the great! At the end of a creative cycle, the universe is enveloped by the deep darkness born of time. The self-effulgent Brahmā manifests the universe by his own brilliance. He creates, governs, and destroys this world on his own, using the three *guṇas*. (26–27) I bow down to the original seed, the very form of knowledge and its application. You bring about the visible cosmos by the transformation of life breath, senses, mind, and intellect. (28) You control both moving and stationary beings by the primordial life breath. You are the lord of creatures and the great lord of consciousness, intellect, mind, and senses. You are the master of the elements, the *guṇas*, and the heart. (29) You reveal the succession of seven Vedic sacrifices through the verses of the Vedas and the knowledge of the four Vedic priests. You alone are the self of the self-possessed. You are without beginning, the inner self, the poet with endless breadth! (30) You alone are unblinking Time, who decreases people's life span by seconds, minutes, and other units. You are the great unborn, changeless, highest, self, and you are the living self of the living world. (31) Nothing is separate from you—neither what is far nor near, the moving nor nonmoving. Your bodies are all the sciences and the arts. You are the great Hiraṅyagarbha, who stands beyond the three *guṇas*! (32) Great lord! You are this manifest, tangible body, by which you experience the senses, life breath, mind, and *guṇas*. You are (also) the unmanifest self, the ancient person, situated in the highest abode. (33) I bow to that blessed lord who has power over matter and spirit. By his limitless, unmanifest form, he extends throughout this world. (34)

"O best of benefactors! Please grant me the wishes that I long for: May I not die because of any beings created by you, Master. (35) May I not die inside or outside, by day or night, by others or by weapons, on the earth or in the sky, by humans or animals, by living or nonliving beings, or by gods, demons, or serpents. May I have no rival on the battlefield. May I be the sole master of living beings, as mighty as all world rulers, whose power is born of austerity and yoga. That power is never lost." (36–38)

THE DEMON KING CONQUERS THE WORLD

Chapter 4

Śrī Nārada said: Śatadhṛti (Brahmā) was pleased with Hiraṇyakaśipu's austerity, and being so petitioned, he gave Hiraṇyakaśipu favors that are very difficult to obtain. (4.1)

Śrī Brahmā said: "My child, the favors you have asked of me are rarely obtained by human beings. Nevertheless, I will indeed grant you these favors, although they are rarely achieved." (2) The powerful and glorious lord, whose benediction never fails, then left. He was worshipped by the best of demons and praised by the gods, the lords of creatures. (3)

Thus the golden-figured Daitya received his wish. Remembering the death of his brother, he (now) showed his hatred for Bhagavān (Vishnu). (4) The great demon conquered all directions and the three worlds. He subdued the gods, demons, human kings, Gandharvas, the celestial birds and serpents, *siddhas*, *cāraṇas*, *vidyādharas*, sages, the chief forefathers, Manus, *yakṣas*, *rākṣasas*, *piśācas*, and even the rulers of ghosts and the spirits of the dead. (5–6) He conquered all the rulers of living beings and brought them under his control. Hiraṇyakaśipu, the conqueror of everything, seized the positions and influence of the world protectors. (7) He occupied heaven, including the beautiful gardens of the gods. He lived in Indra's palace—personally built by Viśvakarmā—the abode of all good fortune and the wealth of the three worlds. (8) In that palace, the staircases were made of coral, the floors of great emeralds, and the walls of crystal. There were rows of *vaidūrya* pillars, wonderful canopies, and seats encrusted with rubies. The beds, bordered with rows of pearls, appeared like the foam of milk. (9–10) The anklets of goddesses made tinkling sounds as they went here and there (in the palace) and saw their beautiful faces with lovely teeth (reflected) on the surface of gems. (11) The mighty and arrogant monarch, the unrivaled conqueror of the world, sported in great Indra's palace, his feet venerated by the gods and others who were tormented by his exceedingly cruel demands. (12) Except for the three (Vishnu, Shiva, and Brahmā), all the directional rulers waited upon him, gifts in hand. Indeed, that pillar of austerity, yoga, strength, and energy remained drunk on strong-smelling liquor, his copper eyes rolling. (13)

Son of Pāṇḍu! Viśvāvasu, Tumburu, myself, and others, including the *vidyādharas*, *apsarās*, *gandharvas*, *siddhas*, and sages, continuously sang the praises of Hiraṇyakaśipu, who sat on great Indra's throne by his own power. (14) He alone was propitiated with sacrifices and generous gifts by all segments of society, and he alone forcefully seized the shares of sacrificial oblations. (15) For him, the earth, with its seven islands, produced harvest without being plowed. Similarly, the cows gave milk as desired and the sky held various wonderful things. (16) The oceans of saltwater, liquor, clarified butter, sugarcane juice, yogurt, milk, and freshwater, together with their wives (the rivers), delivered heaps of gems through their waves. (17) Mountains and valleys provided place for sport, and trees offered their particular qualities (i.e., fruits and flowers) in every season. Hiraṇyakaśipu single-handedly took up the different functions of the gods who look after the world. (18) Thus that autocrat conquered all directions, enjoying sense pleasures as much as he wanted. And yet he was not satisfied, for he had not conquered his senses. (19) Hiraṇyakaśipu passed a long time in this way—arrogant, drunk with power, and transgressing the scriptures—and thus met with the curse of *brāhmaṇas.* (20)

All the worlds, along with their guardians, were terrified of Hiraṇyakaśipu's severe rule. They sought refuge in Acyuta, not finding refuge anywhere else. (21) "Obeisance to that highest region where resides Lord Hari, the Self! The peaceful, pure renunciants go there and do not return." (22) Thus they waited upon Hṛṣīkeśa with steady mind, self-restrained, and pure, without sleep, and living only on air. (23)

Those virtuous persons heard a voice, without form, which rumbled like clouds and resounded in all directions, making them fearless. (24) "Fear not, O best among the wise! Blessings to all of you! Indeed, seeing me is the cause of all good fortune for living beings. (25) I know about the wicked ways of Diti's degraded child, and I will put an end to them. Until that time, you should wait. (26) When one is contemptuous of the gods, Vedas, cows, *brāhmaṇas*, virtuous persons, dharma, and me—that person meets his end very soon. (27) When Hiraṇyakaśipu tries to harm his own son, Prahlāda, who is a great soul, peaceful and without enmity, then I will kill Hiraṇyakaśipu, even though he is empowered by (Brahmā's) boons." (28) Thus addressed by the guru of the world (Vishnu), the heavenly deities offered obeisance to him and returned. Their anxiety was relieved, for they considered the demon already dead. (29)

Śrī Nārada said: That lord of Daityas had four most wonderful sons, of whom Prahlāda was the greatest. He was a great devotee with noble qualities: (30) He was brahmanical in nature, possessed of good character, devoted to truth, and master of the senses. Seeing all living beings like his own self, he was their best friend and most beloved. (31) He touched the feet of noble persons like a servant, he was kind to the poor like a father, he was affectionate to his equals like a brother, and he regarded his teachers as he would the Lord. Although he was blessed with education, wealth, good looks, and social status, he was free of conceit and arrogance. (32) His mind was not disturbed by misfortune, and he had no desire for pleasant things to see or hear, for he saw the *guṇas* as insubstantial. His senses, life breath, body, and intellect were always restrained and his desires were quieted. Although a demon, he did not have the nature of a demon. (33)

King! Poets have always recognized Prahlāda's great virtues, which are not obscured even today, just like the virtues of the supreme Lord, Bhagavān. (34) Monarch! In assemblies where the lives of saints are narrated, even the gods, who are the demons' enemies, put forward Prahlāda as an ideal example. How much more then (would he be praised) by other esteemed persons like yourself! (35) But enough of such description! These innumerable qualities reveal the greatness of one who has unimpeded love for Bhagavān Vāsudeva. (36) Because he was absorbed in Krishna, Prahlāda gave up sport, as if her were a dull child. His mind was overcome by the influence of the planet 'Krishna,' and thus he did not understand such worldly things. (37) While seated, walking, eating, lying down, drinking, or speaking, Prahlāda did not pay attention to these activities, for he was embraced by Govinda. (38) Sometimes he would cry, his mind unsettled by thoughts of Krishna. Sometimes he would laugh, feeling happy thinking of Krishna. And sometimes he would sing loudly. (39)[4] Sometimes he cried out in longing for Krishna, and at other times he danced with no embarrassment. Sometimes in his meditation on Krishna, Prahlāda identified with the Lord and imitated him. (40) And sometimes he remained silent, delighted by the Lord's close touch. His hair stood on end and his eyes were half-closed, with tears of joy born of his unwavering love. (41) To the unfortunate souls who keep bad company, Prahlāda gives peace of mind and the highest bliss of service to the lotus feet of Uttamaśloka. That service is obtained by the company of persons who are completely disinterested in the world. (42) King! It was that great soul, the great devotee of Bhagavān, the greatly fortunate Prahlāda—his own son!—whom Hiraṇyakaśipu tormented. (43)

Śrī Yudhiṣṭhira said: Sage among the gods! Nārada of steady vows! We wish to know from you how the father tormented his pure and saintly son. (44) Fathers scold their disobedient sons in order to teach them a lesson, but they certainly do not torment them like an enemy. Fathers are affectionate to their sons. (45) How much more true this would be for obedient, saintly sons like Prahlāda, who regard their elders like God. A father hates his son, with the intent to kill him—this is a conundrum! Please resolve it for me, O *brāhmaṇa*, O master! (46)

HIRAṆYAKAŚIPU TORMENTS HIS SON PRAHLĀDA

Chapter 5

(Nārada said:) When the child Prahlāda bowed at his father's feet, Hiraṇyakaśipu received him with blessings. Clasping Prahlāda in his arms for a long time, the demon felt the greatest joy. (5.20) Yudhiṣṭhira! Hiraṇyakaśipu placed Prahlāda on his lap and kissed his head. Moistening his son's bright, smiling face with his tears, Hiraṇyakaśipu spoke thus: (21)

Hiraṇyakaśipu said: "My dear son, long-lived Prahlāda, tell me—what is the best thing that you have learned from your teacher after all this time (in school)?" (22)

Śrī Prahlāda said: "Hearing about Vishnu, singing his name, remembering him, serving his feet, worshipping, praising, servitude, friendship, and offering one's very self to him—these are the nine methods of bhakti that a person can offer to Vishnu. If one performs bhakti in these ways, I consider that to be the best education." (23–24)

Hearing this speech from his boy, Hiraṇyakaśipu turned to Śukra's son (Prahlāda's teacher) and spoke these words, his lips quivering in rage. (25) "You excuse for a *brāhmaṇa*! What is this? You have taken the side of my enemy and indoctrinated my son with unwholesome ideas. You despicable fool! (26) Indeed, there are devious people in this world, enemies in the garb of friends. Their evil is exposed in time, even as disease exposes a sinner." (27)

Śukra's son said: "Enemy of Indra! This son of yours—what he speaks was not taught by us, nor was it taught by anyone else. These ideas come naturally to him. Please contain your anger, King! Do not find fault with us." (28)

Śrī Nārada said: When he received this report from the teacher, the demon turned again to his son: "Rascal! If these bad ideas were not taught by your teacher, where did you get them from?" (29)

Śrī Prahlāda said: "Those engrossed in family affairs cannot set their heart upon Krishna, whether on their own, or by (help from) others, or by a combination of both. With unrestrained senses, they enter dark regions, again and again chewing what they have already chewed. (30)[5] They do not know that Vishnu is the means to obtain what is truly valuable for themselves. Instead, they place value in external objects and pursue awful ambitions, like the blind leading the blind. Thus, they remain bound by the strong fetters of God's laws. (31) Their hearts will not touch the feet of wide-striding Vishnu, nor will they see value in getting rid of useless attachments, so long as they do not seek out and anoint themselves with the dust from the feet of great souls who are without any possessiveness." (32)

After speaking thus, Prahlāda became quiet. Hiraṇyakaśipu, blinded by rage, threw his son off his lap and onto the ground. (33) Hiraṇyakaśipu became possessed by anger and indignation, and his eyes turned bloodshot. "This boy deserves to be killed!" he said. "Kill him immediately! Take him away, demons! (34) This vile Prahlāda is the murderer of my brother, for he has rejected his caring family to worship like a slave at the feet of his uncle's killer, Vishnu. (35) It is difficult to abandon one's parents' care, and yet this five-year-old boy has done it. Indeed, let us see whether this traitor remains loyal even to Vishnu. (36) One should adopt a child from another family if he will do good, just as one takes foreign medicine. On the other hand, one should reject a biological son if he is no good, even as one amputates a diseased, unbeneficial limb so that the remainder of the body can flourish by that sacrifice. (37) Kill him by any means—while sitting, sleeping, or eating! He is an enemy in the guise of a friend, even as uncontrolled senses are enemies of an ascetic." (38)

Those demons had sharp fangs, gaping mouths, and copper-red hair and mustaches. They held iron pikes and made horrible sounds. Thus directed by their master, they stabbed Prahlāda's tender body everywhere with iron pikes, shouting, "Chop him up! Impale him!" Prahlāda, however, remained seated. (39–40) Even as the religious rituals of a wicked person are fruitless, so the demons' efforts were futile against Prahlāda, for his mind was focused on the indescribable Bhagavān, the self of all and the supreme reality. (41) Yudhiṣṭhira! The demon king became apprehensive when that attempt failed. He tenaciously tried other means to kill Prahlāda—with powerful elephants, large snakes, and magical spells; by throwing him (off a cliff), conjuring tricks, imprisoning him, feeding him poison, and starving him. He tried killing Prahlāda with snow, wind, fire, and water, and by crushing Prahlāda with boulders. When he was unable to kill his sinless son, the demon became deeply worried that he had not even come close to accomplishing his goal. (42–44)

Hiraṇyakaśipu marvels at his son's strength and begins fearing for his own life. Seeing the king's anxiety, his guru's sons, Ṣaṇḍa and Amarka, suggest a solution: they will take Prahlāda to their school and teach him the ways of wealth and pleasure. Hiraṇyakaśipu agrees to the plan, but when Prahlāda arrives at the school, he does something even more unexpected and problematic.

When the teacher was busy elsewhere with household work, the children at the school, Prahlāda's friends, would seize the opportunity and call him (to play). (54) The enlightened and wise Prahlāda responded to their call with a smile and gentle words. He spoke compassionately to them about their priorities. (55) Out of respect for Prahlāda, they all abandoned their toys. Because they were children, their minds were not polluted by the actions and instructions of their teachers, who were fond of worldly pleasures. (56) The children sat around Prahlāda, their eyes and hearts fixed upon him. The loving, compassionate Prahlāda—the demon prince who was a great devotee of Bhagavān—spoke thus. (57)

PRAHLĀDA TEACHES HIS FRIENDS

Chapter 6

Śrī Prahlāda said: "A wise person should follow the path of Bhagavān from childhood. This human birth is rare, and although it is transient, it is meaningful. (6.1) In other words, a human being should seek refuge at the feet of the supreme person, Bhagavān, for he is the friend of all beings and the beloved Lord of the self. (2) Descendants of Diti! By divine arrangement, living beings can get sensual happiness anywhere, just because they are embodied, even as they get misery without trying for it. (3) Therefore one need not endeavor for sensual happiness. That is a complete waste of human life, for it does not lead one to the joyous abode that is Mukunda's lotus feet. (4) An intelligent person in this temporal world should strive for that joyous state. As long as the body is strong and energetic, one should not misuse it. (5) A human being lives for a mere hundred years, and an unrestrained person wastes half of that sleeping at night, overcome by darkness and ignorance. (6) In the innocence of childhood and youth, a person passes twenty years playing, and when the body is overcome by old age, one helplessly passes another twenty. (7) Finally, a person who is attached to household concerns heedlessly wastes the remaining years, bewildered by powerful and insatiable desires. (8) Attached to household concerns, bound by the strong fetters of affection, senses unrestrained—what man has the ability to liberate himself? (9) Indeed, what person can renounce the thirst for money, which is more beloved than life itself? Merchants, servants, and thieves acquire money at the risk of their dear lives." (10)

In verses 11–18, Prahlāda continues to warn his classmates about the danger of unrestrained desire and the error in thinking, "This is mine, and that is another's." Starting with verse 19, he explains the antidote to this divisive worldview.

"Children of demons! It is not difficult to please Acyuta (Vishnu), for he is the self of all beings and the ever-present reality in this world. (19) The great master Bhagavān, the imperishable self and the supreme Lord, can be analyzed through logical inference, but in fact he is unanalyzable and indivisible. His form consists of pure perception and bliss, but his majestic power remains concealed by *māyā*—namely, the created world consisting of the three qualities (*guṇas*). He is one alone, but in his form as the inner self and in his form as the visible world, he dwells both near and far. Indeed, he dwells in all beings, from plants and trees to Brahmā; in the subtle and gross elements, and in their products; and in the three qualities, both when they are in equilibrium and when they are interacting. (20–23) For this reason, you should be kind and affectionate to all beings. Abandon your demonic natures! This will please Adhokṣaja (Vishnu)." (24)

Prahlāda's classmates ask him where he acquired this wisdom, and so in the next chapter Prahlāda relates his encounter with the sage Nārada and his transformative instructions. Once when Hiraṇyakaśipu was away performing lengthy austerities to please Brahmā, the gods took the opportunity to subdue the demons. As the gods were dragging away Hiraṇyakaśipu's pregnant wife, intent on killing her unborn child, they were stopped by Nārada, who explained that the child was in fact a great devotee of Vishnu. Nārada takes Prahlāda's mother to his hermitage, where he teaches her about the temporal world and the eternal self. Prahlāda, still in the womb, listens carefully and remembers everything, conveying that teaching now to his friends in the demon school. "A person toils for pleasure and wealth in this world, but invariably gets the opposite of what one desires. The body can give one only minimal, fleeting pleasure, and after death it becomes the property of others. Therefore, a person's true benefit lies in pleasing Vishnu, who is impressed not by knowledge, ritual, or social status but only by selfless bhakti." The children are moved by Prahlāda's words, and they reject the instructions of their demonic teachers.

Soon the teachers discover Prahlāda's traitorous behavior and take him back to his father (chapter 8). Hiraṇyakaśipu is now uncontrollably angry and confounded by Prahlāda's fearlessness. "From where comes your strength?" he asks. Prahlāda's response angers his father even further, "The source of my strength is the same as the source of yours—Bhagavān Vishnu." Prahlāda explains that the notion of "friend" and "enemy" is a figment of one's imagination, for there is no enemy other than one's own uncontrolled mind.

"Where is your God," Hiraṇyakaśipu finally asks, "and if he is everywhere, why is he not in this pillar?" Hiraṇyakaśipu angrily strikes his fist against the pillar and picks up his sword to kill Prahlāda. Just then a terrifying sound emerges from the pillar and Nṛsiṁha, the man-lion *avatāra* of Vishnu, appears to slay the demon king.

NṚSIṀHA SLAYS HIRAṆYAKAŚIPU

Chapter 8

To make true the words of his devotee (Prahlāda)—that he is present in all things—the Lord appeared from a pillar in the assembly hall, taking on an extraordinary form that was neither man nor animal. (8.17) Hiraṇyakaśipu carefully examined this being as he emerged from within the pillar. "How strange! He is neither an animal nor a human. The man-lion form—what is this?" (18) Hiraṇyakaśipu studied the truly awesome form of Nṛsiṁha that towered above him. The Lord's fierce eyes glowed like molten gold, his shining mane made his face appear even larger, his razor-tipped tongue moved like a sword between his terrible teeth, his enormous mouth had a frown, his ears stood erect, his striking nose and open mouth appeared like mountain caves, his gaping jaws were terrifying, his body touched the sky, his neck was short and stout, his chest was broad, and his waist was slim. (19–21) The hair on Nṛsiṁha's body was white like the rays of the moon, his hundred arms reached like an army in all directions, and his nails were like weapons. He was impossible to approach as he routed the *daitya* and *dānava* demons with an array of exceptional weapons, including both his personal weapons and others. (22)

"Hari is probably planning to kill me with his great illusive power. But of what use are such plans?" Speaking thus, the elephant among demons let out a cry and attacked Nṛsiṁha with his club weapon. (23) Like a moth flying into a fire, Hiraṇyakaśipu became invisible because of Nṛsiṁha's brilliance. This is not surprising; after all, the Lord who is the fount of luminosity swallowed the darkness at the beginning of creation by his own radiance. (24) The mighty demon rushed at Nṛsiṁha with great speed and angrily attacked with his club, displaying his valor. But the Lord who carries a club caught the demon along with his club, as Garuḍa (Vishnu's eagle carrier) catches a snake. (25) Scion of Bharata! Then Nṛsiṁha playfully let the demon slip from his hand, as Garuḍa plays with a snake. The gods thought this was terrible, as they hid among the clouds. The homes of all these celestial rulers had been seized (by the demon). (26)[6] Hiraṇyakaśipu thought that Nṛsiṁha had released his grip because he was afraid of the demon's prowess. And so the mighty demon recovered from his fatigue in battle, seized his sword and shield, and again rushed at Nṛsiṁha. (27) Hiraṇyakaśipu moved high and low with the speed of a hawk, avoiding injury by means of his shield. Hari then let out a shrill, loud, and powerful laugh and swiftly caught the demon, who shut his eyes (in fear). (28) Pained by Hari's grip, the demon—who could not even be scratched by Indra's thunderbolt—struggled mightily, just as a rat struggles against a snake. At the entrance (to the palace), Hari threw Hiraṇyakaśipu upon his lap and easily tore him apart with his nails, as Garuḍa kills a venomous serpent. (29)[7]

After Nṛsiṁha slays the demon Hiraṇyakaśipu, none of the several celestial beings who approach him are able to pacify the enraged Lord with their prayers. Then Brahmā requests Prahlāda to come forward, and when Nṛsiṁha sees him, he blesses the boy with his hand on Prahlāda's head. Prahlāda then offers several prayers, in which he shows humility, requests the Lord to give up his anger, expresses fearlessness of Nṛsiṁha's terrifying appearance (and fearfulness of worldly existence), his resolve to serve the Lord, and his concern for the well-being of persons who refuse to serve him (chapter 9).

Pleased with Prahlāda, Nṛsiṁha wishes to give him a benediction, but the only gift that Prahlāda will accept is the blessing that he shall harbor no worldly desires, and that his father, Hiraṇyakaśipu (who had just been slain by Nṛsiṁha), be forgiven for all his transgressions. Granting these wishes, Nṛsiṁha then hints at the explanation for his—Bhagavān's—(apparent) partiality to his votaries: it is *they* who are impartial and equipoised with respect to all creatures, and hence Vishnu is always ready to protect them (chapter 10).

With the story of Nṛsiṁha and his devotee Prahlāda concluded, the remainder of Book Seven shifts attention to the subject of dharma while continuing Yudhiṣṭhira's and Nārada's dialogue. Yudhiṣṭhira wishes to hear Nārada's explanation of "eternal dharma" (*dharmaṁ sanātanam*), associated with practices of social organization and occupation (*varṇa*) and life stages (*āśrama*) for bringing about human fulfillment. Nārada lists several general obligatory practices for all persons (such as practicing truthfulness, mercifulness, and austerity), and then outlines briefly the characteristics of the four *varṇas*—the *brāhmaṇas, kṣatriyas, vaiśyas*, and *śūdras.* Then follows a brief description of a virtuous woman's or faithful wife's (*sādhvī*) characteristics and duties. Chapter 11 concludes with the significant statement that it is a person's characteristics—*not* one's birth in the family of a particular *varṇa*—that ought to determine to which *varṇa* he or she belongs.

An outline of the first three of the four *āśramas* follows. First comes celibate student life (*brahmacārya*), followed by householder life (*gṛhastha*), in turn followed by the life of retirement (*vānaprastha*—literally, "situated in the forest"). Each of these life stages has its specific requirements (including regulations about interaction with the opposite sex), but the general aim is to progress toward comprehension of Vishnu's presence in all things, enabling one to quit one's body at the end of life by a process of meditatively bringing all the body's elements and senses to their respective original source elements and divinities, such that only the atemporal self remains with the supreme self (chapter 12). Like the *vānaprastha*, the *saṁnyāsī* is directed to lead an extremely austere life; however, he (always male) must also give up stationary residence to permanently wander, deepening his understanding of ultimate reality; he should avoid becoming a professional teacher, and he should gradually adopt the python's way of life (of eating what is obtained with no endeavor and remaining always satisfied in any condition), thus aiming for the highest level of spiritual culture, that of the *paramahaṁsa* (chapter 13).

Chapter 14 offers further prescriptions for householder dharma, with emphasis placed on the cultivation of detachment and minimizing of worldly pursuits, without neglecting the needs of family and community members. *Gṛhasthas* are enjoined to regularly perform sacrificial rites as worship of Vishnu, make food offerings to their ancestors, welcome guests in their homes, and offer sacrificial food remnants (*prasāda*) to others before partaking themselves. The best places for performing religious rites, including several places of pilgrimage, are listed, with emphasis on the importance of worshipping Vishnu and remembering his presence within all creatures. Then, in Book Seven's final chapter, Nārada provides further details on how the *gṛhasthas* should perform rites on behalf of ancestors (*śrāddha*), avoiding the use of animal flesh for such offerings. He also lists and elaborates on five types of deviant religious practice to be avoided—namely, obstructions to the observance of one's own religious practice (*vidharma*); practices introduced by others (*para-dharma*); activities of proud heretics (*upadharma*); pretentious religion (*chala-dharma*); and whimsical semblances of religious culture (*ābhāsa*). The virtues of self-satisfaction and the dangers of greed are enumerated, and, to highlight the necessity of keeping one's focus on human life's ultimate purpose, an extended analogy of the body as a chariot is elaborated: the senses are like a chariot's horses, the mind is like the reins, and so on. Nārada advises Yudhiṣṭhira to learn to direct this chariot toward its proper goal under the guidance of knowledgeable superiors. By so doing, one comes to realize nonduality in three aspects: *bhāvādvaita* (nondual existence), *kriyādvaita* (nondual activity), and *dravyādvaita* (nondual substance for worship). Nārada concludes by reminding Yudhiṣṭhira of his and his brothers' good fortune at having the supreme *brahman* in human form, Bhagavān (Krishna), residing in their home.

SUGGESTED READINGS

Meister, Michael W. 1996. "Man and Man-Lion: The Philadelphia Narasiṁha." *Artibus Asiae* 56, no. 3/4: 291–301.

Meister traces the early history of Nṛsiṁha (Narasiṁha) in India, focusing on a fourth-century Nṛsiṁha sculpture in the Philadelphia Museum of Art.

Soifer, Deborah A. 1991. *The Myths of Narasiṁha and Vāmana: Two Avatars in Cosmological Perspective.* Albany: SUNY Press.

Soifer compares the Bhāgavata's Nṛsiṁha story with that of other Purāṇas, concluding that the Bhāgavata's version is "richer, multivalent, and portrays bhakti at perhaps its fullest expression," as the Purāṇa attempts to synthesize bhakti with dharma (98–99).

Valpey, Kenneth R. 2013. "Purāṇic Trekking along the Path of the Bhāgavatas." In *The Bhāgavata Purāṇa: Sacred Text and Living Tradition*, edited by Ravi M. Gupta and Kenneth R. Valpey, 21–35. New York: Columbia University Press.

Valpey uses the Nṛsiṁha story to introduce the reader to the narrative structure of the Purāṇas, focusing on the Bhāgavata's aim of celebrating Prahlāda as the paradigmatic *bhāgavata*.

Vemsani, Lavanya. 2009. "Narasiṁha, the Supreme Deity of Andhra Pradesh: Tradition and Innovation in Hinduism—an Examination of the Temple Myths, Folk Stories, and Popular Culture." *Journal of Contemporary Religion* 24, no. 1:35–52.
Vemsani explores the popular worship of Nṛsiṁha in Andhra Pradesh, examining regional pilgrimage texts, temple imagery, ritual practices, and folk narratives, comparing them with classical Purāṇic accounts of the *avatāra*.

BOOK EIGHT

Churning the Ocean of Milk, and Shiva Drinks Poison
Vāmana Dwarfs the Universe

Two episodes are the focus of Book Eight. First is the churning of the cosmic ocean by the gods and demons to produce *amṛta*, the nectar of immortality. In the second episode, the dwarf *avatāra* of Vishnu, Vāmana, subdues the demon king Bali by a ruse, thereby restoring cosmic order and raising Bali to glory as an exalted *bhāgavata.*

Book Seven concludes a long excursus on the story of Prahlāda and appearance of Nṛsiṁha with Nārada's teachings on brahmanical ideals of social order and practice. In Book Eight, the Bhāgavata's description of successive lordships of humankind (Manus, or *manvantaras*) resumes. Up to this point, beginning from Book Three, most of the narrative has been of personages and episodes within the first *manvantara* (of Yajña as Svāyambhuva Manu). Book Eight commences with a brief listing of subsequent Manus: Svārociṣā ("self-luminous," the second Manu); Uttama ("superior," son of Uttānapāda, mentioned in 4.8.9, the third Manu); and Tāmasa ("darkness," the fourth Manu).

An account of Gajendra, an elephant, begins in chapter 2, in a paradisiacal valley near Mount Trikūṭa. Similar to the deer who recalled his previous life as Bharata (Book Five, chapter 8), under the duress of being attacked by a crocodile, Gajendra is able to remember his previous life as King Indradyumna, enabling him to recall and pronounce prayerful strophes he had learned at that time. Here, the central theme is remembrance of Bhagavān in times of emergency.

The next chapter explains how Gajendra and the crocodile came to be born as animals. Because of absorption in meditation, King Indradyumna had neglected to welcome his visitor, the sage Agastya, who therefore cursed the king to become an elephant. Similarly, King Hūhū, a Gandharva, had been cursed by Devala Ṛṣi to become a crocodile when Hūhū pulled him by the leg underwater while frolicking with women in a lake. Included in the curse was a blessing that he would be liberated by Bhagavān, or Vishnu, when he would come to rescue his devotee, Gajendra.

After naming the fifth and sixth Manus (Raivata, "wealthy," and Cākṣuṣa, "son of Cakṣu"), Śuka alludes to an occasion when Bhagavān, as Ajita, son of Vairāja and Devasambhūti, assists the gods in producing the nectar of immortality by churning the milk ocean. This prompts Parīkṣit to request elaboration: Under a curse from the sage Durvāsā, the gods were defeated in battle by the demons. In their helpless condition, the gods had approached Brahmā for help. Brahmā had proceeded to lead them in addressing the invisible Vishnu in prayerful praise; Vishnu then appeared to Brahmā and the other gods, advising them to make a truce with the demons and, together with them, to produce the nectar of immortality by churning the milk ocean, using Mount Mandara as a churning rod. With Vishnu's help (assisted by his eagle carrier, Garuḍa) the gods and demons are able to position themselves to begin the process of churning. The churning of the ocean is one of the most widely attested narratives in Hindu history, found throughout South and Southeast Asian art, performance, architecture, and literature.

CHURNING THE OCEAN OF MILK, AND SHIVA DRINKS POISON

Chapters 7 and 8

Śrī Śuka said: Descendant of Kuru! The gods asked the serpent-king Vāsuki (to participate in the churning) in return for a share of the outcome. They wrapped Vāsuki as the churning rope around Mount Mandara and began working intently for nectar. (7.1) First Hari (Vishnu) took hold of the front portion of the snake, and then the gods followed suit. (2) The demon kings did not appreciate the Great Lord's behavior. "We will not take the tail, the snake's inauspicious part, for we are learned in the Vedas and are famous for our heritage and deeds." (3) And so, seeing the demons standing silently, the supreme person smiled and let go of the snake's head. He and the gods took hold of the tail instead. (4) After assigning their stations in this way, the sons of Kaśyapa (the gods and demons) churned the ocean of milk, completely intent upon acquiring nectar. (5)

Son of Pāṇḍu! As the ocean was being churned, the mountain sank into the water, despite being held up by powerful gods and demons, for it was heavy and had no footing. (6) Having lost their virility by the indomitable force of destiny, the gods and demons became depressed in mind and the radiance of their faces faded. (7) Observing the obstacle ordained by providence, the Lord, whose prowess is limitless and whose determination never fails, took the wondrous form of a great turtle, entered the water, and raised up the mountain. (8) Seeing that the great mountain had been raised, the gods and demons again became eager to churn. The Lord supported the mountain on his back, which extended for a hundred thousand leagues, like a new continent. (9) The primeval turtle bore the rotating mountain upon his back as the gods and demon chiefs moved it vigorously with their arms. Indeed, the immeasurable Lord considered the mountain's rotation as a means for scratching his body. (10)

Thereafter, Vishnu entered the demons in the form of demonic energy in order to excite their strength and virility. To inspire the gods, he entered them with godly energy, and he entered the serpent-lord in the form of ignorance. (11) The thousand-armed Lord stationed himself atop the great Mount Mandara, appearing like another magnificent mountain, and steadied Mandara with one hand. The gods in heaven, including Brahmā, Shiva, and Indra, praised Vishnu and showered flowers upon him. (12) Strengthened by the supreme Lord, who had appeared both above and below, in the mountain and in the churning rope, and in their own selves, the gods and demons passionately and rapidly churned the ocean with the mountain, thus disturbing the many crocodiles. (13) But as he breathed, the serpent-king spewed smoke and fire from his thousand fearsome mouths. The demons, including Pauloma, Kāleya, Bali, and Ilvala, lost their splendor, like pine trees burned by a forest fire. (14) The gods also lost their brilliance because of the serpent's flaming breath, and their faces, clothes, fine flower garlands, and armor became covered in soot. But by Bhagavān's will, clouds rained down upon them and breezes blew mist from the ocean's waves. (15)

When the ocean, churned in this way by the leaders of the gods and demons, did not produce the elixir, the unconquered Vishnu himself began churning. (16) With a complexion like a dark rain cloud, golden garments, earrings brilliant like lightning, radiant hair in disarray, a flower garland around his neck, and reddish eyes—the Lord looked beautiful, like a mountain supporting another mountain, as his victorious arms, which grant fearlessness, held the serpent and agitated Mount Mandara, the churning rod. (17)[1] The ocean churning disturbed the fish, *makaras*, water serpents, and turtles; it also troubled the whales, porpoises, crocodiles, and *timiṅgilas*. The first thing that emerged from the churning was a vicious poison called *hālahala*. (18) That poison flowed in every direction with terrible velocity, spreading upward and downward, unstoppable and intolerable. Indeed, the vulnerable, frightened people, together with the Lord, hastened for refuge to Sadāśiva (Shiva). (19) The best of gods, seated with Goddess Satī on Mount Kailāsa, assures the well-being of the three worlds, and he is honored by sages who intently practice austerity in order to achieve liberation. Thus observing Shiva, the people bowed before him with words of praise. (20)

The intervening verses, spoken by the Prajāpatis, the first progenitors of creation, describe the cosmos as contained within Shiva's body—the mountains are his bones, plants are his hair, the seas are his abdomen, his shadow is adharma, and the three qualities of nature are his three eyes. The Prajāpatis praise Shiva's work of dissolution at the end of time, and they chide those who criticize Shiva for being unclean or uncouth as he wanders in crematoriums. Despite Shiva's antinomian behavior, he brings goodness wherever he goes.

Śrī Śuka said: Lord Shiva, who is a friend to all beings, was deeply pained to see their suffering, and so he compassionately spoke thus to his beloved wife, Satī. (36)

Śrī Shiva said: "Alas! Bhavānī! See the disaster that has befallen the people as a result of the poison born from churning the ocean of milk. (37) I must eliminate the danger facing these people as they try to save their lives. Caring for the weak—this indeed is what it means to be a master. (38) At the risk of their own transitory lives, virtuous persons protect the lives (even) of people who display hostility, deluded by the self's *māyā*. (39) Hari, the self of all, is pleased with a person who is compassionate, and when Bhagavān Hari is pleased, then I and all beings are also pleased. Therefore, gracious lady, I will drink the poison. Let me make the people happy!" (40)

Śrī Śuka said: Thus addressing his wife, Bhavānī, the blessed Lord who brings prosperity to the world began consuming the poison. Bhavānī gave permission, for she knew Shiva's abilities. (41) Mahādeva (Shiva), who brings prosperity to all beings, then compassionately took that pervasive poison, *hālāhala*, into the palm of his hand and drank it. (42) The toxic fluid showed its power even on Shiva, for it made a dark-blue mark on his neck—an ornament for the virtuous Lord. (43) Virtuous persons often suffer themselves because (they wish to relieve) the world's suffering. This indeed is the best way to worship the supreme person, the self of all. (44) When they saw this feat, Dakṣa's daughter (Bhavānī), Brahmā, Vaikuṇṭha (Vishnu), and the people all praised the generous Śambhu (Shiva), god of gods. (45) Scorpions, snakes, poisonous plants, and other venomous beings seized whatever poison spilled from Shiva's palm as he was drinking. (46)

The gods and demons became happy after Shiva, who rides a bull, drank the poison, and they vigorously churned the ocean. At that time emerged the cow who provides butter for sacrifice. (8.1) King Parīkṣit! The sages who teach the Veda took the sacrificial cow so that they could have pure butter for sacrifice that leads to heaven.(2)[2] Then arose a horse, white as the moon, named Uccaiḥśravā, whom Bali (king of the demons) wanted. On the advice of the Lord, Indra did not covet the horse. (3) Next, the king of elephants named Airāvata came forth. With his four tusks, he eclipsed the greatness of the blessed Shiva's white mountain (Kailāsa). (4)[3] From the great ocean emerged a ruby-hued gem called Kaustubha, which Lord Hari desired as an ornament for his chest. (5)[4] Then emerged the Pārijāta tree that decorates the world of the gods. This tree forever fulfills the wishes of the needy, even as you (the king) do on earth. (6) Next the *apsarās* were born, wearing golden necklaces and fine clothing. With their attractive gait and playful glances, they enchant the gods in heaven. (7) And then, in plain sight, emerged Śrī, Ramā (Lakṣmī), who is devoted to Bhagavān. She delighted all directions with her loveliness, like a brilliant flash of lightning. (8) Everyone desired her—the gods, demons, and humans—for she stole their hearts with her beauty, noble manner, youth, complexion, and majesty. (9)

At this point in the narrative all of creation comes forth to honor Lakṣmī, for it is she—the goddess of fortune, beauty, and grace—who is the source of the world's abundance and prosperity. The sacred rivers offer their water to Lakṣmī, the earth brings herbs, cows offer dairy products, the gods bring ornaments, and the sages perform a consecration ceremony. Once the reception is complete, the goddess begins to consider whom she might choose as her husband.

Lakṣmī carefully sought a permanent home for herself—someone blameless, whose good character never wavers. But among the *gandharvas, siddhas*, demons, *yakṣas, cāraṇas*, or other gods, she did not find anyone to marry. (19) "Indeed, someone has austerity but has not mastered anger. Another person has knowledge but is not free of worldly attachment. Yet another has status but has not mastered lust. (20) Someone is religious but is not kind to other beings. Another person is renounced but does not know the path to liberation. A powerful person succumbs to the force of time. Indeed, no second person (other than Vishnu) is free of the *guṇas*' influence. (21)[5] Someone is long-lived but does not have a pleasing disposition. Another has a pleasing disposition, but one cannot tell how long he will live. And while another person has both a pleasing disposition and a long life, he is still inauspicious. And indeed, the one who is most auspicious does not desire me." (22)[6]

Thus deliberating on who might be the most excellent person with unwavering good qualities, Ramā chose as her husband Mukunda (Vishnu), who is independent of the *guṇas*, depending only upon himself. He is desirable, for all good qualities can be seen in him, and yet he remains aloof. (23) Lakṣmī placed on his shoulders a beautiful garland of lotus buds that was surrounded by the hum of nectar-seeking bees. Then, with beaming eyes and bashful smile, she stood near Vishnu's chest, which is her abode. (24) The father of the three worlds made his chest the supreme abode of Śrī, who is the glorious mother of the three worlds. Residing there, she looks mercifully upon her children, bestowing prosperity on the three worlds along with their rulers. (25)

Everywhere sounded conch shells, bugles, drums, and musical instruments, as the celestial attendants and their wives sang and danced. (26) Brahmā, Rudra, Aṅgirā, and all other world creators showered flowers and praised the great Vishnu with authentic mantras that speak of his characteristics. (27) Regarded kindly by Śrī, the gods, progenitors, and human beings were blessed with moral conduct and other good qualities, and they attained the highest bliss. (28) But Lakṣmī ignored the Daityas and Dānavas (demons), and thus they became mean, destructive, frustrated, and shameless. (29) Now emerged the lotus-eyed Vāruṇī, goddess (of liquor). With Hari's permission, the demons seized the young woman. (30)

Emperor! Then, as the children of Kaśyapa (the gods and demons) were churning in search of nectar, there arose from the ocean a most wondrous person. (31) He was youthful, with long, strong arms; his neck was marked with lines like a conch shell; his eyes were like the rising sun;

and he had a dark complexion. He was decorated with a flower garland and all manner of ornaments. (32) The ends of his hair were curled and anointed with oil; he was decorated with bracelets and bright pearl earrings; he wore yellow clothing; his chest was broad; his gait was like a lion's; and he carried a pitcher brimming with nectar. (33) Indeed, he was directly Bhagavān, consisting of a portion of a portion of Vishnu. He is celebrated as Dhanvantari, knower of Ayurveda (medical texts), and he is entitled to a share of sacrificial offerings. (34)

Seeing the pitcher filled with nectar, all the demons wanted its entire contents, and they quickly snatched the pitcher. (35) When the demons carried away that pitcher of nectar, the gods became despondent and sought refuge in Hari. (36) Seeing their pitiful state, Bhagavān, who fulfills the desires of his dependents, said, "Do not lose hope! By my illusive power, I will accomplish your goals through discord." (37) King! A quarrel arose among the demons, whose minds were set on having the nectar. "Me first! Not you! Me first! Not you!" (38) "The gods deserve their own share here, because they put in equal effort, just as (shares are distributed) in a *soma* sacrifice. This is the eternal dharma." (39) In this way, O king, the jealous, weaker demons repeatedly forbade the stronger ones who had grabbed the pitcher. (40)

At this moment, Lord Vishnu, who is skilled in every strategy, assumed the incomparable, most wonderful form of a woman. (41) She had a lovely complexion like a dark-blue lotus; all her limbs were beautiful; she wore matching earrings; she had fine cheeks and a prominent nose; her waist seemed thin because of her large breasts, blossoming in the freshness of youth; her eyes were restless because of the humming of bees attracted by the fragrance of her mouth; she wore a wreath of blooming jasmine flowers in her thick hair; her beautiful neck and arms were adorned with necklaces and bracelets; her buttocks, concealed with unblemished cloth, appeared like beautiful islands; and as she walked gracefully, her anklets and girdle glittered. (42–45) With a bashful smile and glances from playful eyebrows, she inflamed passion in the hearts of the demon leaders. (46)

Vishnu, in the form of a beautiful woman (Mohinī, "she who bewilders"), proceeds to easily win all the demons' confidence to act as their mediator for their internal dispute over who shall receive the nectar first. Taking the vessel of nectar, she then delivers it to the gods, while the spellbound demons watch in disbelief. One demon, Rāhu, manages to disguise himself as a god and to sit between the moon and sun gods, receiving a mouthful of the nectar before being discovered and instantly beheaded. Henceforth, with this immortalized, disembodied head, Rāhu chases the sun and moon (thus causing solar and lunar eclipses).

After the nectar of immortality has been quaffed by the gods, fighting resumes between the gods and demons. Further endangered, the gods resort again to Vishnu for help, and they are then advised by sage Nārada to desist further harassment of the demons. Thereafter Shiva, having heard of Bhagavān's appearance in the female form, out of curiosity requests Vishnu to be allowed to see him in this form. This request granted, Shiva becomes immediately enamored by the beautiful, naked Mohinī: chasing and attempting to embrace her, he discharges semen (the cause of gold and silver mines), and then, seeing his own folly, Shiva pulls himself together to humble himself before Vishnu, who had resumed his original form.

Book Eight continues (in chapter 13) to list the remaining eight Manus and then summarizes how the Manus function as cosmic rulers. Then, once again, conflict between the gods and demons resumes as Bali, the demon king, assumes increased power, forcing the gods to abandon their celestial realms. Aditi, the mother of the gods, then follows the advice of her husband, Kaśyapa, to observe a particular vow (*vrata*) to help her sons regain their celestial positions.

On the twelfth day of Aditi's careful observance of the *payovrata* vow, Vishnu appeared before her and promised to become her son, as the dwarf *avatāra* Vāmana. As the story unfolds, Vāmana comes to be known by another epithet, Trivikrama, "he who took three great strides." In this episode, the powerful demon king Bali shows himself to be a true *bhāgavata* by giving land—and ultimately everything, including himself—to Trivikrama-Vishnu. There are numerous versions of this episode, beginning from the Ṛgveda; but in contrast to other accounts, the Bhāgavata Purāṇa celebrates both this *avatāra* of Vishnu, who initially appears as a *brāhmaṇa* dwarf, Vāmana, and King Bali, a powerful opponent of the gods. We enter the narrative after Vāmana has approached Bali while the latter is preparing a sacrificial rite. Bali has respectfully received the young, charming Vāmana by offering him a seat and washing his feet.

VĀMANA DWARFS THE UNIVERSE

Chapters 18–22

The illustrious Bali said, "Welcome to you; obeisance to you, noble *brāhmaṇa*! What can we do for you? I believe you to be the direct embodiment of the *brāhmaṇa* sages' austerity. (18.29) Today our forefathers are satisfied; today our clan is purified; today this sacrificial rite is correctly done—because you have arrived at our residence. (30) O son of a *brāhmaṇa*! Today my sacrificial fires have received good, properly offered oblations; indeed, this world is not only freed from anxiety by the water that has washed your feet but also purified by the touch of those delicate feet. (31)[7] Little son of a *brāhmaṇa*, I regard you as a supplicant, and whatever you desire I will grant. Most deserving one, please accept from me a cow, gold, a fine residence, as well as savory food and drink, or else the daughter of a *brāhmaṇa*, prosperous villages, horses, elephants, and chariots." (32)

The venerable Śuka said: Hearing the righteous, pleasing words of the son of Virocana, Bhagavān Vāmana was gratified. Indicating acceptance, he spoke as follows. (19.1)

The venerable Lord said: "Ruler of the people, your grandfather is the peaceful elder, Prahlāda, and in matters of the afterlife, the Bhṛgus are your mentors; thus your pleasing manner of speech, full of righteousness, is befitting your family and will bring you renown. (2) In the history of your family, there has never been a hypocrite or a miser; no one has refused a *brāhmaṇa*'s request or broken a promise. (3) Moreover, O king, your family, in which Prahlāda appeared with brilliant fame, like the moon in the sky, is devoid of imprudent persons who decline to give charity to petitioners in places of pilgrimage or to fight when challenged on the battlefield. (4)[8] Hiraṇyākṣa, born in your family, wandered this earth alone, bearing a war club to conquer the directions. He found no hero equal to himself. (5) At the time of delivering the earth, when Hiraṇyākṣa arrived, Vishnu defeated him with difficulty. Repeatedly remembering Hiraṇyākṣa's valor, Vishnu took pride in his victory. (6) Long ago, hearing of Hiraṇyākṣa's death, the furious brother, Hiraṇyakaśipu, went to the abode of Hari to kill him who had killed his brother. (7) Beholding him with a trident, approaching like death personified, Vishnu, the knower of time and the greatest magician, thought, (8) 'As death follows all living beings, Hiraṇyakaśipu follows me everywhere. I will enter his heart because he can see only externally.' (9) King of the demons! Having made this decision, Vishnu, greatly alarmed by the pursuit of his enemy, entered Hiraṇyakaśipu's body through his nostril. His intangible body was invisible in Hiraṇyakaṣipu's breath. (10) Searching Vishnu's vacant abode and not finding him, Hiraṇyakaśipu roared angrily. Investigating in all directions—earth, heaven, sky, intermediate space, and oceans—the hero (still) did not see Vishnu. (11) Thus not seeing, he exclaimed: 'I have sought the killer of my brother throughout this universe. Doubtless he has gone (to that place) from which no person returns.' (12) In this world, so much enmity among embodied beings persists up to the time of their death; anger is born of ignorance and is invigorated by self-conceit. (13) When the gods, disguised as *brāhmaṇas*, approached your father—Prahlāda's son (Virocana), who was always kind to the *brāhmaṇas*—and entreated him to grant them the remainder of his life, he gave it to them, although he knew well who they were. (14) You have performed those religious duties undertaken by *brāhmaṇa* householders, ancestors, heroes, and others of exceptional reputation. (15) O best of benefactors, lord of the *daityas*, I therefore request a little piece of land from you—three steps measured by my foot. (16) O munificent king, lord of the world, I desire nothing else from you! Surely a learned person who accepts charity according to his need does not incur sin." (17)

The illustrious Bali said: "Son of a *brāhmaṇa*, your words are surely approved by the elders; but regrettably you are a child, whose thinking is immature and who lacks wisdom in regard to his own best interest. (18)[9] You have endeared me by your sweet words, and yet you are foolish, for you are asking the absolute monarch of all the worlds for only three steps of land, although I can grant entire islands. (19)[10] Having once approached me, one should not have to beg again. So, little fellow, be sure to take enough land from me to sustain your livelihood." (20)

The illustrious Bhagavān said: "O king, all the pleasing objects in all the three worlds cannot bring fulfillment to one whose senses are unconquered. (21)[11] Unsatisfied with three steps, even an island containing nine regions would not be enough, nor even all seven islands. I would still desire more. (22)[12] We have heard: 'Kings such as Pṛthu and Gaya, lords of the seven islands, never reached the end of their longings for wealth and pleasures.' (23) One can be satisfied with whatever destiny provides; one who has not conquered oneself is never satisfied and cannot find happiness even in possessing the three worlds. (24) This insatiability of ambition and desire causes one to undergo perpetual transmigration, whereas contentment with what one receives naturally is considered to be the means of liberation. (25) When a *brāhmaṇa* is content with adventitious gain, his ascetic power is enhanced; but as water poured on fire extinguishes a flame, discontent dims one's brightness. (26) Therefore I request only three steps (of land) from you who are most munificent. With just as much property as I need, my purpose will be fulfilled." (27)

Śrī Śuka said: Thus addressed, Bali replied, smiling, "Let your wish be fulfilled!" and took up a water pot to grant land to Vāmana. (28)[13] Shrewd Uśanā (Śukra), understanding Vishnu's scheme, addressed his disciple, the lord of the *asuras*, as he prepared to grant Vishnu his land. (29)

The illustrious Śukra said: "Son of Virocana, this is the immortal Bhagavān, Vishnu himself, born of Kaśyapa and Aditi. He is an agent for the gods. (30) Not knowing this, your promise to him is a mistake. I think it is not right. Great calamity is near at hand for the demons. (31) This is Hari (Vishnu) in the guise of a young lad. Snatching away your residence, sovereignty, glory, power, fame, and learning, he will give it all to Indra. (32)[14] He, whose body is the universe, will span these worlds with three steps. Fool! Having given everything to Vishnu, how will you survive? (33) By the Almighty's one step—the earth; by a second step—the heavens; and then, with his cosmic body, he shall bestride all of space. Where shall he place his third step? (34) You are powerless to fulfill this promise! I am quite sure that, having failed to keep a promise, you shall end up in hell. (35) The learned do not approve of charitable acts that threaten one's livelihood: Charity, sacrifice, austerity, and religious rituals are all meant for those who are able to earn a livelihood. (36) By dividing one's assets into five parts—to be used for dharma, reputation, wealth, pleasure, and relatives—one can be happy in this life and the next. (37) O best of *asuras*, listen to this (evidence) from the *Bahvṛca* hymn concerning this matter: 'A true promise is preceded by the sacred syllable *oṁ*, whereas a promise not preceded by *oṁ* is surely false.' (38)[15] The Veda confirms: One should understand that the flowers and fruit of the treelike body are real. If the body does not live, there will be no fruit and flowers (and hence it must be maintained by any means). Untruth is the root of the body. (39)[16] So, as an uprooted tree soon dries up and dies, undoubtedly one who is without untruth must also immediately wither. (40) *Oṁ* is a syllable of distance, emptying, or incompleteness. By uttering *oṁ*—I shall donate such and such,' a person will surely become destitute. And making such a pronouncement to give everything to a beggar, there will not be enough for the giver's own pleasure. (41) Hence one draws wealth toward oneself by saying the untruth no. But one who always lies, refusing to give in charity, becomes infamous, a breathing corpse. (42) It is not wrong to be untruthful when among women, when joking, at a wedding, for livelihood, in a life-critical condition, for cows and *brāhmaṇas*, and in a situation of violence." (43)[17]

Śrī Śuka said: King! The householder Bali, being thus advised by his family mentor, remained silent for a moment and then spoke carefully to the guru. (20.1)

The venerable Bali said: "As Your Honor has stated, the correct execution of dharma for householders should never hinder their pursuit of wealth, pleasure, reputation, and livelihood. (2) Yet how can I, a descendant of Prahlāda's, behave like a cheater, greedy for wealth, having already declared to this twice-born, 'I shall give'? (3) 'I consider there to be nothing more immoral than untruthfulness; I can endure everything except a person who lies.' These are the words of the goddess Earth. (4) I fear not poverty, unfathomable misery, downfall, or even death as much as I fear deceiving a *brāhmaṇa*. (5) All worldly gains abandon us at the time of death, so why not give up my wealth if I can please this *brāhmaṇa* (Vāmana) with it? (6) While saints like Dadhīci and Śibi sacrifice their very lives for the sake of mortal creatures, why should I hesitate to give a little land? (7) O *brāhmaṇa*! Although the force of Time took away the fortunes of those brave demon kings who enjoyed this world, their reputation remained. (8) *Brāhmaṇa*-seer! It is easy to find brave warriors willing to give up their lives in battle; but rare are those who willingly give their wealth when visiting a sacred place. (9) It is glorious when a wise and kind person undergoes difficulty in order to provide for those in need, especially when he provides for knowers of *brahman* such as your good self! Therefore I shall give to this little fellow whatever he requests. (10) O sage! The one whom you adepts in sacred rites attentively worship as *yajña* (sacrifice) with ritual offerings is Vishnu! Whether he gives benedictions upon me, or whether he abuses me—I shall give to him the land he desires! (11) Even if he were to unlawfully capture me, who am blameless, I would not harm my dreaded enemy, because he is in the guise of a *brāhmaṇa*. (12)[18] Because he is *uttamaśloka*—one whose character is perfectly praised—he never loses his fame. Killing me in battle, he may take this land, for I could never kill him." (13)

The venerable Śuka said: Thereupon Śukra, prompted by destiny, cursed his unsubmissive disciple who, wisely adhering to truth, would not heed his instructions. (14) "You who are so resolved, thinking yourself learned, are ignorant and stubborn with disregard for us. You who defy my control shall soon be deprived of good fortune!" (15)

Thus cursed by his own guru, the great Bali, undeviated from truth, proceeded to give the land to Vāmana, having first worshipped him with water. (16) Bali's wife, Vindhyāvali, wearing a pearl necklace, brought a golden pot filled with water for washing the feet. (17) Joyfully washing Vāmana's blessed feet, Bali, the patron of the sacrifice, then sprinkled on his own head that water which purifies the universe.[19] (18) The hosts of gods from above—*gandharvas*, *vidyādharas*, *siddhas*, and *cāraṇas*—released a shower of flowers in jubilation, praising the *asura* king for his honest behavior. (19) Thousands of drums sounded continuously, and *gandharvas*, *kiṁpuruṣas*, and *kinnaras* exclaimed, "The illustrious Bali has accomplished a difficult deed: he has knowingly given the three worlds to his enemy!" (20)

Then that dwarf form of the unlimited Hari miraculously expanded, until the entire creation existed within him—the earth, sky, directions, heaven, intermediate spaces, seas, animals, humans, gods, and seers. (21) Standing there with Śukra and his assembly of priests, Bali saw, within the great Lord's cosmic body, this triple-*guṇa* universe, with all its gross elements, sense objects, senses, seat of consciousness, and living beings. (22) Indrasena (Bali) saw the lower world on the Lord's soles, the Earth on his feet, the mountains on his calves, winged creatures on the cosmic form's knees, and the host of winds on his thighs. (23)

The next nine verses—24–32—elaborate on what Bali sees—namely, further cosmic features located within various features of Vishnu's form; he also witnesses Vishnu being eulogized by several of his chief associates.

O king, wide-striding Bhagavān shone, bedecked with a forest garland encircled by honeybees; with one step he traversed Bali's domain (the earth), with his body he crossed the sky, and with his arms he filled the directions. (33)[20] With his second step the Lord encompassed the threefold heavenly realm: surely there was not a speck of space left for his third step. Yet higher and higher, the Wide Strider's foot reached beyond the Mahar, Jana, and Tapa realms. (34)

In the first twenty-four verses of chapter 21, Brahmā and sages from the higher realms (mentioned at the end of chapter 20) joyously approach and worship Vāmana (Urukrama), with water that thereafter becomes the river Ganges. Meanwhile, without Bali's approval, the *asuras* (demons) resolve to attack and kill Vāmana. Rebuffed by Vishnu's associates, Bali then stops the *asuras* from continuing to fight, arguing that time and destiny are no longer in their favor.

The venerable Śuka said: O king, hearing their master's words, the commanders of the *daitya* and *dānava* armies entered the lower realm, propelled by the agents of Vishnu. (21.25) Then, on the day of the sacrifice when *soma* is extracted, Garuḍa, the king of birds, son of Tārkṣya, understanding the objective of his master, Vishnu, bound Bali with Vāruṇa's ropes. (26) A great cry resounded from every direction of heaven and earth as the king of the *asuras* was restrained by the mighty Vishnu, pervader of the universe. (27)

O protector of the people! Bhagavān Vāmana spoke to the noble Bali, bound by Vāruṇa's ropes, who, though his wealth was gone, remained fixed in wisdom. (28) "O *asura*! You have granted me my three steps of land; with two steps the entire earth is covered. Arrange now for the third! (29) As far as the sun shines with rays of light, as far as the moon glows together with the stars, and as far as the clouds rain down—all this land has been yours. (30) With my first step I have spanned the earthly realm, my body covering the sky and the directions; and, as you witnessed, with my second step I have spanned your celestial realm. (31) Residence in hell is the place for you for not fulfilling your promise; so, as also intended by your guru, you shall enter hell! (32) One who disappoints a supplicant by not giving what was promised falls down; his chances of reaching heaven are remote and his hopes dashed. (33)[21] Having promised to give to me, you have cheated me, due to pride in your possessions. Hence may you suffer several years of hell as the fruit of your hypocrisy." (34)

In a gesture of complete submission Bali invites Vāmana to place the third step upon his own head. Bali insists that he will do whatever is necessary to retain his reputation for truthfulness, and he welcomes Vāmana's punishment as an opportunity to recover a sense of humility. While Bali is considering his good fortune, his grandfather Prahlāda appears on the scene and, offering respects to Vāmana, praises him for appropriately punishing his grandson. Similarly Bali's wife, Vindhyāvali, praises Vāmana for his acts. Then the cosmic lord Brahmā speaks.

The venerable Brahmā said: "O guardian and lord of beings, Lord of lords, pervader of the universe—please release this man who is now bereft of everything. This punishment is no longer necessary. (22.21) He has given you everything—this earth, other worlds, all that was gained from the sacrificial rite, and his very body—all offered with a forthright attitude. (22) An honest person, having reverentially offered water at your feet and having honored you with sacred grass and shoots may surely attain the highest, most glorious destination in the three worlds. How can anyone who worshipped so sincerely deserve harassment?" (23)

Śrī Bhagavān said: "Brahmā! I take away the possessions of one whom I favor, for such a conceited, obtuse person disdains both the world and me. (24) Sometimes when a helpless living being is evolving through various bodies because of its own actions, it may eventually progress to the human form. (25) If one remains without pride despite exceptional birth, good deeds, youthful vigor, handsome form, knowledge, power, or wealth—this is evidence of my favor. (26) Behold! The chain of causes for conceit and arrogance, such as birth (in a respected family), which impede true fortune, does not bewilder one who is dedicated to me. (27) Of the demons and antigods this Bali of increasing renown is foremost. Although dispossessed, he is not perplexed, having subdued *māyā*. (28) Bereft of wealth, fallen from stature, reviled and bound by enemies, abandoned by kinsfolk and subjected to torment, threatened and cursed by his guru—the steadfast Bali did not give up truth nor did he reject true speech when I misrepresented dharma. (29–30) By my will this Bali has gained a place inaccessible even to the deathless gods. Under my charge he shall become Indra during the reign of Sāvarṇi Manu. (31) Until then let him rule Sutala, the realm created by Viśvakarma. Under my supervision its inhabitants are free from pain, disease, lethargy, weariness, defeat, and natural evils. (32)

"O great King Indrasena (Bali)! Good fortune to you! Make haste to Sutala—longed for by heaven's denizens—where you shall be amid your kinsfolk! (33) No celestial rulers—not to mention others—will surpass you; my disk weapon will slay any demons who spurn your rule. (34) In all respects I will protect you, your entourage, and your property. Hero! There, nearby, you will always behold me. (35) There, just by being in my presence, your foolish, diabolical attitude will promptly vanish, freed from the influence of antigods and demons." (36)

SUGGESTIONS FOR FURTHER READING

Bedekar, V. M. 1967. "The Legend of the Churning of the Ocean in the Epics and the Purāṇas: A Comparative Study." *Purāṇa* 9, no. 1:7–61.
A study of the development of the churning story in the Mahābhārata and several Purāṇas, with particular attention given to the items that arise from the ocean during its churning.

Gupta, Ravi M., and Kenneth R. Valpey. 2013. "Churning the Ocean of Līlā: Themes for Bhāgavata Study." In *The Bhāgavata Purāṇa: Sacred Text and Living Tradition*, edited by Ravi M. Gupta and Kenneth R. Valpey, 1–17. New York: Columbia University Press.
This chapter unpacks the various motifs found in the churning narrative and uses them to introduce key themes of the Bhāgavata Purāṇa as a whole.

Heim, Maria. 2004. *Theories of the Gift in South Asia: Hindu, Buddhist, and Jain Reflections on Dāna*. New York: Routledge.
A systematic overview of premodern textual reflections from each of the three traditions, highlighting their points of convergence and departure, from four perspectives (each of which is the subject of one chapter): the donor, the recipient, the ritual, and the gift.

——. 2010. "Gift and Gift Giving." In *Brill's Encyclopedia of Hinduism*, edited by Knut A. Jacobsen et al., 2:747–52. Leiden: Brill.
A brief overview of aspects of giving in Hindu traditions, drawn largely from the author's book (see previous entry; both entries are relevant to chapters 18–22).

Soifer, Deborah A. 1991. *The Myths of Narasiṁha and Vāmana: Two Avatars in Cosmological Perspective*. Albany: SUNY Press.
Soifer discusses key motifs in the Vāmana narrative and traces its development across several Purāṇas. The appendixes include translations of the Vāmana story from nine different Purāṇas.

BOOK NINE

Sage Durvāsā Flees Vishnu's Fiery Weapon
Rāma's Victorious Homecoming
Krishna's Life Story in a Nutshell

The Bhāgavata is by no means finished with cosmic dynastic details. Of the fourteen Manus—lords of humankind—appearing in one day of Brahmā, the Bhāgavata identifies Vaivasvata Manu, the son of the sun god, Vivasvān, and the seventh of the fourteen (and hence, during the "noontime" of Brahmā's day), as the Manu of our current aeon. Book Eight, chapter 13, had briefly described the remaining seven future Manus, and here, in Book Nine, our attention is brought back to the present. Descendants of Vaivasvata are listed in chapter 2, following a curious account, in chapter 1, of Ilā, a daughter of Vaivasvata's, becoming transformed into a male, Sudyumna, and then later becoming again a woman. Several narratives follow about some of Vaivasvata's descendants, leading up to a brief account of Rāma, the famous *avatāra* of Vishnu celebrated in numerous *Rāmāyaṇas*. Thereafter, twelve further chapters describe more dynasties, some of which are descended from Vaivasvata. Then the book's final chapter (24) details dynastic relationships ending with Vasudeva and two of his wives, Devakī and Rohiṇī, mothers of Krishna and Balarāma, respectively. This final chapter prepares us for Book Ten, which is focused entirely on Krishna's life.

The Purāṇas are replete with stories illustrating the dangerous consequences of offending a *brāhmaṇa*. The following story (from chapters 4–5), however, describes a different scenario—a *brāhmaṇa* sage, Durvāsā, loses his temper at King Ambarīṣa, who is praised as a *bhakta* (devotee) of Vishnu, *sādhu* (virtuous person), and a *bhāgavata* (worshipper of Bhagavān). As a result of Durvāsā's misbehavior, he is pursued throughout the universe by Vishnu's lethal disk (chakra) until the sage seeks forgiveness from Ambarīṣa.

Chapter 4 of Book Nine opens with a description of Ambarīṣa's wholehearted devotion—he uses his mind to meditate on Krishna, his words to praise Krishna's qualities, his hands to clean the temple, his ears to hear accounts of Krishna's *līlā*, his eyes to see the Lord's sacred image in the temple, his feet to walk to places of pilgrimage, and his head to bow down to Krishna. Ambarīṣa performed his duties as king and yet did not cling to the possessions and pleasures of kingship.

Once Ambarīṣa performed a particularly difficult fast without food or water, beginning on the day of Ekādaśī (the eleventh day of the waning or waxing moon) and ending a year later on Dvādaśī (the twelfth day) in the sacred lunar month of Kārtika (generally October or November). As the fast was nearing completion, however, the sage Durvāsā arrived as an unannounced—and therefore, highly honored—guest (*atithi*). Ambarīṣa invited him to dine, but the sage wanted to bathe first in the Yamunā. As the king waited for Duvāsā to return, the designated period for breaking the fast had nearly passed and thus the king found himself in a dharmic bind—it would be disrespectful to eat before his *brāhmaṇa* guest and yet his fast would be unfruitful should it not be broken at the right time. The solution to these conflicting obligations, the king decides, is to drink water, which is considered "both eating and not eating" (9.4.40).

Upon his return, Durvāsā is furious that the king would drink water before his guest had eaten, and in a fit of rage, the sage uproots a clump of his own hair, by which he creates a fiery demon that should devour Ambarīṣa. But Lord Vishnu's disk weapon, the Sudarśana chakra, instantly comes to Ambarīṣa's aid, consuming the demon "as fire consumes an angry serpent" (9.4.48). The spinning chakra then pursues Durvāsā, who flees near-certain death.

SAGE DURVĀSĀ FLEES VISHNU'S FIERY WEAPON

Chapters 4 and 5

Durvāsā fled in every direction—in the sky and on the earth, in canyons and oceans, to heaven and to other worlds, and to the worlds' rulers. But wherever he ran, Durvāsā saw there the intolerable Sudarśana. (4.51) Continually seeking refuge but finding no protector anywhere, the sage, with fearful heart, went to Lord Viriñca (Brahmā): "O self-born creator!

Save me from the fire of invincible Vishnu!" (52) Śrī Brahmā said: "When the Lord, as Time, wishes to incinerate this universe at the end of his play—a period called *dviparārdha*—everything, including my abode, will vanish by the mere furrowing of his eyebrows. (53) Divinities like Shiva, Bhṛgu, Dakṣa, and I, as well as the rulers of gods, people, and other beings—all of us are surrendered to the law of the Lord, which is good for the world, and which we carry out with bowed heads." (54)

Refused by Viriñca and pained by the heat of Vishnu's chakra, Durvāsā sought refuge with Śarva (Shiva), who lives on Mount Kailāsa. (55) Śrī Śaṁkara (Shiva) said: "Son, we have no power over the magnificent, supreme Vishnu, in whom thousands of universes like ours, inhabited by Brahmā and other living beings, come into being and go out of being in the course of time. We, too, circulate in these universes. (56)[1] I, Sanatkumāra, Nārada, the blessed Brahmā, Kapila, Vyāsa, Devala, Dharma, Āsuri, Marīci, and other such perfected masters have seen all things, and yet none of us understand the Lord's *māyā* (illusive power), for we are covered by *māyā*. (57–58) This weapon belonging to the Lord of the universe is intolerable even to us. So seek refuge with Hari (Vishnu), for he will look after your welfare." (59)

Now losing hope, Durvāsā went to Bhagavān's abode, called Vaikuṇṭha, where Śrīnivāsa (Vishnu) resides with Śrī (Lakṣmī). (60) Scorched by the fire of the invincible weapon, Durvāsā fell down trembling at the Lord's feet and said: "Infallible, unlimited master! You are sought by the virtuous and you provide for everyone. Protect me, an offender! (61) Not knowing your supreme power, I committed an offense toward those you love. Now please prescribe the atonement for that offense. Even a person fit for hell can be liberated by chanting your name." (62)

Śrī Bhagavān said: "Twice-born *brāhmaṇa*! I am subordinate to my devotees; I am not at all independent. My heart has been stolen by virtuous devotees, for I love my devotees dearly. (63)[2] I do not want limitless fortune for myself without my virtuous devotees, for whom I am the highest destination. (64) When they relinquish their homes, wives, children, friends, lives, wealth, and even what is beyond this and seek refuge in me, how can I possibly abandon them? (65)[3] Virtuous persons, their hearts bound to me, see all impartially. They control me by devotion, as a faithful woman controls her faithful husband. (66) They do not desire the four (kinds of liberation), including *sālokya*, that become available by serving me, for they are satisfied by the service itself. Why then would they want other things that perish in time? (67)[4] Virtuous persons are my heart, and

I am the heart of virtuous persons. They know no one but me, and I do not know anyone at all besides them. (68) I will tell you the solution—listen to it, *brāhmaṇa*! Go without delay to the person whom you targeted with that harmful magic. Power that is directed against virtuous persons brings danger to the one who deploys it. (69)[5] Austerity and knowledge both create good fortune for *brāhmaṇas*, but those very things have the opposite effect when the person who uses them is ill behaved. (70) So go to Ambarīṣa, son of Nābhāga, and ask forgiveness from the illustrious king. Then you will find peace. Good luck to you, *brāhmaṇa*!" (71)

Thus directed by Bhagavān, the distressed Durvāsā, scorched by the chakra, returned to Ambarīṣa and clasped his feet. (5.1) The king was deeply pained to see Durvāsā's exertion and embarrassed to have his feet touched. As so he compassionately prayed to Hari's weapon. (2) Ambarīṣa said: "You are fire and the blessed sun. You are the moon, lord of luminaries. You are water, you are earth, sky, the elements, and the senses. (3) Obeisance to you, Sudarśana of a thousand spokes! Beloved of Acyuta! Destroyer of all weapons! Lord of the earth! I beseech you—please be gracious to the *brāhmāṇa*." (4)

After further eloquent verses of praise, Sudarśana relents and releases Durvāsā from the burning heat. The sage is relieved and grateful.

Durvāsā said: "Ah! Today I have seen the greatness of the Infinite Lord's servants! Although I was an offender, you, O king, still looked after my welfare. (14) What is impossible to do or impossible to relinquish for virtuous, great souls who have caught hold of Bhagavān Hari, chief of the Sātvatas? (15) Merely by hearing the name of Hari, whose feet create holy places, a person becomes pure. So what more do his servants need to do? (16) King, you are exceedingly kind and I am much obliged to you, for you ignored my offense and saved my life." (17) Ambarīṣa had not eaten because he was hoping the sage would return. Now the king touched Durvāsā's feet, had him seated, and fed him well. (18) After eating all that he desired—food fit for a guest that was served attentively—the satisfied sage respectfully asked the king to eat. (19)

The story concludes with further praise of King Ambarīṣa as an exalted *bhāgavata*, promising the attainment of liberation and bhakti for Bhagavān for one who recites or reflects upon this narrative. More dynastic details follow, leading to an account of descendants whose adventures are instrumental in causing the Ganges to descend to the earth from higher realms (chapters 8–9, summarizing the account given in the Vālmīki Rāmāyaṇa).

Then follows the Bhāgavata's retelling of the Rāmāyaṇa, an epic story that has been recounted and performed in cultures across Asia. The Bhāgavata makes no attempt to compete with other Rāmāyaṇas. At the beginning of his narration, Śuka affirms that the story of Rāma and Sītā has been told by "many sages and seers of the truth, and you (Parīkṣit) have heard it many times" (9.10.3). And so Śuka recites the Rāmāyaṇa in brief, summarizing many events in a single verse and reviewing the entire story in only two chapters. Yet Śuka pauses to reflect and elaborate at several points in the narrative, and it is these occasions that reveal the Bhāgavata's priorities and distinctive approach to the Rāmāyaṇa. Two themes emerge clearly: First, the Bhāgavata focuses on the devotional relationships shared between Rāma and other persons in the story, particularly his wife, Sītā, his brothers Bharata, Lakṣmaṇa, and Śatrughna, his mothers, and the residents of Ayodhyā city. When Rāma is exiled to the forest and eventually separated from Sītā, the Bhāgavata takes care to describe the emotions of these devotees, particularly their love in absence (*viraha*), which is a sustained marker of the Bhāgavata's theology. Second, the Bhāgavata spends much time elaborating on Rāma and Sītā's ideal, dharmic reign after they return from exile. The joyous lives of Ayodhyā's people and their affection for their king and queen receive far greater attention than the sad, final episode of Sītā's exile. Indeed, Śuka mentions Sītā's banishment in a few verses and then swiftly returns to Rāma's love for Sītā, the people's devotion to Rāma, and the dharmic nature of Rāma's rule. Taken together, these two distinctive characteristics reveal a perennial theme of the Bhāgavata: selfless bhakti transcends physical limitations and yet is still compatible with social order (dharma).

We enter the story near its end, just after the demon king Rāvaṇa has been killed by Rāma. Śuka has already described the major events of the Rāmāyaṇa: Rāma strings Shiva's great bow in order to win Sītā's hand in marriage; Rāma, Sītā, and brother Lakṣmaṇa are exiled to the forest for fourteen years; Sītā is kidnapped by the demon king Rāvaṇa; Rāma is overwhelmed with grief and begins searching for Sītā; he befriends the monkey chiefs Sugrīva and Hanumān, who help Rāma locate Sītā, build a bridge to the island kingdom of Laṅkā, and fight Rāvaṇa's powerful army; and finally Rāma meets Rāvaṇa on the battlefield and, after rebuking him with sharp words, kills the demon with a single arrow. The wives of the demons who died in the battle come running from Laṅkā, grieving for their dead husbands and vilifying Rāvaṇa for causing such devastation. Rāma permits Rāvaṇa's brother, Vibhīṣaṇa, to perform the funeral rites for his fallen relatives. At last Rāma is reunited with his beloved wife, Sītā, whom he finds living in a grove of Aśoka trees. (The Bhāgavata makes no mention of Sītā's trial by fire.)

RĀMA'S VICTORIOUS HOMECOMING

Chapter 10

Then Bhagavān (Rāma) saw Sītā in a cottage in an Aśoka grove. She lived at the foot of an Aśoka tree, and the affliction of separation from Rāma had made her thin. (10.30) Seeing her forlorn condition, Rāma felt compassion for his dearly beloved wife. Sītā's lotuslike face blossomed with joy when she beheld Rāma. (31) After giving Vibhīṣaṇa (Rāvaṇa's brother) the city of Laṅkā, kingship over the Rākṣasa demons, and a life spanning an aeon, Bhagavān Rāma helped Sīta get onto the aerial car and then got on himself, along with his brother Lakṣmaṇa, his close friend Sugrīva, and Hanumān. His vow (to spend fourteen years in exile) now completed, Rāma left for the city (Ayodhyā). (32) Along the way, kings and princes showered fragrant flowers on Rāma, while Śatadhṛti (Brahmā) and other gods sang about his deeds. (33)

The most merciful Rāma was pained to hear that (in his absence his brother) Bharata was sleeping on the ground, wearing bark, keeping matted hair, and eating barley cooked in cow urine. (34) When he heard that Rāma had arrived, Bharata placed Rāma's shoes on his head and left his camp at Nandīgrāma to meet his older brother. He went with the townspeople, ministers, family priests, *brāhmaṇas* reciting the Veda, musicians singing and playing instruments, and the continuous chanting of Vedic mantras. Bharata brought with him manifold royal accoutrements, including golden chariots with thoroughbred horses, fine golden reins, gold-embroidered flags, and colorful banners; soldiers with golden armor; and a procession of servants, attendants, and courtesans. Bharata fell down at Rāma's feet, his heart and eyes moistened with love. Placing Rāma's shoes on the ground, Bharata stood before him with joined palms and tears in his eyes. Rāma embraced Bharata for a long time, bathing him with tears. (35–40)

The people bowed down to Rāma, while Rāma himself, together with Sītā and Lakṣmaṇa, bowed down to *brāhmāṇas* and other virtuous, venerable persons. (41) Seeing their Lord return after a long time, the people of Northern Kosala (Ayodhyā) waved their scarves, threw flowers, and danced for joy. (42) Protector of the people! Bharata held Rāma's shoes; Sugrīva and Vibhīṣaṇa held an excellent fan and a yak-hair whisk; Hanumān, son of the Wind, held a white parasol; Śatrughna (Rāma's youngest brother) held a bow and quivers; Sītā held a water pot with water from sacred places; Aṅgada (the monkey prince) carried a sword; and the king of bears (Jāmbavān) carried a golden shield. (43–44) With women praising him and reciters extolling his virtues, Rāma shone upon Puṣpaka (the celestial aerial car) like the moon rising among the planets. (45) Thus welcomed by his brother Bharata, Rāma entered the festive city. When he entered the royal palace, he was honored by the elder women and his own mother, as well as by his seniors, equals, and juniors. In turn, he honored them. Sītā, princess of Videha, and Lakṣmaṇa also greeted everyone appropriately. (46–47) The mothers rose to greet their sons, like (dead) bodies coming to life. Placing their sons on their laps, the mothers bathed them with tears, thus relinquishing their grief. (48)

After shaving off Rāma's matted hair, the priest, together with family elders, consecrated him as king, just as Indra (king of the gods) was consecrated—with the waters of the four oceans and proper ritual procedure. (49) After taking a full bath, Rāma wore fine clothes and was adorned with a flower garland. He looked beautiful with Sītā and his brothers, who were also well dressed and decorated. (50) When Rāma became king, Tretā (the Silver Age) was in progress, but the period became like Kṛta (the Golden Age), for Rāma knew dharma and brought happiness to all beings. (51) Best of the Bharatas! The forests, rivers, mountains, valleys, islands, and oceans all yielded whatever the people desired. (52) When the transcendent Lord Rāma was king, there was no anxiety, disease, old age, depression, pain, sorrow, fear, or fatigue. There was no death for those who did not want it. (53) Rāma vowed to have only one wife, and he was pure in behavior like a philosopher-king. He taught the dharma of a householder by practicing it himself. (54) The virtuous and deferential Sītā, by her love, proper behavior, good character, modesty, and shyness understood her husband's mind and stole his heart. (55)

Rāma's reign as the ideal monarch is described in chapter 11, followed by accounts of other kings in Rāma's dynasty, including a rendition of the ancient love story of Purūravā and Urvaśī. Chapters 15 and 16 narrate the story of a "partial" *avatāra* of Bhagavān named Paraśurāma. This vengeful son of the *brāhmaṇa* sage Jamadagni is famous for slaying countless misguided *kṣatriyas*. First he kills the thousand-armed Kārtavīryārjuna, along with his armies, for having stolen his father's wish-fulfilling cow (*kāmadhenu*); then later, after Kārtavīryārjuna's sons had murdered Jamadagni in revenge, Paraśurāma attacks and kills all the sons (making a mountain of their heads) and then repeatedly (twenty-one times) rids the entire earth of *kṣatriyas*.

The story of King Yayāti is told in chapters 18 and 19, echoing a similar account in the Mahābhārata. Yayāti is cursed by his father-in-law to lose his youth, but his youngest of five sons, Pūru, agrees to exchange his youth for his father's old age, making it possible for Yayāti to resume conjugal enjoyment. Eventually, however, he becomes disgusted with himself for his indulgent ways, and both he and his wife, Devayānī, become renounced and devoted to the service of the supreme Lord.

As Book Nine comes to a close, we hear of King Duṣmanta and his wife, Śakuntalā, who parent Bharata (an episode also recounted in the Mahābhārata, made famous as a great love story by the later Sanskrit drama of Kalidāsa, *Abhijñānaśakuntalam*). Finally, at the very end of chapter 24, Śuka prepares Parīkṣit to hear about the life of Krishna in Book Ten and the beginning of Book Eleven, summarizing in only two stanzas his entire life.

KRISHNA'S LIFE STORY IN A NUTSHELL

Chapter 24

Born (as Vasudeva's son), Krishna departed from his father's house to Vraja in order to gladden (its residents). He killed his enemies, accepted many excellent wives, and begot hundreds of sons by them. The supreme person Krishna worshipped himself by sacrificial rites and spread his own teachings among the people. Then, by inducing enmity among the Kurus, who had become a great burden on the earth, Krishna caused them to be destroyed. By his mere glance on the royal armies, he purged them in battle and declared victory (for the Pāṇḍavas). Finally, after teaching Uddhava, he proceeded to his supreme abode.[6] (24.66–67)

SUGGESTIONS FOR FURTHER READING

Black, Brian. 2007. *The Character of the Self in Ancient India: Priests, Kings, and Women in the Early Upaniṣads*. Albany: SUNY Press.

Chapter 3, "Kings and Brahmins: The Political Dimensions of the Upanisads," provides a wider perspective on relationships between *kṣatriyas* and *brāhmaṇas* treated in Book 9, chapters 4 and 5, of the Bhāgavata.

Goldman, Robert, trans. 1990. *The Rāmāyaṇa of Vālmīki*. 6 vols. Princeton: Princeton University Press.

Richman, Paula, ed. 1991. *Many Rāmāyaṇas: The Diversity of a Narrative Tradition in South Asia*. Berkeley: University of California Press.

This includes the classic article by A. K. Ramanujan, "Three Hundred *Rāmāyaṇas*: Five Examples and Three Thoughts on Translation."

BOOK TEN

Krishna Eats Dirt, and Yaśodā Has a Vision
Yaśodā Binds Krishna After He Steals Butter
Krishna Frees Nalakūvara and Maṇigrīva from a Curse
The Worship and Lifting of Mount Govardhana
Krishna Calls the *Gopīs*
The *Rāsa* Dance
Singing to a Bee

By far the largest of the Bhāgavata's twelve books, Book Ten, with its ninety chapters, focuses almost exclusively on the adventures of Krishna with his close relatives and companions, and on his battles with several enemies. It recounts Krishna's childhood and youth as a cowherd in Vraja-Vrindavan, his maturing youth in Mathurā as the slayer of the demon king Kaṁsa, and his later years based in Dvārakā as the favorite prince of the Yadu clan.

In response to the gods' prayers to Vishnu to relieve the earth of its burden of demonic kings, Vishnu had promised to descend, together with his divine associates and the several celestial divinities. Soon thereafter, Krishna is born under the trying circumstances of King Kaṁsa's tyrannical rule of Mathurā. During the wedding of Vasudeva and Devakī, Kaṁsa had been informed by an invisible celestial voice that their eighth child would slay him. In his effort to circumvent the prophecy, Kaṁsa plans to kill Krishna just after his birth; but his plan is foiled when Krishna is secreted away to the cow-herding community of Vraja-Vrindavan (chapter 3), where the chieftain, Nanda, and his wife, Yaśodā, very lovingly raise Krishna as their own son. As he grows from a charming baby and mischievous child to an even more charming boy and attractive youth, Krishna delights the Vraja villagers in various ways, including a daily contest with Kaṁsa's formidable agents sent to kill him. Krishna easily vanquishes each of Kaṁsa's shape-shifting henchmen and then resumes playing with his young cowherd friends.

The following episode, occurring during Krishna's days as a toddler, is much celebrated as a playful demonstration of Krishna's supreme divinity. Like the subsequent episode (chapter 9), it highlights the loving mother-child relationship between Yaśodā and Krishna.

Just prior to this incident, while still a baby, Krishna had slain two agents of Kaṁsa's. Krishna had killed the first, the ogress Pūtanā, by sucking her life from her breast—she having disguised herself as a beautiful woman to offer him her poisoned breast milk. He then killed Tṛṇāvarta (Tornado—literally, "grass spinner") by pounding him to death with his fist while suspended high in the sky by that whirlwind. Thereafter Krishna had learned to crawl and then to walk, soon playing with other small boys, sons of the village cowherds.

KRISHNA EATS DIRT, AND YAŚODĀ HAS A VISION

Chapter 8

Once while playing, Balarāma and other cowherd boys reported to mother Yaśodā, "Krishna has eaten dirt!" (8.32)[1] Desiring his well-being, Yaśodā reproachfully took Krishna in her arms. Eyeing him anxiously, she spoke: (33) "You unruly fellow, why have you eaten dirt on the sly? These boys say this, as do your buddies and even your big brother." (34) (Krishna said:) "Mother, I didn't eat (dirt). They are all liars! If (you think) they speak the truth, then look right into my mouth." (35)[2] (Yaśodā said:) "If it is so, then open wide!" That said, Bhagavān Hari, playing as a human child, freely opened (his mouth), revealing his lordly might. (36)

There Yaśodā saw the universe; moving and stationary beings; the firmament; the directions; mountains; oceans with islands; the earth globe; fire and wind; the moon, planets, water, light, atmosphere, and the sky; the senses with their perceptual functions; the mind; and the totality consisting of three qualities (*sattva*, *rajas*, and *tamas*). She saw in the open mouth of her son's delicate body this wonderful variety, along with living beings, time, dispositions, the stock of karmic effects, and bodily differences. Seeing (there) Vraja village as well as herself, she became awestruck. (37–39)

(Yaśodā thought:) "My goodness! Is this a dream, some divine magic, or the bewilderment of my own understanding? Or is all this really the inherent yogic power of my child? (40)[3] In any case, he is truly inaccessible as he is by reason, heart, mind, endeavor, or words. From him (the world) appears, by him (it is sustained), and in him (it finally) rests. I bow to the feet of him who is very difficult to comprehend. (41) '*I* am the fabulously wealthy wife of Vraja's king.' 'He is *my* husband.' 'This is *my* son.' 'The cowherd men and women, with their herds of cows, are *mine*.' He by whose *māyā* I have such silly sentiment is my refuge." (42)[4] Thus, within that cowherdess who had comprehended reality, the great Lord expanded Vishnu-*māyā* in the form of affection for her son. (43)[5] Just then, taking her son on her lap, Yaśodā Gopī forgot the matter. She became as before, her heart brimming with increased affection. (44) That Lord, whose glory is sung by the three Vedas, the Upaniṣads, Sāṁkhya, Yoga, and Vaiṣṇava *tantra*, she considered to be her own child. (45)

Concluding his account of Krishna's "eating dirt," Śuka explains to Parīkṣit the good fortune of Yaśodā and Nanda to witness the childhood pastimes of Krishna: Brahmā had blessed the ascetic couple Droṇa and Dharā to appear as Krishna's parents, in Vraja, in their next lives. In the next chapter Śuka continues to report about Krishna's divinely mischievous character. Still a small child, Krishna charms Yaśodā and other village women with his pilferage of milk products, prompting Yaśodā to restrain him by tying him to a large and (she presumes) immovable grinding mortar.

YAŚODĀ BINDS KRISHNA AFTER HE STEALS BUTTER

Chapter 9

Śrī Śuka said: Once, while her maidservants were busy with other duties, Nanda's wife, Yaśodā, took to churning yogurt herself. (9.1) While churning the yogurt she sang various songs recollecting Krishna's childhood exploits. (2) She wore a linen dress fastened with a cord about her broad hips, and as she drew the churning rope back and forth her bracelets and ear ornaments moved with her arms' effort. Her face perspiring and *mālatī* flowers falling from her bound hair, out of affection for her son milk flowed from her shaking breasts. Thus she of beautiful eyebrows went on churning. (3)[6] Coming to his mother for her breast milk, grabbing the yogurt churning stick Hari (Krishna) stopped her churning, bringing her delight. (4) He climbed on her hip and drank from her breast that flowed with affection as she gazed upon his smiling face. But then, leaving him unsated, she rushed over to where milk was overflowing from a vessel placed over a fire. (5) Feigning tears, anger upsurging, biting his trembling reddish lips with his teeth, Krishna smashed the pot of churned yogurt on a millstone, then went into the house and stealthily ate fresh butter. (6)[7] Setting aside the cooked milk, Gopī Yaśodā returned and saw the broken yogurt vessel. Although she did not espy him there, taking this to be her own son's stunt, she smiled. (7)

He was perched atop the base of a wooden mortar, his eyes anxious with a thief's guilt, apportioning out from a suspended pot as much butter as he pleased to a monkey. Spotting her toddler from behind, Yaśodā approached slowly. (8) Then, seeing her with stick in hand, Krishna, as if afraid, scrambled down and darted off. *Yogīs'* minds, honed by austerity to undertake hardship, fail to reach him whom Yaśodā followed, running. (9)[8] As the slim-waisted mother pursued Krishna, her movement was hampered by the weight of her large hurrying hips, and flowers fallen from her loosened hair trailed behind. Yet due to her speed, she caught him. (10) She grasped that culprit by the hand, and when she scolded him, he became anxious. She saw him begin to cry, rubbing with his hands his collyrium-lined eyes, which were overcome with fear. (11) Noting her son's fear and feeling affection for her child, she dropped the stick. Yet unaware of his power, she desired to bind him with a rope. (12) He who has neither interior nor exterior, neither beginning nor end, yet who is the beginning and end, exterior and interior of the world, and who is the world— (13) that unmanifest Lord Adhokṣaja, disguised as a mortal, Yaśodā began to bind with a rope to a wooden mortar like an ordinary child, considering him her son. (14)[9] For her culprit child to be bound, that rope was two finger widths short; so the cowherd woman fastened it with another (rope). (15) When that rope was still too short, she joined yet another with it. Even that—whatever more was added—was two fingers short. (16) In this way Yaśodā tied together all the ropes in her home, and yet . . . (it was still too short). For the highly amused, smiling cowherd women, it became a matter for wonder. (17) Seeing his mother's constant exertion—her every limb perspiring and flowers falling from her braid—out of kindness Krishna yielded to his own binding. (18)[10]

Dear Parīkṣit, this world and its masters are under the control of Krishna, who is controlled only by himself. Yet here the Lord has shown the principle of (the master's) submission to the servant's control. (19) Neither Brahmā, nor Shiva, nor even the Lord's better half, Lakṣmī, have received such mercy as Gopī Yaśodā received from the giver of liberation.

(20)[11] For those who are filled with bhakti, this Lord, Yaśodā's son, is easily accessible; not so for the worldly minded, the sophists, or the self-seeking yogis. (21) But while his mother was engrossed in household duties, Lord Krishna noticed two *arjuna* trees, previously celestials who were sons of the bestower of wealth (Kuvera). (22)[12] Formerly, by Nārada's curse, the wealthy brothers named Nalakūvara and Maṇigrīva had, due to their excesses, gained the forms of trees. (23)

At the end of the previous chapter Śuka noted that sage Nārada had cursed Nalakūvara and Maṇigrīva to become trees. In the next chapter (10), Śuka continues this topic, explaining the circumstances that brought a curse upon the two sons of Kuvera, the god of treasures. Intoxicated by strong liquor, the two youths had been carousing with maidens in the waters of Shiva's mountain pleasure garden when Nārada happened by. Though the girls, upon seeing Nārada, hastened to cover themselves and show him respect, the boys, naked, ignored him, prompting the sage to reflect on the blinding effect of wealth and its tendency to breed arrogance. Wanting to see them rectified, Nārada pronounces a curse—for Nalakūvara and Maṇigrīva to endure long lives as motionless and naked trees—that would end in a great blessing—to meet Krishna and be freed by him from their arboreal forms and from their pride. Krishna, having been bound to a grinding mortar by his foster mother, Yaśodā, now moves to liberate them.

KRISHNA FREES NALAKŪVARA AND MAṆIGRĪVA FROM A CURSE

Chapter 10

To validate the words of that foremost godly sage Nārada, the Lord inched softly to where the two *arjuna* trees stood. (10.24)[13] "Because the celestial sage is most dear to me, therefore these two sons of the Wealth Giver (will receive my attention). I shall make happen just what the august Nārada pronounced." (25) (Thinking thus), Krishna then proceeded between those two *arjuna* trees. Just by his passing between them, the grinding mortar wedged crosswise. (26)[14] His waist tethered to the mortar behind him, little Krishna pulled, straightaway freeing those imposing root-bound trees. Trunk, branches, and leaves quaking, with a terrific sound they fell. (27)[15] Like fire gods, two perfected beings emerged from those trees, shining everywhere with stunning beauty, freed from passion. Bowing before Krishna, Lord of all worlds, with joined palms they uttered this prayer: (28)[16]

"Krishna! Krishna! O great yogi! You are the primeval transcendent person. *Brāhmaṇas* know this manifest and unmanifest universe to be your very form. (29) You are the one and only lord of the senses, mind, vital airs, and bodies of all beings; you alone are time, the perpetually pervasive Lord Vishnu, the supreme being. (30) You are the great and subtle primordial nature (*prakṛti*), consisting of the *guṇas*—passion (*rajas*), illumination (*sattva*), and darkness (*tamas*). You alone are the supervising person who is cognizant of the transformations in all bodies. (31)[17] You are not comprehensible by means of things that are comprehensible—the transformations of nature's *guṇas*. Indeed, who in this world, being shrouded by nature's *guṇas*, is able to know you, the innately perfect person? (32) Obeisance unto him—unto you!—the Lord, Vāsudeva, the absolute being, the cosmic arranger, whose glory is hidden by your own brilliant virtues! (33)[18] You, who are not embodied, are known to be among embodied beings as embodied *avatāras* with various unequaled, superhuman, heroic, improbable activities. (34)[19] You are that Lord who has now appeared with your powers and expansions for the well-being and liberation of the whole world, fulfilling devotees' desires. (35)[20] Obeisance to you, most excellent one! Obeisance to you, who are ultimate well-being itself! Obeisance unto you, Lord of the Yadus, gentle Vāsudeva! (36) Bhūman (Krishna), kindly allow us, servants of your follower (Nārada), to go. By that sage's grace we have obtained the sight of you. (37)[21] May our words narrate your virtues and may our hearing be of sacred narrations; may our hands do your works and may our minds remember your feet. May our heads bow to all the world as your abode and may our sight be for seeing the saints, who are your very self." (38)[22]

Śrī Śuka said: Thus praised by those two while bound with a rope to the mortar, the Lord, master of Gokula, grinning broadly, spoke to these Guhyakas. (39)

Śrī Bhagavān said: "I know this favor was done previously by that compassionate sage Nārada; by his curse, you who were blind with the madness of wealth became ruined. (40) As a person's eyes are released from darkness by the light of the sun, one may become released from bondage by seeing equipoised sages who are thoroughly dedicated to me. (41) Nalakūvara, being dedicated to me, you two may go home. Your affection for me has been engendered, for you have desired the nonworldly supreme." (42)[23]

Śrī Śuka said: Thus addressed, these two, repeatedly circumambulating and bowing to him who was (still) tethered to the mortar, took their leave to depart toward the north. (43)

In the next several chapters of Book Ten, the child Krishna continues to amaze and charm his friends and family members in Vrindavan. Krishna's ongoing adventures include being attacked by and slaying more demons sent by the tyrant Kaṁsa (following the deaths of Pūtanā and Tṛṇāvarta prior to the dirt-eating incident) and being tested by the demiurge Brahmā; taming the ferocious water serpent Kāliya and swallowing a forest fire that began to consume Vrindavan forest. Chapter 20, a description of Vrindavan's rainy and autumn seasons, serves as a poetic interlude to Krishna's adventures, and the next three chapters treat of romantic and playful interactions with the local young cowherd maidens and then with the devotional mood of some local *brāhmaṇas*' wives. In all these events, Krishna prevails as the carefree, charming, and merciful winner of his devotees' hearts.

Similarly, in the following episode, Krishna proves himself the charming hero of Vrindavan. This time it is he who provokes the celestial king Indra into a test of powers, simultaneously poking fun at brahmanical orthodoxy through his parody of Mīmāṁsā philosophy (which argues, from a nontheistic position, for the observance of Vedic sacrificial rituals for their own sake). Krishna's feat of lifting and holding aloft Mount Govardhana for seven days and nights remains to this day a favorite motif for much performative and graphic arts in South Asia.

THE WORSHIP AND LIFTING OF MOUNT GOVARDHANA

Chapters 24 and 25

Śrī Śuka said: Staying just there (where Krishna had previously met some *brāhmaṇa* men and their wives) the Lord and Baladeva saw the cowherd men diligently preparing a sacrificial rite for Indra. (24.1)[24] The all-seeing Lord, self of all, was quite aware of their intention. Still, bowing respectfully, he solicited the elders led by Nanda: (2)

"Father, please explain to me what is this flurry of activity you are busied with? Whose prescription is this sacrifice, how is it accomplished, and what shall be the result? (3) Father, tell me, who am eager to hear. This is my great wish! Good people—who are the self of all in this world, who do not distinguish self from other, nor between friends, enemies, and neutrals—should not keep secrets. It is said that one who is indifferent may be avoided like an enemy, but a friend is like oneself. (4–5) The people perform (ritual) actions with or without understanding. There will be fruition of action for those with understanding, whereas there will not be for those without understanding. (6) This being so, tell me clearly about that which I inquire. Is your ritual enterprise the product of deliberation (by the wise), or else is it an ordinary custom?" (7)

Śrī Nanda said: "The powerful lord Indra is rain; clouds are his own forms; they shower forth delightful life, like milk for living beings. (8)[25] Dear boy, by means of sacrifices with products gained by his discharge, we as well as other people worship this lord, master of the rain clouds. (9)[26] They subsist by the remnants of sacrifices performed for the three types of gain. Human effort is fruitful because of rain. (10)[27] A person who would reject this practice received through tradition—out of whim, aversion, fear, or greed—surely does not obtain well-being." (11)

Śrī Śuka said: Hearing the words of Nanda and other Vraja folk, to provoke Indra's anger Keśava (Krishna) replied to his father. (12)

Śrī Bhagavān said: "By karma a creature is born; by karma alone it perishes. By karma alone a creature experiences happiness, misery, danger, and security. (13)

"Even if there is some lord who assumes the form of results to persons' actions, it is still to one who *acts* that he grants (results). He is surely not the master of one who does not act. (14)[28] What's with Indra? He is powerless to change what is fixed by the inherent disposition of human beings subject to their own various actions in this world. (15)[29] A person follows inherent disposition, being ruled only by inherent disposition. All this world, with its gods, demons, and humankind, is grounded in inherent disposition. (16) It is by karma that a creature gains and loses elevated and lowly bodies. Karma alone is one's enemy, friend, outside observer, teacher, and lord. (17) So, grounded in inherent disposition, doing one's own (prescribed) occupation, one should honor that occupation. Indeed that occupation (karma) by which one can easily subsist is one's only deity. (18)[30] One who relies on a person other than the one who sustains life does not enjoy well-being, just like an unchaste woman who relies upon her paramour. (19) *Brāhmaṇas* can subsist by (custodianship of) sacred texts and rulers by protecting the earth; *vaiśyas* can live by enterprise and *śūdras* can live by serving the twice-born. (20)

Cultivation, trade, cow protection, and, fourth, banking are said to be the fourfold enterprise (of *vaiśyas*). Of these, we have always been cowherds. (21) (The *guṇas*) 'illumination,' 'passion,' and 'darkness' are the causes of sustenance, generation, and termination. The universe is generated by passion, and permutations constitute the variegated world. (22)[31] Blown by the wind, clouds shower waters everywhere. By these alone creatures thrive. What will Big Indra do? (23)[32]

"Dear father, not cities, nor territories, nor villages, nor fixed homes are for us. We are forest dwellers, ever residents of forests and mountains. (24)[33] So let a festival commence—for the cows, *brāhmaṇas*, and the mountain (Govardhana)! Please accomplish this festival with the requisites meant for the Indra sacrifice! (25) Let varieties of food be cooked—sweetened milk rice, sweet wheat cakes, sweet breads, sweet rice cakes, soups, and the like—and let all the milk be used. (26) Let the *brāhmaṇa* expounders of Veda properly invoke the fires. Then you should give them top-quality food and cows as gifts. (27) And after giving food appropriately to others—including fallen beings such as dogs and *caṇḍālas* (outcastes)—and grass to the cows, let an offering be made to this mountain. (28)[34] Then, having eaten well, being well dressed, ornamented, and smeared with sandalwood paste, you should circumambulate the cows, *brāhmaṇas*, ritual fires, and the mountain. (29) Father, this is my idea. Please do it if you approve. This festival of cows, *brāhmaṇas*, and mountain is also pleasing to me." (30)

Śrī Śuka said: The Lord, who is Time itself, spoke with a desire to quash Indra's pride. Hearing Krishna's words, Nanda and his cohorts accepted them as appropriate without, however, knowing Krishna's intention. (31) And then everything was done just as Madhusūdana (Krishna) had advised: Getting (*brāhmaṇas*) to recite auspicious hymns, the people of Vraja respectfully offered all those ingredients (originally meant for Indra) as tributes to the mountain and the *brāhmaṇas*. They provided grass for the cows, and, keeping their herds of cows in front, they circumambulated the mountain. (32–33) The well-ornamented cowherd women rode along in wagons drawn by oxen, singing Krishna's exploits as *brāhmaṇas* voiced benedictions. (34) Then Krishna, saying, "I am the mountain!" assumed a different form, inspiring the cowherds' confidence. With a giant body he consumed the enormous tribute. (35) Together with the Vraja folk, Krishna himself offered obeisance to himself (as the mountain), saying, "Oh, look! That personified mountain has bestowed mercy upon us! (36)[35] For the cows' and our own well-being, let us offer obeisance to this mountain: taking any form at will, the mountain surely kills forest-resident mortals who neglect (him)." (37)[36] Then those cowherds returned with Krishna to Vraja, having duly arranged this festival for the mountain, cows, and *brāhmaṇas*, as inspired by Vāsudeva (Krishna). (38)

Śrī Śuka said: O king, when he learned that his own worship had been usurped, Indra became incensed with Nanda and the other cowherds, whose lord was Krishna. (25.1) Indeed, angered Indra, thinking himself the Lord, dispatched what is called the Sāṁvartaka mass of world-destroying clouds, and he uttered this speech to them: (2)[37]

"How amazing is the pride born of prosperity in these forest-dwelling cowherds! Trusting in mortal Krishna, they have slighted the gods! (3)[38] Having spurned metaphysical reasoning, it is as if they tried to cross the ocean of temporal existence with the unstable so-called boats of ritual sacrifices constituted of action (for selfish benefit). (4)[39] Taking shelter of Krishna—a foolish mortal who thinks himself a pandit (but who is merely) a talkative, arrogant little boy—the cowherds have acted adversely toward me! (5)[40] Bolstered by Krishna, these cowherds are insolent because of their fortune! Oust their stubbornness born of pride in wealth! Lead their animals to destruction! (6) With the greatly forceful storm gods I, too, will head over to Vraja, riding the elephant Airāvata, to raze Nanda's cow stables." (7)[41]

Śrī Śuka said: And so, on bountiful Indra's command, those unleashed clouds pounded Nanda's cowherd settlement with their force of driving rains; fomented by the violent storm gods, with flashing lightning and resounding thunder they flung down hailstones. (8–9)[42] As those water bearers incessantly released pillar-thick shafts of rain, submerging the earth with floods, low and high became indistinguishable. (10) The animals, cowherd men, and cowherd women, shivering and distressed from excessive rain, wind, and cold, approached Govinda for shelter. (11)[43] They fell at the feet of the Lord while covering their heads and children with their bodies that were battered and trembling from the rain. (12)[44]

"Krishna! All-fortunate Krishna! Lord! Affectionate guardian of your devotees! You are the master of the cowherd settlement (Gokula)! We beseech you to save us from the vengeful god." (13)[45] Seeing them stunned from the attack by hailstones and fierce wind, Bhagavān Hari thought this had been done by angry Indra. (14)[46]

"For destruction Indra rains down this unseasonal, extremely fierce and windy hailstorm because of our usurping his sacrifice. (15) So by my own yogic power I will launch a fitting countermeasure; I shall obliterate the ignorance of those who, out of stupidity and pride in power, think themselves world lords. (16)[47] The gods, endowed with the disposition of illumination, have no pride of lordship. I break the pride of those lacking illumination to afford them relief (from their illusion). (17)[48] So by my own yogic power I shall safeguard this cowherd settlement that has resorted to me—my own family for whom I am lord. This is the vow I have taken." (18)[49] Having thus considered, Krishna, being Vishnu, took up Mount Govardhana with one hand and playfully held (it), like a child holds up a mushroom. (19)[50] Then the Lord addressed the cowherds: "O mother! Father! Vraja folk! If it pleases you, do enter under this mountain with all your cows. (20)[51] In this place you need have no misgivings that the mountain might fall from my hand. Enough with this distress from wind and rain! I have arranged shelter from all this trouble just for you." (21)

And so, their minds relieved by Krishna, the cowherd folk entered that ample space with their cows, carts, and dependents. (22) The residents of Vraja gazed upon Krishna, who held up the mountain, not budging from that position for seven days. He set aside all consideration of his own (dis) comfort—the pain of hunger and thirst. (23)[52] Seeing that demonstration of Krishna's yogic power, Indra was utterly shocked. His pride collapsed, his resolve broken, he commanded his clouds to turn back. (24)[53] Seeing the violent wind and rain abated, the sky cleared, and the sun risen, the lifter of Govardhana (Krishna) addressed the cowherd folk. (25)

"Cowherd men! Let fear be gone! With your wives, children, and goods, you may go out. The wind and rain have ceased, and the rivers are nearly dry." (26) The cowherd men then proceeded out, each with their cows and carts loaded with their effects; and the women, children, and elderly gradually followed. (27) And while all beings watched, their master, Bhagavān, effortlessly replaced that mountain in its own original position. (28)[54] Beside themselves with love, those delighted Vraja folk gathered together. The cowherd women affectionately embraced him and so on, as appropriate, and joyfully extended well-wishing benedictions with yogurt, whole grains, and water. (29)[55] Overcome with affection, Yaśodā, Rohinī, Nanda, and the best of the strong, Balarāma, embraced Krishna and bestowed their blessings. (30)[56]

O king! The gods in heaven, the perfected beings (Siddhas), and other celestials (Sādhyas, Gandharvas, and Cāraṇas)—all pleased—offered praises and released showers of flowers. (31)[57] Protector of humankind!

By the gods' command, conch shells and kettledrums boomed in the sky; led by Tumburu, the Gandharva lords sang. (32)[58] King! Hari then sauntered back with Balarāma to his own cow settlement, surrounded by his affectionate cowherd friends. The *gopīs* departed, cheerfully singing about such deeds of him who touched their hearts. (33)[59]

The next two chapters describe devotional responses to Krishna's lifting of Mount Govardhana—first by the amazed cowherd companions of Krishna's foster father, Nanda, and then by the heavenly king Indra, who, deeply apologizing to Krishna for having harassed the Vraja residents with torrential rain, appears before him and offers humble prayers. Thereafter (in chapter 28), the cowherds are further astonished when Krishna gives them a glimpse of the transcendent realm after he rescues Nanda from the watery abode of Varuṇa, god of the seas and rivers.

Chapter 29 is the first of five chapters, 29 through 33, which later tradition refers to as the *rāsa-līlā* (the play of *rāsa*), in which Śuka narrates a drama of love between Krishna and the young cowherdesses (*gopīs*) in the Vrindavan forest. This five-chapter episode constitutes what many readers consider *the* central passage of the Bhāgavata Purāṇa; it has been considered as such by later Vaiṣṇava traditions, and it has been the most celebrated portion of the text in performative and fine arts and in Indian vernacular poetry and song (see Schweig, chapter 7, and Beck, chapter 10, in Gupta and Valpey 2013). It has also received attention by the largest number of Sanskrit commentators from medieval times to the present. They all affirm that the *rāsa-līlā* demonstrates the transcendent, selfless love between the Lord and his devotees, devoid of any worldly lust. We include here this drama's opening scene, as well as a short passage from the concluding chapter, in which Krishna and the *gopīs* joyously perform a grand circle dance (*rāsa*) while observed from above by gods and goddesses.

KRISHNA CALLS THE *GOPĪS*

Chapter 29

Śuka, the son of Bādarāyaṇa, said: Seeing those autumn nights, filled with blooming jasmine flowers, even the glorious Lord turned to thoughts of love, resorting to his illusive power of yoga. (29.1)[60] Then the comforting rays of the moon, king of stars, anointed the eastern horizon with a reddish hue, even as a dear husband—returning after a long absence—applies saffron upon his beloved wife's face with his comforting hands. The rising moon relieved the sorrows of all who saw him. (2)[61] The full moon appeared beautiful like the face of Ramā (Lakṣmī) freshly anointed with saffron. The gentle moonlight illuminated the forest and brought the white lotuses to bloom. Seeing all this, Krishna played (his flute) sweetly, captivating the hearts of the lovely-eyed *gopīs*. (3) Krishna had stolen the hearts of Vraja's women, and so when they heard his passion-igniting song, they hastened to where their beloved waited, their earrings swaying. Each *gopī* was unaware of the others' coming. (4) In their eagerness, some *gopīs* left while milking the cows, leaving their milk pails behind. Some had milk on the stove, while others left cakes in the oven. (5)[62] Some stopped serving food, feeding their children milk, or attending to their husbands, and some left in the middle of their meal. (6) Some *gopīs* were applying cosmetics, cleansing themselves, or applying kohl to their eyes. With their clothes and jewelry in disarray, they ran to be close to Krishna. (7) Their husbands, parents, brothers, and other relatives forbade them from going, but the spellbound *gopīs* did not turn back, for their hearts had been stolen by Govinda. (8)[63] Some *gopīs* could not leave, and so they remained at home, meditating on Krishna with their eyes closed, absorbed in love for him. (9)[64] The intense pain of separation from their beloved was unbearable, and that pain burned away all inauspiciousness. Through their meditation, the *gopīs* experienced Krishna's embrace, and the joy of that embrace made all auspicious things worthless. (10)[65] Krishna alone is the supreme self, and yet the *gopīs* regarded him as their paramour. Their attachment to him destroyed their worldly bondage at once and they relinquished their bodies made of the *guṇas*. (11)[66]

In a brief interlude to the story, Śuka assures Parīkṣit that the *gopīs*' attraction toward Krishna is entirely spiritual and not mundane, by virtue of the fact that it is Krishna, the all-pure Bhagavān, to whom they are attracted. Upon the arrival of the *gopīs* before him, Krishna initially welcomes them and then coyly urges them, as respectable young women, to respect the strictures of dharma by returning immediately to their homes and families. But upon listening to the *gopīs*' persuasive protests of faithful devotion to him as the best form of dharma, Krishna graciously reciprocates their love, dallying with them on the white sands of the Yamunā riverbank.

After a short time, however, perceiving an upsurge of pride in the *gopīs*, Krishna suddenly disappears from their midst, with the dual aim (as he later explains) of humbling them and increasing their longing for him. In their acute feeling of anxiety and longing because of his absence, the *gopīs* then take to imitating and even identifying themselves as Krishna, and they undertake a concerted and maddened search for Krishna in the forest, inquiring from trees and animals as to his whereabouts. Eventually, seeing footprints and reading their significance, the *gopīs* detect that Krishna has indeed been present there, together with "a certain *gopī*" (identified by later tradition as Krishna's principal consort, Rādhā) whom he has also subsequently abandoned, having registered her pride at receiving Krishna's special attention. Soon finding the lone, abandoned *gopī*, the other *gopīs* commiserate with her, and then they all return together to the Yamunā riverbank, where they ardently sing Krishna's praises (chapter 30).

Chapter 31 consists of what might be called a choral monologue, in which the *gopīs*, as a group, address the absent Krishna. In these nineteen verses, they celebrate Krishna's beauty, his power, and his auspicious presence in Vrindavan, and they request him to bless them with his presence in intimate contact. They also express anxiety for Krishna's well-being, especially regarding the danger of his delicate bare feet being harmed as he traverses the Vraja countryside herding his father's cows. In their eagerness to gaze constantly on Krishna's beautiful form whenever he is visible to them, the *gopīs* chide the cosmic creator, Brahmā, for having contrived the blinking of eyelids, by which their viewing of Krishna becomes momentarily interrupted.

In the next chapter, Krishna reappears before the *gopīs*, each of whom react in varied ways to express their overwhelming love for him. United in their joy at being again with their beloved, the *gopīs* surround Krishna and, despite their happiness, challenge him to explain his absence. Krishna responds with a short discourse on different types of friends and lovers. He concludes that his own love for the *gopīs*, unconditional as it is, had impelled him to disappear from their midst, knowing that their love for him would thereby become further intensified by experiencing his absence. But then Krishna confesses that the *gopīs*' love for him is so perfect—demonstrated by their having given up all ordinary social considerations—that he is unable to fully reciprocate with them; rather, he requests them to regard their pure devotion as its own reward. With Krishna's speech concluded, all are ready to commence the great *rāsa* dance.

THE *RĀSA* DANCE

Chapter 33

Śrī Śuka said: Thus, having heard Bhagavān's delightful words, the *gopīs* gave up sorrow born of separation, their longing fulfilled by the touch of his limbs. (33.1)[67] There and then Govinda began the *rāsa* dance surrounded by those beloved, faithful jewels of women interlocking their arms with one another. (2)[68] The *rāsa* festival commenced, graced by the circle of *gopīs*, with the master of yoga, Krishna, positioned between each two of them. Embraced by him around their necks, each girl was thinking he is with her alone. (3)[69] At that time the sky was filled with hundreds of celestial airships of the gods and their wives, their minds caught up with excitement (to witness the dance). (4) Then kettledrums resounded, showers of flowers descended, and the chief Gandharvas with their wives sang Krishna's flawless glory. (5)[70] In the *rāsa*-dance circle with their beloved, the girls' armlets, ankle bells, and waist bells sounded tumultuously. (6) Bhagavān, Devakī's son, shone brilliantly among the *gopīs* like a fine emerald amid golden ornaments. (7)[71] As Krishna's consorts sang his praises, by their dancing steps, gesturing hands, sportive eyebrows and smiles, swaying waists, tightened braids and belts, shifting blouses, ear ornaments swinging against their cheeks, and faces perspiring, they shone like streaks of lightning amid a circle of clouds. (8)[72] The world was suffused with their resounding melodic voices as they sang and danced, rapt in amorous pleasure, thrilled by Krishna's touch. (9) One prominent *gopī* sang in a free and unaccompanied way, along with Mukunda (Krishna), who, pleased with her, said, "Excellent, excellent!" (Another *gopī*), to whom Krishna showed great regard, sounded a *dhruvam* (a melody set to a fixed metric pattern) to the same song. (10)[73]

As this final chapter of the Five Chapters of Rāsa concludes, Śuka compares Krishna to a child playing with its own reflection, fully satisfied with himself (*ātmārāma*) as he expands himself into as many forms of himself as there are *gopīs* with whom he dances. Concluding the dance, Krishna leads the *gopīs* into the Yamunā River, where together they all frolic, splashing one another and laughing; finally, they all wander for some time together in the midnight forest.

At this point, Parīkṣit voices concern: how can Krishna, who appears in the world to reestablish the principles of dharma, so flagrantly violate those same principles by dancing with other men's wives? Śuka replies by reminding Parīkṣit of Krishna's transcendent position, beyond considerations of piety and impiety. Similarly, he argues, Krishna's associates—such as the *gopīs*—are beyond such considerations because of the purity of their devotion to their Lord (implying, according to the commentator Viśvanātha, that it is only reflections of the *gopīs*—*māyā*-fabricated facsimiles—that consort with their apparent husbands). Moreover, Krishna is present within all beings (including the *gopīs*' husbands) as the supreme self, and so he acts in such a way as to attract all beings to himself. Indeed, Śuka concludes, by hearing about this particular *līlā* of the *rāsa* dance, one can become freed from all sensual desire and gain perfect bhakti, devotion for Krishna.

Sometime later Krishna again meets the *gopīs*, when he kills Śaṅkhacūḍa as the demon attempts to pursue the young women. The same *gopīs* are then presented singing together in praise of their beloved Krishna as he wanders with his friends and cows during the daytime (chapter 35). And in the course of Krishna's wanderings he encounters and sportingly slays three more attackers sent by Kaṁsa—Ariṣṭa, the bull-demon, Keśi, the horse-demon, and Vyoma, the air-demon.

Chapters 38 through 44 mark an important turn in Krishna's life as he and his brother Balarāma, now blossoming youths, are summoned to Mathurā for a public wrestling match by King Kaṁsa, with the aim of having the boys killed. Instead, they both easily kill their (much larger) wrestler opponents, and then Krishna renders Kaṁsa lifeless, using his bare fists. The two brothers remain away from Vrindavan, taking up formal studies under their preceptor, Sāndīpani, having first seen to the reinstatement of their maternal grandfather, Ugrasena, on the throne of Mathurā. Sometime thereafter, being greatly concerned for the Vrindavan residents' suffering the pangs of his long absence, Krishna sends his cousin Uddhava to Vrindavan with a message of consolation (chapter 46).

The following brief passage, spoken by one of the *gopīs* who have gathered around Uddhava to hear his message, consists of her distracted expressions of love in separation from Krishna. Her words are addressed to a bee that hovers about her, which she takes to be Krishna's messenger.

SINGING TO A BEE

Chapter 47

The *gopī* said: Nectar-drinking honeybee, friend of a cheater! Do not touch my feet with your hair, which is colored by saffron from (Krishna's) garland after it was crushed by the breasts of another lover. Let the honey-sweet Lord show favor to the women (of Mathurā), who think highly of him! One who has a messenger like you will be ridiculed in the Yadu assembly. (47.12)[74] After allowing us to drink the nectar of his lips just once, Krishna abandoned us like you, sir, abandon flowers. Why then does Padmā (Lakṣmī) serve his lotus feet? Oh, no doubt she, too, must have had her heart stolen by Uttamaśloka's (Krishna's) deceitful words. (13) Six-legged bee, why do you sing so much about the Lord of the Yadus in front of us homeless women? You should sing of these bygone affairs in front of the (new) girlfriends of Arjuna's friend! He has relieved the pain (of desire) in the breasts of his beloveds, and so they will give what (gifts) you desire. (14) In heaven, on earth, or in lower worlds, what women are unavailable to him? He makes them all his own, with his deceitful, charming smile and arched eyebrows. Even the Goddess of Fortune, Lakṣmī, worships the dust of his feet. Who are we (in comparison)? He is called Uttamaśloka because he is partial to the unfortunate (yet we remain unfortunate). (15) Do not place your head on my feet! I know you are skilled in the art of conciliation and you have come with flattering words sent by Mukunda (Krishna). We abandoned our husbands, children, and all others in this world for his sake, but he ungratefully abandoned us. Why then should we make up with him? (16) (In an earlier *avatāra* as Rāma:) Abandoning the (warrior's) code of ethics, he shot Vāli, king of the monkeys, like a hunter (hiding in the trees). And he was so henpecked that he disfigured a woman (Śūrpaṇakhā) who desired him. (In another *avatāra* as Vāmana,) he tied up King Bali like a crow, even after he consumed the king's offerings. Enough of friendship with dark-hued Krishna! And yet it is difficult to give up the need to speak about him. (17) Krishna's playful deeds are like nectar for the ears, and those who have tasted even a drop of that nectar abandon proper worldly behavior. Many such wretched, ruined persons have promptly relinquished their pitiable homes and families, and like birds they pursue the life of beggars here. (18) We believed his deceptive speech as if it were true, just as foolish does, wives of the antelope, fall for the hunter's song. We fell for this many times, for we were afflicted by the sharp pangs of love because of the touch of his nails. O messenger, please talk about something else! (19)[75] Friend of our beloved, you have returned! Were you sent by our dearest? What would you like? Please say! I should honor you, my friend. Now, gentle sir, how can you take us back to him whose intimacy is so difficult to give up when his consort Śrī forever stays with him, upon his chest? (20) Does Krishna, son of the noble Nanda, now live in Mathurā? Indeed, does he remember his father's houses, his family, or his cowherd friends? Gentle sir! Does he ever speak about us, his maidservants? Oh, when will he place his agar-wood-scented hand upon our heads? (21)[76]

Uddhava, who had listened to the *gopī*'s song to the bee, then expresses his admiration for all the *gopīs*' intense love for Krishna. He then delivers Krishna's message to them, to the effect that actually he is constantly with them and that his purpose in remaining apparently distant from them is to heighten their longing for him. Uddhava remains in Vraja for several months, consoling the residents while speaking about Krishna. By the time he leaves to report back to Krishna, his regard for the people of Vraja has become boundless, seeing them as most glorious because of the boundless character of their love for Krishna.

Book Ten continues with another forty-three chapters, describing Krishna's continuing adventures in Mathurā, Dvārakā, and other locations. As powerful demons and their armies continue to plague the land, Krishna (henceforth generally referred to as Vāsudeva, the son of Vasudeva) pursues the fulfillment of his purpose in descending to the world, as he had promised the gods prior to his appearance: Kaṁsa's father-in-law, Jarāsandha (chapter 72); Kālayavana (chapter 51); the earth goddess's son Naraka (chapter 59); Krishna's envious cousin Śiśupāla (chapter 74); Śālva (chapter 77); Dantavakra (chapter 78); and others, along with their armies, are battled and killed either by Krishna, Balarāma, or (in the case of Jarāsandha), by the Pāṇḍava brother Bhīma.

In the course of ongoing clashes with Jarāsandha and his armies, Krishna arranges, with the help of the celestial architect Viśvakarma, an island fortress surrounding a grand city, Dvārakā (chapter 50). Here, by mystic yoga, Krishna transfers his entire clan, the Yadus, from Mathurā and settles down to enjoy life as a prince. In the course of his exploits with his enemies, he wins many wives, among whom Rukminī and Satyabhāmā are the chief (chapters 54, 58). Also, by wondrously multiplying himself into sixteen thousand identical forms, Krishna marries an entire group of sixteen thousand maidens who had been abducted by the demon Naraka (chapter 59). He duly provides each of his wives with separate palaces in Dvārakā and fathers with each of them ten sons. The sage Nārada visits each of Krishna's palaces to witness how he and his wives happily carry on daily routines as perfect, pious householders (chapters 70, 90).

Beginning with chapter 71, several chapters describe interactions between Krishna and the Pāṇḍavas, referring to events that lead to the devastating fratricidal war between the Pāṇḍavas and their cousins the Kauravas. This account, highly abridged and "retold" from the Mahābhārata, focuses on the Rājasūya rite conducted by the Pāṇḍava eldest brother, Yudhiṣṭhira, culminating in Krishna's slaying of his antagonist, Śiśupāla (chapter 74), one of the two Vaikuṇṭha doorkeepers who had been cursed to descend to the mortal world as demons for three lifetimes (see Book Three, chapter 15, "Four Sages Curse the Gatekeepers of Heaven"). Significantly, a key episode in the Mahābhārata leading eventually to the war—namely, the gambling match between Duryodhana and Yudhiṣṭhira—is bypassed, presumably because Krishna was not present at that occasion. Instead, during that time he was fighting against Śālva, Śiśupāla's friend. Also noteworthy is the absence of any reference in Book Ten to Krishna's participation in the Mahābhārata war as Arjuna's charioteer and adviser. Rather, there is (in chapter 79) an account of Balarāma's long pilgrimage tour that (according to the Mahābhārata) he undertook to avoid participating in the war, since he had friends on both sides of the dispute.

After the description of a warmhearted exchange in Dvārakā between Krishna and his old schoolmate the *brāhmaṇa* Sudāmā (chapters 80–81), the final nine chapters include an intriguing account (in chapters 82–85) of a reunion of Krishna and Balarāma with the Vrindavan residents that takes place during a solar eclipse at Samanta-panchaka (in Kurukṣetra, where the Mahābhārata war would be fought). There Krishna meets Nanda, Yaśodā, and the *gopīs*, assuring the latter of their good fortune by virtue of their constant remembrance of him. Others—members of the Kaurava clan—are also mentioned as being present, suggesting that this event would have had to take place prior to the Kurukṣetra battle, in which those warriors would be killed.

A further highlight of Book Ten's closing chapters is the Prayers by the Vedas (*veda-stuti*) in chapter 87, wherein Śuka responds to Parīkṣit's question (v. 1) "How do the Vedas, the scope of which are the (world-bound) *guṇas*, approach directly to the indescribable *brahman*, which is beyond both being and nonbeing?" Śuka relates how the same question had been put by the sage Nārada to Nārāyaṇa Ṛṣi, who, in turn, recalls the same question having previously arisen among sages in the celestial realm Janaloka, to whom one of the sages, Sanandana, replied by quoting a series of twenty-eight prayers sung by the Śrutis—the Vedas—as they awakened Vishnu from his cosmic slumber to begin creation anew.

Although space constraints prevent us from including a translation of this wonderful series of prayers, we can still touch on a few of its features. First, we can keep in mind that the prayers serve as a response to Parīkṣit's question, broadly, of whether it is at all possible for human language—even the sacred, "revealed" language of the Vedas—to describe the transcendent reality that is designated by the term *brahman*. Taken in this context, it is significant that the Vedas (in "personified" form) are offering prayers to Vishnu as that transcendent reality. By this action they affirm that *brahman* is a sentient, willful being—the supreme person, elsewhere referred to as Bhagavān. Therefore the question becomes whether, or how, the Vedas can lead one to that supreme being. Collectively, these stanzas serve as a densely arranged summary of the entire Bhāgavata's devotional theology; they also serve as a commentary on the Vedas, particularly the Upaniṣads. As had been argued in Book Two, in the "Four-Verse Bhāgavata" (vv. 2.9.33–36), the supreme being, while existing independently of the world, is simultaneously intimately connected to it and is, indeed, in a sense, nondifferent from the world. The personified Vedas humbly admit (in v. 14) that "sometimes" (*kvacit*)—not always—they can "approach" (*anucaret*) the supreme being, the Lord, "who acts on his own and with his illusive power." However, because the Vedic seers (*ṛṣis*) understand that "the Great" (*bṛhat*, indicating *brahman*, the supreme reality) is the basis of all existence, they cannot help but direct their minds, words, and actions toward that supreme (v. 15). Moreover, the personified Vedas are optimistic: they anticipate relishing the "nectar of the lotuslike feet" of the Lord because of being regarded by him in the same way as he regards his consorts and beloveds (v. 23).

Ordinary persons can surely not know the supreme, who exists before creation (v. 24). But being themselves grounded in knowledge of the supreme *brahman*, the *ṛṣis* provide a variety of methods for progressing to that ultimate reality, depending on the qualifications of various aspirants (v. 18). Indeed, some persons whose minds have been mesmerized by the Vedic incantations become bewildered, not understanding that all Vedic sacrifices are meant to please the Lord; thus they become bound "like animals" (*paśūn iva*) by their own folly (vv. 20, 27, 36). However, if one accepts guidance from a guru who is a proper descendant of Vedic tradition and who comprehends the Vedas' purport, one can learn to direct the mind to be constantly attentive to the Lord's glories (vv. 33, 40) and can thus reject all the various materialist theories of the self's identity (v. 25). Such persons will also understand that although this world is unreal, it is not to be rejected, for, just as gold objects possess the full value of the gold metal they contain, this world has value as the Lord's creation, into which he has entered (v. 26). The Vedas conclude their prayers joyfully, proclaiming that the Lord's glories, being unlimited, cannot be fully described by anyone, not even by the Lord himself. The Vedas' success, they feel assured, is in their ability to reveal the Lord's glory to be their final conclusion, arrived at by their method of eliminating as unworthy of ultimate regard everything that is separate from the supreme being.

SUGGESTIONS FOR FURTHER READING

Bryant, Edwin F. 2004. *Krishna: The Beautiful Legend of God.* London: Penguin.
A complete translation of Krishna's biography as told in the ninth, tenth, and eleventh books of the Bhāgavata Purāṇa.

Haberman, David L. 1994. *Journey Through the Twelve Forests of Vrindavan.* Oxford: Oxford University Press.
Chapter 3, "Hungry Mountains and Ponds of Love," has a lively account of present-day pilgrimage around Mount Govardhana, relevant to chapters 24 and 25.

Hawley, John Stratton. 1983. *Krishna, the Butter Thief.* Princeton: Princeton University Press.
This monograph on the theme of Krishna's butter-stealing acts, relevant to chapter 9, focuses particularly on the sixteenth-century saint-poet Surdas's lyrical meditations on this subject.

Mason, David. 2009. *Theatre and Religion on Krishna's Stage: Performing in Vrindavan.* New York: Palgrave Macmillan.
Chapter 3 refers to the butter-stealing *līlā* (chapter 9), provides a good overview of Krishna's life, and situates his acts in the context of performance. Mason explores the notion of *līlā* as divine freedom from social norms.

O'Flaherty, Wendy Doniger. 1984. *Dreams, Illusion, and other Realities.* Chicago: University of Chicago Press.
Chapter 3, "Inside the Mouth of God," explores the event described in chapter 8 in relation to wider Indic literary expressions of extraordinary visions.

Schweig, Graham M. 2005. *Dance of Divine Love: India's Classic Sacred Love Story; The Rāsa Līlā of Krishna.* Princeton: Princeton University Press.
A full translation of the celebrated *rāsa-līlā*, chapters 29–33 in Book Ten, as well as

the "Song of the Flute" (Veṇu-gīta), chapter 21, and the "Song of the Black Bee" (Bhramara-gīta), chapter 47. Schweig's beautiful verse translation is accompanied by an accessible introduction, theological analysis, and notes from Sanskrit commentaries.

—. 2013. "The Rāsa Līlā of Krishna and the Gopīs: On the Bhāgavata's Vision of Boundless Love." In *The Bhagavata Purāṇa: Sacred Text and Living Tradition*, edited by Ravi M. Gupta and Kenneth R. Valpey, 117–41. New York: Columbia University Press.

This chapter provides an overview of the *rāsa-līlā* and an analysis of its ethical implications, reflecting on the Bhāgavata's portrayal of divine love's dramatic qualities.

Vaudeville, Charlotte. 1980. "The Govardhan Myth in North India." *Indo-Iranian Journal* 22:1–45.

This article, relevant to chapters 24 and 25, traces various accounts of the Govardhana story in sources other than the Purāṇas.

BOOK ELEVEN

Lessons from the World
The Formal Worship of Vishnu

Already in Book One, as a retrospection, the news of Krishna's departure from the temporal world had been reported (in chapter 14). Now, after Krishna's life has been extensively narrated in Book Ten, Book Eleven concludes that account, its final two chapters (30–31) describing first the self-annihilation of the Yadu clan (Krishna's direct relatives) in a drunken brawl, followed by Krishna's apparent death on the pretext of an accidentally shot arrow from a hunter.

The book opens with the story of how, in accord with Krishna's secret plan, the Yadu clan had been cursed by sages, whom young Yadu princes had attempted to embarrass by a ruse. Sāmba, dressed as a woman and made to appear pregnant, came with his friends before the sages to ask whether she (he) would give birth to a girl or a boy. Understanding their impudent intentions, the sages angrily declared, "Fools, she will bear a club that will be the destruction of the clan!" After a narrative interlude (four chapters) in which Nārada instructs Krishna's father, Vasudeva, on a wide variety of topics centered around the effective practice of bhakti, the story resumes briefly (in chapter 6), setting the stage for the Yadus' destruction by their leaving Dvārakā for Prabhāsa-kṣetra, a nearby beach resort where they would eventually take to heavy drinking and lose all self-restraint. Just as Krishna intends, the enraged Yadus annihilate themselves in a drunken melee.

Meanwhile, Krishna's cousin and close friend, Uddhava, sensing what was about to happen and that Krishna would also be departing the world, approaches Krishna and humbly appeals to him for final instructions on ultimate truth. Krishna obliges with an extensive discourse (covering 22 chapters) that has come to be known in later tradition as the "Uddhava Gītā." Krishna draws his initial lesson from a recollected conversation between the Yadu clan's patriarch, King Yadu, and a certain *avadhūta* ascetic. The latter relates how he had learned valuable lessons for self-cultivation from twenty-four "gurus." Among a variety of teachers that include natural phenomena and animals, one teacher is a certain prostitute, Piṅgalā, whose story and example of worldly detachment is featured in the next reading.

LESSONS FROM THE WORLD

Chapter 8

The glorious *brāhmaṇa* said: O king, as the senses give pleasure in heaven, so also they cause suffering in hell. Therefore, one who discerns this should not wish (for sense satisfaction). (8.1)[1] Like the passive python, one should eat only food obtained gratuitously, whether it be fine or flavorless, or whether it be plentiful or meager. (2)[2] If food is not forthcoming for several days, (nonetheless), fasting and unassertive, one should be quiescent like the python, taking only what providence has given. (3)[3] Even though weakened, reclining and awake, one should not exert oneself, sustaining the body's sensory, mental, and physical strength without goal-oriented action. (4)[4] Like the sea's calm water, the unperturbable sage's placid gravity is verily unlimited, unfathomable, and unsurpassable. (5)[5] Like the sea, into which rivers' waters flow or do not flow, a sage devoted to Nārāyaṇa need not swell (with elation) or shrink (with despair), whether he is fulfilled or failing in his needs. (6)[6] Like a moth (flying) into fire, one with unbridled senses, allured by the sight of God's *māyā* appearing as a seductive woman, falls into murky blindness. (7)[7] As a moth is to be consumed (in the fire), a fool's better judgment is spoiled by the desire to enjoy, driving him to be seduced by the contrivances of *māyā*—a woman with her golden ornaments, dress, and so on. (8)[8] Like a honeybee's occupation (drawing nectar from flowers), a sage's practice should be to meekly approach householders, accepting what little food sustains his body. (9)[9]

The chapter continues with further lessons for the ascetic sage to be learned from nature. Continuing with the honeybee (which, like the moth, is attracted to enjoy—in this case through smell), one learns not to imitate them in their habit of collecting and storing food. Nor should one make the mistake of acting like the male elephant, which, to feel the pleasure of touching a female elephant's body, subjects itself to the murderous wrath of other male elephants. Further, the ascetic sage is warned not to fall victim to sensual music, as the deer is attracted to the hunter's whistle; nor should he make the mistake of the fish that is caught by a hook through its attraction for tasting. Indeed, the *avadhūta brāhmaṇa* declares, if a sage can learn to tolerate the demands of his tongue, he will have thereby prevailed over the demands of all his other sense organs. The chapter concludes with the lesson learned from the prostitute named Piṅgalā.

O prince (Yadu), there was once a prostitute named Piṅgalā who lived in a town in Videha. Learn what I learned from her. (22)[10] One evening, that unchaste woman stood outside her door seeking to lure a customer into her bedroom by displaying her fine shapeliness. (23) My good man! Viewing men coming along the way, that woman, wanting money, scanned (potential) moneyed customers who would be able to pay her price. (24)[11] While those men passed by Piṅgalā, whose livelihood depended on her bedroom (she thought), ". . . Maybe this is another man of means! . . . Is there any generous fellow who will approach me?" (25) Thus with vain hope, sleeplessly anxious, she would go in and out of the doorway as midnight arrived. (26) Dispirited, her countenance withered by her want of money, her anxious brooding precipitated an awakening to utterly joyful detachment. (27) Like a sword, detachment (cuts) the bonds of vain expectation. Now hear from me Piṅgalā's song of remorse. (28)[12] Dear king, as a human being who lacks wisdom lacks the willingness to abandon possessiveness, so one in whom detachment is not engendered is unwilling to give up the bondage that is the body. (29)[13]

Piṅgalā said: "Alas, just see the extent of my folly! Lacking all self-control, like an idiot, I long for a lover! (30) Foolish me! While rejecting him who is closest, dearest, most pleasing, munificent, and eternal, I instead pursue a good-for-nothing who gives no pleasure, who only inflicts misery, fear, anxiety, and delusion. (31) It's so! Vainly subjecting myself to abuse by doing this nasty whoring business, I, keen for cash, have been itching for profit from sex, hiring my body out to a wretched womanizer. (32) What other woman than I dedicates herself to this house (body) of nine leaking portals, full of urine and excrement, which is made with bones—spine ribs and femur—wrapped with skin, hair, and nails? (33)[14]

Most surely I am the only dimwit in this town of Videha, an unchaste woman who desires something other than Acyuta (Vishnu), the self-giver. (34)[15] This Lord is the most dear friend and the very self of embodied beings. Purchasing him by (offering) myself, I will surely enjoy with him as does Ramā (Lakṣmī). (35)[16] Sense objects, pleasure-giving men, and even the gods have beginnings and ends, sundered by time. How much pleasure can women get from these? (36)

Surely by some (previous) act of mine Bhagavān Vishnu has been pleased, for this joyful detachment has arisen in me, despite my vain hopes. (37) Thus it cannot be the case that I am an unfortunate woman, for, impelled by my troubles, I have become detached; by such (detachment) a person gains freedom from passion, eliminating bondage. (38)[17] Renouncing vain hope for sensual encounters, I take refuge in the supreme Lord, welcoming his care with bowed head. (39) I am (now) completely satisfied, living by whatever comes to me, having faith in the Lord's care. I shall enjoy life with only him, the truly delightful (supreme) self. (40) Who else but the supreme Lord can deliver one who has been seized by the serpent of time, fallen in the well of repeated death, his vision blinded by sensuality? (41) One is surely one's own protector when one becomes weary of everything and soberly sees that this world is swallowed by the snake of time." (42)[18]

The glorious *brāhmaṇa* said: Her mind thus resolved, cutting off vain hopes born of hankering for lovers, Piṅgalā settled peacefully in her bed. (43) In this way Piṅgalā completely broke off her longing for lovers and happily slept. Longing is surely the greatest misery; absence of longing brings the greatest joy. (44)

The remaining teachers for the ascetic include further members of the animal kingdom—an osprey, a snake, a spider, and a wasp—and three humans—a lazy child, a young girl, and an arrow maker (the latter demonstrating perfect concentration, having been so absorbed in his arrowmaking task that he failed to notice the royal procession passing his workshop). Finally, the ascetic had drawn a lesson from his own mortal body about the urgency to employ it for the pursuit of one's ultimate good.

The next several chapters continue with Krishna's teachings to Uddhava, providing a concentrated review and loosely structured elaboration on the Bhāgavata's approach to a variety of subjects, including the nature of the human condition, the practice of yoga and a comparison of *karma-jñāna-* and bhakti yoga approaches to enlightenment, a recollection by Krishna that he had previously similarly taught these subjects to Arjuna (the Bhagavad Gītā), principles of social order (*varṇāśrama-dharma*), and an overview of the Sāṁkhya system of cosmic structure. Just prior to the next reading selection, Krishna recites a song that had once been sung by King Purūravā (whose story is told in Book Nine, chapter 14), in order to underscore a lesson on bad association: by keeping the company of hedonists, one descends into the utter darkness experienced by one who is blind.

To avoid the pitfalls of worldly life and bad association, Krishna recommends the devotional practices known collectively as *arcana*—ritual worship of the supreme Lord as present in a sacred image or other appropriate sacred object. He summarizes this process in the next reading.

THE FORMAL WORSHIP OF VISHNU

Chapter 27

Glorious Bhagavān said: O Uddhava, there is hardly any limit to the vast ritual portion (of the Veda), so I will provide a fitting and sequential summary. (27.6) There are three sorts of my ritual worship—Vedic, Tantric, and mixed. Of these three, one may surely worship me with one's preferred sort. (7)[19] Hear from me with faith how, when a person gains twice-born status as enjoined in one's own Vedic school, one may worship me with devotion. (8)[20] In an image, on the ground, or in fire; in the sun, in water, or in one's own heart, the twice-born, imbued with devotion, may forthrightly worship me—one's own guru—with physical objects and substances. (9) To purify the body, one should first cleanse the teeth and perform ritual bathing. A second ritual bath is then done by smearing the body with clay and so forth while chanting both (Vedic and Tantric) mantras. (10)[21] With thorough resolve, one should arrange worship of me by ritual acts such as daily prayer during the sidereal junctures. These practices, enjoined in the Vedas, purify one from reactions to (selfish) acts. (11)[22]

It is declared that there are eight types (of sacred images appropriate for worship)—namely, those formed of stone, of wood, of metal, of clay, of sand, of jewels, as a painting, and in the mind. (12) Uddhava! The sacred image, abode of all beings, is consecrated in two ways—as movable or as immovable. (The ritual processes of daily or occasionally) invoking and sending away are not to be done in the worship of an immovable image.

(13) But these two rituals are to be done in the case of an image formed on the ground and could optionally be done for temporary images. An image not made of clay can receive ritual bathing; for other types there should be thorough cleansing (without water). (14)[23] The ritual worship of me in images and so on is done with prescribed items; yet for the desireless devotee, (ritual worship is done) with whatever items can be readily obtained, as well as by mentally fashioned offerings. (15)[24] O Uddhava, for worship of an image, ritual bathing and ornamentation are most pleasing; for an image inscribed on the ground, *tattva-vinyāsa* (ritual invocations with mantras) is most pleasing; for worship in sacred fire, oblations of food grains soaked in ghee is most pleasing. (16)[25] Offerings (such as *arghya* and flowers) are preferred in worship of the sun; worship in water is best performed with water oblations accompanied with mantras. Even a little water presented with faith by my devotee is most pleasing, (17)[26] whereas abundantly offered (items) of a nondevotee do not bring me satisfaction, much less (a nondevotee's offering of) scents, incense, flowers, lamps, and edibles. (18)

Having purified oneself and assembled items (for worship), and having arranged one's seat with *darbha* grass, the tips of which point eastward, one should sit facing east or north, or facing the image (to be worshipped). (19)[27] After performing invocations with mantras on oneself and on my image, one should use one's hands to clean the image (by removing previously offered materials, such as flowers). A vessel (into which the deity has been invoked) and a pot of water for sprinkling should be properly prepared. (20)[28] With the water from the sprinkling vessel one should sprinkle the area where the image is situated, the items for worship, and oneself. One then arranges three water vessels with the appropriate (additional) substances for each. (21) The adept should consecrate the three vessels—(containing water) for foot bathing, for *arghya*, and for refreshing the mouth—with the heart, head, and hair-tuft mantras, respectively, followed by the Gāyatrī mantra. (22)[29] When the gross body has been purified by air and fire, one should meditate on my supreme, subtle presence on the lotus of the heart—the Lord of all beings who is apprehended by perfected beings in the reverberation that concludes the syllable *oṁ*. (23)[30] Having honored (me) as manifest like oneself, pervading one's body, and, having invoked and established (this form) in a sacred object such as a sacred image, one should worship me, having first consecrated my limbs with mantras. (24)[31] To gain success in both (pleasure and liberation) one should mentally arrange my eight-petaled lotus seat—its whorl radiant with saffron filaments—with (personified) *dharma* and so on and with the nine (divine powers). Then, following both Vedic and Tantric injunctions, one should make offerings such as foot-washing water, water for refreshing the mouth, and *arghya*. (25–26)[32] (Next), one is to venerate, in sequence, Vishnu's Sudarśana (disk weapon), Pāñcajanya (conch shell), club, sword, arrows, bow, plow, and *muṣala* (mace), as well as his Kaustubha gem, Śrīvatsa emblem, and flower garland. (27) (Also to be venerated are Vishnu's associates)—Nanda, Sunanda, Garuḍa, Caṇḍa and Pracaṇḍa, Bala, Mahābala, Kumuda, and Kumudekṣaṇa. (28)[33] With ritual sprinkling (*prokṣaṇa*) and the like, one venerates Durgā, Vināyaka, Vyāsa, Viṣvaksena, the gurus, and gods—in their respective positions facing (the image of Vishnu). (29)[34] Then, assets permitting, one bathes (the image of Vishnu) daily, using waters scented with sandalwood paste, khuskhus, camphor, vermilion, and aloewood, while chanting mantras such as the Svarṇa-gharma, the Mahāpuruṣa Vidyā, the Puruṣa Sūkta, and Sāma Veda hymns such as the Rājana and the Rohiṇya. (30–31)[35]

Next, following injunctions, my loving devotee may decorate me with garments, a sacred thread (*upavīta*), ornaments, painted designs, garlands, and unguents. (32)[36] The worshipper may then offer me water for washing the feet, water for refreshing the mouth, fragrant oil, flowers, unbroken grains, and other items such as incense and lamps. (33) If possible, one then arranges food offerings (such as) molasses, *pāyasa* (sweetened rice boiled in milk), ghee, fried cakes, biscuits, sweets, *saṁyāva* cakes, yogurt, and soups. (34) On days of lunar transition, or else daily, there can be oil massage, a mirror, cleansing of the teeth, bathing, chewable and soft foods, singing, and dancing. (35)[37] One may then build up a blazing fire, having installed it in a ritual fireplace constructed according to prescription, with surrounding steps, fire pit, and raised ritual ground. (36) According to the rules, (around the fireplace) one scatters (*kuśa* grass) and sprinkles (water); placing fuel on the fire, arranging the items for offering (in the fire), sprinkling the items with water for this purpose, one should then invoke me within the fire. (37)[38] The adept may then meditate on my serene form as having the hue of molten gold, with four arms, bearing conch, disk, club, and lotus flower, and wearing brilliant garments the color of lotus filaments. I bear a glittering helmet, bracelets, belt, and precious armbands; and the Śrīvatsa emblem, shining Kaustubha gem, and forest-flower garland adorn my chest. While thus meditating, one proceeds to offer worship: throwing ghee-soaked wood (into the fire), one then sprinkles the fire with two portions of ghee and offers ghee-soaked oblations to sixteen divinities, beginning with Dharma (Yama), accompanied with the appropriate *mūla-mantra* and appropriate verse from the sixteen-verse Puruṣa Sūkta, followed by "*sviṣṭi-kṛte svāhā.*" (38–41)[39]

Having thus worshipped, one then makes obeisance to the Lord's associates and renders them offerings. He then softly chants the root mantra, remembering *brahman* to be Nārāyaṇa himself. (42) Having offered water for refreshing the mouth, one then places the remnants (of the Lord's food offering) before Viṣvaksena. Then one may present (to me) a fragrant mouth freshener and a betel-nut preparation. (43) One may (then) be my entertainer for a while—singing, reciting praises, dancing, acting out my activities, and hearing or narrating about me. (44) Eulogizing (me) with formal and informal hymns and prayers—from the Purāṇas and even from folk traditions—one may then pray, "O Bhagavān, be pleased (with me)!" while lying prone in obeisance. (45) One's head placed at my feet, with hands together (one may pray), "O Lord, please protect me, a supplicant. I am terrified by this ocean wherein lurks the crocodile that is death." (46) Thus praying, respectfully placing on one's head the remnants I have given, if (the image is) to be dismissed, one may now dismiss it, its light again placed within the light (of the lotus within one's own heart). (47)[40]

One should surely worship me in my sacred image or elsewhere—wherever one has faith—for I, the self of all, abide in all beings, as well as (independently) in myself. (48)[41] Thus worshipping with the Vedic and Tantric processes of ritual activity, one obtains from me one's cherished fulfillment in both (this life and the next). (49) To fully establish my image, one may build a solidly constructed temple (with) pleasing flower gardens dedicated to (daily) worship, processions, and (annual) festivals. (50)[42] One who offers land, markets, cities, and villages for the perpetual daily and occasional worship and maintenance (of my image and temple), gains plenitude equal to mine. (51) By establishing (my image), (one may gain) lordship over the entire earth; by (building) a temple, (one may rule) the three worlds; by worship and service (of my image), (one may gain) the realm of Brahmā; and by doing all three of these activities, one gains equality with me. (52) I am won simply by unmotivated bhakti (devotional) yoga, and one who thus worships me achieves bhakti yoga. (53)[43] (On the other hand), one who takes away the property of the gods or *brāhmaṇas*—whether given by oneself or by others—will be born (repeatedly) as a worm in excrement for one hundred million years. (54) The (theft's) perpetrator, assistant, instigator, and sympathizer all share in the action's resulting reaction in the next life, proportionate to their participation (in the crime). (55)[44]

Two further chapters complete Krishna's discourse to Uddhava, summarizing the practices of *jñāna-yoga* and bhakti yoga, respectively, after which Uddhava proceeds to Badarikāśrama in the Himalaya Mountains. Then follows the conclusion to the annihilation narrative introduced in Book Eleven's opening chapters.

The male members of the Yadu clan, having arrived at Prabhāsa-kṣetra, take to drinking *maireya* liquor and, heavily intoxicated, quarrel among themselves and then resort to violent fighting with their weapons. Eventually, uprooting tall *erakā* grass stalks, which immediately turn to iron, in a mad rampage they all begin killing one another, thus making come to pass the curse that had been pronounced by the sages in Dvārakā. In their madness, the Yadus even attack Krishna and Balarāma, who, retaliating, slay the remaining male clan members.

Balarāma then sits down on the seashore, absorbs himself in meditation, and departs the human realm, after which Krishna sits down under a nearby banyan tree, manifesting his four-armed form, surrounded by his weapons and insignia in personified form. At that moment, Jarā (old age), a hunter, approaches and, seeing only Krishna's left foot raised and held by Krishna on his right thigh, thinking it to be the face of a deer, releases an arrow that hits its mark. Coming closer, Jarā is horrified as he sees his mistake and falls at Krishna's feet, begging forgiveness and requesting to be immediately killed for his offense. Krishna assures the hunter that this has been according to his own plan, and then he sends the man by celestial airplane to Vaikuṇṭha. Krishna then instructs his charioteer, Dāruka, to report what had happened to the survivors who had remained in Dvārakā, and then to bring them out of Dvārakā to Indraprastha (the capital city of the Pāṇḍavas) with Arjuna's help. Then, while countless celestial beings in the sky watch, Krishna closes his eyes and, meditating on himself, departs to his atemporal realm.

Śuka briefly reports the bereavement of the surviving residents of Dvārakā, and how many of the surviving women came to Prabhāsa-kṣetra to enter into the funeral pyres of their husbands' remains. Śuka ends the final chapter (31) of Book Eleven by reminding Parīkṣit of Krishna's absolute supremacy over his own creation; hence his apparent demise is naught but the play of his own *māyā*.

SUGGESTIONS FOR FURTHER READING

Eck, Diana L. 1998. *Darśan: Seeing the Divine Image in India.* 3rd ed. New York: Columbia University Press.

This is a modern "classic," highly accessible introduction to Hindu culture and ideas about divine images—relevant to chapter 27.

Khandelwal, Meena. 2009. "Research on Hindu Women's Renunciation Today: State of the Field." *Religion Compass* 3, no. 6:1003–14.

Relevant to chapter 8, this is a fine overview and analysis of current field-based research on Hindu women's renunciation, challenging the notion that locates renunciation as an almost exclusively male prerogative in Hindu cultures. Includes bibliography.

Valpey, Kenneth Russell. 2006. *Attending Kṛṣṇa's Image: Caitanya Vaiṣṇava Mūrti-sevā as Devotional Truth.* London: Routledge.

Relevant to chapter 27, this is a close study of two Vaiṣṇava temples and their current practices and ideas of image worship, focused on the *sevā* (constant devotional attendance) of Krishna.

Waghorne, Joanne Punzo, and Norman Cutler, eds. 1996. *Gods of Flesh, Gods of Stone: The Embodiment of Divinity in India.* New York: Columbia University Press.

This collection of essays covers a rich range of perspectives on ideas and practices related to images as embodiments of divinity in Hindu traditions. Especially noteworthy in relation to chapter 27 (as a description of Vaiṣṇava worship practices) may be the chapter by William H. Deadwyler III, "The Devotee and the Deity: Living a Personalistic Theology," and another by Vasudha Narayanan, "Arcāvatāra: On Earth as He Is in Heaven."

BOOK TWELVE

The Earth Sings
The Unsurpassed Bhāgavata

As the Bhāgavata Purāṇa arrives at its conclusion, Book Twelve serves largely as an extended meditation on worldly temporality, with an account of Parīkṣit's demise at the conclusion of his seven-day audition of the Bhāgavata (chapter 6) as a dramatic narrative high point. Just prior to Parīkṣit's death, Śuka, the sage who had been reciting the Bhāgavata to Parīkṣit, leaves the assembly, and the dialogical frame consisting of Śaunaka (leading the group of sages at Naimiṣāraṇya) and Sūta (Ugraśravās) resumes. After a brief survey of Purāṇic literature (chapter 7), Sūta narrates the story of the sage Mārkaṇḍeya, who, in contrast to Parīkṣit (whose life had been foreshortened by a curse), is blessed by Shiva to remain alive for millions of years, up to the time of cosmic annihilation (chapters 8–10). The last three chapters offer, respectively, a means of attaining immortality by practicing worship of the Lord as the *mahāpuruṣa* (the great person), a summary of important themes in the Bhāgavata, and a eulogy of the Bhāgavata as the best of the Purāṇas.

The first two chapters of Book Twelve elaborate on the unfortunate characteristics of the Kali age, said (in Book One) to commence with the departure of Krishna from the world. Chief among the difficulties of this degenerate age are the decreasing qualifications of kings, the dynasties of which Śuka names in anticipation of their future dominance despite their complete lack of piety. Lacking spiritual direction, people in this age suffer deeper and deeper degradation, up to a time when the final *avatāra* of Vishnu for the cycle of four ages, Kalki, appears and annihilates countless rogues with his sword. Bhūmi, the goddess of the earth, muses over the folly of kings in their futile efforts to subdue her and establish themselves permanently as territorial lords.

THE EARTH SINGS

Chapter 3

Śrī Śuka said: Seeing kings intent on conquering her, the earth herself laughed, "Ah! Kings who are playthings in the hands of death seek dominion over me. (3.1) This ambition is bound to fail, even for rulers who are learned. Driven by ambition, these kings place great faith in the body, which is (ephemeral) like froth. (2) 'First, I will discipline my senses and mind. Then I will subdue my royal ministers, counselors, citizens, close friends, elephant keepers, and enemies of the state. Thus I will systematically conquer the earth, with its seas and valleys.' Their hearts bound by such aspirations, the kings do not see death approaching. (3–4) After conquering all my land, bounded by the seas, they forcefully enter the ocean. Of what use is their self-discipline? The result of self-discipline should be liberation. (5) Leader of the Kurus! All human beings have quit the earth, departing (empty-handed) just as they came, and their children do the same. Still, fools try to conquer me in battle! (6) Base men, their minds enslaved by possessiveness, fight even with brothers, fathers, and sons for the sake of dominion over me. (7) 'All this land is mine,' they declare. 'Not yours, fool!' Kings vie with one another over me, killing and dying. (8) There was Pṛthu, Purūravā, Gādhi, Nahuṣa, Bharata, Arjuna, Māndhātā, Sagara, Rāma, Khaṭvāṅga, Dhundhuhā, Raghu, Tṛnabindu, Yayāti, Śaryāti, Śantanu, Gaya, Bhagīratha, Kuvalayāśva, Kakutstha, Naiṣadha, Nṛga, Hiraṇyakaśipu, Vṛtra, Rāvaṇa—who made the world cry—Namuci, Śambara, Bhauma, Hiraṇyākṣa, and Tāraka. (9–11) And there were many other demon kings, great rulers. All were brave heroes, all were invincible. They knew everything and they conquered everything. They loudly proclaimed possession over me. But they were mortal, and with the passage of time, all that is left of them are legends. Your Majesty, they all failed in their goals." (12–13)

(Śrī Śuka said:) Mighty lord! Extraordinary kings have spread their fame throughout the world and then perished. I narrated their histories to you because I wanted to teach wisdom and dispassion. Their histories add power to my words, but they do not constitute the ultimate point.

(14) Narrations of Krishna's qualities, on the other hand, are sung continually (in the Bhāgavata), for they destroy misfortune. One who desires pure bhakti for Krishna, who is praised in choice verses, should regularly and forever hear those narrations. (15)

King Parīkṣit said: Blessed sage, by what means can people born in the age of Kali eradicate the burgeoning vices of this age? Please explain this to me, as you see fit. (16)

In response to Parīkṣit's request, Śuka describes the characteristics of each of the four ages—Satya, Tretā, Dvāpara, and Kali. The passage of these cosmic seasons brings a gradual reduction in the moral order, the earth's abundance, people's life span, and personal contentment. After an extended description of Kali's vices, Śuka describes the antidote for the ills of this terrible age.

(Śrī Śuka said:) When human beings sing together, hear about, meditate upon, worship, or even just honor Bhagavān, he—abiding in their hearts—scrubs away the filth collected over thousands of births. (46) Just as fire, when applied to gold, removes impurities caused by (traces of other) metals, so Vishnu, abiding in the self, destroys the yogis' stock of past sins. (47) By scholarship, austerity, breath control, generosity, bathing in sacred waters, ritual vows, charity, or chanting of mantras, the mind is not as thoroughly cleansed as it is when the infinite Bhagavān abides in the heart. (48) Therefore, O king, with all your soul, install Keśava (Vishnu) in your heart! If you are thus focused at the time of death, you will go to the supreme destination. (49) Those who are dying should meditate upon the supreme Lord Bhagavān, the soul of all and refuge of all, for he will certainly guide them to their own true nature. (50)[1] In the ocean of vice that is the Kali age, there is but one great virtue: merely by singing Krishna's name, one becomes free of selfish attachment and attains the Supreme. (51)[2] Whatever (result) was attained in the Satya age by meditation on Vishnu; in Tretā by performing sacrifice, and in Dvāpara by temple worship, that (very result) is attained in the age of Kali by singing Hari's name. (52)

As the time for King Parīkṣit's anticipated death rapidly approaches, Śuka imparts to him final teachings aimed to prepare him for that moment.

By reciting "The Earth's Song," Śuka has urged Parīkṣit to comprehend the meaninglessness of his designation as "king," and next, resuming the theme of time's divisions (from Book Three, chapter 11), Śuka describes four processes of annihilation—namely, continuous (*nitya*), occasional (*naimittika*), elemental or cosmic (*prākṛtika*), and final or ultimate (*ātyantika*). None of these affect the atemporal self, which, by directing all attention to the supreme self, Vāsudeva (Krishna), will become permanently free from bodily fetters (chapters 4–5).

In chapter 6, as a result of carefully attending to Śuka's profound words, King Parīkṣit finds himself to be entirely fearless of death. Expressing deep gratitude to his preceptor, he requests his permission to fasten his full attention on Bhagavān and thus give up his life. As Sūta describes, Śuka grants Parīkṣit's request and then departs, leaving Parīkṣit to sit alone, absorbing himself in yogic trance, at which time the serpent-king Takṣaka bites and kills his already abandoned body, thus fulfilling the curse Parīkṣit had received seven days before (see 1.18.37).

Some details on Vedic and Purāṇic literary traditions and contents constitute the substance of chapter 7; Sūta elaborates an account of the sage Mārkaṇḍeya's adventures in the next three chapters. Mārkaṇḍeya is awarded the audience of the divine beings Nara-Nārāyaṇa after having performed ascetic practices through the lifetimes of six Manus and then, during the seventh Manu, having resisted the allurements of Kāmadeva (Cupid) and his female associates. As the fulfillment of a wish to directly see the Lord's magical power, *māyā*, Mārkaṇḍeya becomes witness to a cosmic deluge in which he wanders alone for millions of years. Happening upon a small island on which a lone banyan tree grows, he discovers a luminous, humanlike baby lying alone in one of the tree's leaves, sucking on its toe. When Mārkaṇḍeya approaches, the child inhales him into his body, revealing there the entire universe with all its varied wonders. When, within this vision, Mārkaṇḍeya also sees before him the same infant on the banyan leaf, as he approaches the infant, the infant and the entire universe, and the deluge, all disappear, leaving Mārkaṇḍeya back in his *āśrama*, just as he had previously been. Later Shiva blesses Mārkaṇḍeya with freedom from old age and death until the final dissolution of the universe, along with great renown and wisdom that qualifies him to be a teacher of the Purāṇas (*purāṇācārya*). He is understood to be presently alive, absorbed in devotion to the supreme Lord as he travels about the world (chapters 8–10).

The next chapter outlines how one might pursue a spiritual stature similar to that of Mārkaṇḍeya, by worshipping—especially in the early morning—the supreme Lord, particularly in his expansion as the divinity of the sun. Associated specifically with the annual cycle of Vedic rites, Lord Hari (Vishnu), as the sun, is identified with nine aspects of such rites—namely, time (*kāla*), place (*deśa*), activity (*kriyā*), agent (*kartā*), instruments of activity (*karaṇa*), the rite that must be performed (*kārya*), the sacred texts directing the rite (*āgama*), materials offered in the rite (*dravya*), and the result of the rite (*phala*). Then, in the Bhāgavata's penultimate chapter (chapter 12, prior to our final reading selection), Sūta provides a brief summary of the entire Bhāgavata, up to and including the demise of King Parīkṣit and the adventures of Mārkaṇḍeya. Further, he explains that he has now fully responded to all the questions posed by the sages in Naimiṣāraṇya Forest (Book One, chapter 1). Sūta then reiterates the value of hearing about the supreme Bhagavān, especially as presented in this compilation from the Purāṇas (*purāṇa-saṁhitām*). Finally, he offers obeisance to the ever-existent (*sanātana*) Bhagavān and to Śuka, Vyāsa's son, whom he praises as the "destroyer of all obstacles."

The first few verses of chapter 13, leading up to our final selection, include a list of other Purāṇas with their verse lengths. Thereafter, Sūta further praises the Bhāgavata Purāṇa, proclaiming its superiority to all other Purāṇas.

THE UNSURPASSED BHĀGAVATA

Chapter 13

In an assembly of virtuous persons, other Purāṇas appear brilliant only as long as the supreme Purāṇa, the beautiful Bhāgavata, is not seen. (13.14)[3] Indeed, the Śrīmad Bhāgavatam is accepted as the essence of all Vedānta (the Upaniṣads and Brahmasūtra). One who has found fulfillment in the Bhāgavata's immortal emotions (*rasa*) can no longer find pleasure in any other literature. (15) As the Ganges is (unsurpassed) among rivers, Acyuta (Vishnu) among the gods, and Śambhu (Shiva) among devotees of Vishnu, so this Bhāgavata is among the Purāṇas. (16) Brāhmaṇas! As Kāśī (Vārānasī) is unsurpassed among all sacred places, so also is the Śrīmad Bhāgavatam among the multitude of Purāṇas. (17)[4] Śrīmad Bhāgavatam is a flawless Purāṇa, dearly loved by devotees of Vishnu, for it narrates only the highest, pure wisdom of perfected souls. The Bhāgavata reveals knowledge, detachment, devotion, and selfless action. One who is devoted to hearing, reciting, and deliberating upon the Bhāgavata with bhakti becomes fully liberated. (18) Let us meditate upon the pure, flawless, sorrowless, immortal Supreme Truth, who long ago illuminated this unparalleled lamp of wisdom to Brahmā. Through Brahmā, he taught it to Nārada, and through him to the sage Vyāsa. Through Vyāsa, he taught it to the best of yogis, Śuka, and Śuka compassionately taught it to Parīkṣit, who is protected by Bhagavān. (19)[5] Obeisance to the all-seeing Bhagavān Vāsudeva (Krishna)! He mercifully narrated the Bhāgavata Purāṇa to Brahmā, who desired liberation. (20) Obeisance to the best of yogis, Śuka, the embodiment of Vedic knowledge, who liberated Viṣhṇurāta (Parīkṣit) from the snakebite of repeated birth (*saṁsāra*). (21)[6] O master, God of gods! Grant us bhakti at your feet, birth after birth, for you alone are our Lord. (22)

nāma-saṁkīrtanaṁ yasya sarva-pāpa-praṇāśanam
praṇāmo duḥkha-śamanas taṁ namāmi hariṁ param

Singing Krishna's name destroys all sins, and prostrating before him dispels suffering. I bow down to that supreme Hari. (23)[7]

This concludes the Bhāgavata Purāṇa, in 12 books, 335 chapters, and, according to tradition, 18,000 verses. Śrīdhara Svāmī ends with a plea for devotion and an expression of humility, "I have explained the confidential Bhāgavata with a desire for the highest bliss and love—not to display my intellectual prowess. Indeed, where are the manifold, profound meanings of the Śrīmad Bhāgavatam, and where am I, so slow witted!"

SUGGESTIONS FOR FURTHER READING

Dāsa, Gopīpāraṇadhana, trans. 2013. *Śrī Tattva-sandarbha by Śrīla Jīva Gosvāmī.* Vrindavan: Girirāja.
A traditional (sixteenth century) Bhāgavata commentator's systematic analysis of the Bhāgavata Purāṇa's preeminence as a source of valid knowledge (*pramāṇa*), relevant to Book Twelve's concluding praises of the work.

Kloetzli, Randy, and Alf Hiltebeitel. 2007. "Kāla." In *The Hindu World*, edited by Sushil Mittal and Gene Thursby, 553–86. London: Routledge.
Provides an overview of the concepts and narratives of time found in several contexts of Hindu traditions, relevant to Book Twelve's theme of temporality and cosmic annihilation.

Sardella, Ferdinando, and Abhishek Ghosh. 2013. "Modern Reception and Text Migration of the Bhāgavata Purāṇa." In *The Bhāgavata Purāṇa: Sacred Text and Living Tradition*, edited by Ravi M. Gupta and Kenneth R. Valpey, 221–47. New York: Columbia University Press.
In the context of the Bhāgavata's self-praise, this chapter sketches recent reception history of the text.

COMMENTARIAL EXCURSIONS

1

Diving Into the Bhāgavata: Śrīdhara's Commentary on the First Verse

"Let us inquire into the supreme truth, the origin of this world." Thus begin two classics of the Indian religious traditions—the Brahmasūtra (also called Vedāntasūtra) and the Bhāgavata Purāṇa. The former is a collection of some five hundred succinct prose aphorisms (*sūtras*) that systematically argue for the philosophical doctrines of the Upaniṣads. These aphorisms have become the subject of a vibrant tradition of commentary and debate known as Vedānta. The Bhāgavata Purāṇa, on the other hand, is a marvel of poetry that—in more than fourteen thousand verses—expresses a sophisticated theology of devotion to Krishna. The Bhāgavata has served as the inspiration for works of literature, art, and architecture in both popular culture and elite circles of Sanskrit learning.

The Bhāgavata Purāṇa and the Brahmasūtra differ significantly in their literary styles, teaching methods, and historical origins, but readers have drawn connections between them for some eight hundred years. In the thirteenth century, for example, the Vedānta philosopher Madhva quotes a verse from the Garuḍa Purāṇa stating that the Bhāgavata Purāṇa contains the meaning of the Brahmasūtra. Śrīdhara Svāmī makes similar connections in the fourteenth century, followed by the Caitanya Vaiṣṇava theologian Jīva Gosvāmī in the sixteenth century.

An inspiration for such connection making is the Bhāgavata's first verse, one of the most philosophically rich passages in the Purāṇa. The verse is a meditation on the supreme truth (*satyaṁ param*), describing that truth in clearly Vedāntic terms. The verse is dense and difficult, rather like a string of metrically arranged *sūtras*, and it employs the long meter called tiger's play (*śārdūla-vikrīḍitam*), thus hinting at the poetic nature of the Purāṇa. Commentaries on the first verse tend to be extensive and involved, wherein a commentator sets the tone for his entire commentary. Indeed, in Sanskrit commentary, the first verse of a text is often seen as a microcosm of the entire work. Thus, a deeper look into commentaries on the first verse is indispensable for any student of the Bhāgavata Purāṇa. Here we focus on the venerable Śrīdhara Svāmī, whose commentary has shaped how generations of commentators have read the Bhāgavata. Here is the first verse again:

janmādy asya yato'nvayād itarataś cārtheṣv abhijñaḥ svarāṭ
tene brahma hṛdā ya ādikavaye muhyanti yat sūrayaḥ
tejovārimṛdāṁ yathā vinimayo yatra trisargomṛṣā
dhāmnā svena sadā nirastakuhakaṁ satyaṁ paraṁ dhīmahi

"From him this (world) is born, etc. That cognizant and self-luminous one is (known) by meanings inferred from positive and negative reasoning. He is the one who revealed the Veda through the heart to the first seer, but the gods are confused about him. In him the threefold creation—such as the interplay of fire, water, and earth—is not false, for he has removed all deception by his own power. Upon that supreme truth let us meditate."

Śrīdhara begins his commentary with the word *atha*—literally, "now." "Now, the main objective of the Bhāgavata Purāṇa is to describe the qualities of the beautiful Bhagavān." The word *atha* resonates deeply across Sanskrit literature; perhaps its most famous use is at the beginning of the Brahmasūtra: "Now let us inquire into the supreme truth." Centuries of commentators have asked, "When is now?" The answers have been varied: now that you have gained a human birth, with the ability to investigate the truth; now that you have relinquished the useless pursuit of sensual pleasure and religious ritual; now that you find yourself at this opportune moment for study. But all agree that the humble word *atha* is a harbinger of auspiciousness, a good way to begin a text: "Now, at this auspicious moment."

Like many other commentators, Śrīdhara then plunges directly into the final statement of the verse and its overarching exhortation—*satyaṁ paraṁ dhīmahi* (upon that supreme truth let us meditate). The immediate question arises, what is the supreme truth upon whom we should meditate? The rest of the first verse, says Śrīdhara, provides a definition of that supreme being. The definition comes in two parts—the essential characteristics of the supreme being and those characteristics that are only contingent. (An example might be useful here: if we were to define a chair for someone who had never seen one, we might say that a chair's essential characteristic is its ability to provide a raised sitting place for human beings, whereas its contingent characteristic would be the fact that it is located in my bedroom. If I took the chair out of my bedroom, it would still be a chair, but if I removed its ability to serve as a seat, it would no longer be a chair.) The essential characteristics (*svarūpa-lakṣaṇa*) of the supreme being, says Śrīdhara, are indicated by the word *satya*, "truth" or "reality." God is reality itself and all other beings are real only by virtue of his reality. This is expressed in the first verse as follows: "In him the threefold creation—such as the interplay of fire, water, and earth—is not false, for he has removed all deception by his own power." In other words, God's ability to bestow reality on what is fleeting (i.e., this world), by virtue of his own being, is essentially what makes him God. Thus, the verse calls him cognizant and self-luminous.

The contingent characteristics of the supreme being are expressed in the phrase "From him this (world) is born, etc." This phrase is identical to the second aphorism of the Brahmasūtra, and nearly every commentator unpacks the "etc." as follows: "From him this world is born, upon him it rests, and in him it is finally dissolved." Śrīdhara quotes a variety of passages from the Upaniṣads to further corroborate the Bhāgavata's claim that everything comes from God. Nevertheless, although the creation of the world is an important identifier of God, it is still a contingent characteristic, for if the world did not exist, this would not threaten God's existence or nature.

In a manner typical of Sanskrit commentaries, Śrīdhara then raises various objections to his interpretation and rebuts those objections by using phrases from the verse itself. In this process, Śrīdhara attempts to reveal the internal logic of the Bhāgavata's first verse.

"Could matter alone be the cause of this world?" asks the objector. "Is the verse asking us to meditate on matter?"

"No," Śrīdhara responds, "because the verse clearly states that the cause of the world is 'cognizant' (whereas matter is unaware and inert)."

"Then is the verse asking us to meditate on the individual living beings (like us humans, who are cognizant)?"

"Wrong again," says Śridhara, "because the object of meditation is called 'self-luminous,' which means that he does not rely on anyone else for his wisdom (whereas human beings suffer from ignorance that must be dispelled by wisdom received from others)."

"Then is the verse asking us to meditate on Brahmā (the secondary creator-deity, who is the highest-ranking divinity in this world)?"

"No," says Śrīdhara, "because the verse says, 'He is the one who revealed the Veda through the heart to the first seer (Brahmā), but the gods are confused about him.' So clearly Brahmā's knowledge is also dependent upon another."

"The only person whose knowledge is self-luminous," concludes Śrīdhara, "is the supreme Lord (*parameśvara*), and so he alone is the cause of this world." Earlier in his commentary, Śrīdhara specifies Vishnu as that supreme Lord—the main subject of the Bhāgavata Purāṇa.

Throughout these arguments, Śrīdhara quotes profusely from the Upaniṣads, Brahmasūtra, and other Purāṇas, thus drawing connections between the Bhāgavata and the rest of Sanskrit sacred literature. Indeed, Śrīdhara is gradually building a case for what the Bhāgavata will itself claim in its second and third verses, "What is the use of other books? (This is) the fruit of the Vedic desire tree. . . ."

Śrīdhara concludes his commentary on the first verse by drawing one last connection—between the Bhāgavata Purāṇa and the famous Gāyatrī mantra of the Ṛgveda. This far-reaching connection is sparked by the last word of the verse, *dhīmahi*, "let us meditate." The word *dhīmahi* is the heart of the Gāyatrī. Śrīdhara points out that *dhīmahi* is a Vedic form of the verb *dhyai*; the proper grammatical form in classical Sanskrit is *dhyāyema*. The Bhāgavata's use of the Vedic form, therefore, could only indicate its intention to recall and explain the Gāyatrī.

Śrīdhara offers another connection with the Gāyatrī, using the following line from the first verse: "He is the one who revealed the Veda through the heart to the first seer (Brahmā)." The Gāyatrī is a prayer asking the Lord to inspire the intellect, and the first person to be thus inspired was Brahmā. Since he heard the Bhāgavata at the dawn of creation (see 2.9.33–36), the Bhāgavata can be considered a form of the Gāyatrī.

In his commentary to the first verse, Śrīdhara has attempted to accomplish several tasks. First, he has introduced his readers to the key philosophical concepts of the Bhāgavata. This is a Vedāntic text that shares the same assumptions and scriptural canon as the rest of the Vedāntic tradition. Second, Śrīdhara has made clear the Bhāgavata's position relative to that canon: the Bhāgavata is the fruit that contains the meanings of the Vedic and Vedāntic traditions. And last, Śrīdhara has specified the primary subject matter of the Bhāgavata: this text focuses on no one less than the supreme Deity, Bhagavān Vishnu, the origin of the world.

A less-tangible but nevertheless crucial function of Śrīdhara's commentary on the first verse is to set the mood with which he and his readers ought to approach the text. It is obvious that Śrīdhara, like other commentators on the Bhāgavata, takes great delight in drawing a world of meaning from a single verse and then arranging those meanings into systematic arguments. The connections are far-reaching—the Ṛgveda, Upaniṣads, Brahmasūtra, and several Purāṇas. Each word of the first verse becomes a repository for an entire body of texts, concepts, discussions, and debates. This delight and fearless exegesis arise from a deep conviction in the inherent value and profundity of his text, the Bhāgavata Purāṇa. Indeed, such conviction is the defining characteristic of a religious reader and commentator. Paul Griffiths describes this well:

> The first and most basic element in these relations [between religious readers and sacred texts] is that the work read is understood as a stable and vastly rich resource, one that yields meaning, suggestions (or imperatives) for action, matter for aesthetic wonder and much else. It is a treasure house, an ocean, a mine; the deeper religious readers dig, the more ardently they fish, the more single-mindedly they seek gold, the greater will be their reward. . . . There can, according to these metaphors, be no final act of reading in which everything is uncovered, in which the mine of gold has yielded all its treasure or the fish pool has been emptied of fish. Reading, for religious readers, ends only with death, and perhaps not then: it is a continuous, ever-repeated act. (1999, 41)

For religious readers, the variety and depth of meaning in a sacred text are limited only by the limitations of the human intellect. Thus, we find Śrīdhara Svāmī reflecting before beginning his commentary on the Bhāgavata,

Where am I, so slow witted?
And where is this task of churning the milk ocean?
Indeed, what can an atom do
where even Mount Mandara sinks?

Nevertheless, Śrīdhara Svāmī dives into the ocean of the Bhāgavata, confident that Lord Vishnu will support his effort, even as he supported the Mandara Mountain upon his back in his *avatāra* as the great turtle, Kūrma. The churning was difficult and the gods often stumbled in the process, but with Vishnu's assistance they eventually extracted the sweet nectar of immortality. Śrīdhara prays here that his commentary will succeed in extracting the nectar that is latent in the verses of the Bhāgavata.

2

Who Is to Blame? The Fall of Vishnu's Gatekeepers

Curses are frequent events in the Bhāgavata Purāṇa. Typically, a curse is uttered by a *brāhmaṇa* who has witnessed a transgression (toward himself or toward others) by a *kṣatriya* king. The curse of a *brāhmaṇa* is a feared weapon that can lead to loss of fortune, rebirth in lower life-forms, or physical harm. The purposes of curses are manifold—to punish a perceived offense, to protect someone from harm, to reform the cursed individual, to predict something untoward that is about to happen, or even to simply vent (inappropriate) anger. Victims of curses also respond in manifold ways—some accept blame (and the curse), others reject blame and hurl a countercurse, and yet others demonstrate their blamelessness but still humbly accept the effects of the curse.

Despite the presence of all these curses, the Bhāgavata is rather nonchalant about the entire matter of cursing. Indeed, there is no consistent correlation between a curse and culpability. Those who are cursed are rarely blamed and sometimes even praised. Curses often turn out to be redeeming (and thus serve as blessings in disguise), or they are shown to be groundless (and thus the curser is blamed), or they merely serve as catalysts for what is inevitable. In only a few instances is the curse truly effective and the cursed truly culpable.

Nowhere is the question of a cursed person's culpability brought into greater focus than in the story of Jaya and Vijaya's fall from grace. The two serve as Vishnu's attendants, guarding the innermost gates of Vaikuṇṭha, the supreme heaven where Vishnu dwells with his consort, Lakṣmī. When four child sages, the Kumāras, arrive at these gates seeking to see the Lord, the gatekeepers turn them away, not recognizing the boys' greatness. The sages become angry and curse the gatekeepers to fall to earth and take three successive births as demonic enemies of Vishnu. Jaya and Vijaya instantly recognize their folly and repent, as Vishnu hastens to the scene to resolve the situation and give the sages what they longed for—an audience with the Lord. At this point, the sages are also feeling deeply repentant for their angry behavior, and they request the Lord to punish them appropriately. But Vishnu is undisturbed by the situation; he reassures both sides that all this was part of his divine plan. He asks Jaya and Vijaya to accept the curse and requests the sages to ensure that the gatekeepers' return to Vaikuṇṭha is swift.

The story of Jaya and Vijaya's fall from Vaikuṇṭha has intrigued commentators because it demonstrates what is said to be impossible—a liberated devotee of God falling from the transcendent world to earth. How, then, can the personal attendants of Vishnu stumble from his eternal abode, Vaikuṇṭha? Indeed, the story of Jaya and Vijaya is one of the few narratives to be told twice in the Bhāgavata, in Books Three and Seven. In its second telling, the story serves as part of an answer to the question of whether God behaves partially when he kills some and saves others. Krishna's slaying of the hateful king Śiśupāla, we are reassured, was in fact a blessing in disguise, because Śiśupāla was one of the two gatekeepers, and this was his last birth on earth as a demon. But this explanation of Śiśupāla's death simply pushes the question further back in time—did Jaya and Vijaya truly deserve to be cursed and to fall from their posts in heaven? Who is to blame for their cursing—the four child sages, the gatekeepers, Vishnu himself, or some combination of the three parties?

It is this question that engages commentators for much of chapters 15 and 16 of Book Three. Who is to blame? The Bhāgavata itself incriminates different individuals at various points in the story, and the commentators faithfully follow the text's attributions of guilt. But each commentator also has his own sense of what went wrong and who is truly at fault. Here, we reread the story along with several commentators and attempt to trace the contours of culpability.

Vallabha is the first to raise the question of culpability in his commentary to chapter 15, verse 27:

tasminn atītya munayaḥ ṣaḍ asajjamānāḥ
kakṣāḥ samāna-vayasāv atha saptamāyām
devāv acakṣata gṛhīta-gadau parārdhya-
keyūra-kuṇḍala-kirīṭa-viṭaṅka-veṣau

"Here the sages passed through six gates without lingering, but at the seventh they saw two celestial beings holding clubs. Both were of equal age, and they were beautifully dressed with the most excellent crowns, earrings, and armlets."

Purāṇic descriptions inform us that Vaikuṇṭha has seven gates, each of which is guarded by a pair of gatekeepers. Thus, Vallabha raises a pertinent question: why were the sages able to pass through six gates without obstruction but were stopped at the seventh? Each of the six gates, Vallabha explains, proffers one of Bhagavān's six excellences—majesty, strength, fame, beauty, wisdom, and renunciation. Because the sages had already acquired these excellences, they did not see the gatekeepers for the first six gates. But the seventh gate represents bhakti, devotion for Vishnu, which the sages did not yet possess, and so they were stopped. (The Bhāgavata tells us in the sixteenth chapter that the sages were dedicated to a nondualist understanding of Vishnu as the ever-present reality, and their devotion was evoked only when they saw the Lord's beautiful form.) Thus, even before the sages have uttered any curse, Vallabha makes it clear that the sages did not deserve to be there, and so the gatekeepers cannot be blamed for obstructing their path.

What, then, do we make of the Bhāgavata's statement, in verse 31, that the sages were most deserving (*svarhattamāḥ*) of visiting Vaikuṇṭha? Vallabha explains that because the sages were *jñānīs* (men of wisdom), they were certainly more deserving than mere ascetics or others with good behavior. Even for them, however, entering Bhagavān's inner chambers would have been a major transgression (presumably because they were not yet devotees, as mentioned), and allowing this to happen would have been a mistake on the part of the gatekeepers. To protect both sides from this offense, the sages were forbidden entry into the Lord's private chamber.

But the gatekeepers were not without fault, says Vallabha. After all, the Bhāgavata itself says in verse 30 that "the gatekeepers' conduct was displeasing to the Lord."

tān vīkṣya vāta-raśanāṁś caturaḥ kumārān
vṛddhān daśārdha-vayaso viditātma-tattvān
vetreṇa cāskhalayatām atad-arhaṇāṁs tau
tejo vihasya bhagavat-pratikūla-śīlau

"Seeing the four boys—clothed by the wind, ancient but (appearing only) five years old, knowers of the truth of the self—the gatekeepers laughed at their boldness and blocked them with maces. The gatekeepers' conduct was displeasing to the Lord, for the boys did not deserve such treatment."

The gatekeepers' flaw, according to Vallabha, is that they harbored pride (in their status as the Lord's chief gatekeepers), and pride is the characteristic quality of demons. Thus, they had to give up their posts and suffer birth as demons on earth. Śrīdhara, on the other hand, identifies their disagreeable quality as disrespect of *brāhmaṇas*, who are dear to Vishnu (as Vishnu will himself emphasize in chapter 16).

Jīva, elaborating on Śrīdhara's explanation, states that the Lord can tolerate someone's flouting his own rules, but he cannot tolerate a transgression against those who are dear to him. In this instance, the sages may have transgressed the rules of Vaikuṇṭha by trying to enter the Lord's private chamber, but obstructing them was a far greater offense on the gatekeepers' part.

All through chapter 15, Śrīdhara sticks closely to the Bhāgavata's own attribution of guilt, by emphasizing the sages' qualification and the gatekeepers' mistake. In Śrīdhara's eyes, there is little need to work at justifying the gatekeepers' behavior—as we have read, the sages were "most deserving," the gatekeepers' conduct was "displeasing to the Lord," and the reason for the displeasure will be made clear in chapter 16—namely, insulting the *brāhmaṇas*. The Gauḍīya commentators tend to agree with Śrīdhara's position. Viśvanātha states that Vishnu is fond of the *brāhmaṇas*, and yet the gatekeepers behaved in a contrary way. "A competent servant is one whose behavior is in accord with his master's intention" (3.15.30). Bhaktivedanta explains that the child sages' attempt to enter Vaikuṇṭha, and their subsequent anger at being obstructed, was a result of their childlike innocence. "They were not at all duplicitous, and they entered the doors exactly as little children enter places without any idea of what it is to trespass. That is a child's nature. . . . Indeed, a child is generally welcome in his attempts to go places, but if it so happens that a child is checked from entering a door, he naturally becomes very sorry and angry" (3.15.29).

Still, the Gauḍīya commentators cannot resist the urge to defend Jaya and Vijaya, particularly when the Bhāgavata softens its stance toward them near the end of chapter 15 and the beginning of chapter 16. After all, from a theological perspective, the gatekeepers are Vishnu's devotees, whereas the sages are not (as yet), and thus the commentators never pass up an opportunity to defend the Lord's attendants. For instance, in verse 35 of chapter 15, we read of the attendants' reaction to the curse:

teṣām itīritam ubhāv avadhārya ghoraṁ
taṁ brahma-daṇḍam anivāraṇam astra-pūgaiḥ
sadyo harer anucarāv uru bibhyatas tat-
pāda-grahāv apatatām atikātareṇa

"When the sages uttered these terrible words, the gatekeepers realized that this was a *brāhmaṇa*'s curse, which cannot be counteracted by any number of weapons. The servants of Hari became very fearful and immediately fell to the ground, grasping the sages' feet in desperation."

Here both Jīva and Bhaktivedanta explain that the gatekeepers' offense was unintentional. According to Jīva, the word *avadhārya* ("realized" or "understood") indicates that the gatekeepers had not known that the boys were *brāhmaṇas*. Along the same lines, according to the Mādhva commentator Vijayadhvaja, the fact that the gatekeepers reacted "immediately" indicates that they were not at fault. And when the attendants pray (in verse 36) that they might never forget the Lord when they take birth on earth, Viśvanātha explains that by making this request, the gatekeepers were transforming the curse into a blessing.

The story's tone shifts significantly as soon as Vishnu arrives on the scene. Vishnu sides with the sages and approves of their curse but clearly does not relinquish his commitment to his attendants. When he tells the sages, "I would cut off my arm if it were adverse to you!" this has a double-edged meaning—the attendants are closely connected to him, but he is willing to accept the pain of their departure (3.16.6). He then beseeches the sages, "Please arrange my servants' exile to be short—that would be a great favor to me" (3.16.12).

By this time, the sages are deeply repentant for retaliating against Jaya and Vijaya, blaming themselves for the entire situation. "Master! . . . We will accept whatever punishment you consider appropriate for us, for we have implicated two innocent persons." (3.16.25). Vishnu, however, ends the discussion by taking "blame" upon himself:

etau suretara-gatiṁ pratipadya sadyaḥ
saṁrambha-sambhṛta-samādhy-anubaddha-yogau
bhūyaḥ sakāśam upayāsyata āśu yo vaḥ
śāpo mayaiva nimitas tad aveta viprāḥ

"You should know that I alone ordained this curse. These two will now become demons, but through intense yogic concentration born of anger, they will soon return close to me." (3.16.26).

At this point in the narrative, each person has volunteered to accept responsibility for the difficult situation. The gatekeepers accepted blame for insulting *brāhmaṇas*, the sages pronounced themselves guilty of cursing innocent gatekeepers, and now Vishnu claims responsibility for preordaining the entire event. Viśvanātha explains that Vishnu here is reassuring both sides that they are faultless, for the gatekeepers are his steadfast devotees and the boys are perfectly self-controlled sages. The entire event, says Viśvanātha, was set into motion by the Lord for the purpose of intensifying his loving relationships with his devotees and increasing their happiness by appearing as different *avatāras* (to fight the gatekeeper-turned-demons). After all, Viśvanātha asks, what better opponent can the Lord have in battle sport than his own powerful guards? And how else would he satisfy his devotees' desires for loving exchange if he were not to descend to earth?

And this indeed is the Bhāgavata's resolution to many such theological quandaries. Why would two dedicated devotees fall from Vishnu's eternal abode? While we might lay blame in any number of places, the Bhāgavata's final resolution lies in the eternal play (*līlā*) of Bhagavān, which is inscrutable and yet perfectly beneficial for all who participate in it.

The Lord's *līlā* is endless, and along with it, the Purāṇic narrative. In a final twist to the story, the Bhāgavata reattributes guilt one last time. Just before leaving the scene, Vishnu tells his attendants, "This (curse) was foretold by Ramā (Lakṣmī) a long time ago. She was angry, for she was turned away at the door while I was sleeping" (3.16.30). The narrative has come full circle now, with another (very deserving!) person refused entry and the gatekeepers (presumably) again culpable. But we receive only this tantalizing tidbit of a story, with the rest left to commentators to fill in. And so the Purāṇic narrative continues—another story for another time.

3

A Cosmic Debate on the Power of Divine Names

The importance of the Ajāmila narrative, in Book Six, for later Vaiṣṇava traditions is due largely to the inspirational lesson it conveys about divine names (specifically the name Nārāyaṇa in this episode): when pronounced, these names have special, incomparable salvific power as vehicles for divine grace. This message is embedded in discourses on the nature and source of dharma, a theme that pervades the Bhāgavata in its treatment of bhakti as dharma's foundation. Drawing on some of the early Bhāgavata commentaries, here we revisit five verses from Book Six, chapters 1 through 3, to gain further insight into how the Bhāgavata and its subsequent commentarial tradition approach issues related to righteousness and unrighteousness, transgression and punishment, "accidental" liberation, divine grace, and the power of divine names.

The critical moment in Ajāmila's story is the time of his death, when he remembers and calls out the name of his youngest son, whose name is Nārāyaṇa (6.1.27):

sa evaṁ vartamāno'jño mṛtyu-kāla upasthite
matiṁ cakāra tanaye bāle nārāyaṇāhvaye

"And so, as the time of death drew near, that ignorant Ajāmila absorbed his mind in his young son named Nārāyaṇa."

Despite Ajāmila's ignorance, which had deepened over time because of his worldly preoccupations, by the Lord's grace at this moment his knowledge became again manifest. In effect, writes Vijayadhvaja, Ajāmila was able to invoke the Lord into the form of his young son, and therefore his calling to his son was in fact calling to the Lord. This explanation is somewhat in contrast to that of Śrīdhara, who suggests a more cumulative process: bhakti—devotion—for the name's original owner, the Lord, manifested only after Ajāmila repeatedly and affectionately called his son by (the Lord's) name. These considerations are relevant to the ensuing discussion between the Yamadūtas—Yamarāja's minions—and the Vishnudūtas—servants of Vishnu, Nārāyaṇa. The Yamadūtas have begun to remove Ajāmila from his body, dragging him to their master for punishment, and the Vishnudūtas, hearing the name of *their* master, Nārāyaṇa, arrive to bring Ajāmila to Nārāyaṇa's transcendent realm, Vaikuṇṭha. Having been obstructed and questioned by the Vishnudūtas, the Yamadūtas begin their reply (6.1.40):

yamadūtā ūcuḥ
veda-praṇihito dharmo hy adharmas tad-viparyayaḥ
vedo nārāyaṇaḥ sākṣāt svayambhūr iti śuśruma

"Yama's messengers replied: 'Dharma is enjoined in the Veda, and adharma is dharma's opposite. We have heard, 'The Veda is directly the self-born Nārāyaṇa (Vishnu).' "

For the Yamadūtas, the case was clear: Ajāmila had blatantly and repeatedly transgressed the rules of dharma—the collective (and often apparently contradictory) set of ordinances and regulations governing behavior for particular groups of people, and for human beings in general. Since the Vishnudūtas had challenged the Yamadūtas to explain "the true character of dharma and its opposite, adharma" (1.38), the Yamadūtas now begin their argument to justify the punishment of Ajāmila. Here they affirm the broadly brahmanical view that the source of dharma is the collection of sacred texts known as Veda. Then, after discussing the general notion of action (karma) and how its effects are registered and perpetuated, the Yamadūtas recount the story of Ajāmila's sudden fall from brahmanical behavior, despite having been "well versed in the Veda . . . a reservoir of good character, conduct, and qualities" (1.56). Concluding their argument that Ajāmila deserves to be punished, they accuse him of being "in violation of scripture, irresponsible, and thoroughly contemptible" (1.67). As violation of scripture (*śāstram ullaṅghya*) implies violation of Vedic injunctions, it is important for the Yamadūtas to establish that "dharma is enjoined in the Veda."

Commentaries on this verse elaborate on how its first half can be understood in light of the Mīmāṁsā (or Pūrva Mīmāṁsā) exegetical tradition. Mīmāṁsā (literally, "deliberation") literature developed as a means to defend the authority of the Veda against its critics, and as a way to analyze and determine the meaning of Vedic passages. With its emphasis on the preeminent authority of Vedic injunctions, Mīmāṁsā aims to facilitate the proper execution of those injunctions, especially with respect to the performance of ritual acts.

Since it is essential for Mīmāṁsakas (followers of Mīmāṁsā) to establish the Veda as the epistemological foundation for all discussion of right action (dharma), Śrīdhara begins his commentary to this verse by noting that its initial phrase means "Veda is that which makes (or constitutes) authoritative evidence" (*veda-pramāṇaka*) and hence "that which is Vedic authoritative evidence is dharma; what is dharma is Vedic authoritative evidence." Further, "authoritative evidence is the essential form (*svarūpam*) (of Veda)." Śrīdhara's proof text for this claim is a quote from the foundational text of Mīmāṁsā, the Mīmāṁsā Sūtras attributed to the sage Jaimini (1.1.2): "Dharma is an object (*artha*—aim, purpose) characterized by an injunction (*codanā*)." Again, Mīmāṁsā's emphasis on the Veda's injunctive character is highlighted, and Vaṁśīdhara provides an example (from an unspecified Vedic source): "Daily one must perform worship during the days' junctures (*saṁdhyā*)." Here, dharma is characterized by the injunction to perform *saṁdhyā* worship. In turn, this injunction serves as the authoritative evidence or proof (*pramāṇa*) that this is indeed what is to be done (the implication being that, as a Vedic injunction, its function as "evidence" trumps any apparently countervening evidence, such as one's own experience or perception—*pratyakṣa*—that this activity should not be done, or such as some argument based on inference—*anumāna*—that it should not be done). Both Śrīdhara and Vaṁśīdhara make similar arguments regarding adharma: what the Veda explicitly forbids or rejects (such as the killing of a *brāhmaṇa*—Vaṁśīdhara's example!) is adharma, and its forbidding or rejecting of something serves as evidence or proof that it is not to be done.

Turning to the second half of this verse (6.1.40), Śrīdhara says that the Yamadūtas give the reason (*hetu*) why Veda is regarded as the decisive *pramāṇa*: "The Veda is directly the self-born Nārāyaṇa," or, in other words, the Veda issues forth directly from Nārāyaṇa. Specifically, Śrīdhara notes, according to Bṛhadāraṇyaka Upaniṣad (2.4.10), "Thus, indeed, the Ṛgveda, Yajurveda, Sāmaveda, Atharva-Aṅgirasa, the Itihāsas and Purāṇas, the sciences, Upaniṣads, verses, aphorisms, explanations, and glosses—all this is the breath of this Great Being (Nārāyaṇa)." Again, the concern here is over the authority of the Veda, with an allusion to the Mīmāṁsā explanation of why the Veda is to be regarded as infallible. Mīmāṁsakas claim that the Vedic texts are infallible because they have no personal origin; rather, they are *apauruṣeya*—nonpersonal, ever-existent revelation. Followers of the Bhāgavata maintain that whereas Nārāyaṇa is the supreme person, he is not subject to the faults of human beings, and therefore the *apauruṣeyatva*—the nonpersonness—(and hence infallibility) of the Veda is upheld in the understanding that it issues forth from him.

Vīrarāghava calls attention to the Yamadūtas' employment of the word "self-born" (*svayambhū*) as dispelling doubt regarding the Veda's possible temporality (and hence imperfection) owing to being identified as an effect of a prior cause. He notes that cause and effect are "nondifferent" (*abheda*) and then defines *svayambhū* as "appointed by oneself alone: without deviation, primordially and in orderly fashion, one manifests." Since the cause of the Veda, Nārāyaṇa, is understood to be "self-born," his divine (infallible) nature is underscored, implying, in turn, that the scripture that issues forth from him (the Veda—the effect) can confidently be taken as the authoritative, infallible source of knowledge about dharma and adharma.

At this point, Vaṁśīdhara anticipates our burning question: what about the various scriptures of the Buddhists, Arhats, Vāmas (Tantrikas), Paśupatas, and the like? Are they not also providing authoritative guidelines for upholding dharma? After all, they contain quite reasonable exhortations to observe such practices as "sport, pleasure, making of *maṇḍalas*, dispassion, meditation, concentration, nonviolence, truthfulness, self-restraint, charity, and compassion." No, says Vaṁśīdhara: according to the Mīmāṁsakas, these scriptures cannot be accepted as authoritative and therefore do not teach dharma (even though, we may note, several such practices and principles are praised in the Bhāgavata Purāṇa!).

The Yamadūtas fall silent after presenting their case for Ajāmila's punishment by their master, Yamarāja. Then, in the beginning of Book Six, chapter 2, the Vishnudūtas commence with their defense of Ajāmila. After rhetorically lambasting their counterparts, the Yamadūtas, the Vishnudūtas declare (6.2.8),

etenaiva hy aghono'sya kṛtaṁ syād agha-niṣkṛtam
yadā nārāyaṇāyeti jagāda catur-akṣaram

"When the sinful Ajāmila called out, 'Come, Nārāyaṇa,' he pronounced the four-syllable name of Hari. By this action alone, his sins would have been nullified."

Thus begins the Vishnudūtas' declaration about the power of the divine name "Nārāyaṇa" (and of other names of Vishnu) for the atonement of sinful acts—power far greater than that of any other acts of atonement. The commentators are concerned to support this claim, arguing that the divine name's effectiveness extends to cases when it is pronounced with intentions other than to praise or address the supreme Lord, as was apparently the case with Ajāmila.

Beginning with Śrīdhara, commentators again refer to the Mīmāṁsā *darśana* ("school"; literally, "viewpoint"), alluding to a technical reference from Mīmāṁsā regarding *khādira*—a certain type of wood used in Vedic rituals—to argue that there can be more than one result simultaneously by the invocation of divine names. In the case of Ajāmila, while calling the name of his son, he was (inadvertently) calling the name of Vishnu, Nārāyaṇa. Indeed, even by a mere "semblance of (divine) names" (*nāmābhāsa*), one may be freed from all reactions to sinful actions. To support this claim, Śrīdhara quotes from the Viṣṇu Purāṇa (6.8.19): "When one pronounces the Lord's name even unconsciously, one is immediately freed from all sins, which flee away like animals frightened by a lion."

In his own characteristic style, Viśvanātha enriches the verse's meaning with an embellishment of the Yamadūtas' and Vishnudūtas' dialogue: The Yamadūtas, objecting to the Vishnudūtas' claim that Ajāmila's sins are nullified simply by his pronouncing "Nārāyaṇa," say, "But Ajāmila was not pronouncing the divine name with the attitude of atonement, thinking, 'This is the Lord's name.' Rather, seeing us, he became fearful and just called his son." The Vishnudūtas reply, "Phaw! You don't know the truth; materialists that you are, you don't understand! Even by this calling for his son, his sins were certainly nullified, despite the absence of an intention to nullify sin." Viśvanātha continues, "(The portion of the verse) beginning with 'When' means 'calling his son at that moment is atonement for all his sins.' But not only this. When, previously, at the time of his son's name-giving ritual, Ajāmila would say in ungrammatical language, 'O Nārāyaṇa! Come from your mother's lap to my lap,' even then, his sins were atoned. Not only by the four syllables of the name Nārāyaṇa but even by two syllables or one syllable (of the Lord's name) can all sinful reactions be destroyed—this is the sense (of this verse)."

For the next several verses, the Vishnudūtas continue to expound on the power of Vishnu's names to remove all traces of sinful reactions from one who pronounces or recites them (see 6.2.9–18). The Vishnudūtas conclude (6.2.19):

yathāgadaṁ vīryatamam upayuktaṁ yadṛcchayā
ajānato'py ātma-guṇaṁ kuryān mantro 'py udāhṛtaḥ

"As a powerful medicine will act by its own potency even if ingested inadvertently and unknowingly, similarly a mantra will act when pronounced (even in ignorance of its power)."

In addition to the several ways in which the power of Vishnu's names are iterated in the Vishnudūtas' speech, commentators are keen to add further references to underline the message. In particular, we can note some points of elaboration by Giridhara, who addresses several possible doubts one might have on this subject, responding with scriptural proof texts (only a few of which we include here). One such doubt has to do with the qualification of one who chants divine names: is one's position in the *varṇāśrama* social order and life stages of relevance? No, says Giridhara. He quotes the Bhaviṣya Purāṇa: "Wherever *brāhmaṇas*, *kṣatriyas*, *vaiśyas*, *śūdras*, women, or tribals carry out the proclamation of Vishnu's names, they become free from all sin and proceed to the eternal realm." Giridhara (a follower of Vallabha's, who taught the worship of Krishna) highlights the particular effectiveness of chanting Krishna's name, quoting (among other scriptural sources) the Brahmavaivarta Purāṇa: "One may obtain the result of remembering one thousand divine names merely by pronouncing (one time) the name of Rāma. But a person who once recites Krishna's name can obtain the result of reciting one thousand divine names three times. And for one who betakes to the auspicious name 'Krishna,' millions of sins are immediately turned to ashes. Even performance of one hundred thousand sacrificial rites and observance of all vows, ritual bathing in all sacred places, austerities, fasting, reciting the Veda one thousand times, and circumambulating the earth one hundred times—all these acts do not equal one-sixteenth (the benefit) of the quiet recitation (*japa*) of Krishna's name."

Giridhara answers various further possible doubts about the efficacy of uttering divine names. After recalling the concern voiced in Śrīdhara's commentary regarding two simultaneous functions of one object (in this case the divine name), Giridhara raises the question whether the divine name could remove the reactions to one's future improprieties. "Yes," he writes, quoting from the prominent Caitanya Vaiṣṇava, Rūpa Gosvāmī (in his *Laghubhāgavatāmṛta*): "The fire of uttering Govinda's (Krishna's) name and glory quickly burns away all sins of the present, past, and future."

Well (one might wonder), then what is the point of performing counteractive and other expiatory acts (*prāyaścitta*)? Answer: because, although all sins cease by only once performing *nāma-saṁkīrtana* (chanting, uttering, singing divine names) and the like, still, fearing that sins may again occur, one does expiatory acts. But actually one ought to do counteractive acts only for the purpose of strengthening one's devotion (*bhakti-dārḍhyārtham*), since it is well known that uttering divine names eliminates all sorts of sins.

But why do some people who do *nāma-saṁkīrtana*, by which the root fault (*mūla-doṣa*, the root cause of sinful action) is removed, thereafter again engage in sinful acts? Reply: because of the force of the habit to enjoy and the like, there is the possibility of acting sinfully.

But then won't there be reactions to such sins? No, such understanding goes against the statements of many authorities, because it is not true that the claimed great result of even minimal practice of *nāma-saṁkīrtana* is impossible.

But isn't this just hyperbole (*arthavāda*)? No. The Nāradīya Purāṇa states, "For those wretches (*narādhama*) who say, 'the Purāṇas are full of hyperbole,' by those words the pious credits they have gained become only that (namely, so much empty talk)." Further, other authoritative texts state that to think these statements about the power of divine names is mere hyperbole earns one a place in hell.

But in that case, since we know that *nāma-saṁkīrtana* and so on does not have the power to free one from the offense (*aparādha*) of such thinking, how can it be said that it removes all sins? Giridhara proposes an analogy: in essence, as one is unable to pardon those who commit a crime against oneself (i.e., a judge must decide whether a punishment is necessary), similarly the divine name will not pardon offense to itself. Those who, in their offensive mentality toward Bhagavān's name, turn away from Bhagavān, surely will continue to undergo the cycle of repeated births and deaths (*saṁsāra*), by no fault of the divine name. The glory of the divine name is not compromised by its being disrespected or disregarded by some persons. Giridhara concludes that, in any case, it is clear that Ajāmila did not commit this offense (*nāmāparādha*), because nowhere in the Bhāgavata text is it mentioned, and, to the contrary, it describes the wonderful result of his uttering the divine name "Nārāyaṇa."

Quite dazed and confused by their encounter with the Vishnudūtas, the Yamadūtas return—without their intended victim, Ajāmila—to their master, Yamarāja. The Vishnudūtas' firm and authoritative words have turned the Yamadūtas' world topsy-turvy, and they are eager to get explanations from their master, whom they had assumed wields ultimate authority. Yamarāja explains that above him and all other lords is Vishnu, the independent "great self" (*mahātmā*), and it is by him that dharma is established. Including himself in a list of twelve sages and celestial beings who "know well this dharma established by the Lord," he then specifies the highest dharma (6.3.22):

etāvān eva loke'smin puṁsāṁ dharmaḥ paraḥ smṛtaḥ
bhakti-yogo bhagavati tan-nāma-grahaṇādibhiḥ

"Thus the highest dharma for human beings in this world is deemed to be the yoga of devotion to Bhagavān, beginning with invoking his names."

By these comments on dharma, the discussion returns to the issue that had engaged the Yamadūtas and Vishnudūtas in the beginning of their meeting (6.1.40). Now Yamarāja is voicing the Bhāgavata's conclusion, that the heart of dharma is bhakti yoga intent upon Bhagavān. Ajāmila has served Śuka's purpose of underlining this message by virtue of his apparent disqualifications as a practitioner of dharma. Indeed, for the commentators, the story of Ajāmila, because it is present in the Bhāgavata, becomes itself authoritative proof (*pramāṇa*) of the power of divine names, the superiority of bhakti as perfect dharma, and of Vishnu and his servants as the final arbiters of proper dharma.

4

Righteous Indignation in Longing for Krishna

One of the Bhāgavata Purāṇa's most poetically rich passages is the celebrated monologue of a particular cowherdess (*gopī*) beloved of Krishna, in which she addresses a bee that she assumes has approached her as a messenger from Krishna. In this final commentarial excursion we revisit this passage, focusing on verses 12, 15, and 21, to give a sense of how commentators derive multiple meanings from the text, wherein they explore the aesthetics of separation (*viraha*)—the devotionally artful experience and expression of the divine lover's absence (see Book 10, "Singing to a Bee," for the translation of all ten verses). Several commentators have elaborated on each of the song's verses, often embellishing them with explications of various possible ways to appreciate the intense and often contradictory emotions of the speaker, sometimes "filling in" between verses or between lines in a verse with explanatory or oratory additions. In the absence of Krishna, the singer of these verses contemplates her own plight; she bemoans the good fortune of other women with whom, she assumes, Krishna is presently enjoying company; she decries the deceptive but irresistible nature of Krishna as the best of lovers; and she eagerly questions the bee for news about her lover's state of mind. The entire display of one-pointed devotion for Krishna serves as a lesson in exalted bhakti for Uddhava, Krishna's cousin, who observes from nearby.

One day, sometime after Krishna and his brother Balarāma had departed from Vrindavan to Mathurā, and after Krishna had killed the tyrant Kaṁsa, Krishna sent his cousin and friend Uddhava as a messenger to console the Vrindavan residents in his absence. Seeing him in the early morning and noting the similarity of his features to those of Krishna, the young *gopīs* were eager to question him. Hardly had they seated him in a secluded place when one of the cowherd women, seeing a honeybee hovering about, imagined it to be Krishna's messenger and addressed it thus (10.47.12):

gopy uvāca
madhupa kitava-bandho mā spṛśaṅghriṁ sapatnyāḥ
kuca-vilulita-mālā-kuṅkuma-śmaśrubhir naḥ
vahatu madhu-patis tan-māninīnāṁ prasādaṁ
yadu-sadasi viḍambyaṁ yasya dūtas tvam īdṛk

"The *gopī* said: Nectar-drinking honeybee, friend of a cheater! Do not touch my feet with your hair, which is colored by saffron from (Krishna's) garland after it was crushed by the breasts of another lover. Let the honey-sweet Lord show favor to the women (of Mathurā), who think highly of him! One who has a messenger like you will be ridiculed in the Yadu assembly."

In this first of the ten Bhramara Gītā verses, the *gopī* (identified by commentators as Śrī Rādhā, the preeminent beloved of Krishna) addresses the bee in ways that allude to both Krishna's sweetness and his deceptiveness. In his *Bṛhad-vaiṣṇava-toṣanī* commentary on Book Ten of the Bhāgavata, Sanātana Gosvāmī notes that she considers the bee to be the friend of a cheater by similarity of appearance (black with saffron), similarity of name (*madhupa, madhupati*), and similarity of behavior (drunkenness—typically seen in the company of cheaters—and fickleness). Whatever message the bee intends to deliver, its very appearance—with saffron-colored hair—discloses to her that Krishna has been *firmly* embraced by a rival lover whose breasts, smeared with kumkum powder, had crushed Krishna's forest-flower garland, within which the bee had obviously been lingering.

In regard to the bee's form, Sanātana wishes to dispel what he considers a misconception of some commentators—namely, that the saffron-colored hair refers to Uddhava's having a red mustache. This cannot be so, he writes, because Uddhava is described in the beginning of the chapter (verse 2) as being very handsome (implying that anyone with a red mustache would not be considered handsome). On the other hand, Sanātana continues, it would be no mistake to read the passage as indicating that Rādhā identifies Uddhava with the bee.

With Rādhā's negative pronouncements about the bee messenger's association with Krishna, she displays her indignation, forbidding the bee to touch her feet, which, says Sanātana, the bee considers to be flowers (because of her red toenails) from which it may draw nectar, or which the bee approaches in order to propitiate her with flattery. "We don't need your flattery," says the *gopī* proudly. "We already have a high reputation and are thoroughly self-willed, so what is the use of your touching my feet?"

Sanātana continues: the *gopī* expresses her mood of jealousy in this verse. Essentially she says, "Alas, he enjoys with our rival, forgetting us altogether." And her jealousy is sharpened with contempt, which is expressed by the phrase "Let the honey-sweet Lord show favor to the women (of Mathurā), who think highly of him." Sanātana, paraphrasing the *gopī*'s derision, asks rhetorically, "What has all this effort to gain Krishna's favor given us?" Hence, "Let him give his favor to them; after all, this is appropriate, since he is a king (*pati*), the lord of the Yadus. In any case (playing on the meaning of the verse's first word, *madhupa*), it is well known that 'there is no friendship with a drunkard.'" Taking the final line of the verse in a different way, Sanātana has the *gopī* say, "Actually, in the assembly of those sophisticated ladies, his (charming but insincere) conduct is laughable, to be derided."

Viśvanātha identifies each of the ten verses of the Bhramara Gītā as instances of ten different types of artful speech (*citra-jalpa*) exhibited by a lover. Thus, this verse exhibits *prajalpa*, which is characterized by rude expression of disrespect, indignation, jealousy, and pride toward the beloved.

We may also note the ironic juxtaposition of lovers' messengers in this verse and in the passage as a whole. Krishna's official messenger, Uddhava, who, later in the same chapter, will attempt to appease the *gopīs* on Krishna's behalf with theological observations about Krishna's omnipresence, is warmly welcomed by the *gopīs*. At the same time, the bee messenger (whom the one *gopī* is sure has been sent by Krishna, though we are never quite sure—*maybe* Krishna has also sent this little creature, or is indeed himself present in the form of the bee) receives considerable rebuke before finally being submissively questioned. It is by virtue of the bee messenger's presence that we, the listeners and readers, become privy to the *gopī*'s turbulent sentiments of longing for her lover.

In verse 13, the *gopī* makes a further negative comparison of the bee messenger and Krishna and then, in verse 14, dismissively advises it to perform its song of praise before Krishna's new urbanite girlfriends. In the following verse, she broods over Krishna's too-attractive nature (10.47.15):

divi bhuvi ca rasāyāṁ kāḥ striyas tad-durāpāḥ
kapaṭa-rucira-hāsa-bhrū-vijṛmbhasya yāḥ syuḥ
caraṇa-raja upāste yasya bhūtir vayaṁ kā
api ca kṛpaṇa-pakṣe hy uttamaḥ-śloka-śabdaḥ

"In heaven, on earth, or in lower worlds, what women are unavailable to him? He makes them all his own, with his deceitful, charming smile and arched eyebrows. Even the Goddess of Fortune, Lakṣmī, worships the dust of his feet. Who are we (in comparison)? He is called Uttamaśloka because he is partial to the unfortunate (yet we remain unfortunate)."

Like all other verses in this passage, this verse can be read variously, as expressive of differing, and even contrasting, moods of the *gopī* singer. According to the commentator Jīva Gosvāmī, in one reading, in her maddened state, the *gopī* suddenly and completely gives up her conceit of lover's anger, *māna* (expressed in previous verses)—the anger of one who has been separated from her lover following a quarrel. Thus, in a remorseful mood, she asks rhetorically, "In heaven, on earth, or in lower worlds, what women are unavailable to him?" She speaks in the mood of humble attendance about his inaccessibility to her by contrasting herself with all other women: "Who are we (in comparison)?"

Still, according to Jīva, one can just as well read this verse as an expression of the *gopī*'s anger (*māna*). In this case, he suggests that the bee is challenging her, "In your initial meeting with him, why were you not careful?" "It was not our fault," she insists, "we were swept away by his magic (*māyayā*), and now he has given us up." Displaying both a sense of lowliness and jealousy, she says, "He makes them all his own, with his deceitful, charming smile and arched eyebrows. Even the Goddess of Fortune, Lakṣmī, worships the dust of his feet."

Jīva goes a step further with his interpretation. The *gopī*'s talk about how any and all women of the universe are available to Krishna is indicative of her indignation at the fact that he is ungovernable. And along with indignation, she expresses feelings of lowliness, jealousy, pride, and a measure of irony. "Whomsoever he wishes to attract, those women are all available to him. Even Goddess Lakṣmī follows him wherever he goes, serving the dust of his feet, so who are we in comparison?" She concludes with a touch of harshness: "Unfortunate persons speak of Krishna as Uttamaśloka (one who is praised with choice verses), but, although we *gopīs* are unfortunate, we refuse to call him by that name."

Similar to *prajalpa* instantiated in verse 12, according to Viśvanātha, this verse is an example of *ujjalpa*, which includes expression of the lover's duplicitous nature as well as insulting words born of jealousy. Viśvanātha summarizes this verse's structure in this way: the first two lines ("In heaven . . . eyebrows") describes the lover's duplicitous nature; the third line ("Even . . . comparison") indicates her prideful jealousy; and the fourth line ("He is called . . . unfortunate") expresses her insulting indignation.

We can make two further observations about this verse and Jīva's commentary. First, the *gopī*'s explanation of Krishna's attracting power as being because of his *māyā* ("magic," in this instance) is significant, in that considerable attention is given to this term both in the Bhāgavata and beyond, in the wider Vedānta discourse. Suffice it to note here that in his systematic treatise on the philosophy of the Bhāgavata Purāṇa, the *Bhāgavata Sandarbha* (also known as *Ṣaṭ Sandarbha*; in the second treatise, the *Bhagavat-sandarbha*, Anuccheda 22), Jīva discusses the nature of *māyā* as a principal energy of Bhagavān, the supreme Lord. It is he who activates *māyā*, which (or who—understood to be a female person) then brings about the creation, maintenance, and annihilation of the temporal world. However, the irony here is that the *gopīs*, and all other women with whom Krishna has a conjugal relationship, are understood to be forms of a different, "internal" power of Bhagavān, who are ever beyond and untouched by his "external" power, *māyā*. Indeed, *māyā* is identified as the external, subordinate counterpart to the energy that is hypostasized as Krishna's consorts, who, according to Jīva's reading, are bemoaning their subjection to that energy to which they are ontologically superior.

Krishna's incomparable power of attraction is both his glory and his "fault." And Krishna's fault—his impropriety—runs deep, as the *gopī* insists (in v. 17) by citing various questionable acts of Krishna's in his previous *avatāras*. All this goes to show that one should not hear about Krishna at all, because to do so, one's worldly life is sure to be ruined (v. 18). It is best not to hear about him, and certainly not to hear his direct words: in effect (v. 19), "We *gopīs* have been victims of his charms repeatedly, but now we have learned our lesson, so let there be no more talk about Krishna!"

The commentators write that at this point the *gopī* seems to have lost sight of the bee, causing her considerable anxiety; but then the bee reappears (or else, writes Jīva, perhaps another bee appears), and the *gopī*'s attitude softens. She wants to reward the bee (v. 20), and, in the next verse, she becomes submissively inquisitive (10.47.21):

api bata madhu-puryām ārya-putro'dhunāste
smarati sa pitṛ-gehān saumya bandhūṁś ca gopān
kvacid api sa kathā naḥ kiṅkarīṇāṁ gṛṇīte
bhujam aguru-sugandhaṁ mūrdhny adhāsyat kadā nu

"Does Krishna, son of the noble Nanda, now live in Mathurā? Indeed, does he remember his father's houses, his family, or his cowherd friends?

Gentle sir! Does he ever speak about us, his maidservants? Oh, when will he place his agar-wood-scented hand upon our heads?"

Coming to the end of the song to the bee, in the final two verses the *gopī* puts aside her pretense of lover's anger and jealousy to show the simple and complete purity of her love for Krishna. Viśvanātha identifies this final verse as an example of *sujalpa*, consisting of honest questioning with gravity, humility, and nervous eagerness. Here we can note how Jīva and Viśvanātha treat each of the *gopī*'s four questions as indicative of her anxious anticipation.

According to Jīva, the *gopī* is here addressing Uddhava ("Gentle sir"), rather than the bee. Because she and her companions had not heard any news about Krishna for such a long time, she is not at all sure that he is in Mathurā (though when he had departed Vraja long before, he was certainly on his way there). Perhaps, as she had heard, he was far away in Avantī, attending a *gurukula* (residential school for Vedic learning), keeping this a secret out of fear that Kaṁsa's friend Jarāsandha, vengeful of Krishna's relatives for Krishna's having killed Kaṁsa, would attack Mathurā if he knew of Krishna's absence from the city (knowing that Krishna's presence there would guarantee the city's residents' protection). Krishna's secrecy about being in faraway Avantī was also, Jīva notes, owing to his concern for the residents of Vraja, who would be sad if they knew of his distant whereabouts.

Viśvanātha's explanation for the first question is quite different: Hoping that Krishna may be about to return to Vraja, the *gopī* reasons that Krishna may be ready to leave Mathurā just as he had previously left Vraja. Then again, he may be staying there out of a sense of obligation to his father, the noble Nanda, whose well-meaning simplicity led him to let his son be taken in by the Yadus in Mathurā.

But, writes Jīva, fearing that the answer to her first question might be "yes, Krishna is happily living in Mathurā," she hastens to ask the next question: "Does he remember his father's houses . . . ?" (Jīva notes, incidentally, that the plural "houses" indicates that Nanda had built several residences for his son's pleasure). Viśvanātha indicates that the question expresses the *gopī*'s genuine concern for Krishna's father, noting that since Krishna's departure, Nanda had remained completely stunned, leaving his residential quarters completely neglected.

Again, with the final two questions, Viśvanātha reads a sense of high anticipation based on recognition of the *gopīs*' superiority to the Mathurā women in matters of pleasing Krishna. He has the speaker imagining that

Krishna tells the women of Mathurā, after finding them unable to perform the several arts of which the *gopīs* are thoroughly skilled, "O ladies of the Yadu clan, go back to your families. I've had quite enough of you. Instead, I'm going back to Vraja early tomorrow morning!" And, whereas such an attitude might suggest a sense of pride on the part of the *gopī* speaker, Jīva writes to the contrary, that the *gopīs* see their particular qualification as being only that they identify themselves as Krishna's maidservants, and thus that the *gopī* here expresses her humility.

Viśvanātha ends his comments on this last of the ten Bhramara Gītā verses by noting that, altogether, they demonstrate the most exalted form of devotional fervor, referred to technically as "divine madness" (*divyonmāda*), of which the ten types of artful speech (*citra-jalpa*) are a key characteristic. Again, he notes that the exalted nature of the *gopī*'s behavior points to Rādhā as the speaker, for it is only she, Krishna's first and dearest consort, who has the capacity to experience such devotion (*mahābhāva*)—perfect, transcendent love.

We may note further that the commentator Jīva Gosvāmī elsewhere (in his systematic Bhāgavata Purāṇa commentary, the *Ṣaṭ Sandarbha*) expounds extensively on the Bhāgavata's theological underpinnings to counter the view that this or similar passages in the Bhāgavata are accounts of worldly romance between ordinary—or even extraordinary—human beings. From Jīva's exposition we briefly relate two relevant points.

First, to emphasize the transcendent, atemporal identity of Krishna as the original supreme divinity, *svayaṁ bhagavān*, Jīva affirms (in his *Bhagavat Sandarbha*, Anuccheda 29) that Krishna's form (*vigraha*) is integral to his identity (*svarūpa*), and hence even when he appears as an "ordinary" human in this world, his transcendence is not compromised. In light of this understanding, Krishna's agar-wood-scented hand is neither a figurative hand nor a mortal hand subject to the vulnerabilities of all mortal bodies.

In a similar vein, as a further reminder of the Bhāgavata's concern that its readers or listeners not misunderstand, Jīva quotes (in his *Bhakti Sandarbha*, Anuccheda 338) Śuka's promise at the end of his description of the *rāsa-līlā* episode (10.33.39) that "a steady-minded person who faithfully hears or describes Vishnu's sporting with the Vraja *gopīs* gains perfect devotion (*bhaktiṁ parām*) to the Lord, freed very rapidly from the heart disease of lust." Jīva adds that these are "confidential pastimes" (*rahasya-līlā*) and, as such, are not to be mistaken for worldly activities.

NOTES

INTRODUCTION

1. Here we employ "the Rāmāyaṇa" in a generic sense to refer to the many vernacular versions and adaptations as well as film and television renditions. The Bhāgavata Purāṇa includes its own highly abridged rendition of the Rāmāyaṇa (in Book Nine), explicitly referring to other Rāmāyaṇa versions as being commonly known, justifying a very brief summary within the Bhāgavata.
2. Readers unfamiliar with classical Indian literature may find the profusion of strange names found in the Bhāgavata to be rather daunting. We encourage patience while grappling with these names; gradually some familiarity with at least the more important names will develop, and this knowledge can be useful in relating to other classical (and some later) Indian texts.
3. Bhagavān means, literally, "possessor of fortune," from which is derived the sense of "possessor of plenitude," sometimes referring, in the Bhāgavata Purāṇa, to any superhuman being but mainly to the supreme divinity, identified as Krishna or one of his many forms. Unlike other texts, such as the Viṣṇu Purāṇa, which identifies Krishna as a form or "expansion" of Vishnu, the Bhāgavata (specifically in 1.3.28) identifies Krishna as the origin of Vishnu, Nārāyaṇa, and all the *avatāras*.
4. *Rasa* means, literally, "taste," "juice," or "that which is aesthetically relished" or "aesthetic mood" and is a term of great significance for the Bhāgavata's later commentarial tradition and for followers of the various sectarian devotional traditions that regard it as canonical. See Gupta and Valpey (2013), especially chapter 7, for further explanation.
5. See Jarow (2003), chapters 2 and 3, for further discussion on the Bhāgavata as an antidote to the sense of loss and absence, particularly the absence of Krishna.
6. While it is reasonable to assume that the Bhāgavata Purāṇa was compiled with a specific community of listeners or readers in mind, the identity of such a community is a matter of conjecture. See Colas (2003, 230–34), for a discussion of epigraphic evidential traces of a Bhāgavata cult.

7. Purāṇic tradition (alluded to in 12.7.10) makes a distinction between greater and lesser Purāṇas, the latter said to include five topics and the former, ten. The Bhāgavata Purāṇa names its ten topics at 2.10.1. Lists of the main Purāṇas usually include eighteen, some of which are named after *avatāras* such as Varāha, Kūrma, Matsya, and Vāmana.
8. Allusions to *maṇḍala* formations in the Bhāgavata are evident particularly in sacrificial rites (in which the fire rituals would be performed within a ritually demarcated symmetrical space that may include a circular boundary or fire pit) and in references to assemblies of persons (typically sages) surrounding a single leader sage or divinity. On the macrocosmic level, Book Five, chapter 16, describes the universe as being in the form of a *maṇḍala*.
9. To quote Noel Sheth (1984, 108), "When we turn to the Bhāgavata Purāṇa, we find that it is literally saturated with devotion; every page drips with the juice (*rasa*) of devotion. In its variety, elaborateness and intensity, it leaves the *Harivaṁśa* and the *Viṣṇu Purāṇa* far behind."
10. According to Soifer (1991, 98), the Viṣṇu Purāṇa also makes Prahlāda the central character of the story and argues for the supremacy of bhakti, and yet the Viṣṇu Purāṇa's understanding of bhakti differs markedly from the Bhāgavata's. The former sees bhakti as transcending and thus trivializing the world of dharma, whereas the Bhāgavata attempts to synthesize the two realms by demonstrating bhakti's ability to encompass the world, fulfill dharma, and yet move beyond it.
11. The Sanskrit term *dharma* carries a wide range of meanings, some of which will be encountered occasionally in this book. Rooted in the notion of "sustaining" or "upholding," in the present context it refers to the faithful observance of one's duties as circumscribed by one's social position.
12. Hospital (1995, 30); see his essay for elaboration on the Bhāgavata's presentation of *līlā* in relation to earlier texts.
13. The different types of bhakti practice are further discussed in Sheth (1984, 108–43).
14. Ashutosh Sarma Biswas has exhaustively documented the Bhāgavata's use of Vedic grammar and archaic words in his *Bhāgavata Purāṇa: A Linguistic Study* (1968). Biswas organizes his work as a verse-by-verse commentary on the Bhāgavata, pointing out unexpected grammatical forms, meanings, and etymologies as they occur.
15. Take, for example, the word, *apīcya*, which is used thrice in the Bhāgavata, always in the sense of "beautiful" or "charming." Biswas (1968) points out that *apīcya* is a Vedic word, virtually unknown in classical Sanskrit, and is never used to mean "beautiful" except in the Bhāgavata. (See Biswas's comments on 1.19.28 and 3.28.17.) Another example can be found at 3.15.22, where the word *uccheṣitam* occurs. Biswas writes that this is an "unusual obscure word used in the sense of 'kissed', for which no other parallel instance is available."

BOOK ONE

1. 1.1 Invocation. "*Oṁ!* Obeisance . . . Bhagavān!" translates *oṁ namo bhagavate vāsudevāya*—a line that appears in modern editions of the Bhāgavata here and again at the beginning of Book Two. (It is also found at 4.8.54, where Nārada

instructs Dhruva). In present-day Bhāgavata recitation events this mantra is typically recited as an initial invocation.

2. 1.1 This initial verse of the Bhāgavata Purāṇa consists of a series of dense, metrically arranged *sūtras* (aphorisms) that echo the famous opening lines of the Brahmasūtra. The reader is encouraged to consult this volume's concluding chapter, "Commentarial Excursions," where we provide a more detailed explanation of the first verse, drawing from the Sanskrit commentary of Śrīdhara Svāmī. The first verse speaks of the supreme truth by freely mixing both masculine and neuter pronouns (*yaḥ*, *yat*, "who," "which," and *asya*, "his" or "its") and introducing other ambiguities. For example, the phrase *trisargomṛṣā* can be read as "**the threefold creation . . . is not false**" or "the threefold creation is false." The parenthetical phrase **(upon him it rests, and in him it dissolves)** is supplied in place of the word *ādi*, "etc." Nearly all commentators explain *ādi* as shorthand for "rest" and "dissolution," which—along with "birth"—constitute the three cyclical phases of this world. The **first seer** is identified by Śrīdhara as Brahmā, the four-faced demiurge who is born from Vishnu. According to Jīva Gosvāmī, **positive and negative reasoning** refers to *anvaya-vyatireka*, a method of defining the Supreme by compiling scriptural statements about what he is and what he is not. For a fuller discussion of this verse, see Gupta (2007, 105–12).
3. 1.2 In the present context, **dharma** can be understood as "expressions of righteous disposition and behavior." The **three miseries** are those caused by other beings, by oneself, and by natural occurrences. These constitute a standard Purāṇic typology of human misery.
4. 1.3 The Bhāgavata Purāṇa here promotes itself not only as a philosophical text (stated in the previous verses) but also as a work of poetry. This verse contains an extended metaphor: as the fruit of the Veda tree, the Bhāgavata Purāṇa is both a direct product of and also very different from the Vedic corpus of texts. Fruits are said to become sweeter when they are tasted first by a parrot, and here the first speaker of the Bhagavata is the sage **Śuka**, whose name means, literally, "parrot." The Bhāgavata fruit is bursting with *rasa* (literally, "juice" or "sap")—an exceptionally difficult word to translate in its fullness. In Indian aesthetics, the word usually denoted the intensified emotion born of human (or divine) relationships. For a brief history of *rasa* and a discussion of its use in the Bhāgavata Purāṇa, see Haberman (1994). For a discussion of Śuka's identity as sage-parrot, see Doniger (1993).
5. 2.2 Śrīdhara explains the compound *sarvabhūtahṛdayam* as "he who has entered the hearts of all beings by the power of yoga," while Jīva Gosvāmī explains it as "one who has (captured) the hearts of all beings," as evidenced by the fact that even the trees felt the pain of separation from him.
6. 2.11 The Upaniṣads often identify *brahman* as *jñāna*—knowledge, **consciousness**, or awareness.
7. 2.12 **The self** refers to the nondual consciousness (*jñānam advayam*) defined in the previous verse—i.e., Bhagavān, who is the self within the self.
8. 2.13 **Social orders and life stages** translates *varṇāśrama*, the Hindu social system that organizes society into four occupations (priests, warriors, farmers and merchants, and workers) and life stages (celibate student, householder, forest dweller, and wandering ascetic).

9. 2.14 The **Sātvatas** were a royal clan related to the Yadus and were thus part of Krishna's larger family. Viśvanātha gives a theological interpretation, deriving *sātvata* from *sattva*, the quality of illumination: "The Sātvatas are those among whom lives Krishna, who is pure *sattva*."
10. 2.16 **Devoted . . . virtue** translates *puṇyatīrthaniṣevaṇāt*, which Viśvanātha and Vaṁśīdhara interpret as service to the guru. Vaṁśīdhara also explains it as studying scriptures like the Bhāgavata Purāṇa and visiting places of pilgrimage like the Ganges and Vrindavan.
11. 2.18 The phrase *bhāgavata-sevā* can be interpreted two ways in this context, according to Śrīdhara: **service to devotees of Bhagavān** and service to (i.e., hearing) the Bhāgavata Purāṇa.
12. 2.19 The three qualities (*guṇas*) described in this verse—**illumination (***sattva***)**, **passion (***rajas***)**, and **darkness (***tamas***)**—are frequently used in the Purāṇas to describe and classify the psychophysical nature of persons, actions, and objects in this world. The quality of *sattva* is characterized by clarity and knowledge, *rajas* by ambitious activity, and *tamas* by lethargy and ignorance.
13. 2.21 The **knot in the heart** is a metaphor—found several times in the Bhāgavata—for the unbreakable bond of attachment, particularly the attachment between man and woman. **The Lord, the self**: The Sanskrit term *ātman* is a reflexive pronoun that can refer variously to the individual self (body, mind, or spiritual essence) or the ultimate Self (the self of selves, and the self of the universe). Often in the Bhāgavata there is ambiguity as to its referent (either individual or ultimate Self). Although one might make a distinction in translation with the words "self" and "Self," throughout this volume we retain the ambiguity in the Sanskrit (which makes no such distinctions in writing) with the lowercase "self."
14. 8.18 **The primordial supreme person** translates *puruṣaṁ param*, and **material nature** translates *prakṛti*. These terms belong to Sāṁkhya philosophy, which sees the universe as consisting of two primordial principles—the individual conscious self, *puruṣa*, and the inert material nature, *prakṛti*. The Bhāgavata teaches a theistic form of Sāṁkhya, wherein Krishna is the supreme self (*puruṣa*) who stands above all individual selves and gives rise to *prakṛti* by his own power. The Bhāgavata Purāṇa sees this original *puruṣa* as a personal and playful Deity—namely, Bhagavān Krishna or Vishnu. For a more detailed discussion of the Bhāgavata's Sāṁkhya, see Book Three, chapter 26.
15. 8.19 While the word ***māyā*** is often explained in nondualist Vedānta as "illusion" or "unreality," in the Bhāgavata Purāṇa, *māyā* is the real power of God to create and act in wondrous ways. This power often obscures the Lord from the ignorant and reveals him to the devotee. For further discussion of *māyā*, see Book Ten, chapter 8, including the suggested readings in that chapter.
16. 8.20 **How then can we women see you?** The irony, of course, is that while Kuntī repeatedly explains how Krishna is invisible to all people, *she* is able to see Krishna with her own eyes and describe him in personal detail, as the following verses reveal.
17. 8.21 This verse includes epithets that describe Krishna in relation to his birth parents in Mathurā (Vāsudeva and Devakī) as well as his foster parents in Vrindavan (Nanda and Yaśodā). According to Viśvanātha, the order of epithets in the verse

suggests an ever-deepening hierarchy of love. All those whom Krishna regards as his family are blessed, especially his father, Vāsudeva. More blessed, says Viśvanātha, is Krishna's mother, Devakī, who possessed greater love for her son and had the privilege of bearing him in her womb. More blessed is Nanda, Krishna's foster father, and beyond him Mother Yaśodā, whose love was yet deeper. Both of them had the opportunity to relish the sweetness of Krishna's childhood play in Vrindavan. But greater even than Krishna's childhood play is the sweetness of his youth, when he captivated the hearts of Vraja's people by his beauty and charm. The final epithet, **Govinda**, Viśvanātha says, refers to the sweetest, youthful Krishna.

18. 8.22 **Lotus navel**: Vishnu/Krishna is called *pankaja-nābha* because at the dawn of creation a lotus grows from his navel, upon which the first created being, Brahmā, is born. The Lord is also said to have a navel that resembles the whorl of a lotus. Krishna's **eyes** are shaped like lotus petals, while his **feet** are soft like a lotus and marked with lines in the shape of a lotus.
19. 8.24 The Bhāgavata Purāṇa begins where the Mahābhārata ends, and here Queen Kuntī reminisces about the many adversities she has faced with the Pāṇḍavas. The events are listed here in their approximate order of occurrence, thus providing a one-verse summary of the Mahābhārata.
20. 8.28 Here, Kuntī offers a resolution to the problem of human suffering. As we have seen in preceding verses, she does not blame Krishna for the troubles that she and her sons endured; Krishna, as **eternal time**, moves equally among all beings. Rather, Kuntī says, the blame for strife lies in individual free will. In his comments on this verse, Jīva further explains Krishna's involvement in the world: "First, the Lord is impartial. Second, although he is impartial, he bestows grace upon his devotees and restrains their enemies. Third, for this purpose, the Lord descends (to earth) and performs his playful activities (*līlā*). But fourth, the Lord is nevertheless beyond all of this." For a further discussion of the Bhāgavata Purāṇa's theodicy, see Book One, chapter 9, as well as Gopal K. Gupta, "The Bhāgavata's Response to the Problem of Evil," in Gupta and Valpey (2013).
21. 8.29 **They think that you are partial**: Bhaktivedanta offers an explanation for apparent differences in the Lord's treatment of human beings: "The sun rays are open to everyone but the receptacles differ. . . . Those who are completely against the service of the Lord are considered to be in abject darkness, those who ask for the Lord's favor only at the time of necessity are partial recipients of the mercy of the Lord, and those who are cent-percent engaged in the service of the Lord are full recipients of the mercy of the Lord. Such partiality in receiving the Lord's mercy is relative to the recipient, and it is not due to the partiality of the all-merciful Lord."
22. 8.32 **Like sandalwood grows in Malaya**: King Yadu was Krishna's ancestor, and thus Krishna is often addressed using the patronymics Yādava and Yadunandana. While aristocratic birth may elevate an ordinary person, here it is Krishna who gives glory to the dynasty, even as the presence of sandalwood trees in the Malaya hills makes the latter famous.
23. 8.39 **Your footprints, which are distinguishable by their characteristic markings**: Krishna's feet are said to be marked with many unique signs, including a flag,

lotus, thunderbolt, disk, and elephant goad. As he walks, Krishna leaves the impressions of these symbols upon the earth, bringing auspiciousness and good fortune.

24. 8.41 **The Pāṇḍus and the Vṛṣṇis**: Bhaktivedanta comments, "The Pāṇḍavas are her [Kuntī's] own sons, and the Vṛṣṇis are the members of her paternal family. Krishna was equally related to both families. Both the families required the Lord's help because both were dependent devotees of the Lord. Śrīmatī Kuntīdevī wished Śrī Kṛṣṇa to remain with her sons the Pāṇḍavas, but by His doing so her paternal house would be bereft of the benefit. All these partialities troubled the mind of Kuntī, and therefore she desired to cut off the affectionate tie. A pure devotee cuts off the limited ties of affection for his family and widens his activities of devotional service for all forgotten souls."
25. 9.10 The Sanskrit term ***māyā*** appears several times throughout the Bhāgavata, with various shades of meaning, usually with philosophical import. Here it is used in its broadest sense as **divine power**. It often carries the sense of "magic" or "illusion."
26. 9.12 A possible alternative translation of this verse is, "Oh what hardship! What injustice! You sons of dharma did not deserve to live in such distress, but you had the shelter of the *brāhmaṇas*, dharma, and the infallible Lord." The difference turns on two senses of the verb *arh* as "deserve" and "be able." The chosen translation emphasizes the hardship they endured, whereas this alternative translation highlights the injustice of their suffering.
27. 9.15 **Voracious** translates *vṛkodara*, literally. "wolf bellied."
28. 9.16 **Krishna's plan** translates *asya vidhitsitam*. Since *asya* is simply a demonstrative pronoun signifying a nearby masculine entity, it could also refer to the masculine noun *kāla* (time), which was mentioned two verses ago, leading to a plausible alternative translation, "Time's plan." However, the closest possible referent of the pronoun is Krishna, who appears in the last line of the previous verse and is the main subject of the chapter's remainder.
29. 9.23 **From the karma of selfish desires** translates *kāma-karmabhiḥ*. Karma—literally, "action"—refers to all kinds of activities that implicate the actor in some form of "reaction," usually with a moral implication of being good, bad, desirable, or undesirable. *Kāma* means, in the broadest sense, "desire," with a general implication of self-interest, selfishness, and the pursuit of goods deemed gratificatory for a person's own senses or for persons one identifies as one's "own," especially family members and friends.
30. 9.30 *Sahasraṇī*: Śrīdhara offers many explanations of this epithet for Bhīṣma—he was **leader of thousands,** protector of thousands in battle, and his words carried a thousand meanings.
31. 18.26 Commentators agree that **beyond the three states** refers to "the fourth" (*turīya*) state of consciousness, beyond wakefulness, dreaming, and dreamless sleep—a classic Upaniṣadic formulation taken up by later Vedāntic discourse to articulate the liberated state. Vijayadhvaja adds that in this case it means the sage had "gained" (*praptam*) Hari, the Lord.
32. 18.28 These are standard, minimal items of reception offered to a guest by a householder, according to Dharma texts. As a king, Parīkṣit would be entitled these tokens of respect at the very least. **Ceremonial water** refers to *arghya*—a

ritual water offering (possibly containing various ingredients considered auspicious) presented to an honored guest, who would sprinkle some drops of the *arghya* on his own head.

33. 18.32 **Great brahmanical power** translates *atitejasvī*. As the son of a *brāhmaṇa*, he is considered to have powers similar to those of the father, such as the power to bless and to curse.
34. 18.33 As elaborated in the next verse, the sage's son represents the view that *kṣatriyas* (royalty) are always to behave as subordinates to *brāhmaṇas*. The examples of crows and dogs—both considered highly impure animals—suggest that the transgression is one of impurity (of royalty) upon purity (of *brāhmaṇas*).
35. 18.35 **Boundaries of propriety have been laid asunder** translates *bhinna-setūn*. A *setu* is something that binds or ties, and it can also mean "a bridge" or "a boundary." Here, according to commentators, it is the boundary of propriety that has been broken. Also suggested is that with appropriate decorum for *kṣatriyas* having been broken, their social connection with *brāhmaṇas* had been destroyed. Commentators note that here the sage's son addresses his young friends.
36. 18.36 To touch water, especially of a sacred river, is a ritual act of purification (usually involving ritual sipping of the water while reciting a mantra) observed prior to the incantation of sacred hymns. Vamṣīdhara comments that **Kauśiki** could be understood as an allusion to the Gāyatrī mantra (see note 40). In this reading, the boy first chanted this essential mantra pronounced by *brāhmaṇas* before uttering the curse.
37. 18.37 **Takṣaka** is a leader of the snakes, said to be able to fly. It is understood that his bite will be lethal. Commentators mention that some versions of the text indicate that Parīkṣit will be burned to ashes.
38. 18.39 Śaunaka is the leading interlocutor among the sages to whom Sūta (Ugraśravās) speaks.
39. 18.46 **The horse sacrifice** (*haya-medha*, or *aśvamedha*) is an elaborate Vedic ritual, the performance of which was a means for a king to demonstrate his preeminence in relation to neighboring kings. This yearlong rite would begin with the king setting a wild horse free to wander where it chose, accompanied by an army prepared to fight any resisting king along the path of the horse. At the end of one year all the submitting kings would be invited to witness the sacrifice of the horse and thus affirm the sacrificing king's preeminence.
40. 19.3 According to Vaṁśīdhara, **twice-born, gods**, can be read as "twice-born gods," meaning that the *brāhmaṇas* are the gods of the earth. "Twice-born" (*dvija*) identifies those who have undergone a ritual "second birth," *upanayana*, which initiates *brāhmaṇas*, *kṣatriyas*, and *vaiśyas* into study and recitation of the Veda and into the daily recitation of the Gāyatrī mantra, a mantra from the Ṛgveda considered central to brahmanical life.
41. 19.5 **River of immortality** refers, for most commentators, to the Ganges River. However, Jīva suggests that it must refer to the Yamunā River, since the mention of **service to Krishna's feet** indicates that Parīkṣit went to Vrindavan—Krishna's home—through which the Yamunā River flows, and because of the mention, in the next verse, of the river's **waters, mixed with dust from Krishna's feet and blessed *tulasī* leaves.**

42. 19.6 **Destined to die** translates *mariṣyamāṇaḥ*, literally, "being about to die." The sacredness of rivers in India is closely associated with preparing for death. Especially the river Ganges is celebrated in Purāṇic texts as an opportunity, or even guarantee, to achieve liberation for one who dies in its close proximity. ***Tulasī***, "sacred basil" (*Ocimum tenuiflorum*), is revered in Vaiṣṇava traditions, being considered especially dear to Krishna. **Both worlds** indicates, according to commentators, "within and without." Vaṁśīdhara adds that, alternatively, **purifies both worlds** indicates purification in this world from worldly characteristics, and purification in the next world (following death) from being subject to reaching hellish realms and from being subject to returning to this world.
43. 19.8 **Sacred places** translates *tīrtha*, literally, "crossing" or "ford," coming to mean any place (especially where a body of water is present) that enables crossing over from this to the next world, or to the realm beyond all mundane worlds. The verse suggests that the sages' pretexts of being on pilgrimage were unconvincing, since pilgrimage is typically undertaken with hopes to gain purification for oneself. These sages, Sūta notes, had no such need, for they were themselves, by their mere presence at sacred places, capable of purifying them from the accumulated sins of ordinary pilgrims.
44. 19.9–10 These two verses constitute a roll call of the most celebrated sages in Puranic literature, several of whom are mentioned, described, or heard from elsewhere in the Bhāgavata Purāṇa.
45. 19.25 Vaṁśīdhara notes that Śuka's being **without visible signs of *āśrama*** (*alakṣya-liṅga*) indicates that he belonged to none of the four *āśramas* (student, householder, forest dweller, and renouncer). His being **negligently dressed** translates *avadhūta-veśaḥ*, literally, "having the dress of an *avadhūta*," which can mean, says Vaṁśīdhara, that he was naked (as is stated explicitly at 1.19.27). An *avadhūta* is an ascetic who identifies with no *āśrama*, not even *sannyāsa*, the *āśrama* of final renunciation.
46. 19.29 **Whose life was granted by Vishnu** translates *viṣṇu-rātaḥ*, literally, "given by Vishnu," alluding to Parīkṣit's having been protected by Vishnu while still in the womb of his mother, Uttara, from Aśvatthāmā's attempted murder. This episode is described in the Mahābhārata (Sauptika Parvan, chapters 11–16, though without mention of Vishnu entering Uttara's womb) and, very briefly, in 1.12.7–12 of the Bhāgavata.
47. 19.30 **Seers . . . celestial** translates *brahmarṣi-rajarṣi-devarṣi*, three types of *ṛṣis*—"seers" or "visionaries"—associated with these three categories (two *varṇa* categories and one of divine beings).
48. 19.32 **We lowly *kṣatriyas*** translates *kṣatra-bandhavaḥ*. By referring to himself as a mere friend of the royal order, Parīkṣit shows modesty. At the same time, he uses the royal "we" (*vayam*) and also refers to Śuka with the respectful (and plural) form *bhavadbhiḥ*, literally, "by all of you."
49. 19.35 Viśvanātha comments that Parīkṣit here implies that because of his relationship with Krishna and his family, Krishna must have sent Śuka to Parīkṣit at this time in order to deliver him from worldly existence.
50. 19.36 **You, who were previously unseen**: Śuka's having disappeared from home is alluded to at 1.2.2, wherein is remembered that Vyāsa, Śuka's father, had called

after him in vain when Śuka had left for a life of renunciation in the forest. This story is elaborated in the Mahābhārata (see Doniger 1993).

51. 19.38 **Shared** translates *bhajanīyam*. Connotations of *bhajana* include "worship" and "adoration," and in current usage suggests the regular, typically daily, routine of an individual's religious practices such as recitation of prayers, chanting of mantras, and performance of worship rites.

BOOK TWO

1. 1.1 **Benefits the world** (*loka-hitam*): Śrīdhara notes that the specific benefit is liberation (*mokṣa*); Jīva adds that the inquiry's excellence is equally due to its expression of interest in the love (*prema*) that is fixed completely upon Krishna.
2. 1.2 **Pursue domestic happiness** refers to the *gṛhamedhī*, one who maintains brahmanical domestic rituals and who, according to Śrīdhara, is bound to commit violence against unseen living beings by five routine activities (namely, the use of fire, the grinding of spices, sweeping, pounding with pestle and mortar, and filling a water vessel). Ascetics, especially of Jain traditions, typically strive to avoid or minimize such activities as far as possible.
3. 1.5 **Peace** translates *abhayam*, literally, "absence of fear," but which also has the sense of safety, security, and peace, the last word being, in our view, the most inclusive.
4. 1.8 **When the Dvāpara age began**: Some commentators write that here **began** means "ended," offering an illustrative analogy: the top portion of a tree, though technically its "end," is viewed first. Hence the verse locates this transmission event at the commencement of the age that immediately *follows* Dvāpara—namely, the Kali age. Regarding the Bhāgavata's "equivalence" to the Veda, see Holdrege (2006).
5. 1.15 **Body and what is related to it**: Śrīdhara offers elaboration—namely, "sons, wife, and so on," for what is related to (literally, "those who follow") one's body. The Bhāgavata's emphasis on the need for freedom from involvement with family as crucial to spiritual accomplishment is indicated here at the beginning of Śuka's answer to Parīkṣit.
6. 1.17 **Three-part syllable (*a-u-m*)**: The syllable *oṁ* is much celebrated in the Veda and Upaniṣads as the **seed of the Veda**, in the sense that it is understood to contain in potential form the entirety of the Veda and its wisdom.
7. 1.18 **Guide** translates *sārathi*, literally, "driver." This alludes to an extended analogy in the Katha Upaniṣad 1.3.3–4, of a chariot, passenger, charioteer, horses, and reins—signifying the human body, the self within the body, the intelligence, the senses, and the mind, respectively—employed to illustrate the predicament of worldly existence. **Upon realizing felicity** translates *śubhārthe*, which Śrīdhara (and others) identify as "the form of God," suggesting continuity with the direction in verse 11 to praise the name of God as well as with the direction given in the next verse (19) to meditate on the Lord's bodily limbs.
8. 1.20 Vijayadhvaja comments that **concentration** (*dhāraṇā*) is "like the flow of sesamum oil," suggesting a state of awareness that is steady, undisturbed, and yet

dynamic. **Them** refers to the two lower *guṇas*—namely, **passion** (*rajaḥ*) and **darkness** (*tamaḥ*).

9. 2.7.1 This event is elaborated in Book Three, chapters 13 and 17–19. **First demon** translates *ādi-daityam*. The *daityas* are powerful progeny of Diti who generally oppose and frequently fight against the gods.
10. 7.3 **Self's sojourn** translates *ātma-gatim* and **Kapila's refuge** translates *kapilasya gatim*. The word *gatim* connotes both senses. Kapila's refuge calls attention to the devotional character of liberation espoused in the Bhāgavata: as Kapila is identified as an *avatāra* of Vishnu, and as his instructions to his mother have their locus in bhakti, her spiritual perfection is understood to be the taking of complete refuge in her divine son. However, *kapilasya gatim* could also be read as "Kapila's path," emphasizing his teachings as the "path" that Devahūti follows to achieve liberation. Kapila's appearance, instructions, and departure from the world are related in Book Three, chapters 22–33.
11. 7.4 The *avatāra* referred to here is Dattātreya, or Datta, the son of the sage Atri. Further—very brief—mention of Dattātreya is found in 4.1.15, 4.1.33, 4.19.6, 6.8.16, 6.15.14, 8.14.8, 9.15.17, 9.23.24, and 11.4.17. More extensive description of Dattātreya is found in other Purāṇas. Similarly, many personages and events mentioned only briefly in the Bhāgavata are given more extensive accounts in other Purāṇas, or significantly different versions of narratives contained in the Bhāgavata may be given in other Purāṇas.
12. 7.5 These four sages are sometimes referred to collectively as the Four Kumāras. Their appearance as sons of Brahmā is elaborated in 3.12.4–5. See also 3.15–16, narrating how these sages encountered difficulty upon entering Vaikuṇṭha. Instructions by these sages to King Pṛthu are in Book Four, chapter 22.
13. 7.6 **Dharma's wife**: Generally, the divinity Yama, or Yamarāja, is identified as the personification of dharma, known also as the lord of death and the judge of persons' wrongful activities (adharma) at the time of death. However, here the commentators are silent as to Dharma's identity. An account of this failed attempt to seduce the sages Nara-Nārāyaṇa and thus break their vows of celibacy is found in 11.4.6–16. Anaṅga means "who is without body," a name of Kāmadeva, the god of erotic love, who is usually accompanied by celestial beauties called *apsarās*. Kāmadeva's body was burned to ashes by Shiva's angry glance when the former attempted to incite Shiva's desire for Parvatī. This event is also alluded to in verse 7.
14. 7.8 The story of the child Dhruva's pursuit of a kingdom greater than that of his grandfather (Brahmā) is recounted in Book Four, chapters 8–12. **Position of *dhruva*** translates *dhruva-gatim*, identified as the polestar; it is understood that celestial sages reside in realms situated **above and below** this star.
15. 7.9 **The position of heir apparent** translates *putra-padam*. Śrīdhara takes this as meaning "the position of son." The idea is that a son's duty is to free (*tra*) his father from hell (*pu*). The account of **King Vena**, his being killed by *brāhmaṇas* for his tyrannical ruling, and his replacement by the virtuous King **Pṛthu** (considered an *avatāra* of Vishnu) is given in Book Four, chapters 14–23.
16. 7.10 ***Paramahaṁsa* state** translates *pāramahaṁsyam padam*. The *haṁsa* bird—a goose, gander, or swan—is said to be able to separate *soma* juice (see the glossary) or milk out of a mixture of these with water, and hence the *parama* (superior or

exalted) -*haṁsa* is a person able to draw (spiritual) essences from the temporal world. By extension, a *paramahaṁsa* is a spiritually advanced person considered to live beyond ordinary social rules.

17. 7.11 **Hayaśirāḥ** is also referred to as Hayaśīrṣā and Hayagrīva. Prayers to this *avatāra* that describe some of his characteristics are found in 5.18.2–6.

    A ***satra*** (usually spelled *sattra*) is an elaborate ritual sacrifice involving the offering and partaking of *soma* juice, which is much praised in the Vedas for its exhilarating and apparently hallucinogenic effects.
18. 7.12 The story of **Matsya** *avatāra*, Vishnu in the form of a giant fish, is elaborated in Book Eight, chapter 24. In this account, Hayagrīva is the name of a demon who seeks to steal the Vedas from Brahmā, but his plan is foiled by Matsya.
19. 7.13 See Book Eight, chapters 6–10, for the Bhāgavata's elaboration of the cosmic-churning narrative, in which Kurma *avatāra* plays a pivotal role.
20. 7.14 See Book Seven, chapters 2–9, for the Bhāgavata's full account of the **man-lion** (Nṛsimha) appearance and his protection of Prahlāda and killing of Hiraṇyakaśipu. This narrative is discussed in chapter 1 of *The Bhāgavata Purāṇa: Sacred Text and Living Tradition.*
21. 7.16 See Book Eight, chapters 2–3, for an elaboration of the story of Vishnu protecting the elephant king Gajendra.
22. 7.17 **Even lords . . . by begging**: The point is that the dwarf *avatāra* (Vāmana), being the supreme Vishnu, might have simply confiscated the kingdom of King Bali (not referred to by name until the following verse); but instead he respected the dharmic principle that no one, whatever one's position, can take the property of another. By playing the part of a begging *brāhmaṇa*, Vāmana induces Bali to give in charity what ends up being his entire kingdom (the entire world), including himself, since Vāmana's three steps (as he expands to cosmic dimensions) cover all creation.
23. 7.18 See Book Eight, chapters 18–21, for the Bhāgavata's full account of this story of Vāmana's begging from King Bali.
24. 7.19 Most commentators identify the form of Vishnu implied in this verse to be that of Haṁsa (Swan), who is mentioned in 11.13.16–40 as having instructed Brahmā and his "mental sons"—the Four Kumāras—about yoga and *sāṅkhya* (the philosophical analysis of matter and spirit that is associated with yoga theory and practice). Here, unlike in Book Eleven, **Nārada** (also a son of Brahmā's) is mentioned as the recipient of this lesson, rather than the Kumāras.
25. 7.21 **The knowledge of preserving life** translates *āyuṣya-vedam*, which is related to the traditional Indian medical system, Ayurveda. The Bhāgavata and other Purāṇas identify **Dhanvantari** as the divine founder of this medical system. His appearance is recounted in 8.8.31–34.
26. 7.22 **That oppressive thorn** refers to the military order, the *kṣatriyas*. The Bhāgavata's account of **Paraśurāma**'s exploits is given in Book Nine, chapters 15 and 16. Paraśurāma's immediate reason for killing the *kṣatriyas* is to avenge the death of his father, Jamadagni, at the hands of the sons of Kārtavīryārjuna. The unjust killing of his father was, for Paraśurāma, the sign of a larger cancer of disrespect to *brāhmaṇas* spreading throughout the world; thus he weeds out the martial order repeatedly.

27. 7.24 **Like Shiva . . . the enemy's city**: This alludes to Shiva's destruction of three aerial cities constructed by Maya Dānava, narrated briefly in 7.10.51–69. Verses 23–26 summarize the story of Rama. See Book Nine, chapters 10 and 11, for the Bhāgavata's (very brief) version of this famous story, known in its classical form as the Vālmīki Rāmāyaṇa and in numerous other versions.
28. 7.26 This and the next nine verses refer in briefest outline to the activities of Krishna elaborated extensively in the whole of Book Ten. Commentators indicate that each of the nine following verses are meant to show that the acts described could be performed by no other than the supreme Lord in his ultimate form as Krishna. **He whose way is uninferable by common folk** translates *janānupalakṣya-mārgaḥ*, which Viśvanātha suggests indicates the path of *rāgānugā-bhakti*—devotional practice driven by emotional inclination (rather than by rules). This reflects the notion suggested by several commentators that Krishna's "acts" are characterized by "sweetness" (*mādhurya*), in contrast to those of the other *avatāras* mentioned here, whose acts are demonstrative primarily of "lordship" (*aiśvarya*).
29. 7.27 For the Bhāgavata's elaboration of this episode of Krishna uprooting the two ***arjuna* trees**, see Book Ten, chapter 10.
30. 7.28 **He will bring to life**: Although the verb is in the past tense (possibly to indicate that this event happens before the next one), in general these verses are in the future tense. Śrīdhara notes these changes of tense (in his comment to v. 38), indicating that Brahmā is referring to the appearance of certain *avatāras* as happening before his speaking to Nārada, during, and later. The implication is that Brahmā anticipates a repetition of events he has already witnessed, during Krishna's previous descent, possibly during Brahmā's previous cosmic "day." The Yamunā River flows through eastern **Vraja** (roughly north to south). Vraja (Hindi Vraj or Braj) is an area said to have a circumference of approximately 185 miles, situated south of present-day Delhi and northwest of Agra, encompassing portions of three present-day states—Haryana, Uttar Pradesh, and Rajasthan.
31. 7.30 **Awakened** translates *pratibodhitā*. In this episode (elaborated in 10.8—see Book Ten), the child Krishna's foster mother looks inside her son's mouth, prompted by **Balarāma**'s complaint that Krishna had been eating dirt. What she sees in his mouth is the entire universe, and thus she becomes for that moment aware, awakened, instructed, or enlightened (all possible translations of *pratibodhitā*) that her son is actually Lord Nārāyaṇa.
32. 7.33 This refers to the *rāsa*-dance episode (elaborated in Book Ten, chapters 29–33), in which young Krishna meets with, disappears from, and then again meets the young damsels of **Vraja** during an autumn full-moon night that is mystically extended to the length of a cosmic night of Brahmā. For a detailed account of this important section of the Bhāgavata Purāṇa, see Schweig's chapter in Gupta and Valpey (2013). Although described in Book Ten in chapter 34 (just after the *rāsa*-dance episode), based on a variant reading of the Sanskrit, Viśvanātha indicates that it is after the killing of **Śaṅkhacūḍa** that Krishna performs the *rāsa* dance. Here as elsewhere in the Bhāgavata (as also in other Purāṇas), chronology is not a primary concern, as is often the case in ordinary conversation.

33. 7.34–35 These two verses list names of several opponents of Krishna and his associates. The associates **Pārtha (Arjuna)** and **Bhīma** are two of the Pāṇḍava brothers central to the Mahābhārata epic. Accounts of Krishna's victorious battles constitute much of Book Ten, especially the latter half.
34. 7.37 Regarding the first half of this verse, see note 27. The mention of Buddha as an *avatāra* of Vishnu is not elaborated in the Bhāgavata. In the Vishnu Purāṇa (3.16) Vishnu is described as manifesting a "magical deluding form" who mixes with the *daityas* and *asuras* (demons) and persuades them to adopt Jain, Buddhist, and other nontheistic or anti-Vedic doctrines, so that they will abandon Vedic rituals by which they had gained power to subdue the gods. These persuasions include presenting arguments that reflect (or parody) Buddhist ideas, **subdharmic principles**. This is one of the ways brahmanical Purāṇas explain the existence of groups they consider heretical, especially Buddhist and Jain persuasions. The personage **Maya** is a celestial architect known for his fantastic architectonic creations, not to be confused with the term *māyā*, meaning "power," "magic," or "illusion."
35. 7.38 ***Svāhā, svadhā, vaṣaṭ*** are incantations pronounced when oblations are offered in Vedic ritual sacrifices. That these incantations are **not heard anywhere** suggests that the most essential ritual activities of the *brāhmaṇas* have been curtailed and that as a result dharmic (dutiful, religious) activity has become lost to human society. **Kalki** is the *avatāra* who ends the Kali age and ushers in the next cycle of four ages, beginning with the Kṛta age.
36. 7.40 This verse alludes again to Vishnu's dwarf *avatāra*, Vāmana, described previously (vv. 17 and 18), who took three steps from the nether regions to the highest realm of the universe. An alternative translation of the first sentence is, "Although a scholar may count all the earth's dust particles, who in this world is able to enumerate the powers of Vishnu?"
37. 7.41 In the Bhāgavata **Śeṣa** (literally, "remainder" or "surplus"), also referred to as Ananta (without end), is regarded as an expansion of Vishnu, appearing as a snake with one thousand heads to serve as a couch for Vishnu. He is said to be occupied constantly in praising Vishnu with each of his thousand mouths.
38. 7.46 As a continuation of the three previous verses, this verse suggests the Bhāgavata's sense of inclusiveness—that any and all beings may be benefited from knowledge of **the supreme's wondrous opulence** (vv. 43–45). While the more orthodox brahmanical currents of early Indic religion tended to claim considerable social exclusivity, the Bhāgavata, while positioning itself close to orthodoxy in many respects, also exhibits a degree of at least theoretical social liberality. **Hūnas** is a blanket term for "barbarous people," and **Śabaras** is used here also as a generic term for "mountain tribes."
39. 7.47 This verse indicates that realization of *brahman* is, so to speak, included in realization of the supreme Lord.
40. 7.48 Just as **Indra**, the storm god, being the controller of rain, has no need to dig a well, similarly ascetics who know *brahman*, the Absolute, as Bhagavān, need make no separate endeavor of self-control to attain yogic perfection, typically considered to be a position of **nondifference** between the self and *brahman*.

41. 7.49 Commentators indicate that this verse intends to emphasize that because the Lord is the giver of reward for one's actions, and because the self continues after the death of the body, it is assured that right action in this life will be rewarded with an appropriate heavenly destination hereafter.
42. 7.53 This verse plays on the double meaning of the term ***māyā***, as both **enchanting** power and **illusion**. Vīrarāghava notes that the first mention of *māyā* indicates the Lord's way of bringing about cosmic creation, sustenance, and destruction; and the second instance refers to the *guṇas* (clarity, passion, and darkness). As the final verse of this chapter, it declares the "fruit" of hearing the chapter—namely, to be freed from illusion, provided the hearing is done regularly and **with faith** (*śraddhayā*).
43. 9.31 **Application, secrets, and supplements** translate *vijñāna*, *rahasya*, and *aṅga*, respectively. Commentators differ on the meaning of these technical terms. Most follow Śrīdhara in glossing *vijñāna* as *anubhava*, "experience," although Vallabha reads it as "varieties of knowledge" and Vīrarāgha as "scripture" and "yoga." Furthermore, Śrīdhara glosses *rahasya* as bhakti, so that Vishnu is offering knowledge of himself, along with devotion and its experience.
44. 9.33 According to most commentators, the essential four-verse Bhāgavata begins with this verse, as do Vishnu's answers to Brahmā's four questions. Vallabha, however, regards the entirety of Vishnu's speech (comprising seven verses) as the essential Bhāgavata. **I alone existed**: Jīva argues that Bhagavān's existence includes his associates, abode, and other paraphernalia, for several reasons: Brahmā has just seen Vishnu (before creation) with all these accompaniments; Vishnu has promised in the previous verse that he will speak of himself with his "form qualities and activities"; and when a person uses the first-person pronoun, it is reasonable to assume that he means himself as he stands before the person being spoken to. Vishnu uses the first-person pronoun as he stands before Brahmā in his full majesty, not in an abstract, depersonalized sense. **Beyond cause and effect** translates *sad-asat-param*. The words *sat* and *asat* (the first *t* changed to *d* for grammatical reasons) have a multitude of meanings, including "existence" and "nonexistence," "conscious" and "nonconscious," "gross," and "subtle." The main point being made here is that Vishnu existed before any primal entity that might have been the source of this world's dualities.
45. 9.34 Among commentators, interpretations of this verse differ widely depending on their particular understanding of ***māyā***. Some take *māyā* as an illusive power, which leads them to read the verse along the lines given here, while others take *māyā* as the substance of this world and its living beings (*prakṛti* and *jīva*). Viśvanātha describes *māyā* as having two facets—namely, knowledge and ignorance and suggests that the verse gives an example of each facet: *yathā bhāso*, "like light" (instead of *yathā ābhāso*, **like a reflection**), and *yathā tamaḥ* (**like darkness**). Śrīdhara reads *tamaḥ* as Rāhu, the dark planet that is invisible and yet makes its presence known during a solar or lunar eclipse.
46. 9.35 The idea here is that the five great **elements**—earth, water, fire, air, and sky—transform into various created objects, and yet none of these created objects contains the totality of the elements. Similarly, the Lord is present within all beings and yet maintains his independent identity.

47. 9.36 This verse reinforces what was stated in the previous verse: Vishnu is within all things and yet separate from them. Those who seek the truth should see Vishnu's dual relationship everywhere.
48. 9.38–39 Both these verses offer epithets for Vishnu that reflect the immediate context: *ajanaḥ janānām*, **who moves all people**, has just succeeded in moving Brahmā to create. Similarly, verse 39 suggests Brahmā's sense of loss when it mentions how *indriyārtha*, **the goal of the senses**, has just become imperceptible to Brahmā.

BOOK THREE

1. 10.1 Commentators indicate that **corporeal and mental progeny** means progeny produced both from Brahmā's body and from his mind (or mental resolve). The sense is that Brahmā creates by various means, and Vidura wants to know about all types of beings originating from him.
2. 10.4 **Toward the self**: Viśvanātha identifies this "self" as Nārāyaṇa.
3. 10.6 **Drank . . . water**: Commentators agree that this refers to the process of periodic cosmic annihilation, which Brahmā brings to an end by swallowing the destructive winds and waters.
4. 10.8 **Threefold . . . division**: This refers to two schemas of cosmic order found widely in Puranic literature. The threefold division consists of earth, middle region, and heaven (*bhūḥ*, *bhūvaḥ*, and *svāḥ*), while the **fourteenfold division** adds four regions above and seven below these.
5. 10.9 **Differences in nature**: Brahmā is contrasted with all other living beings, in that the latter require places to pursue their various desires for gain in the world, which is repeatedly annihilated. Because Brahmā is constitutionally **mature** (literally, "well done," "cooked"), he is not subjected to the vicissitudes of his own creation. Giridhara notes that this verse gives reason for there being three divisions and that Brahmā, though a *jīva*, is exceptional because his dharma—the aggregate of duties he performs—is free from the binding effects of karma.
6. 10.10 **Since you have mentioned**: Maitreya has referred to time in verse 5.
7. 10.12 Rādhāramaṇadāsa points to this verse as a proof text for the Vedāntic doctrine of transformation (*parināma-vāda*): the world is a product of the transformation of the energy (time) of *brahman*, which is real, and hence the world is real, not unreal.
8. 10.13 **As . . . hereafter**: Śrīdhara comments that this verse points out the unlimited, perpetual character of the universe as time's repeatedly recurring creation. Also it indicates the general feature of time, whereas the specific characteristics of time (or its product, the universe) are indicated in the following verses. Rādhāramaṇadāsa notes that the verse also indicates the nonillusory character of the universe. It is periodically destroyed and remanifested, but it is not unreal.
9. 10.14 Śrīdhara and other commentators elaborate on the **dissolution** as having three causes or types—namely, **time** (*kāla*) as the cause of the repeated cosmic dissolution, **matter** (*dravya*) as the fire emanating from Saṁkarṣaṇa (Ananta Śeṣa), and **qualities** (*guṇa*) as the workings of individuals' actions.

10. 10.16 Vaṁśīdhara notes that the fourth creation is the function of the "I-maker" (*ahaṁkāra*) associated with the quality of passion (*raja-guṇa*). The fifth creation is the function of the "I-maker" associated with the quality of purity (*sattva-guṇa*).
11. 10.18 For an explanation of *prakṛti*, see note 57. **Imbued with passion**: Vaṁśīdhara calls attention to verse 14.10 in Book Ten, in which Brahmā apologizes to Krishna for an impropriety, due to his being imbued with the quality of passion (*rajas*). Viśvanātha says that here **primary products of nature** refers to *māyā*, the Lord's creative power that suggests magic and illusion. **Wonder work** translates *līlā*, a term often appearing in the Bhāgavata to indicate divine sport, play, or pastime but here associated with the work of creation, also identified as divine purposeless action.
12. 10.21 Giridhara comments that **ignorant** means "lacking awareness of yesterday, today, tomorrow, and the like"—i.e., lacking a sense of continuity from past into future; **deep in darkness** means "predominantly angry; set only upon eating, sleeping, mating, and fearing"; **perceiving by odor** means "perceiving what they desire only by smell"; and **without purposefulness of heart** means "devoid of inquiry about the extent of happiness, distress, and the like."
13. 10.22–24 **Makara**: Monier-Williams identifies this beast as "a kind of sea-monster (sometimes confounded with crocodile, shark, dolphin, etc.; regarded as the emblem of Kāma-deva . . .)."
14. 11.1 Śrīdhara and Viśvanātha point out that although objects are constituted of innumerable atomic parts, people nevertheless think of objects as simple wholes without parts. At 5.12.9 it is stated that such "atoms" are ultimately unsubstantial, for they are continuously created and dissolved. Thus at times the Bhāgavata appears to argue against Vaiśeṣika philosophy (see glossary), which holds to the classical Indian "atomic" theory of material composition.
15. 11.4 Commentators explain **macrocosmic time** as the period of the sun's traversing through the twelve zodiacal mansions, or one solar year.
16. 11.5 According to Monier-Williams, an **atom** is said to equal 1/54,675,000 of a *muhūrta* (48 minutes). Vallabha, to emphasize the shortness of ***paramāṇu*** time, indicates that its duration is measured by the length of time it takes the sun's chariot to traverse a *paramāṇu* particle as it speeds along its cosmic pathway.
17. 11.6 According to Vaṁśīdhara (who quotes an early Sanskrit text on astronomy, the *Sūryasiddhānta*) a ***truṭi*** is the time it takes for a lotus flower petal to split.
18. 11.7 Monier-Williams gives the duration of a ***kṣaṇa*** as 4/5 or 24/35 of a second, and the duration of a ***kāṣṭhā*** as 1/450 of a *muhūrta*.
19. 11.8 Commentators explain the variation **six or seven** by the shortening and lengthening of days and nights. Thus, in this account, the basic determinant of periods is understood to be the movement of the sun in relation to the earth, as perceived by human beings.
20. 11.9 According to Monier-Williams, a ***pala***, 32 of which equal 1 ***prastha***, is equal to 4 *karṣas*, which "in common use" would each be about 280 grains troy, or approximately 2.16 troy ounces; a ***māṣa*** "in common use is said to be about 17 grains troy." (One grain troy equals 0.0648 g.)
21. 11.12 Śrīdhara mentions that **twelve months** is the period of a day and night of the gods. Vaṁśīdhara notes that in standard astrological treatises the length of

human life is classified into three categories—short (up to thirty years), medium (up to sixty years). and long (generally up to one hundred years). He further notes that a person's life span is dependent exclusively on sinfulness or piety, especially with respect to sexual behavior. Sinful sexuality is practiced against scriptural injunctions, during the day (causing a shortened life span), whereas pious sexuality is practiced at night, in accord with scripture (leading to a longer life span).

22. 11.14 Viśvanātha explains that the sun's completed orbit is a ***saṁvatsara***, Jupiter's orbit is a ***parivatsara***, the moon's orbit is an ***anuvatsara***, the orbit of lunar mansions (12 × 27 days) is a *vatsara*, and the procession of the countless stars, calculated in terms of months having thirty days, is an *iḍā-vatsara*.
23. 11.16 **Aeon**: Commentators here identify a ***kalpa*** as the length of time the three worlds—earth, middle region, and heaven—endure before a cosmic partial destruction takes place, during which realms above heaven—Maharloka, Janaloka, Tapaloka, and Satyaloka—and their residents, such as the four Kumāra sages, Bhṛgu, and Brahmā, are unaffected. According to the Bhāgavata and other Purāṇas, a partial cosmic destruction occurs every day of Brahmā, or every 4,320,000,000 terrestrial years. Each type of being mentioned here (**ancestors, gods, and humans**) is gauged as living up to 100 years, in terms of the corresponding type among the five types of years listed in verse 14.
24. 11.17 **Blessed one**: Maitreya is addressed reverentially as *bhagavān* by using the grammatical third person, indicating, according to Giridhara, that because he practices *bhagavat-bhakti*—devotion to Bhagavān—he is identifiable as *bhagavān*, and therefore he certainly knows the identity of Bhagavān's movement as time.
25. 11.18 The names of the four ages (*yuga*) are those of the four possible throws of a die (Indian dice being oblong, with four sides and two short ends, rather than cubicle).
26. 11.19 The Kṛta-yuga is reckoned thus: 4 × 1,000 = 4,000 + 2 × 100 × 4 = 4,800 celestial years. Similarly the Tretā-yuga is 3,600, the Dvāpara-yuga 2,400, and the Kali-yuga 1,200 celestial years in duration, making a total of 12,000 celestial years for one complete cycle of cosmic ages. Commentators note that 1 celestial year is equal to 360 terrestrial (human) years, making a fourfold cosmic age equal to 4,320,000 terrestrial years in duration. The next verse indicates that the hundreds place marker in the lengths of the four ages (in celestial years) represents the sum of the two junctures—before and after—associated with each age. Thus, for example, the junctures of the Kṛta age are each 400 celestial years long, hence 800 celestial years together, while the Kṛta age proper is 4,000 celestial years in length.
27. 11.20 Śrīdhara explains that while specific **prescribed duties** for particular *varṇas*, such as protection of cows by *vaiśyas*, are observed during the ages proper, general duties for all persons are observed at all times, including the junctures.
28. 11.21 **Comprehensively**: literally, "four parted," glossed by Vaṁśīdhara and Vijayadhvaja as "austerity, truthfulness, mercy, and cleanliness." Vallabha comments that in the Kṛta age all four of the *varṇas* are present—*brāhmaṇas*, *kṣatriyas*, *vaiśyas*, and *śūdras*—while in the Tretā age there are no *brāhmaṇas*, and in the present Kali age only *śūdras* remain. Several commentators note that the incremental reduction in dharma over the ages spurs one to renunciation.

29. 11.29 **Saṅkarṣaṇa . . . Janaloka**: Saṅkarṣaṇa is a form or aspect of Nārāyaṇa, identified with Ānanta Śeṣa, the cosmic serpent that breathes out fire to burn the worlds at the time of cosmic devastations. Maharloka is a realm above the three worlds, Janaloka (the realm of people) is above Maharloka, and Brahmāloka is above Janaloka.
30. 11.40 **Universe** in this and the previous verse translates *āṇḍakośa*, literally, "egg-shell." Commentators specify the number of layers enclosing each universe as seven. Counting eight elements (earth, water, fire, air, space, mind, intelligence, and ego), the innermost covering layer is that of water; then comes fire, and so on, progressing outward to ego.
31. 11.41 **Body** translates *dhāma*, following Viśvanātha (quoting the *Amarakośa* dictionary). Vallabha adds that it can mean either "body functioning as place" or "residence functioning as place." Just as the universe is the imperishable self's body functioning as place, so the imperishable (*akṣara-brahman*) is a "body" with respect to Bhagavān, whose life span is therefore immeasurable. **Cause of every cause**: According to Vallabha, this refers to the two types of causes—namely, *puruṣa* (person) and *prakṛti* (nature). Giridhara notes that Vishnu is **great** because he is not dependent on anything outside himself.
32. 15.13 Both Vishnu and his abode are called **Vaikuṇṭha**, even as a king is often addressed by the name of his kingdom.
33. 15.14 **Vaikuṇṭha bodies** (*vaikuṇṭha-mūrtayaḥ*): Nearly all commentators (Śrīdhara, Vīrarāghava, Vijayadhvaja, Viśvanātha, Vallabha, and others) explain that the residents of Vaikuṇṭha have forms (*mūrtayaḥ*) that resemble the form of Vishnu (*vaikuṇṭha*). The Bhāgavata elsewhere (3.29.13) identifies this state as a specific kind of liberation (*sārūpya*).
34. 15.19 ***Pārijāta*** is a celestial flowering tree that is said to have emerged during the churning of the ocean and claimed by Indra, king of the gods, for the gardens of heaven. Later, Krishna brought the prized tree to earth to please his wife, Satyabhāmā. **Greatly honor the austerities of *tulasī***: Other Purāṇas tell of *tulasī*'s wish to have Vishnu as her husband. She practices asceticism to gain the Lord's favor, and the two are married. *Tulasī* always stays close to Vishnu in the form of the holy basil plant, and Vishnu prefers her fragrance over all others. According to Bhaktivedanta, this verse shows the absence of envy among Vishnu's devotees, as each flower appreciates the success of another.
35. 15.20 ***Vaidurya* gems** are said to change color, like alexandrite or certain kinds of garnet and spinel.
36. 15.23 **Hari** translates *aghabhid*, literally, "destroyer of sins." There is symmetry in the verse, contrasting topics of Vishnu, which destroy sin, and other topics, which destroy good judgment.
37. 15.25 **Leave far away the punishments of hell** translates *dūre yamāḥ*. Śrīdhara and Viśvanātha interpret this phrase as "they give up rules and restrictions." The idea here is that those who have deep love for Vishnu naturally possess all virtues, and thus they do not need to pursue the eightfold yogic path of *yama, niyama, āsana, prāṇāyāma, pratyāhāra, dhāraṇā, dhyāna*, and *samādhi*. Variant readings for this verse are given by Śrīdhara, Vīrarāghava, and Viśvanātha, as follows: *dūre'hamā, dūre yamādyupacitaślāghyaśīla*, and *dūre yamādy upari na ślāghyaśīla.*

38. 15.27 **The sages passed through six gates**: According to Vallabha, the six gates proffer six excellences, beginning with majesty and ending with detachment. The seventh gate presents bhakti, but because the sages still lacked devotion, they saw the guards of the seventh gate. This will change, of course, when the sages meet Vishnu. **Without lingering**: Śrīdhara, Vīrarāghava, and Viśvanātha define *asajjamānāḥ* as "without attachment." Because of their eagerness to see the Lord, the sages were not attracted by the rich decorations they observed as they passed through the various gates. **Both were of equal age**: Vallabha and Bhaktivedanta explain that because time has no influence in Vaikuṇṭha, people do not age, and so it is impossible to tell who is older.
39. 15.29 **Without asking . . . for they see all places equally**: The four sages were born at the beginning of creation, but they had decided to remain always as small boys. According to Bhaktivedanta, the sages' free behavior was a characteristic of their childlike nature: "They were not at all duplicitous, and they entered the doors exactly as little children enter places without any idea of what it is to trespass. That is a child's nature. . . . Indeed, a child is generally welcome in his attempts to go places, but if it so happens that a child is checked from entering a door, he naturally becomes very sorry and angry."
40. 15.30 **The gatekeepers' conduct was displeasing to the Lord**: Śrīdhara identifies the disagreeable quality as disrespect of *brāhmaṇas*, who are dear to Vishnu, whereas Vallabha points to pride as the problem. According to Vallabha, pride is the characteristic quality of demons, and thus the gatekeepers will be cursed to take birth as demons. Jīva points out that the Lord can tolerate transgressions of his own rule (such as the sages' alleged trespass), but he cannot tolerate any offense toward his own servants, his portions, or those he has appointed to positions of management and maintenance.
41. 15.31 **Certainly most worthy** translates *su-arhat-tama*, "the very best of *arhats*." The word *arhat* is a standard title for Jain and Buddhist adepts. The Bhāgavata may be alluding to these traditions in a polemical fashion to highlight the Kumāras' superiority. Again, the next verse refers to the Kumāras as *munis*, a common term for Jain renunciants. **Anger** here translates *kāmānujena*, which literally means "the younger brother of desire." The idea is that when a person's desire is unfulfilled, anger soon follows. According to Bhaktivedanta, this verse acknowledges the existence of emotions like anger even in a liberated state. Nevertheless, "the difference between the anger of an ordinary person and that of a liberated person is that an ordinary person becomes angry because his sense desires are not being fulfilled, whereas a liberated person like the Kumāras becomes angry when restricted in the discharge of duties for serving the Supreme Personality of Godhead."
42. 15.33 **The sky in the sky** is a reference to a standard Vedāntic metaphor: the sky seen within a pot is actually (part of) the entire sky. Similarly, the self is contained within the supreme self, for the Lord holds everything within him. Vedānta philosophers disagree, however, over the implications of this metaphor. Is the potted sky identical to the great sky, or is it only a part of the great sky? Vīrarāghava and Viśvanātha here argue against the Advaitin claim that the self and the Supreme Self are identical. **Everything in his belly . . . class distinctions**:

This verse plays on imagery of womb and birth. The words *kukṣi* (abdomen) and *udara* (belly) can both mean "womb," and *nabhas* (sky) can mean "navel." The sense here is that since God holds everything in his belly—or gives birth to everyone—the gatekeepers should not see "womb differences," i.e., distinction based upon a person's birth.

43. 15.34 **Where a sinful person has these three enemies**: The majority of commentators interpret the verse along the lines of the translation here. Vijayadhvaja and Jīva, however, offer a compelling alternative interpretation of the second sentence: "Because of your discriminatory vision, you should take sinful bodies, among these three enemies of the Lord (*daityas*, *rākṣasas*, and *kṣatriyas*)." This interpretation anticipates the three births the gatekeepers will take—as Hiraṇyakaśipu and Hiraṇyākṣa (*daityas*), Rāvaṇa and Kumbhakarṇa (*rākṣasas*), and Śiśupāla and Dantavakra (*kṣatriyas*). The Lord appears as Nṛsimha, Rāma, and Krishna, respectively, to vanquish these troublemakers. The Bhāgavata briefly repeats this story in Book Seven, where the sages clearly state that the gatekeepers will take three demonic births.
44. 15.35 **The gatekeepers realized**: Both Jīva and Bhaktivedanta regard the gatekeepers' offense as unintentional. According to Jīva, the word *avadhārya* ("realized" or "understood") indicates that the gatekeepers had not known that the boys were *brāhmaṇas*. According to Vijayadhvaja, the fact that the gatekeepers reacted immediately indicates that they were not at fault.
45. 15.36 **Do not let illusion destroy our remembrance**: Viśvanātha suggests that by making this request, the gatekeepers are transforming the curse into a blessing. Bhaktivedanta writes that the gatekeepers are here indirectly requesting not to be born in animal species, where forgetfulness of the Lord is almost inevitable. "To a devotee, any heavy punishment is tolerable but the one which effects forgetfulness of the supreme Lord." The gatekeepers will be granted their wish, for they will be born as enemies of Vishnu, constantly thinking of him in anger. This meditation on the Lord, the Bhāgavata later says (7.1.47), will help them regain their former positions in Vaikuṇṭha.
46. 15.37 **He immediately . . . walked with those very feet**: According to Śrīdhara, Vishnu was thinking in this way: "The sages' anger was a result of being prevented from seeing my feet, so by showing them my feet, I will pacify their anger." Thus the Lord hastened there on foot, without any conveyance. Bhaktivedanta connects the Lord's hasty arrival to his promise in the Bhagavad Gītā that his devotee never perishes. The Lord wanted "to stop further aggravation, so that His devotees, the doormen, might not be vanquished for good."
47. 15.38 **The goal of their deep meditation**: This translates the phrase *sva-samādhi-bhāgyam*. *Bhāgyam* carries the sense of something that arrives unexpectedly—i.e., good luck or fortune. The word can also be translated as "worshippable." In other words, the sages encountered the object of their worship in a most unexpected way—face-to-face.
48. 15.40 **He twirled a lotus**: Viśvanātha writes, "Under the pretext of twirling a lotus, the Lord stirs the sages' lotuslike hearts, which had been stilled by the experience of (undifferentiated) *brahman*. He does this by showing them his own sweetness."

49. 15.43 **Mixed with the filaments of the lotus feet**: Viśvanātha treats this as an extended analogy—the Lord's feet are like lotuses and his brilliant reddish-white toenails like the filaments of a lotus. **It shook their bodies and minds**: Vallabha points out that the sages had attained complete stillness of mind from their worship of the self as *brahman*, but they had never experienced the bliss of devotion, and thus when they encountered the Lord's qualities, the experience shook them to the core.
50. 15.44 **The sages meditated upon the Lord intently**: Śrīdhara suggests that the sages gazed upon the Lord again and again, but being unable to comprehend the beauty of all the Lord's limbs simultaneously, they simply resorted to meditation.
51. 15.45 **The esteemed object of meditation . . . his human form**: According to Vaṁśīdhara and Bhaktivedanta, this verse makes clear that a yogi should meditate on the personal form of Nārāyaṇa and not on an attributeless Reality. **He possesses the eight pleasures**: Śrīdhara identifies these as the eight yogic perfections (*aṇimā, mahimā, laghimā, garimā, prāpti, prākāmya, iṣitva*, and *vaśitva*—powers such as the ability to change one's size or weight, to shift to another place, to fulfill desires, and to master the world and other beings). Viśvanātha and Vaṁśīdhara agree with Śrīdhara but also suggest a second interpretation. The Lord possesses seven kinds of sweetness that give pleasure to his devotees: his beautiful voice, delicate touch, beauty, sweetness, fragrance, affection, and his playful activities. The eighth quality is his supremacy, encapsulated by the word *bhaga*, which is further analyzed as strength, fame, majesty, beauty, knowledge, and detachment.
52. 15.47 **Repentance**: Viśvanātha explains that the sages are repenting their act of cursing the Lord's devotees. Śrīdhara, on the other hand, glosses *anutāpa* as *kṛpā*, or the Lord's mercy, by which devotion is bestowed.
53. 15.48 **Disregard even the gift of liberation**: The selfless devotee rejects even liberation if that were to preclude the possibility of serving the Lord, as explained later in Book Three (3.29.13).
54. 16.6 **My unbounded fame is due to you**: The Bhāgavata affirms elsewhere (1.13.10) that Vishnu's devotees create sacred places because they carry the Lord within their hearts. **I would cut off my arm**: By this statement, Vishnu is expressing his loyalty to the sages but also reminding them of his fondness for the gatekeepers. Losing the attendants, he says, would be akin to cutting off his own arm.
55. 16.26 **I alone ordained this curse**: At this point in the narrative, each person has volunteered to accept responsibility for the difficult situation. The gatekeepers accepted blame in the last chapter, the sages did so in the previous verse, and now Vishnu claims responsibility. Viśvanātha explains that Vishnu is here reassuring both sides that they are faultless, for the gatekeepers are his steadfast devotees and the Kumāras are perfectly self-controlled sages. The entire event was set into motion by the Lord himself for the purpose of intensifying his relationships (of *rasa*) with his devotees and increasing their happiness when he appears in different *avatāras*. **Yogic concentration born of anger**: The Bhāgavata maintains that any intense emotion—lust, enmity, fear, or familial affection—directed toward the Lord results in liberation, for that emotion leads a person to focus steadily on the Lord. The word used in this verse is *samādhi*, the final stage of yoga. (See also 7.1.30.)

56. 16.30 Śrīdhara explains that long ago Jaya and Vijaya had restricted Lakṣmī from passing through these gates because Vishnu was in deep sleep. Lakṣmī became angry and declared that in the future the gatekeepers would be cursed by *brāhmaṇas* who had also been denied entry.
57. 26.9 ***Puruṣa*** is often translated as "self" or "consciousness." In Sāṁkhya dualism, the individual *puruṣa* is the unchanging, passive witness, enjoyer, and overseer. ***Prakṛti***, "nature" or "materiality," is the primal material cause of the universe. *Prakṛti* consists of three qualities (*guṇas*)—namely, illumination (*sattva*), passion (*rajas*), and darkness (*tamas*). These three qualities interact with one another and transform into all the constituent elements of the material world—from subtle to gross—including intellect, ego, mind, the five senses, the five gross elements, etc. This process of transformation is described in the following verses. In the devotional Vaiṣṇava Sāṁkhya of the Bhāgavata Purāṇa, Vishnu or Krishna is identified as the supreme *puruṣa*, whose illusive power (*māyā*) is identified with *prakṛti*, thus softening the dualism of classical Sāṁkhya. (See, for example, v. 19 in this chapter, along with the accompanying note.)
58. 26.19 **The Supreme Puruṣa placed . . . the golden** *mahat-tattva*: *Mahat-tattva* is the making of outwardness, or grossness—the first time that the universe is made separate from its origins. Note here the theistic, Vedāntic version of Sāṁkhya being taught by the Bhāgavata: the one supreme *puruṣa* pervades the many individual *puruṣas* (the living beings who are the agents of activity); He also encompasses *prakṛti*, which is described here as his own womb, giving the *puruṣa* a central role in creating the world. The classical Sāṁkhya of Īśvarakṛṣṇa is more clearly dualist in nature, with a distant and passive role for the *puruṣa*.
59. 26.37 **The essence of all the senses**: The air carries sound and fragrance, facilitates touch, and causes visible movement.
60. 26.40 **Eating, drinking**: The fire of digestion in the body allows one to consume food and drink. Alternatively, this can refer to fire's own ability to consume both solids and liquids.
61. 26.46 **Constructing (forms of) *brahman***: Commentators offer differing interpretations of the phrase *bhāvanam brahmaṇaḥ*. Śrīdhara, Vallabha, and Viśvanātha all take this to mean that the earth element allows one to construct images or statues of God's form. Jīva says that the earth element provides analogies (*dṛṣṭānta*) that are useful for meditation upon the Lord's form, such as the sapphire (which is deep blue like Krishna's complexion). Alternatively, Jīva says that the phrase can refer to the *virāṭ-rūpa*, which is the entire universe conceived as the body of God. Vīrarāghava, on the other hand, takes *bhāvana* independently to mean "producing objects like pots, etc." and combines *brahmaṇaḥ* with the following word, *sthāna* (**location**), together meaning "providing residence for the *brāhmaṇa* community." The word *brāhmaṇa*, he says, is a synecdoche referring to all beings—i.e., the earth element provides residence for all beings.
62. 28.1 **With its object of meditation** translates *sabīja*, literally, "with seed." In Patañjali's Yoga Sūtra (1.46) the term is used in relation to *samādhi*, the ultimate stage of yoga practice, and is contrasted with *nirbīja-samādhi*. Whereas the latter refers to a state or practice of meditation or "absorption" *without* the presence of any object upon which the practitioner directs attention, *sabīja-samādhi* (of which

four varieties are listed) employs some object as a locus of the state or practice. In the present context, the object of meditation is Vishnu, considered to be located in the heart.

63. 28.2–7 These verses, up to and including verse 11, summarize the classical eight-limbed (*aṣṭāṅga*) yoga system. **Own duties** and **wrongful acts** translate *sva-dharma* and *vidharma*, respectively. Vīrarāghava notes that the former refers to one's obligations in accordance with one's *varṇa* (station) and *āśrama* (stage of life). To neglect these constitutes *vidharma*. **Vulgar conduct** translates *grāmya-dharma*, literally, "village conduct," or worldly preoccupation. **Amid the body's energy vortices** (chakras, Skt. *cakra*): Most commentators agree that the term *sva-dhiṣṇyānām* (literally, "of one's own regions") refers to the six chakras—vortices of subtle energy said in yoga traditions to be located consecutively more or less along the spine in the human body. However, Vijayadhvaja differs, saying it refers to the various limbs of Vishnu's body (perhaps anticipating the main subject of this chapter—namely, the devotional yogic practice of meditating on Vishnu's bodily features). **Meditating on divine pastimes** Vijayadhvaja glosses as "uninterrupted remembrance" of divine acts, including the act of cosmic creation. He also specifies that **complete mental absorption** (*samādhānam*) means "the condition of effortless concentration on Hari."
64. 28.8 Giridhara suggests the bank of the Ganges River as an example of a **sanctified place**.
65. 28.9 Several commentators give details about how to practice controlled breathing (*prāṇāyāma*). Vallabha adds that "*prāṇāyāma* and so on" are the only means to achieve clearance of the life-air passage. **By the reverse** means to first exhale, hold the breath with the lungs empty, and then breathe in, in regular repetitions.
66. 28.11 The four practices listed here are items 4–7 in the classical eightfold *aṣṭāṅga-yoga* system mentioned in the Patañjali Yoga Sūtras.
67. 28.12 **Exquisite form**: Vijayadhvaja, apparently suspecting a textual corruption with the word *kāṣṭhām* (literally, "wooden object"), glosses it as either "entire form"—hence, "one should meditate on a (wooden) form of the Lord"—or "the form of the Lord that is the best of all qualities." Vallabha glosses it as "Vaikuṇṭha" or "heart" or "Vaikuṇṭha in the heart." Considering the description of the Lord's form that immediately follows, we have translated the term as "exquisite form." **While keeping the tip of the nose in sight**: Commentators note that the yogi is advised to keep the eyes half-opened to avoid either sleeping (due to the eyes being closed) or being distracted (by the eyes being fully open).
68. 28.13–18 Vallabha suggests that the **maddened bumblebees** are incessantly humming Vishnu's praise, thereby surpassing in value the six classical Indian philosophical traditions.
69. 28.19 Viśvanātha suggests that this verse could be taken as directions for the meditational practices of Krishna devotees who "pursue devotional attachment" (*rāgānuga*) as well as of Vishnu devotees whose practices are more rule governed: whereas the Vishnu devotee might visualize Vishnu standing in Vaikuṇṭha (the divine majestic realm), Krishna's devotees would visualize Krishna standing under a tree of plenty (*kalpavṛkṣa*) in his pastoral realm of Vrindavan. He offers similar examples for two different ways of visualizing the Lord's walking, sitting, or reclining—in either Vaikuṇṭha or Vrindavan, as either Vishnu or Krishna, respectively.

70. 28.21 The lines in Vishnu's feet are said to form emblems of particular auspicious items. We may note that this and the following verses describing the various bodily features of Vishnu suggest that the meditating yogi sustain a quite literal understanding of form. Hence, Vishnu's divine (humanlike) form has humanlike feet, legs, hands, chest, face, and so on. The *effects* of meditating on the various limbs are often described in figurative terms, as, for example, in the following verse.
71. 28.23 Commentators explain that this verse alludes to the mention in verse 19 of Vishnu's reclining position. Here it is suggested that he is reclining on Śeṣa-nāga—the divine multiheaded snake who serves as Vishnu's couch—as Lakṣmī attends to him by massaging his lower legs. **Lotus-eyed Lakṣmī**: Viśvanātha suggests that the mention of Lakṣmī's eyes indicates her being able to gaze without hindrance upon Vishnu's charming form. He further advises that the meditator appreciate both the "sweetness" (*mādhuryam*) and "majesty" (*aiśvaryam*) of Vishnu's lower legs and knees, and that the same applies to meditation on all his limbs, as they will be described in subsequent verses.
72. 28.24 The instruction **one . . . heart** is, commentators note, implied from previous verses. Vallabha characteristically offers a detailed symbolic reading of the several details of this verse. So, for example, Garuḍa symbolizes time, and Vishnu sitting on Garuḍa's shoulders indicates his transcendence of time. He also notes that this is a meditation on Vishnu as he moves ("walks," in v. 19).
73. 28.26 As described in verse 23, Lakṣmī sits next to Vishnu; yet she is also said to be located on Vishnu's chest in the form of Śrīvatsa—a golden curl of hair. The Kaustubha gem (mentioned again two verses later) is invariably associated with Vishnu as one of his identifying features and is frequently included in descriptions of his form. It is said to have appeared as one of the products generated by the churning of the cosmic ocean (see 8.8.6). That Vishnu's neck **serves to embellish** the Kaustubha jewel is to suggest that, whereas ornaments are generally worn to enhance one's beauty, in the case of Vishnu his beauty enhances that of the ornaments he wears.
74. 28.27 Vishnu is typically described as having four arms. Here the Sanskrit plural form is used rather than the grammatical dual form for **arms**, implying that the form of Vishnu being described here and to be meditated on has four arms.
75. 28.28 **Honeybee** translates *madhuvrata*, literally, "one who is occupied with sweetness" or "one whose vow is to eat (only) honey." **Emblem of the individual self** translates *caityasya tattvam*, literally, "the principle of the individual self." Here, in contrast to verse 21, the literal-figurative divide is more blurred: one is directed to meditate on a visual item, a particular gem, *and* the meditator is encouraged to think of this visual item as representing a nonvisual principle.
76. 28.31 **Threefold torments** (*tāpa-traya*) refers to three types of misery experienced by all living beings, according to cause—the misery of one's own body or mind, that caused by other creatures, and that caused by higher powers. **Augmented** translates *anuguṇitam*, literally, "continuously augmented." Viśvanātha notes that Vishnu's smiling glance represents his sweetness, which is "initially doubled, then tripled, and henceforth multiplied millions of millions of times."
77. 28.32 Both Jīva and Viśvanātha extend the **ocean of tears** image, saying that Vishnu's smile turns it into an ocean of tears of supreme joy. Viśvanātha suggests

that the **severe suffering** is that of the Lord's devotees in their feelings of separation from him. **Humble** translates *avanata*, literally, "bowed" or "bent."

78. 28.34–35 **Hooklike mind**: Commentators note that this verse compares the mind to a device for catching fish. **Withdraws . . . (. . . meditation)**: Śrīdhara suggests that, extending the analogy of the fishhook mind, once the mental effort of "catching" the object of meditation—Vishnu—is accomplished, the mind can withdraw and be "relaxed," such that the meditator can effortlessly continue to be absorbed in Vishnu, who is now "captured" in the heart. Viśvanātha's perspective is quite different: The yogi, foolishly disinclined to cherish the vision of Vishnu and the intense devotion this vision evokes, withdraws his mind (which, like an iron hook, is not easily melted) to settle in the lesser, *nondevotional* state of yogic isolation. This state, he claims, is what is described in verses 35–44.
79. 28.36 **Falsely . . . the cause** refers to the idea that the true self is not an initiator of action in the world and that the sense of being an independent agent is illusory. Some commentators note that this verse and that following describe the state of yogic attainment known as living liberation (*jīvanmukta*), the state of being fully liberated while alive in the present body. Vijayadhvaja further notes that the word **final** (*carama*) indicates the cessation of the cycle of birth and death (*saṁsāra*) and also that a practitioner's **exalted state**, in this level of yogic accomplishment, consists in faultless knowledge and bliss and in perceiving oneself as subservient to Bhagavān.
80. 28.37 **Final body**: Unlike the ordinary person who, it is understood, transmigrates perpetually from one body to the next, the perfected yogi is understood to terminate this process permanently. The analogy of the intoxicated person serves to highlight the yogi's indifference to and detachment from that body that will be his last.

BOOK FOUR

1. 2.11 **Like Sāvitrī**: the allusion to Sāvitrī is based on a Mahābhārata story (in the Vana [3rd] Parvan) wherein she outwits Yama, the lord of death, in her determination to remain with her husband, Satyavān.
2. 2.14 **Ghosts and spirits**: Two categories of beings are mentioned here—*bhūta* (literally, "existent") refers in this context to ghosts, and *preta* (literally, "gone forth") are a deceased person and also the spirit of a deceased person. Shiva is often described and portrayed as being surrounded by a variety of such troublesome beings.
3. 2.16 **Respectable girl** translates *sādhvī*, the feminine form of *sādhu*. As Shiva is seen in many Hindu traditions as the paradigmatic *sādhu*, there seems to be an intended irony by the text's author, with a suggestion that in fact Satī is perfectly matched with Shiva.
4. 2.17 **Touching water** refers to a brahmanical ritual practice, *ācamana*, that involves sipping water that one first infuses with a mantra from the palm of the right hand, as a means of ritual purification enjoined as preliminary to other ritual acts and posterior to contaminating acts or occasions.
5. 2.18 **Entity** translates *bhavaḥ*, which is also a name of Shiva in the Bhāgavata. Dakṣa has previously denied that Shiva is *śiva* (auspicious), and hence referring to him as

Bhava (which can mean "being" or "existence") suggests distance and contempt (while indeed affirming that Shiva actually exists). Viśvanātha notes that this "curse" may be taken as a blessing, freeing Shiva from the need to dine with the **worst of gods**—the ordinary divinities. In this reading, Dakṣa (unintentionally) says, "Let Shiva have his share, since he is the nourisher of all the gods, having fed them."

6. 2.21 **Bereft of the truth**: Commentators suggest "highest" or "absolute" truth as that which, according to the curse, such persons will ignore or turn away from (*vimukha*, here translated as **bereft of**, literally means "whose face is away").
7. 2.22 **Whose good sense is deranged by Vedic pronouncements**: In offering an example of a statement in the Veda that causes one to lose discriminating power, several commentators quote a Vedic passage that promises attainment of immortality for one who performs a particular four-month sacrifice. The idea is that such prescribed ritual activities actually bring about only temporary benefits for the performer, and therefore their performance is a waste of time.
8. 2.28 **Keep vows for Bhava**: Vaṁśīdhara comments that these practices include the keeping of matted hair, smearing ashes on the body, and wearing bones, as is done by the Pāśupatas, one of several Śaivite ascetic traditions. These practices are made explicit in the next verse. **Heretics** refers here to those who stand on the periphery of orthodox brahmanical practices. See chapter 8 in Gupta and Valpey (2013).
9. 2.32 **Blaspheming the Veda**: Viśvanātha notes that Bhṛgu is saying, in effect, "What I say is 'pounding the already pounded' (*piṣṭa-peśa*), since you are already condemned by your action of disrespecting the Veda." Yet we may note the disrespect for the Veda implied in verse 22, spoken by the same followers of Shiva in derision of the *brāhmaṇas* who follow Vedic injunctions.
10. 4.1 **Could die in either case**: Shiva anticipates that Satī's death may occur whether or not she attends Dakṣa's sacrifice. If she attends, she will be angered by her father's insults against him (Shiva), and if she stays home, she will be frustrated by not seeing her relatives. In either case she may immolate herself out of desperation.
11. 4.2 Here Satī is referred to as **Bhavāni**, the female counterpart of **Bhava** (Shiva). With Satī's (seeming) death (vv. 27–29), Shiva becomes apparently without his consort, yet Satī will later be reborn as Parvatī, resuming her position as Shiva's wife and counterpart.
12. 4.3 **Her mind perplexed by her womanly nature**: Commentators explain that *straiṇa*, "femininity," is here identified as the cause of Satī's deciding to leave for her father's house, despite her husband's warnings.
13. 4.10 **Exertions in ritual** translates *dhūma-patha*, literally, "the path of smoke," which commentators gloss as the path of (ritual) action. The text suggests that ritual action, centered in fire sacrifice, creates both literal and figurative smoke, obscuring rather than revealing the way to freedom. The Bhagavad Gītā (8.24–25) also contrasts the smoky path, which keeps one bound to this world, with the path of light, which leads to the supreme destination.
14. **4**.12 Śrīdhara lists four types of persons in relation to faultfinding: (1) those who see only faults in others even when there are good qualities (*adhama*, "the lowest"); (2) those who see both good and bad qualities for what they are but

accept only the good (*madhya-stha*, "situated in the middle"); (3) *sādhus*, who notice only good qualities, not bad (*mahattara*, "greater"); and (4) the greatest of saints (*mahattama*), who magnify a person's good qualities, however minimal, and ignore bad qualities.

15. 4.13 **Dust of the feet of those great souls**: The idea is that finding fault with great persons causes misfortune, in that great souls are seen to be in all respects more exalted than their detractors, such that even the dust from their feet is more exalted. Further, in bhakti traditions foot dust from great souls is associated with mercy: by serving such a person one aspires to receive dust from his or her feet upon one's head.
16. 4.14 **Quite his opposite**: *aśiva*, literally, "else than Shiva," which can also mean "inauspicious," since *śiva* means "auspicious."
17. 4.15 **Exalted ones**: Commentators identify these as the four Kumara child sages (encountered in Book Three, chapter 12; see also Book Three, chapters 15–16), whose aim in approaching Shiva, unlike the **ordinary supplicants**, is to gain **the nectarean bliss of *brahman*** (*brahmānanda*, the bliss of realizing *brahman*). "Nectarean bliss" translates *rasāsava*, suggesting the important Indian notion of aesthetic relish (*rasa*) of an essence (*āsava*) consisting of a relationality between two persons (of whom one may be divine).
18. 4.16 **Whatever falls from his feet**: Some commentators say it is flowers that have been offered to Shiva, while others say it is the dust of his feet that the gods honor. In either case the point is that they all honor Shiva. Satī's acknowledgment here of Dakṣa's points of criticism regarding Shiva's dress and lifestyle (vv. 4.2.14–15) serves rhetorically to bring attention to his exalted status in light of the fact that he is worshipped by such beings as Brahmā.
19. 4.17 Satī alludes to grim injunctions found in Dharmaśāstras (brahmanical law books) about proper or sanctioned behavior in response to blasphemy. According to Vaṃśīdhara, for each *varṇa* there are different appropriate responses. The *brāhmaṇa* is expected to block his ears while remembering Vishnu and then leave the place; the *kṣatriya* may cut out the tongue of the offender; and for the *vaiśya* and *śūdra* it is appropriate to "give up" one's own body—in other words, to kill oneself (as a solution to the problem of implication in the act of blasphemy because of having heard it).
20. 4.18 **The blue-throated Shiva**: As described later (8.7.36–44), Shiva is known for having voluntarily drunk poison for the benefit of the world. Satī's allusion to this incident serves as ironic backdrop to her own resolve to, in effect, reject the "poison" of her father's insults.
21. 4.19 **The way of gods**: The idea is that gods travel in the *ākāśa*, the sky, whereas human beings travel on the earth, each according to its nature. Similarly a **great sage** (*mahā-muni*) such as Shiva, unlike either gods or humans, being self-satisfied, "travels" in the mind, not needing to observe ordinary human social conventions.
22. 4.20 **Engaged and disengaged** refers to an oft-considered distinction (*pravṛtti* and *nivṛtti*) between actions associated with brahmanical traditions centered on the ritual performance of sacrifice for temporal benefits (hence, "engaged") and

("disengaged") ascetic practices associated with *śramanical* traditions (including those of Buddhists and Jains, who reject sacrificial ritual in favor of meditation, in pursuit of liberation).

23. 4.21 **Cherished by *avadhūtas***: An *avadhūta* is an ascetic, considered to be beyond all social restraints and designations—literally, "one who has shaken off" worldly life and hence is discarded by the world. Vijayadhvaja glosses **ritual food** as animal flesh. Since this **smoky path** is separate (from that of Shiva), Shiva's virtues are not diminished by what is said to insult him by the (flesh-eating) ritualists. **Father**: Giridhara notes that Satī's addressing Dakṣa thusly indicates that she is not forgetting her relationship to him, wanting to benefit him by her words.
24. 4.24 **Yoga pathway**: This and the following three verses echo standard practices delineated in the classical *aṣṭānga* (eightfold) and other yoga systems: Satī sat **in silence** and is **blameless** (suggesting the first two yoga practices, *yama* and *niyama*, vv. 24, 25); she was **fixed in posture** (suggesting *āsana*, v. 25), **balancing the life airs** (suggesting *prāṇāyāma*, v. 25); she **directed her concentration** (*dhāraṇā*, v. 26); she **meditated** (suggesting *dhyāna*, v. 27), finally blazing with the fire born of **complete trance** (*samādhi*, v. 27).
25. 4.27 **With her body's impurities removed**: Viśvanātha explains that Satī's identification as the daughter of Dakṣa (which was the source of her anguish) had become removed by her yogic efforts. And since she is understood to be actually the eternally existent *māyāśakti*—the power of *māyā*—only the temporal body, a product of *māyā*, was destroyed.
26. 4.30 **Hater of Shiva**: Shiva is implied from the context of the narration, though only the word "person" (*puruṣa*) appears in the text. Vijayadhvaja comments that by implication Vishnu, the **supreme** person, is also meant. Because Shiva is considered (especially in the Bhāgavata) to be a devotee of Vishnu, Dakṣa's animosity toward Shiva implicates him in being inimical also to Vishnu.
27. 4.33 **Thousands of gods named Ṛbhus**: For details about these semidivine Vedic beings, see Biswas's (1968) comments on this verse. See the glossary for an explanation of ***soma***.
28. 19.8 **The rivers flowed with . . . all juices**: The word *rasa* can mean "juice" as well as "flavor." This term is central to Indian classical aesthetic theory, and the Bhāgavata consciously uses its multiple meanings. Here the idea that rivers carry milk and the like suggests the steady flow of agricultural abundance. Commentators note that **all juices** refers specifically to sugarcane juice, grape juice, and the like. Giridhara suggests that a reference to grains (*anna*) in this verse can be taken to refer to clarified butter (Skt. *ghṛta*, Hindi ghee), a dairy derivative that, always together with grains, is offered in sacrificial oblations.
29. 19.9 **Four kinds of food**: Food is categorized according to how it is eaten—whether by chewing, swallowing without chewing, sucking, or licking. The phrase suggests comprehensive totality: all types of food were abundantly available thanks to Pṛthu's proper execution of ritual sacrifices.
30. 19.12 **Dressed as a heretic**: This chapter serves as an etiological narrative, accounting for the cosmic origins of various groups whose ideologies and practices the Bhāgavata considers heretical because of their rejection of brahmanical principles (e.g., regarding the Vedas as revelatory scripture). In this account, heresy

arises rather ironically as a by-product of human and celestial ambitions from within brahmanical society, pitted against one another.

31. 19.14 Viśvanātha comments that Pṛthu's son saw Indra as Shiva or one of his followers and therefore saw him as **dharma personified**—i.e., as a properly religious person.
32. 19.16 **Just as the king of vultures chased Rāvaṇa**: This alludes to the Rāmāyaṇa episode in which Jatāyu, the vulture friend of Rāma, battles in the sky (to his own death) against the demon Rāvaṇa as the latter carries off Rāma's wife, Sītā.
33. 19.20 **One who bears a skull-topped staff**: This refers to a particular tradition of ascetic Shiva worshippers. See chapter 8 in Gupta and Valpey (2013).
34. 19.23 This verse is offering an "etymology" of the word ***pākhaṇḍa*** (translated in v. 12 as "heretic"). That Indra's various disguises are regarded as "signs" suggests the metonymic character of the explanation: persons who are considered heretics are identified by their dress, and as this account has it, it was the various guises (ways of dressing) adopted by Indra that spawned the various types of heresy.
35. 19.24–25 **Naked** is generally understood to refer to the Jains (particularly those Jain ascetics of the Digambara tradition); **clad in red** is understood to refer to Buddhists.
36. 19.27 **To kill others . . . decreed**: The idea is that it would be against the rules prescribed for the successful execution of the sacrifice for Pṛthu, as its sponsor, to commit an act of killing. Only the priests may perform ritual acts of sacrificial killing, implied in the next verse.
37. 19.42 **Appropriately worshipped**: Vīrarāghava says that each attendee was, literally, "made an object of kindness, (each) as was befitting." As a benedictory declaration (indicated in v. 41), the sense is, "We bless you that you have now sufficiently performed sacrifice, because all those you have summoned have been properly satisfied."

BOOK FIVE

1. 5.2–3 The Bhāgavata's male bias evident here may be explained at least in part by the context: Ṛṣabha speaks to his sons. In general the Bhāgavata speaks from a male perspective, but when negativity with respect to the opposite sex is expressed, it can be understood that the principle applies in both directions. Hence in this context, the **gateway to darkness** for women would be association with women who are overly attached to men.
2. 5.8 **Shared . . . heart**: Commentators note that this mutual "knot" is the second of two, the first being the force of bondage the individual holds to his or her own body.
3. 5.15 The last two lines of this verse are missing from the Ahmadabad critical edition.
4. 5.21 **Pramathas . . . Siddhas**: See the glossary.
5. 5.23 **Oblations . . . (to *brāhmaṇas*)** refers to offering food to *brāhmaṇas*, especially hosting them for a meal. Ṛṣabha's praise of the *brāhmaṇas* in verses 22–25 points to the Bhāgavata's concern to reject the non-Vedic ways of the Jains, who identify Ṛṣabha as one of the Tīrthaṅkaras. See chapter 8 in Gupta and Valpey (2013).

6. 5.26 **Judicious** (*vivikta*) **vision**: Śrīdhara mentions purity and freedom from envy as characteristics of such vision. Vijayadhvaja, however, emphasizes "separateness" suggested by the word *vivikta*: only one who sees that the Lord is different from all beings—in whose bodies he resides—pleases the Lord.
7. 5.27 **From fate's fetters** translates *kṛtānta-pāśāt*. "Fate" also refers to the lord of death, Yama, who is said to hold a noose with which he punishes wrongdoers after death.
8. 5.28 **Brahmāvarta**: Viśvanātha (commenting on this place's reference in 4.19.1), says that it is a place of the gods, located between the rivers Sarasvatī and Dṛśadvatī. The identity and location of both these rivers, associated with Vedic peoples in northern India, remain debated.
9. 5.34 Viśvanātha notes that Ṛṣabha acted like these animals for the sake of persons who have such animal natures.
10. 8.1 The commentators Śukadeva and Giridhara both identify the **Great River** as the **Gaṇḍakī**, a river in present-day Nepal. **Three moments** translates *muhūrta-trayam*. A *muhūrta* is either a "moment" or a period of approximately forty-eight minutes. Here the dramatic aspect of the episode suggests that Bharata had been seated for just a few moments before the accident subsequently described takes place.
11. 8.13 Vīrarāghava notes that while sleeping Bharata would keep the fawn on his chest.
12. 8.14 **Lord of the realm** translates *varṣa-patiḥ*, alluding to Bharata's lordship over the division (*varṣa*) of the "island" Jambūdvīpa, in turn a division of Bhū-maṇḍala (see chapter 16). Later tradition, to the present day, identifies India as Bhāratavarṣa, the realm of Bharata. **With his mind pacified**: having been reassured of the fawn's presence.
13. 8.23 **With . . . sacrifice**: An area where deer are present is considered to be a favorable place for performing religious rites.
14. 8.26 Śrīdhara and Vīrarāghava note that the explanation for Bharata's abandonment and fall from yogic practice was *prārabdha-karma*, "commenced action"—the effect of action from a previous life that becomes assumed in the present life. **His own soul** translates *ātmānam*. Usually we translate this (from the stem *ātman*) as "the self"; here, however, "soul" is preferred to highlight the nature of Bharata's neglect, intentionally resonating with the biblical expression "For what shall it profit a man, if he shall gain the whole world, and lose his own soul?" (Mark 8:36, KJV).
15. 8.30 Giridhara notes that **a place of the Lord** indicates the reason for Bharata's going there: such holy places are known to afford rapid attainment of liberation.
16. 8.31 **Condition . . . deer**: literally, "the cause of the deer state," suggesting Bharata's concern to be free not only from the deer body but also, and especially, from the mentality of worldly absorption that caused him to be born as a deer.
17. 16.4 **Earth sphere**: Although the word *golaka*—"sphere" or "globe"—is used in this verse, from verse 5 onward the impression is given of a more or less flat, circular plane, upon which the central mountain, Meru, is situated and around which several mountain ranges are located.

18. 16.5 Opinions on the equivalence of the *yojana* differ, ranging from about two and a half to eighteen miles, hence we keep the Sanskrit term of measurement, and the possible equivalent distances, untranslated and uncalculated.
19. 16.6 Commentators, beginning with Śrīdhara, are at pains to explain these descriptions of "islands" and mountains, with their various lengths and widths, in order to work out a plausible picture of what is described, each with more or less persuasive arguments aiming toward consistency. For an interesting modern attempt to correlate with, or otherwise explain, this description in light of early and contemporary Western cosmological understandings, see Thompson (1996).
20. 16.7 The earth globe is here being compared to a lotus flower. As a lotus is narrow at its base but opens widely at its top, so Mount Meru has a smaller diameter at its base and a wider surface at its peak.
21. 16.12 The kadamba (*Neolomarckia cadamba*) is a tall, expansive tree native to India that produces fragrant, orange blossoms.
22. 16.18 **Bhavānī** is Shiva's wife, who lives with her husband in Ilāvṛta. As described in the Bhāgavata's next chapter, she permits the presence of no men other than her husband in that region of Jambūdvīpa. **Pious men**: Commentators identify these as Yakṣas—forest beings associated with Kuvera, said to be the god of treasures and regent of the northern quarter.

BOOK SIX

1. 1.21 Commentators offer several explanations (or "etymologies") for the name **Ajāmila**, playing with a variety of possible meanings construed from various ways of parsing the word *ajāmila*. Vīrarāghava, in particular, is concerned to show that the essential themes embedded in the story of Ajāmila (namely, loss and recovery of higher knowledge) are alluded to by his name.
2. 1.26 Śrīdhara notes that while indulging his son, Ajāmila frequently called his name, **Nārāyaṇa**, and thus inadvertently he developed devotion (bhakti) toward the Lord. Vaṁśīdhara adds that the various services Ajāmila provided the boy amounted to acts of worship (*pūjā*), thus hinting that in effect he was inadvertently worshipping the supreme Lord, albeit in the form of his own son.
3. 1.27 Vijayadhvaja suggests that by the grace of the Lord, who removes all faults and sins, Ajāmila's knowledge within the heart was manifest, such that he was able to invoke with devotion the Lord into the particular form of his five-year-old son by his remembrance of his son.
4. 1.41 **Consisting of activity, illumination, or inertia** translates *rajaḥ-sattva-tamomayāḥ*, referring to the three "modalities" or "qualities" (*guṇas*) that in the Saṁkhya thought system constitute the ways by which temporal nature (*prakṛti*) function. That Vishnu **remains in his own realm** implies that his realm is untouched by these states of being.
5. 1.44 See verse 53 in this chapter and note 9 for a further explanation of the notion of the impossibility of being a nonactor.
6. 1.46 Śrīdhara suggests three ways of construing **three kinds of effects**—namely, as three qualities of life in accordance with the three *guṇas*; as happiness, misery,

and a mixture of both; and as the condition of being virtuous (*dhārmika*), non-virtuous, or a mixture of both. **In the other world** translates *anyatra*, literally, "elsewhere," which Śrīdhara glosses as "in the next birth."

7. 1.48 Śrīdhara explains that **Situated . . . unborn lord** can refer to either Yama in his abode or the form of the supreme Lord said to be located in the heart of all living beings (*paramātmā*).
8. 1.50 The numbers in this verse and the next allude to the Sāṁkhya thought system, with its analysis of several constituents of nature (*prakṛti*), and hence the temporal body and its means of enjoyment. The self, distinct from the body, is nevertheless identified here as the seventeenth constituent of enjoyment to suggest that without the presence of the self there would be no experience of enjoyment by the remaining sixteen constituents.
9. 1.53 This verse is almost identical to Bhagavad Gītā 3.5, as part of Krishna's argument for the necessity to perform *karma-yoga* in order to become free from the binding effects of worldly action (karma).
10. 1.58 **Kuśa** is a type of long grass (*Poa cynosuroides*) used in Vedic sacrificial rituals.
11. 2.4 This verse is almost identical to Bhagavad Gītā 3.21. The notion that rulers must lead by exemplary behavior is strongly emphasized as a key principle of kingship in the Mahābhārata as well as in the Bhāgavata Purāṇa and other brahmanical literature.
12. 2.9 **One who has . . . his guru's wife** translates *guru-talpa*-gaḥ, literally, "one who goes to the guru's bed." This is commonly mentioned in lists of heinous crimes in Purāṇic literature and Dharmaśāstras, crimes for which punishment is most severe.
13. 2.14 **To signify something else** (*sāṅketya*) means using a word with the intention of indicating something other than that which it properly signifies. Thus Ajāmila's calling his son would be an example of this kind of chanting.
14. 2.16 **Procedures for atonement** translates *prāyaścittāni*. *Prāyaścitta* literally means "predominant thought," referring to one's anticipation of death and the consequent concern to prepare for it by atonement for sins committed during one's life. Dharmaśāstras—early Sanskrit texts that prescribe specific rules of dharma—as well as Purāṇas, devote considerable attention to detailed prescriptions of atonement for specific transgressive acts.
15. 3.1 Giridhara notes that *all* persons, including Ajāmila, are **under his** (Yama's) **rule**, thus highlighting Parīkṣit's surprise that Ajāmila should be an exception.
16. 3.2 **Punishment was subverted** translates *daṇḍa-bhangaḥ*, literally, "broken stick." The term *daṇḍa* secondarily means "punishment," indicating the connection between an instrument of punishment and the act of punishment.
17. 3.4 **Results** translates *phala*, literally, "fruit," a term typically employed in the context of action (karma) as that which produces "fruits" (that are either sweet or sour, depending on their appropriateness or inappropriateness). **Three types of action** translates *trai-vidhyam*, indicating the Sāṁkhya conception of nature as functioning in three modalities (*guṇas*).
18. 3.5 Bhaktivedanta's translation of this verse elaborates on the reasoning in the Yamadutas' confusion: "If in this universe there are many rulers and justices who disagree about punishment and reward, their contradictory actions will

neutralize each other, and no one will be punished or rewarded. Otherwise, if their contradictory acts fail to neutralize each other, everyone will have to be both punished and rewarded."

19. 3.11 Viśvanātha attributes Yama's being delighted to his having heard the divine name Nārāyaṇa from his servants in the course of their questioning him (v. 10).
20. 3.13 **Names** refers specifically to identifications of social position (*varṇa*). **Rope of (Vedic) language** indicates the complex of Vedic scriptural law by which, according to brahmanical traditions, humanity is bound.
21. 3.18 Vaṁśīdhara comments that **from me** means "from me and mine—namely, from *you*." Yama is speaking to his messengers, so Vaṁśīdhara humorously suggests that Yama wants to make it clear to his own agents that they are particularly objects of Vishnu's messengers' protection for his devotees.
22. 3.19 ***Vidhyādharas*** are said to be supernatural beings that dwell in the Himalayas as associates of Shiva; ***cāraṇas*** are a type of celestial singer. Vaṁśīdhara claims that **directly by the Lord** means "by the Bhāgavata (Purāṇa)."
23. 3.20–21 The acts and teachings of each figure listed here (except **Janaka**) are featured in the Bhāgavata Purāṇa. A nonexhaustive list of where these can be found is as follows: **Brahmā** (2.5–6, 3.9, 10.13–14); **Nārada** (7.1–15); **Shiva** (4.2–5, 4.24, 10.88); **Kumāras** (3.15–16, 4.22); **Kapila** (3.25–33); Svayambhuva **Manu** (3.21, 4.11); **Prahlāda** (7.4–9); **Bhīṣma** (1.9); **Bali** (8.19–22); **Śuka** (1.19–12.13); Yama (6.3). **Enjoys immortality** translates *amṛtam aśnute. Amṛta*, "nondeath," also refers to the ambrosia that, when drunk, is said to afford immortality.
24. 3.22 **Yoga of devotion** translates bhakti yoga.
25. 3.24 **Glorification** translates *saṁkīrtanam*. Śridhara indicates that the prefix *saṁ* (in *saṁkīrtanam*) suggests completeness. Thus Ajāmila, although thinking of his son, had in fact, in all sincerity, pronounced the divine name, and thus he was entitled to its liberating effect.
26. 3.26 **Who makes wide strides**: Urugāya, a name of Vishnu (famous for extending his stride to include the entire universe in his bid for three steps of land from King Bali). See Book Eight, chapters 19–20.
27. 3.28 **Saints** translates *paramahaṁsa-kula*. For an explanation of *paramahaṁsa*, see 2.7.10 and its note.
28. 3.30 **People . . . joined in supplication** translates *racitāñjalīnām*, literally, "of those whose hands are placed together as a gesture of supplication." Monier-Williams explains that the two hands are cupped together, as a beggar would cup the hands to receive alms.
29. 3.35 Commentators identify this person as Agastya, a celebrated sage in Sanskrit epic and Purāṇic literature.
30. 7.36 **The gleaning of neglected grains**: a practice said to be followed by certain *brāhmaṇas* as their sole means of maintaining themselves. Two places for obtaining "neglected" grains are implied by the verse—namely, grains left in the field after harvest and grains left in the marketplace after business hours. The idea is that the occupation of a priest, who performs rituals in expectation of payment, is considered contemptible, whereas for a *brāhmaṇa* to live independently is honorable.
31. 7.39 With two different terms—**(Vishnu) mantra** and **magical technology**—we have translated the word *vidyā* (occurring twice in this verse, in its instrumental

form), as it carries both meanings. The Vishnu mantra referred to here is called the Nārāyaṇa-kavaca ("shield of Nārāyaṇa," which is given fully in chapter eight of Book Six—not included in this translation).

32. 9.39 As we have noted in earlier chapters, the mention of ***rasa*** alludes to a major theme of the Bhāgavata Purāṇa—namely, the aesthetics of devotional relationality, expressed as "taste" or "relish" (*rasa*). For some commentators, this theme finds its culmination in the *rasa* dance of Krishna and the *gopīs*—cowherdesses of Vrindavan (Book Ten, chapters 29–33). **Exalted *bhāgavatas***: again, a major Bhāgavata Purāṇa theme, from which the entire work derives its name; a *bhāgavata* is a person related to Bhagavān, the supreme Lord. **Destroyer of Madhu** alludes to a celebrated feat of Vishnu's, who is said to have killed the demon Madhu as he attempted to steal the Veda from the memory of Brahmā, the cosmic creator.
33. 9.40 **Who took three strides** translates Trivikrama, a celebrated name of Vishnu for his act of prevailing over Bali by claiming the world by taking three steps. See note 26.
34. 12.1 **Kaiṭabha** is often associated with another *asura*, Madhu. See note 32.
35. 13.12–13 **Outcaste woman** translates *cāṇḍālīm*, a term (rarely instanced in the Bhāgavata Purāṇa) used to denote a person (in this case female) of very low social standing.
36. 13.14 **The Mānasa lake**, or Mānasa Sarovara, is sometimes identified with a freshwater lake on the Tibetan Plateau. In Purāṇic literature it is associated with Mount Meru (or Sumeru), the central mountain of Jambūdvīpa (see Book Five, chapter 16).
37. 13.16 Vīrarāghava and other commentators explain that **Nahuṣa**, although a human being, was able to rule heaven by virtue of his being a **possessor of knowledge, austerity, self-discipline, and strength**. But owing to the **madness of wealth and power** he became a snake as a result of being cursed by sages (in turn the result of a ruse by Bṛhaspati) for making advances toward **Indra's wife**, Śacī. For this reason Indra was able to regain his ruling position.
38. 13.17 **Vishnu** is here referred to as Ṛtambhara, "he who preserves truth." Indra received support from several sources for his reinstatement as ruler of heaven—Vishnu, **Rudra** (identified with Shiva in the Bhāgavata Purāṇa), **Lakṣmī** (said to reside in lotuses, amid which Indra resided—see v. 15), and ***brāhmaṇas***. It seems that a combination of his own sense of remorse, his recourse to meditation on Vishnu, and his identity as Indra worked in combination to overcome the effects of what is considered one of the direst of sinful acts—namely, killing a *brāhmaṇa*.
39. 17.30 **As one . . . a curled-up object** translates *śrajivat*, literally, "as in a garland." The root word *śraj* can refer to anything that turns, winds, or coils. Commentators explain that this alludes to the Upaniṣadic analogy of a rope being mistaken for a snake to explain misapprehension (especially of the nature of the world). Śrīdhara and other commentators extend the analogy to that of a sleeping person unable to properly discriminate the actual from the nonactual. Shiva eulogizes Citraketu as being unaffected by common human tribulations of dualistic misperception thanks to his being an exalted *bhāgavata*.
40. 17.34–35 Viśvanātha embellishes these verses, in effect pointing out that in this speech (beginning with v. 27) Shiva is reprimanding Parvatī for having cursed Citraketu: Shiva explains that as close friends (both being devoted to the Lord),

he and Citraketu had been having a friendly, joking exchange when Parvatī interrupted with her inappropriate cursing words, showing her ignorance of the devotional mood that Shiva and Citraketu shared.

BOOK SEVEN

1. 3.3 The verb *tap*, "to heat," and its nominal derivatives are used repeatedly in these verses. The verbal root refers to ascetic practice, which often involves both tolerating heat (along with other methods of self-mortification) and giving off heat (upon accumulating ascetic power). Both senses are applicable here: in this verse, Hiraṇyakaśipu gains power by heating (tormenting) himself, which leads, in the next verse, to the release of ascetic power as fire from his head. Because there is no single verb in English that encompasses both "heat" and "austerity," the various instances of *tap* had to be translated differently according to context, losing much of the verses' alliteration and emphasis.
2. 3.11 Śrīdhara interprets this verse as follows: "I will reverse the order of gods and demons as well as the order of pious and sinful activity in this world. What is the use of Vaiṣṇava worlds like the polestar? I will subdue them too!"
3. 3.21 **You are certainly mortal**: According to Viśvanātha, Vaṁśīdhara, and Bhaktivedanta, this statement serves as a warning to Hiraṇyakaśipu that although he is the greatest of *asuras*, and although his wishes will be fulfilled, he will nevertheless remain mortal.
4. 4.38–39 **He was embraced . . . laugh**: Viśvanātha explains that even as loving parents embrace their child and hold him close, so Krishna did the same with Prahlāda. And as a child cries when his mother leaves his side and becomes happy as soon as she returns, so Prahlāda laughed or cried when Krishna became visible or absent. This affectionate exchange with the Lord was perceptible only to Prahlāda.
5. 5.30 **Chewing what they have already chewed**: The idea here is that human beings have repeatedly pursued sensual pleasures in previous births. Yet people remain anxious to experience such pleasures again in this life, despite their inability to truly satisfy.
6. 8.26–27 **Nṛsiṁha playfully let the demon slip from his hand**: Bhaktivedanta comments, "When a sinful man enjoys material facilities, foolish people sometimes think, 'How is it that this sinful man is enjoying whereas a pious man is suffering?' . . . A sinful man who acts against the laws of nature must be punished, but sometimes he is given a chance to play, exactly like Hiraṇyakaśipu when he was released from the hands of Nṛsiṁha-deva."
7. 8.29 By using this method of killing Hiraṇyakaśipu, Nṛsiṁha honors all the boons that Brahmā granted to the demon (in 7.3.35–38). Hiraṇyakaśipu was killed by neither a man nor animal but by a man-lion; he died neither in the sky nor on the earth but on Nṛsiṁha's lap; he was not slain by any weapon but by the Lord's fingernails; he did not die inside nor outside but at the threshold of the palace; and he died not during the day or night but at twilight. Finally, he was not killed by any created being but by the supreme Bhagavān himself.

In addition to the readings suggested at the end of the chapter, there are two seminal, non-English studies of Prahlāda and Nṛsiṁha that should be mentioned: Biardeau (1975) and Hacker (1959).

BOOK EIGHT

1. 7.16–17 These verses are missing in the Ahmadabad critical edition.
2. 8.1 This celestial **cow** is often called Kāmadhenu or Surabhi, a cow of plenty who can fulfill any desire. The Rāmāyaṇa tells of an instance when King Viśvāmitra attempted to seize Kāmadhenu from the home of the sage Vaṣiṣṭha but found himself defeated by the cow's magical ability to defend herself. For a study of the sacred cow as a source of prosperity in Hinduism, see Biardeau (1993, 99). For a discussion of Kāmadhenu's iconography, with accompanying images, see Smith (2006, 402–4).
3. 8.4 Jīva attests to the existence of a variant reading, wherein there is an additional verse between verses 5 and 6, as follows: "Monarch! Thereafter came eight elephants who guard the directions, led by Airāvaṇa, together with eight female elephants, led by Abhramu."
4. 8.5 This verse is missing from the Ahmadabad critical edition. **A ruby-hued gem called Kaustubha**: Commentators hold different opinions about the relationship between the ruby and Kaustubha gems mentioned in this verse. Vīrarāghava and Giridhara state simply that the Kaustubha is a ruby, while Vaṁśīdhara suggests that the Kaustubha is a gem that is ruby colored. Both Vaṁśīdhara and Bhaktivedanta are open to the possibility that two distinct gems emerged from the ocean—the Kaustubha and the ruby (*padmarāga*).
5. 8.21 **Succumbs to the force of time**: The word *aja* (literally, "leader" or "unborn") can refer to several deities and, in the feminine, to material nature as *prakṛti* or *māyā*. Here commentators are unanimous in glossing the word as "time," which defeats even powerful leaders as they succumb to old age and death.
6. 8.22 Śrīdhara offers examples of each type of person described in the verse. Sages like Mārkaṇḍeya, he says, are long-lived, but because they practice strict sense control, they develop a harsh disposition. Kings like Hiraṇyakaśipu have a pleasing disposition, but their life spans are uncertain, since Vishnu could kill them at any time. Shiva has both a pleasing disposition and the certainty of long life, but he has a few inauspicious attributes. (He frequents crematoriums, for example.) Indeed, Vishnu is the only person who is auspicious in every way, Śrīdhara says, but the Lord does not desire Lakṣmī, since he is satisfied and complete in himself.
7. 18.31 The (twice) mention of Vāmana's **feet** is ironically significant, since it will be the steps of those same feet that will bring loss and defeat, but ultimate devotional victory, to Bali.
8. 19.4 For the story of Prahlāda, see Book Seven, chapters 5–8. **Petitioners . . . battlefield**: According to dharmic laws, a *kṣatriya* is required to give charity to *brāhmaṇas* who solicit it, especially when solicited at a place of pilgrimage; similarly, a *kṣatriya* is required to give battle when challenged by another *kṣatriya* to do so on a field of battle.

9. 19.18 Bhaktivedanta, following Viśvanātha, notes that Bali is correct in saying that Vāmana is not acting in **his own best interest**, because as the self-sufficient supreme Lord, his only concern was for the welfare of his devotees. He adds, "Devotees sacrifice all personal interests to satisfy the Supreme Personality of Godhead, and similarly the Supreme Lord, although having no personal interests, can do anything for the interests of His devotees."
10. 19.19 **Worlds**: *Loka* is another term used in this passage for cosmic regions. Verse 21 refers to **three worlds**—lower, earthly, and heavenly realms—and verse 22 mentions **nine regions**, referring to *varśas*, or "divisions," of the "island" called Jambūdvīpa, described in Book Five, chapter 19. **Entire islands**: Book Five, chapter 20, describes the universe as consisting of seven "islands" shaped like concentric rings, each surrounded by an ocean consisting each of a different substance.
11. 19.21 **Objects** translates *viṣayāḥ*, suggesting "objects of the senses." Thus **one whose senses are unconquered** is so because of being under the control of objects attractive to the senses. As Bali claims to rule the world, the insinuation is that he is yet unable to rule his senses.
12. 19.22 **An island . . . seven islands**: see note 10.
13. 19.28 **Took up a water pot**: The declaration of a vow—particularly a vow to give in charity—is required by ritual texts to be confirmed by the pouring or sprinkling of pure water (see Heim 2004, 88, and, more broadly to this episode as a whole, note her discussion [92–102] of the transforming character of ritual giving and the ritual use of water).
14. 19.32 As a name of Vishnu, **Hari** is traditionally identified as being derived from the verbal root *hṛ*, "to take away or to remove, especially sin or evil." Viśvanātha suggests that the devotional significance of the name is that the Lord "even takes away one's mind" (in the positive sense that a devotee—in this case Bali—becomes positively charmed by the Lord).
15. 19.38 ***Bahvṛca* hymn**: The mantra alluded to is found in *Aitareya Āraṇyaka* 2.3.6: Keith (1969, 39) notes that Āraṇyaka II and III are sometimes referred to as the *Bahvṛca-brāhmaṇa Upaniṣad*.
16. 19.39 To dissuade Bali from fulfilling his promise, in verses 39–43 Śukra contrives an argument ostensibly based on Vedic wisdom. The main force of his argument, based on rational self-interest, is the consideration that one must keep oneself in a position of worldly well-being in order to give in charity (to give **flowers and fruit**). According to Śukra, to sustain well-being in this world requires one, at least sometimes, to be untruthful. Further, pronouncing the promise to give charity using the syllable *oṁ* implies that Bali will give everything he owns, leaving nothing for himself to enjoy. Verse 43 is clearly intended as a parody of the sort of self-serving injunctions likely to be found in brahmanical law books, the Dharmaśāstras.
17. 19.43 This verse echoes an injunction found in the Dharmaśāstric text the Manusmṛti (8.104, Jha p. vol. 6, p. 122): "Where the telling of the truth would lead to the death of a Shudra, a Vaishya, a Kṣatriya or a Brāhmaṇa,—in that case falsehood should be spoken; as that is preferable to truth." It also echoes a verse in the Mahābhārata (1.77.15, translated in van Buitenen 1973, 188): "A lie spoken in jest does not hurt, / Nor a lie to women, or at marriage time, / Or on pain of life, or

of all property— / These five lies are said to be no sins." Many thanks to Anand Venkatkrishnan and Ravi Khangai for pointing out these references.

18. 20.12 **Guise of a *brāhmaṇa*** translates *brahma-tanum*, literally, "whose body is *brahman*." The compound suggests a multiple meaning: *brahma* can indicate both *brāhmaṇa* (a member of the priestly class) and "monk" (*brahmacārin*), a celibate student who "lives in *brahman*"; further, the sense is implied that as an *avatāra* of Vishnu, Vāmana is the transcendent Lord whose body (*tanum*) is the nondifferentiated absolute, *brahman*.
19. 20.18 **Sprinkled . . . that water**: A gesture of respect and self-purification is for the worshipper, having worshipfully bathed the feet of an honored guest, to then sprinkle some of that water on his or her own head.
20. 20.33 **Wide-striding** translates *urukrama*, which Monier-Williams (p. 217) translates as "far-stepping, making wide strides (said of Vishnu)," following the early Indologist Ralph T. H. Griffith's translation of *urugāya* in Ṛgveda 1.154.6.
21. 21.33 The Ahmadabad critical edition has a variant reading for the second half of this verse: *yo viprāya pratiśruty na tadarpayate 'rthinam.*

BOOK NINE

1. 4.56 **Universes . . . inhabited by Brahmā and other living beings**: This phrase translates *aja-jīva-kośāḥ*, which commentators are unanimous in glossing as follows: "The coverings (i.e., the universes) wherein reside Aja (i.e., Brahmā) and the *jīvas* (living beings)."
2. 4.63 **I love them dearly**: As Vīrarāghava points out, the word *bhakta-jana-priya* can be taken as a *bahuvrīhi* compound (the devotees are dearly loved by me) or as a *tatpuruṣa* compound (I am dearly loved by devotees). Jīva and Viśvanātha offer a third interpretation, taking *bhakta-jana* itself as a *tatpuruṣa*: "The followers of my devotees are dearly loved by me." Bhaktivedanta explains, "Therefore Caitanya Mahāprabhu identified Himself as *gopī-bhartuḥ pada-kamalayor dāsa-dāsānudāsaḥ*. Thus he instructed us to become not directly servants of Kṛṣṇa but servants of the servant of Kṛṣṇa."
3. 4.65 **What is beyond this**: Śrīdhara and Vijayadhvaja explain that devotees have no desire to live in heaven (*svarga*), while Jīva precludes even the four kinds of liberation (see v. 67 and note 4).
4. 4.67 The **four (kinds of liberation)** are (1) *sālokya*, residing in Vishnu's abode; (2) *sārūpya*, receiving a form similar to Vishnu's; (3) *sāmīpya*, living near Vishnu; and (4) *sārṣṭi*, receiving opulence similar to Vishnu's. They are listed in Book Three (29.13), where a similar point is made: devotees do not accept liberation if it means being deprived of the Lord's service.
5. 4.69 The first line of this verse is missing in the Ahmadabad critical edition. **You targeted with that harmful magic**: Bhaktivedanta, anticipating what is said in the remainder of the verse, glosses *ātmābhicāraḥ* as a transgression against oneself. Although Durvāsā attempted to harm Ambarīṣa, in fact the sage was targeting only himself, since **power that is directed against virtuous persons** returns to harm the person who deploys it.

6. 24.66–67 These two verses are numbered 46–47 in the Ahmadabad critical edition since the critical edition omits twenty verses earlier in chapter 24.

BOOK TEN

1. 8.32 Jīva notes that **cowherd** (*gopa*) alludes to the boys' concern to uphold Krishna's foster father's order to protect Krishna in all circumstances. The suggestion is that the boys' complaint arises from their affectionate protectiveness, not from a wish to vilify Krishna. To the contrary, they wish to bring Yaśodā joy, perhaps anticipating the vision that Krishna will reveal to her as a consequence of their report.
2. 8.35 Against possible accusations that Krishna or his friends lie to Yaśodā, Vaṁśīdhara discusses ways in which both Krishna's and his friends' truthfulness are vouchsafed. Quoting a Vedic text, he notes that as the self (*ātmā*) of all, Krishna is not subject to the frailties of mortals, nor does he need to eat or drink; hence, he has not eaten earth. But, to preserve the truthfulness of Krishna's friends, who accuse Krishna of eating earth, Vaṁśīdhara suggests that during the cosmic destruction, as the cosmic Lord, Krishna indeed "eats" the entire universe. However, Jīva and Viśvanātha argue that Krishna's lying—if it be seen as such—is not a fault, for it is inspired by his wish to increase the happiness of his devotees.
3. 8.40 **My goodness** translates *bata*, an exclamatory expression of astonishment that can also indicate regret. Here, Yaśodā is clearly astonished; yet this mood could be taken as being mixed with regret for having made unfair assumptions about her son's behavior and honesty, and for having failed to recognize his divinity.
4. 8.42 **Silly sentiment**—literally, "weak intellect" (*kumati*)—is an interesting example of self-reflection or, in contemporary language, the expression of "subjectivity" in which the very act of self-assessment belies the negative sense of having "weak intelligence." Nonetheless, Viśvanātha, followed by Vaṁśīdhara, notes that Yaśodā's reflective reasoning exhibited here is "momentary," for, immediately following these thoughts, she is again, by the power of Vishnu's *māyā*, caught up in her motherly feelings (v. 43).
5. 8.43 The expression **thus** (*ittham*) would seem to be a non sequitur, as Krishna's divine revelation to Yaśodā (vv. 36–42) occurs as he withdraws his *māyā* under which she had always experienced motherly affection, whereas this verse describes his reenveloping her in *māyā*. The expression may, however, be taken as referring to the episode as a whole, in effect saying, "The motherly affection induced by Vishnu's *māyā* was thus temporarily withdrawn and then, after she briefly saw the divine identity of Krishna, was again extended so that her devotional attitude would be no longer disturbed." Jīva identifies **Vishnu-*māyā*** as the *svarūpa-śakti*—the innate power of Vishnu—indicating the ontically real nature of the relationship of mother and child between Yaśodā and Krishna.
6. 9.3 **Linen dress** (*kṣaumam*): Commentators have varied opinions on the meaning of this term. Vijayadhvaja, Satyadharma, Giridhara, and others take it as referring to silk, whereas Sanātana and Baladeva, referring to the classical Amarakośa Sanskrit dictionary, identify it as *atasī*, or "flax," as indicative that it was very fine linen, tied with a golden **cord**. ***Mālatī***: *Aganosma dichotoma*, a vine with fragrant

flowers, similar to jasmine. In Sanskrit literature, these flowers frequently scatter from women's hair, where they are placed for decoration. Sanātana suggests that this verse's description of Yaśodā's great beauty and affection for Krishna serves to emphasize the appropriateness of her being his mother.

7. 9.6 **Fresh butter**: Monier-Williams explains that the term *hayaṁgavīna* is related to the term in the present verse, *haiyaṁgavam*, as "clarified butter prepared from yesterday's milking; fresh butter." Since clarified butter, used commonly in Indian cooking to this day, especially for deep-frying, is not sweet tasting in the same way butter is, we assume that it would be fresh butter that Krishna would have consumed. **Millstone**: specifically the lower, heavier of two stones used for grinding grains, alluding to the superhuman strength that Krishna exhibits on several occasions.
8. 9.9 **As if afraid**: Viśvanātha calls attention to devotees' wonder at the fear—or apparent fear—that Krishna displays here (and in v. 11). As the all-powerful Lord, Krishna is the cause of fear to fear itself, yet Yaśodā is able to instill fear in him with her motherly resolve to correct him. In regard to the sense that Krishna is genuinely fearful, Viśvanātha quotes Kuntī's prayer (1.8.31) that expresses bewilderment about why the all powerful should be fearful. But Viśvanātha also suggests, following Sanātana and Jīva, that Krishna may not actually be feeling fear within himself, only *displaying* fear when actually he was confident in the simple love of Yaśodā.
9. 9.14 Viśvanātha and Vaṁśīdhara highlight the Bhāgavata's message: although it is impossible to bind (or otherwise control) the all-powerful Lord, who is **Adhokṣaja**—imperceivable by the senses—because of her extraordinary motherly devotion, Yaśodā will indeed be able to bind him. Vijayadhvaja shows how the meaning of Adhokṣaja is derived: it refers to "he by whom that knowledge which is born (*ja*) from the senses (*akṣa*) is made inferior (*adha*)." **Began to bind**: Literally, "bound" (past tense), but considering that her success is not immediate (see vv. 15–17), we have rendered it in a past progressive sense.
10. 9.18 **Constant exertion** translates *pariśrama*, which can also mean "fatigue."
11. 9.20 **Brahmā**: Sanātana notes that Brahmā (referred to in the text as Viriñca) is the primordial guru of *bhaktas*—devotees of Bhagavān; **the Lord's better half** is Bhaktivedanta's liberal yet apt translation of *aṅga-saṁśrayā*, literally, "whose complete shelter is (the Lord's) body."
12. 9.22 **Celestials:** *guhyakas*, literally, "makers of secrets or secrecy," a particular type of celestials who, as associates of the god of wealth, Kuvera, are guardians of his treasure (see also vv. 25 and 39).
13. 10.24 **To validate the words**: literally, "to make true the words." As curses and blessings of revered persons are understood to bear real consequences, higher beings and sometimes the supreme Lord display both the power to realize such pronouncements and the inclination to do so, to uphold the honor of those who make the curses or blessings (see the next verse). ***Arjuna* trees**: *Terminalia arjuna* trees are known to have extremely deep and strong roots, making them highly resistant to strong winds or other forces that might bring them down—a feature relevant to the present episode.
14. 10.26 Sanātana notes that Krishna's effortlessness in moving the mortar is implied in this verse, and that the mortar's wedging between the two trees is clearly no

accident. Rather, Krishna's conscious intention is highlighted, as is his *līlā-śakti*—his power to accomplish whatever he likes.

15. 10.27 **His waist tethered** translates *dāmodareṇa*, literally, "by him whose belly is roped." Dāmodara is a celebrated name of Krishna, who is remembered for this *līlā* of being "punished" in this manner by Yaśodā for his butter thievery.
16. 10.28 **Bowing**: Sanātana and Vallabha specify this as "stick bowing"—i.e., making obeisance by stretching full length on the ground—a standard, traditional way to show special deference in South Asia and, in this case, fitting to the circumstance of the two trees falling to the ground.
17. 10.31 **Bodies** translates *kṣetra*, literally, "field," referring to the body as an aggregate of senses, mind, and so on upon which "cultivation" activities (karma) are enacted, producing "fruit" (*karma-phala*).
18. 10.33 **Whose glory . . . virtues**: Śrīdhara compares "brilliant virtues" to clouds covering the "sun" of the Lord's glory. As clouds are ultimately produced by the sun, and their rain-giving function complements the light and energy of the sun, so Vāsudeva's virtues (*guṇa*) complement, even as they "hide" his unlimited glory.
19. 10.34 **Improbable** translates *asaṅgata*, which Sanātana glosses as *aghaṭa*—"incongruous" or "incoherent." In general, he says, these divine activities are "inexpressible" (*anirvacanīya*), a term used frequently in nondualist Vedānta in reference to *māyā*'s reality or nonreality.
20. 10.35 **Fulfilling devotees' desires**: this is Sanātana's and Jīva's gloss for *āśiṣān*, glossed by Sudarśanasūri as *abhyudayāni*—"upliftments." Jīva also notes that **liberation** means "special well-being—i.e., bhakti yoga," to distinguish it from liberation as conceived in nondevotional (especially nondualist) traditions.
21. 10.37 **Sight** translates *darśanam*, which connotes "audience" in the sense of being in the presence of a highly revered person. But rather than aural sense indicated by "audience," *darśanam* indicates, above all, the visual sense—of both seeing and being seen.
22. 10.38 **Remember your feet**: a common idiom throughout bhakti literature. Ordinarily, to be touched by another's feet is reprehensible, but in bhakti traditions, the feet of saints and divine personages are much sought—whether to be touched by them, to see them, or to be approached in humility and with an attitude of service to the person possessing the feet.
23. 10.42 **Nalakūvara**: Commentators explain that Krishna addresses the older of the two brothers while advising both of them. **Nonworldly** translates *abhava*, literally, "nonexistent." Baladeva glosses it as *saṁsāra*, the realm of endless tribulation.
24. 24.1 **Indra**: By far the most hymned god in the Ṛgveda, Indra nonetheless loses much of his stature in later, classical Hindu traditions. He is known as the god of thunder, like Zeus in the ancient Greek pantheon and, also like Zeus, typically associated with excessive sensuality. See also Book Six, "Indra's Grave Mistake." The present episode can be read as a contest between the orthodox brahmanical (Vedic) and the later classical (Purāṇic) traditions, in which the latter prevails.
25. 24.8 Nanda's reply reflects Vedic understanding, that the various gods are manifest as particular natural phenomena or elements. **Milk** is widely referred to in Vedic texts as the essence of nourishment.

26. 24.9 **By his discharge** is from *tad-retasā*, which is literally, "by his semen." A common identification in Vedic hymns is that of rain with the semen of Indra, since the rain brings about fertility on earth.
27. 24.10 **Three types of gain**: literally, "three types of fruit." Śrīdhara identifies these as the three *puruṣārthas*—namely, dharma (righteousness), *artha* (wealth), and *kāma* (pleasure). Sanātana adds that these fruits may be "seen" or "not seen," alluding to an important notion in Mīmāṁsā philosophy, the "unseen fruit" that is promised to be gained in a future birth.
28. 24.14 Jīva notes that unless action (karma) is performed by a person, a lord has no power to give "fruit" (results—*phala*).
29. 24.15 Śrīdhara points to a common analogy in Indic philosophies to highlight noncausal relations: the nipples on the neck of a goat yield no milk; similarly, according to Krishna's argument here, the worship of Indra is not the cause of rain. Rather, the cause (of *any* results in this world) is **inherent disposition** (*svabhāva*) of beings, in turn the results of their **own various actions**. The inherent disposition is, furthermore, **fixed** (*vihita*) by previous "impressions" (*saṁskāra*). Vīrarāghava includes *guṇa* (qualities) with actions as that which fixes, or establishes, one's "inherent disposition." Vijayadhvaja calls attention to the nonindependent character of Indra's lordship and takes "inherent disposition" as that which is fixed by Nārāyaṇa (Vishnu), the only independent Lord (taking *svabhāva* as *svatantra bhāva*—"independent nature").
30. 24.18 Krishna's tongue-in-cheek reasoning in support of his argument for nonperformance of the Indra sacrifice seems to be the Bhāgavata's ironic way of challenging the brahmanical notion that "work is worship" if work is disassociated from service to Vishnu, the supreme Lord. Still, here and in verses 20–21, he is upholding the orthodox brahmanical notion that all persons must follow prescribed duties (*varṇa* and *āśrama* duties in particular). In his commentary to verse 38, Śrīdhara summarizes the six arguments Krishna gives in verses 13–23: an individual's actions (karma) alone determine his or her destiny (13, 17); one's inherent disposition (*svabhāva*) is decisive (15–16); it is the *guṇas* that control all (22–23); divinity—even the supreme Lord—is a mere aspect of karma (14); divinity is subject to karma (15); and that one's own occupation is, for him or her, the worshipable deity (18).
31. 24.22 The argument now shifts, drawing from Sāṁkhya rather than Mīmāṁsā discourse (see Book Three, chapter 26, for the Bhāgavata's main presentation of Sāṁkhya).
32. 24.23 **Wind** translates *rajas*, which also means "passion" in the context of the Sāṁkhya tradition of classifying phenomena in terms of three *guṇas*. In either case, Krishna's argument remains essentially the same—namely, that rainfall is not dependent on divine or semidivine agency.
33. 24.24 The suggestion is that the ritual being planned by Nanda is not necessarily wrong, but it is for city folk. For nomadic cowherds, imitating settled folk in their religious practices would be improper.
34. 24.28 The particular arrangements that Krishna specifies for the new ritual suggest that much is preserved from the orthodox Indra sacrifice: The same implements and ingredients are to be used, (vegetarian) food is to be prepared, the

brāhmaṇas are to be heard, and various beings are to be given an **offering** (*baliḥ*) of food remnants from ritual performance. Only after food is distributed to the various human beings and other creatures is *bali* (also known as *bali-dāna*) to be offered to the mountain.

35. 24.36 **Personified** translates *rūpī*, "one having a form." Jīva notes that a direct perception of the senses (*pratyakṣa*) is indicated here. In other words, the Vraja residents directly saw the giant form consume the food offering. He also notes that several people made this exclamation, not just Krishna. Vīrarāghava, however, opines that it is Krishna alone addressing the cowherd men, saying that the mountain has **bestowed mercy** upon them by accepting their offering. Giridhara suggests that Krishna is contrasting this moment of directly perceiving the mountain personified with their nonperception of Indra, despite having, in the past, made so many offerings to him.
36. 24.37 **Taking . . . will**: Śrīdhara glosses this expression as "the forms of snakes, and other poisonous beasts," and Śukadeva suggests "boa constrictors (literally, 'goat swallowers') and the like," while Vallabha adds tigers and lions as possible forms the mountain can take. Commentators note an alternative reading of the second part: "O forest dwellers, taking any form at will, the mountain surely kills mortals who neglect (him)."
37. 25.2 **Sāṁvartaka . . . clouds**: Sanātana notes that these are clouds that cause final cosmic destruction (a process described in detail in Book Twelve, chapter 4).
38. 25.3 Viśvanātha, taking **pride** (*mada*) as "joy," turns Indra's disdain into admiration: "How wonderful is the joy and prosperity of these cowherds!" Furthermore, he notes that by taking "Sarasvatī's meaning" (interpretation with the aid of the goddess of learning), it is not that Krishna is **mortal** (*martyam*) but rather that Krishna is salutary for those subject to death.
39. 25.4 Vijayadhvaja glosses **metaphysical reasoning** (*ānvīkṣikī*) as "self-knowledge, which is constituted of seeing oneself in relation to the Lord, as one sees a reflection in relation to an object reflected."
40. 25.5 **Thinks . . . pandit** (*paṇḍita-māninam*): Vijayadhvaja elaborates that Krishna thinks himself learned, profiting by propounding deterministic views like "Clouds are blown by the wind" (v. 24.23) that are opposed to scriptures. Viśvanātha converts each apparent insult to Krishna in this verse into praise, as their "real meaning." So, for example, *paṇḍita-mānina* comes to mean "honored by the wise," and **talkative** (*vācāla*) means "because of him even a fool can speak scriptural truth."
41. 25.7 **Airāvata** is Indra's pure-white elephant carrier, said to have four tusks and seven trunks. Satyadharma notes that Indra's destructive aim follows the last of four political means—namely, conciliation (*sāma*), giving gifts or bribes (*dāna*), causing dissension (*bheda*), and punishment (*daṇḍa*).
42. 25.8–9 **Bountiful**: Indra's epithet Maghavān is used here, doubtless with some irony intended, as here his watery "bounty" is intended for destruction.
43. 25.11–14 These verses are missing from the Ahmadabad critical edition.
44. 25.12 **Covering**: Sanātana qualifies this, saying they were *trying* to cover themselves, with little or no success. Vallabha (for whom the notion of "surrender" or "going for shelter"—*śaraṇāgati*—is central in his bhakti theology) calls attention to this verse as an ideal example of how Lord Krishna is to be approached, both

to see him and to receive his grace. He interprets the battering rain as the failed devotional efforts one undertakes. Giving up all such efforts and the attempt to protect oneself, one is advised to follow this example of utter helplessness shown by the residents of Vraja.

45. 25.13 **Affectionate . . . devotees** translates *bhakta-vatsala*, a celebrated epithet and characteristic of Krishna. Vaṁśīdhara, drawing on Viśvanātha, notes that, by addressing Krishna with this epithet, they are recalling a prediction by the priest Garga soon after Krishna's birth: "You (Vraja residents) will easily cross beyond all obstacles by his help" (10.8.16).
46. 25.14 Krishna has, of course, intentionally provoked Indra's anger (see also v. 15), so the basic cause of the storm is, Viśvanātha notes, Krishna's "potency of divine pastimes" (*līlā-śakti*), creating a situation, says Jīva, in which Krishna will simultaneously protect the Vraja residents and remove Indra's pride.
47. 25.16 Sanātana glosses *ātma-yogena* (**by . . . power**) as Krishna's *svābhāvika-śakti*—"innately existing potency" (hence not extraneously acquired by effort). Whereas in Vedic and later texts Vishnu typically supports and defends Indra, here he opposes him for the purpose of teaching him (and the other gods) a lesson.
48. 25.17 In terms of the Sāṁkhya typology of three *guṇas*, the gods are presumed to be situated in illumination (*sattva-guṇa*). Here Krishna declares his intention to bring the gods, who have strayed from their proper sphere, back to their normal ways by demonstrating his superior lordship.
49. 25.18 Again emphasizing that it is Krishna's **own . . . power** by which he will proceed, there is a touch of irony in the contrast with Indra's need for assistance from the Saṁvartaka clouds to accomplish his aim. Viśvanātha claims that the **vow** Krishna here proclaims is actually to protect all beings from the final cosmic destruction. Further, Viśvanātha assures his readers that Krishna remained completely dry as he ran from his home porch to Govardhana, because Saṁhārikī (she who completely removes), an aspect of Krishna's special potency called Yogamāyā, prevented rain from falling on him.
50. 25.19 Vijayadhvaja points out that by this act of lifting Mount Govardhana, Krishna makes himself into a *jayastambha*—"a pillar of victory." Sanātana cites the Viṣṇu Purāṇa and Harivaṁśa to note that the **one hand** was Krishna's left hand. Comparing Krishna's act to that of a child holding up a mushroom serves, Sanātana notes, to illustrate his effortlessness (**playfully**—*līlayā*) and that he has lifted the entire hill, in effect "uprooting" it from its base. Vallabha notes that this example alludes to the way children might play as in a king's court (holding the mushroom aloft as one would hold a ceremonial umbrella for a king).
51. 25.20 Viśvanātha anticipates the doubt that, considering the limited size of Govardhana, not all of Vraja's folk could be accommodated under the mountain: because Govardhana was being touched by the left hand of Krishna, the mountain experienced great bliss, so that with inconceivable increased power, perceiving Indra's angry hundredfold lightning bolt attack like a flower garland, Govardhana expanded himself from three *krośas* to four *yojanas* in diameter at the base. (According to Monier-Williams' Sanskrit dictionary, one *krośa* equals "the range of the voice in calling or hallooing"; a *yojana* is "a distance traversed in one harnessing or without unyoking . . . sometimes regarded as equal to 4 or 5 English

miles.") Moreover, citing the Harivaṁśa, Viśvanātha assures that the animals on top of Govardhana did not suffer, because as the mountain expanded, its peak rose above Indra's warring clouds, providing a safe and dry area for them.

52. 25.23 Sanātana notes that during the time of staying under Govardhana, Krishna did not depend for his happiness on food, drink, or rest. Rather, he was satisfied seeing the Vraja residents and facilitating their seeing him. Sanātana also notes (quoting the Viṣṇnu Purāṇa) that some Vraja residents thought they needed to help Krishna hold up Govardhana. This is often represented in paintings, wherein the cowherds are represented propping up the mountain with their cowherd sticks. Further, Sanātana points out that the effortlessness of Krishna's holding the mountain is indicated by the expression **from that position** (*padāt*), which can also be taken to mean "from that (single) foot," indicating that Krishna was standing throughout the seven days in his artful dancing stance, his "threefold bending form" (*tribhaṅga-rūpam*).
53. 25.24 Vijayadhvaja glosses **his resolve broken** as "his dream lost." Vallabha specifies Indra's resolve—namely, "I shall kill them!" Viśvanātha explains Indra's withdrawal of the clouds as having been because of great fear: "Today Krishna will punish me."
54. 25.28 **Effortlessly**: As in verse 19 (see note 50), this translates *līlayā*, "with pleasure" or "by divine fiat." Sanātana elaborates: Krishna replaced the mountain effortlessly, charming everyone with his lack of endeavor, causing wonder and joy for all beings, for the Vraja residents, and for the celestials who witnessed the event.
55. 25.29 **As appropriate** (*yathā*): Sanātana specifies how social superiors, equals, and inferiors related to Krishna at this moment. Priests spoke benedictions and elders affectionately smelled his head; servants took up his feet and massaged his arms; and friends embraced him and massaged his arms and cracked his knuckles.
56. 25.30 Sanātana gives examples of the kinds of **blessings** Krishna received: "May you enjoy long life! May you always be happy! May your dreams always come true!"
57. 25.31 Giridhara notes that the **celestials** experienced and expressed satisfaction with their minds (**all pleased**), words (**offered praises**), and bodies (**released . . . flowers**). The latter—celestials releasing flowers—is a common indicator of cosmic celebration in Purāṇic literature, typically exhibited when Vishnu or Krishna prevails in his acts of subduing demons, pleasing devotees, and reestablishing dharma.
58. 25.32 **Protector of humankind** translates *nṛpa*, literally, "protector of people"—an address to King Parīkṣit. Sanātana suggests that by addressing Parīkṣit thus, Śuka reminds him what sort of festivity took place—namely, a festival in grand, royal style.
59. 25.33 **Him . . . hearts**: Śrīdhara offers two ways this expression can be taken. Because of their dearness to him, Krishna **touched** the **cowherd girls' hearts**; and, the cowherd girls touched his heart with their love. Sanātana elaborates on a few aspects of this verse: The term **affectionate** means Krishna's friends all shared with him a similar mood, full of tender feeling; also, all the residents of Vraja accompanied Krishna to his home, just as they had all joined him under Mount Govardhana. Further, the cowherd girls were particularly pleased because they had enjoyed the sight of Krishna's moonlike face for seven uninterrupted days, having exchanged affectionate, timid smiles with him. Moreover, Sanātana

opines, his own cow settlement was near or next to Rādhā-kuṇḍa, a sacred pond at the north end of Govardhana.

60. 29.1 This first verse of the *rāsa-līlā* receives extensive commentary, with much attention given to the transcendent nature of the love between Krishna and the *gopīs*. Śrīdhara affirms that the *rāsa-līlā* demonstrates Krishna's victory over Cupid, the god of worldly lust. Viśvanātha explains that the *gopis*' love for Krishna is pure and free of selfish motive, unlike the sexual love of this world, and Krishna honors their love by dancing with them. Similarly, Krishna's love for the *gopīs* is an expression of his inner, ever-satisfied nature, and not the result of an external, selfish need.

   Bhaktivedanta compares worldly lust to iron and the *gopīs*' love to gold; both share certain similarities but differ vastly in beauty and value. Lust is an attempt to gratify one's own senses, while love aims to satisfy Krishna. Bhaktivedanta points to the phrases *bhagavān api*, **even the glorious Lord**, and *yogamāyām*, **his illusive power of yoga**, as clear indicators of the divine nature of Krishna's love.

61. 29.2 As Schweig (2005, 198) points out, this verse serves as a metaphor for the *rāsa-līlā* as a whole. Later in this chapter, Krishna is compared to the **moon** among the starlike *gopīs*, who are comforted by him **after a long absence**. The words **reddish hue** and **saffron** translate *aruṇena*. In Indian custom, the husband applies a reddish powder, made of either vermilion or saffron (*kuṅkuma*), to his wife's forehead and the parting of her hair as a symbol of their marriage. He does this for the first time during the wedding ceremony and then again at special occasions throughout their lives. The reddish color is specified as *kuṅkuma* in the next verse, which continues with the metaphor.

62. 29.5 Viśvanātha explains that the *gopīs* were unable to tolerate even a moment's delay in answering Krishna's call, and in their eagerness, they abruptly stopped their daily routine. The *gopīs*' willingness to abandon their social dharma (duties and propriety) indicates their lack of selfish motivation or worldly desire.

63. 29.8 Bhaktivedanta (2008, 277) explains the *gopīs*' lack of concern for social propriety: "When a person becomes attracted by Kṛṣṇa and is in full Kṛṣṇa consciousness, he does not care for any worldly duties, even though very urgent. . . . This is the test of advancement in Kṛṣṇa consciousness: a person advancing in Kṛṣṇa consciousness must lose interest in material activities and personal sense gratification."

64. 29.9 **Meditating on Krishna with their eyes closed**: Schweig (2005, 152–58, 205–7) demonstrates that the Bhāgavata regards the *gopīs* as the highest yogis—adept in the practice of eight-limbed yoga and absorbed in the final state of *samādhi*.

65. 29.10 The *gopīs* felt great pain in Krishna's absence, and yet that pain also intensified their meditation on Krishna, making him directly present in their meditation. This paradox of presence-in-absence leads to another paradox: the purifying power of love in absence destroys all undesirable things, but the joy of Krishna's presence makes all desirable things appear worthless. The *gopīs* thus transcend all that is desirable and undesirable, fortunate and unfortunate, in this world.

66. 29.11 **They relinquished their bodies**: Viśvanātha argues that this does not refer to physical death. Rather, it indicates that the *gopīs*' bodies became fully spiritual, losing their material impurities and inauspiciousness. The pain of separation from Krishna purified the *gopīs* of all ignorance and karmic bondage. Viśvanātha

quotes a verse from later in the tenth book (47.37), where Krishna uses the word "fortunate" to describe the *gopīs* who could not attend the *rāsa* dance, thus precluding the possibility of their (unfortunate) death.

67. 33.1 **Gave up sorrow born of separation**: This very phrase is employed in the previous chapter (10.32.9), just after Krishna has reappeared following his disappearance from among the *gopīs* soon after the initial commencement of the dance (in chapter 29).
68. 33.2 ***Rāsa* dance**: The term *rāsa* specifies the type of dance—an ancient Indian circle dance—and the devotional relish in a variety of "flavors" being exchanged between Krishna and the *gopīs* in the course of their dancing. For further elaboration on *rāsa*, see chapter 7 in Gupta and Valpey (2013).
69. 33.3 Śrīdhara explains that it is because Krishna is *yogeśvara*, the **master of yoga**, that each *gopī* perceives Krishna as dancing exclusively with her. As the supreme master of yoga, Krishna is understood to wield all mystic powers at will. Alternatively, Viśvanātha credits *yogamāyā*—Krishna's power of illusion for purposes of accomplishing *līlā*—for the *gopīs*' experience. **Circle** translates *maṇḍala*; as noted in the introduction, this is an important key to the structure of the Bhāgavata as a whole, culminating in this particular event of perfect devotional exchange between Bhagavān and his devotees.
70. 33.4 **Chief Gandharvas** might well be translated, as Thielemann (2000, 68, 69) does, as "masters of the heavenly musicians." She also notes that **kettledrums**, *dundubhī*, are "a pair of medium-sized kettledrums, less than three feet in diameter and beaten with sticks. The instrument is played still today in the folk music traditions of Vraja and various other areas in India."
71. 33.7 Śrīdhara glosses **emerald** as "sapphire," but Viśvanātha and Vaṁśīdhara explain that the comparison with an emerald suggests the result of color mixture: as yellow and blue yield green, similarly, while amid the *gopīs*, Krishna's sapphirelike complexion "mixed" with the *gopīs*' golden complexions, giving him a greenish hue.
72. 33.8 As Schweig (2005, 263) points out, the meter of this verse is appropriately named *mandākrāntā*, literally, "approaching slowly." As the first verse to describe the actual dance (a description that ends with v. 20), its rhythm in recitation suggests the tentative beginning cadences of the dance. **Tightened braids and belts**: Śrīdhara and other commentators point out that one could take the word for "tightened" in the opposite way, as "slackened," which seems fitting to the verse as a whole.
73. 33.10 For a discussion of the technical musical terms in this verse, see Gupta and Valpey (2013, 187–88) and Thielemann (2000, 71). **Sang in a free . . . way**: Śrīdhara indicates that this initial performance was a prelude—*ālāpa*—which is characteristically a preliminary, unrhythmed setting forth of the notes and melodic phrases that will then be elaborated with rhythm in the *dhruvam*.
74. 47.12 **The *gopī* said**: Commentators identify this *gopī* as Rādhā, Krishna's dearest consort, who is never directly named in the Bhāgavata. According to commentators, the clearest reference to Rādhā is found in the *rāsa-līlā* narrative (10.30.28), when Krishna elopes with a special *gopī* who has truly worshipped (*anayārādhitaḥ*) and pleased him. **Colored by saffron**: Viśvanātha explains that Rādhā, in divine

madness (*divyonmāda*), attributes the bee's natural yellow color to saffron that has rubbed off of the breasts of rival lovers. **The honey-sweet Lord**: Rādhā addresses the bee as "honey drinker" (*madhu-pa*) and then, in a play on words, addresses Krishna as *madhu-pati*, which is usually translated as "Lord of the Madhu dynasty" or "Lord of Mathurā city" but here can be taken as "Lord of honey."

75. 47.19 Jīva and Viśvanātha explain that at this point the bee momentarily disappears, and Rādhā becomes anxious that it might have returned to Krishna and conveyed her sharp words. When the bee reappears, she continues her soliloquy in a much gentler tone, praising the bee and inquiring about Krishna's welfare.
76. 47.21 **Son of the noble Nanda** translates *ārya-putra*, a respectful form of address often used by a woman for her husband. Jīva suggests that by using this address, Rādhā indicates that Krishna is in fact the *gopīs*' husband, for no one has loved him as they have.

BOOK ELEVEN

1. 8.1 Vaṁśīdhara identifies the ***brāhmaṇa*** (referred to in the previous chapter as an *avadhūta*—a sage indifferent to social constraints) as Dattātreya, the extremely ascetic sage born of Atri (see v. 2.7.4 and its note). Rādhāramaṇa refers to the pleasure of sense objects as "trifling," like the common pleasures experienced by such animals as pigs.
2. 8.2 **Like . . . python**: Vīrarāghava explains that the python serves in this and the next two verses as a model for inaction and hence "indifference." The analogy is perhaps strained, as *ajagara*, here translated as "python," means literally "goat eater," suggesting less than complete passivity in food acquisition. In any case, since it is one's own effort that produces the karmic results that invariably involve suffering, passivity with respect to one's own basic needs is here recommended. **Gratuitously** translates *yadṛcchayā*, which Vīrarāghava glosses as "by destiny, not gained by effort."
3. 8.3 **Nonetheless** is added, following Vijayadhvaja's observance that this verse answers the question, "What if no food is forthcoming?"
4. 8.4 Vijayadhvaja explains that the situation described here is for advanced yogis, for whom it is possible to draw nourishment from the "nectar" (*amṛta*) of meditation on the many qualities of Bhagavān, whose inconceivable power makes this possible. **Without . . . action** translates *akarmaka*, literally, "a nonmaker of action." Since avoiding to act is seen generally as a form of karma (as result-bearing activity) just as much as conscious endeavor to act, we here supply **goal-oriented** (Vijayadhvaja suggests "without endeavor") to highlight the broader sense of the passage.
5. 8.5 This verse is missing from the Ahmadabad critical edition.
6. 8.6 Śukadeva identifies the "womb reason" (the essential cause) for the sage's constancy to be his dedication to Nārāyaṇa. Bhagavatprasādācarya adds, "Implied is that the sage, devoted to Nārāyaṇa, is not devoted to sense objects." Viśvanātha notes that the devoted sage, rather than experiencing joy and sorrow in relation to worldly gain or loss, feels joy or sorrow in relation to his sense of success or failure in attaining the Lord.

7. 8.7 Commentators explain that the example of the **moth** illustrates the first, or foundational, of five senses by which the living being is allured and trapped. The moth is attracted by sight, or "form" (*rūpa*); similarly, other animals are identified (in other texts) for their tendency to be lured by the other four sense functions. These will also be mentioned in subsequent verses of this chapter.
8. 8.8 **Better judgment** translates from *dṛṣṭi*, literally, "sight," but also "wisdom."
9. 8.9 Śrīdhara enlarges on the **honeybee** example: as a bee may enter a particular lotus flower, only to be caught inside when the lotus closes (at night), so the unwary sage who begs from householders may become trapped by attraction to the pleasing features of a particular household if he lingers there.
10. 8.22 **Videha** is the area of present-day Tirhut (northern Bihar), which is identified with the kingdom of Mithilā, ruled in ancient times by the Janaka kings and bearing several associations with religious and philosophical culture. *Videha* can also mean "bodiless" or "dead," but more relevant may be that this area is associated with the important Jain figure, the twenty-fourth Tirthankar, Mahavir (sixth–fifth centuries B.C.E.).
11. 8.24 **My good man** translates the vocative *puruṣarṣabha*, literally, "bull among men." The *avadhūta brāhmaṇa* continues to address King Yadu, and it would seem that he wants to reassure the king that he is not to be compared with the men (*puruṣāṇ*) whom Piṅgalā is assessing as prospective customers.
12. 8.28 The second line of this verse is missing from the Ahmadabad critical edition. **Vain expectation** translates *āśā*, literally, "hope" or "expectation." The context calls for the addition of "vain." Rādhāramaṇa identifies *āśā* with *rāga*, "attachment" or "longing," one of the five afflictions or impediments (*kleśa*) listed in Patañjali's Yoga Sūtras (2.3), the other four being ignorance (*avidyā*), ego (*asmitā*), aversion (*dveṣa*), and clinging to life (*abhiniveśa*). See Bryant (2004, 175).
13. 8.29 The second line of this verse is missing from the Ahmadabad critical edition. **Bondage . . . body** translates *deha-bandham*, glossed by Śrīdhara as *saṁsāra*, the repetitive cycle of rebirth in countless life-forms, each body subjected to miseries culminating in death; the implication is that detachment from one's present body is seen as necessary for achieving a permanent end to this cycle.
14. 8.33 Each of the terms for body parts also refer to elements of house construction.
15. 8.34 **Desires something** translates *icchantī . . . kāmam*, literally, "desires an object of desire." The spectrum of meanings for *kāma* range from "desire" in the broadest sense to "carnal pleasure," and here the connotation leans strongly toward the latter. Yet in juxtaposition with the devotional "object" of desire, Vishnu, the desiring of whom is characterized as being free from lust, there is need for a neutral and nonspecific term in translation. **Self-giver** translates *ātma-da*, which could be taken as "he who gives himself" or as "he who favors the self." Vīrarāghava glosses it as "he who is magnanimous to the entire self" to contrast Vishnu (here Acyuta, "unfallen" or "undeviated") with the lascivious men with whom Piṅgalā had been dealing, whose "magnanimity" was superficial at best.
16. 8.35 **Ramā** is another name for Lakṣmī. Vijayadhvaja explains (quoting an unidentified source) that Piṅgalā is actually a celestial woman (*apsarās*), not an ordinary prostitute, who could not be expected to show such intelligence; hence she is qualified to be a consort of the Lord.

17. 8.38 Commentators suggest that Piṅgalā here continues, from the previous verse, to express her gratitude to Vishnu, interpreting her previous sufferings—caused ultimately by the Lord—as bringing about her good fortune.
18. 8.42 Vaṁśīdhara explains that the self, recognizing the supreme self (*paramātmā*) as its **protector**, becomes able to protect itself.
19. 27.7 **Vedic . . . mixed**: In the context of ritual worship methods, these distinctions are largely with regard to the types of mantras employed. Whereas Vedic mantras, drawn from the hymns and mantras of the Vedic Saṁhitās (collections) may be pronounced only by "twice-born" persons (generally, males who have been born into the three higher *varṇas* and have received *upanayana* initiation); Tantric mantras may be pronounced by one of any *varṇa*, if the person (either male or female) has received tantric initiation. "Mixed," according to Vaṁśīdhara, refers to a combination of mantras from Vedic, Tantric, and Purāṇic (from the Purāṇas) sources.
20. 27.8 This reference to **twice-born status** fits rather poorly to verse 7, which suggested that this status may not be required to perform ritual worship of Krishna.
21. 27.10 **And so forth**: Commentators specify this as cow dung (considered purifying and antiseptic). As Vaṁśīdhara relates in his extensive comments to this verse, bathing rituals can be quite elaborate and detailed. He provides several examples of mantras that might be pronounced at this time, their main theme being one's appeal to be purified of one's previous unfavorable actions along with purification of one's body.
22. 27.11 **Sidereal junctures** refers to the three *saṁdhyas*—dawn, dusk, and midday transitions of the sun. At these times, those who have received initiation into the Gāyatrī mantra (*upanayana* initiation, establishing one as "twice-born") are enjoined to perform worship centered on recitation of the Gāyatrī mantra. **(Selfish) acts** translates *karma*, as the context suggests that it is action, especially ritual action, in pursuance of more or less selfish ends, that calls for purification (see also v. 1.9.23 and its note and v. 5.5.5).
23. 27.14 Images whose material would not be adversely affected by water and other liquids may receive ritual bathing. Otherwise, cleansing, for example, with a dry cloth or simply with mantras is enjoined.
24. 27.15 **Desireless** translates *amāyin*, literally, "void of trick or guile." Śrīdhara glosses the term as "devoid of *kāma*," and Vīrarāghava identifies it as referring to not having a specific aim or intention.
25. 27.16 Especially in Tantric forms of worship, there are numerous types of *vinyāsa* or *nyāsa* prescribed. Typically, these involve the "placement" of particular mantras or single syllables (often with a physical gesture of touching the intended location) on parts of one's own body or on parts of a sacred image or diagram.
26. 27.17 ***Arghya***, literally, "valuable," is an offering consisting typically of water containing certain food grains. It is offered as an honorific gesture to a respected guest.
27. 27.19 ***Darbha*** typically refers to *kuśa* grass—*Poa cynosuroides*—a long-stemmed grass that, usually after being dried, is used in sacrificial rituals, particularly as a ritual seat.
28. 27.20 **Properly prepared**: this would entail, minimally, invoking sacred rivers—especially the Ganges—into the water by pronouncing an appropriate mantra and

visualizing the sacred waters entering the vessel while touching the surface of the water with the right middle finger and bending the index finger at a right angle. This is the *ankuśa-mudrā*, or hand formation indicating an elephant goad.

29. 27.22 **Heart . . . mantras:** Each invocation relates to a part of the human or human-like body, thus emphasizing the notion that all the various items used in the worship rituals are related to or "expansions" of the divinity being worshipped.
30. 27.23 This verse briefly describes a ritual called *bhūta-śuddhi*, "purification of the elements," whereby the worshipper is to purge, by processes involving mantras and visualizations, his or her own body, as preparation to approach the divinity.
31. 27.24 **Manifest like oneself:** Commentators explain that one is advised to think of the Lord within oneself as pervading one's body, like the light of a lamp spreading throughout a room; then the worshipper is to mentally offer the items of worship (*upacāras*) to that form of the Lord within, after which one (mentally) transfers that form into the sacred object such as a sacred image. **Consecrated . . . mantras:** This is the process of *nyāsa*, touching sequentially each part of the image (generally with *kuśa* grass) while pronouncing the appropriate mantra.
32. 27.25–26 Śrīdhara and other commentators fill out the details of which personages are to be represented in the **lotus seat:** *dharma* (righteousness), *jñāna* (knowledge), *vairāgya* (renunciation), and *aiśvarya* (plenitude) are placed (by mantra and visualization), respectively, between the four cardinal directions, beginning with the southeast and moving clockwise. Their opposites, *adharma* (irreligion), *ajñāna* (ignorance), and so on, are placed in the four cardinal directions, beginning with the east. More toward the center of the seat one (mentally) places the **nine (divine powers)** (*śaktis*)—namely, *vimalā, utkarṣiṇī, jñānā, kriyā, yogā, prahvī, satyā, īśānā*, and *anugrahā*.
33. 27.28 With the exception of **Garuḍa**, Vishnu's eagle carrier, the remaining six names apparently refer to gatekeepers of Vishnu's transcendent realm, Vaikuṇṭha.
34. 27.29 **Durgā:** a prominent goddess, usually identified with Pārvatī, wife of Shiva; **Vināyaka:** "remover (of obstacles)," an epithet of Gaṇeśa; **Vyāsa:** "arranger," the sage compiler and key character in the Mahābhārata, introduced in 1.4.15; **Viṣvaksena:** an attendant of Vishnu but also a form of Vishnu to whom remnants of sacrificial offerings are offered.
35. 27.30–31 Commentators identify the **Svarṇa-gharma** mantra by its first words, *svarṇaṁ gharmaṁ parivedanam*; the **Mahāpuruṣa Vidyā** begins with *jitaṁ te puṇḍarīkākṣa namas te viśva-bhāvana*; and the **Rājana** hymn begins with the words *indraṁ naro nema-dhitā*. The well-known **Puruṣa Sūkta** (beginning with *sahasra-śīrṣā puruṣaḥ*, from Ṛgveda 10.90) narrates a cosmic sacrificial rite in which the Cosmic Man's dismemberment as the sacrificial offering generates the cosmos.
36. 27.32 Dressing and ornamenting the image is, in many temple traditions of contemporary India, a prominent feature of the worship procedure, attracting temple visitors to view and appreciate the often artfully done daily display. The injunctions followed for these practices are typically locally prescribed, whether written or, more likely, through local tradition preserved orally by priests and temple managers.
37. 27. 35 Days **of lunar transition:** days of the new and full moon. All the items listed are offerings and services to the Vishnu image.

38. 27.37 This and the next four verses describe a brief fire rite, as part of an elaborate image-worship procedure. Although changing the medium (fire) and materials (especially ghee) of worship, from what has thus far been described in previous verses, the object of worship—namely, Vishnu—remains the same.
39. 27.38–41 A ***mūla-mantra*** is an invocatory incantation for a particular deity. *Mūla* means "root," suggesting that the deity "sprouts" from the mantra when it is properly intoned.
40. 27.47 **Placed . . . heart**: Several commentators agree that, by meditation, the worshipper is to relocate the light that is identified with the presence of the deity into the light that is conceived as situated in the heart, or the lotuslike heart. Viśvanātha notes that **dismiss** means "drawn up" into the heart.
41. 27.48 Śrīdhara explains that this verse intends to counter the notion that one type of worshipable form is superior or inferior to another (see 11.27.9 for a list of these types). Viśvanātha and Vaṁśīdhara elaborate: although the *arcā* image is to be seen as foundational with respect to the practice of ritual worship, with deeper faith one may appreciate the Lord's presence in other forms, knowing that he abides as the self of all. They cite the example of Prahlāda, for whom the Lord appeared (as Nṛsiṁha—see Book Seven, chapter 8) from an apparently inanimate palace pillar because of Prahlāda's complete faith in his presence there. Taking the voice of Krishna, Viśvanātha writes, "While the main emphasis (in this chapter) is worship of the *arcā* image, the cause of my appearance is faith alone. Although I am directly present (in physical forms), one without faith does not comprehend my presence."
42. 27.50 A contrast is implied here between the type of image consecration thus far described and the option to fully establish an image, in the sense of making a permanent arrangement. Further implied is that the practice of building permanent temples is meant for kings and powerful landlords.
43. 27.53 **Thus** refers to the ritual procedure described in this chapter.
44. 27.55 The stern warning of this verse and the previous one seems to be meant as a deterrent for the wily person of means who would build a temple and arrange for the worship of an image, only later to seize wealth that had then accrued to the temple over time through its votaries.

BOOK TWELVE

1. 3.50 **Own true nature**: Śrīdhara glosses *ātma-bhāva* as *sva-svarūpa* (own true form), while Vīrarāghava explains it as *ātma-svabhāva* (self's true nature). Vijayadhvaja takes *ātmā* as referring to *sarvātmā*, **the soul of all**, and *bhāva* as synonymous with bhakti; thus the verse says, "He will certainly lead them to devotion for Bhagavān."
2. 3.49–51 As the Bhāgavata Purāṇa comes to a close and Parīkṣit prepares for impending death, Śuka reassures the king and reminds him of his original prescription in Book Two: "Descendant of Bharata, the self of all, the adorable Lord Hari, is therefore to be heard about, praised, and remembered by one desiring peace. The highest reward of a human birth, by practices such as *sāṁkhya*, yoga, and complete dedication to one's dharma, is remembrance of Nārāyaṇa at the end

of life. . . . O king, for those despairing, for those desiring, and for the disciplined, ongoing recitation of Hari's names is the assurance of complete fearlessness" (2.1.5, 6,11).

3. 13.14–16 These verses are numbered 12–14 in the Ahmadabad critical edition, because of a reorganization of verses in this chapter. (The first two verses of this chapter in Kṛṣṇaśaṅkara Śāstrī's edition become the last two verses of the chapter in the critical edition.)
4. 13.17–23 These verses are omitted in the Ahmadabad critical edition, although they are attested in the commentaries of Śrīdhara and Jīva.
5. 13.19 Jīva regards this verse as the concluding statement of the entire Bhāgavata Purāṇa. Following standard methods of Mīmāṁsā exegesis, he seeks congruence between the opening and concluding statements of the Bhāgavata in order to determine the overall import of the book. This verse serves that purpose well; the phrase *satyaṁ paraṁ dhīmahi*, **Let us meditate upon the . . . Supreme Truth**, matches exactly the first verse of the Bhāgavata, thus demonstrating that the Supreme Truth, Bhagavān, is the import of the entire Purāṇa. See Gupta (2007), chapter 4, for further discussion of this verse.
6. 13.21 Here we return to the frame story of the Bhāgavata Purāṇa. King Parīkṣit was cursed to die of snakebite in seven days, and thus he decided to spend his remaining week listening to the Bhāgavata from Śuka. Now that the Bhāgavata is complete, Sūta points out that Śuka did something far greater than protect Parīkṣit from death by **snakebite**; Śuka liberated Parīkṣit altogether from the suffering of **repeated birth** and death in this mortal world.
7. 13.23 **Singing:** the word *saṁkīrtana* conveys the sense of "singing together," "proclaiming," or "praising fully." Vaiṣṇavas interpret this word as referring to the practice of singing Krishna's names in a public assembly or moving procession.

GLOSSARY

ADHARMA. The opposite of dharma, hence inappropriate or unlawful behavior; deviation from social or religious norms articulated in Indic texts as dharma.

AMṚTA. Ambrosia, said to give immortality for those who drink it; produced from the churning of the Cosmic Ocean and desired by both the gods and demons.

ARCANA. Ritual worship, especially of the supreme Lord as present in a sacred image or other appropriate sacred object.

AŚIVA. Inauspicious, the opposite of *śiva*. The god Shiva, also known by several other epithets such as Mahādeva, is considered the embodiment of auspiciousness.

ĀŚRAMA. A wilderness hermitage where ascetics reside and concentrate on practices of spiritual development. One of four human life stages: (1) celibate student (*brahmacārī*), (2) householder (*gṛhastha*), (3) retired or hermit (*vānaprastha*), and (4) renunciant (*saṁnyāsī*).

ĀŚRAYA. A refuge or shelter. The Bhāgavata Purāṇa identifies Bhagavān as the ultimate *āśraya*. One of the ten subjects of the Bhāgavata Purāṇa.

ASURA. Usually translated as "demon," in opposition to the gods (*suras* or *devas*).

ĀTMĀ (ĀTMAN). Sometimes translated as "breath," "spirit," or "soul" but generally as "self." The atemporal living being, independent of the body; also refers to the supreme being in some contexts in the Bhāgavata Purāṇa.

AVADHŪTA. "Shaken," referring to a person who has "shaken off" worldly duties; typically referring to an ascetic whose behavior is unpredictable and beyond social norms.

AVATĀRA. A descent of Vishnu into the temporal world from his atemporal realm to perform special salvific acts in the world, in one of several forms.

BHAGAVĀN. The supreme, eternal being or Lord; in the Bhāgavata Purāṇa, a prominent epithet for Krishna, Vishnu, Hari, and Nārāyaṇa.

BHĀGAVATA. A worshipper of Bhagavān, especially one regarded as an accomplished adept or immediate associate of Bhagavān.

BHAKTA. A votary of Bhagavān.

BHAKTI. The devotional disposition of one dedicated in service to Bhagavān, typically expressed through varieties of devotional activities, including singing, praising, and meditation. In the Bhāgavata Purāṇa, bhakti is focused especially upon Krishna, as the original, primeval form of Bhagavān.

BRAHMAN. The ultimate, nondual, and all-pervasive reality; Being as such, and the source of all being. A central subject of the Upaniṣads and of Vedānta philosophy.

BRĀHMAṆA. A social category consisting of priests (who typically conduct Vedic fire and other rituals), teachers, and mentors.

DARŚANAS. Schools of thought and philosophy, especially in post–Bhāgavata Purāṇa India classified as six "orthodox" schools—Sāṁkhya, Yoga, Mīmāṁsā, Vedānta, Nyāya, and Vaiśeṣika—which are contrasted with "heterodox" schools of thought—namely, Jain, Buddhist, and Ājīvika.

DEVAS. Gods, lords of celestial yet temporal realms, whose great powers over cosmic functions do not exempt them from mortality (in contrast to Bhagavān).

DHARMA. "That which sustains"—especially an individual's set of duties and obligations according to social position, gender, and stage of life.

GANDHARVA. A semidivine being associated with musicality.

GOPĪ. A cowherdess, especially one of the several young maidens of Vraja whose love is exclusively for Krishna.

GUṆAS. According to Sāṁkhya, three constituents of an individual's nature—namely, (1) ***sattva***, "purity," "illumination"; (2) ***rajas***, "passion"; and (3) ***tamas***, "dullness" or "darkness." All beings are understood to carry and be carried by different proportions of the three ***guṇas***.

ĪŚĀNUKATHĀ. Narrations about the Lord, consisting of activities of Bhagavān and his devotees during Bhagavān's various descents. *Īśānukathā* is one of the ten themes of the Bhāgavata Purāṇa.

JÑĀNA. Knowledge, especially comprehension of atemporal reality, *brahman*.

KALI (KALI YUGA). The last, shortest, and most degenerated age in a cosmic cycle of four ages; the recitation of the Bhāgavata Purāṇa by Śuka to Parīkṣit is set in the beginning of the Kali age, soon after the departure of Krishna to his transcendent realm.

KARMA. Action, especially ritual action, but more broadly any intentional or unintentional action that leads to an eventual "reaction," whether in one's present life or a future life. A person's cumulative karma is presumed to be determinative of the conditions and form of one's next life and is regarded as the cosmic principle sustaining the perpetuation of individuals' bondage in temporal existence, lifetime after lifetime.

KṢATRIYA. A member of the martial or ruling order.

LĪLĀ. The karma-free, atemporal, and playful activity of the supreme person, Bhagavān, with his votaries and his acts of cosmic creation.

LOKA. One of the various realms or planets of the cosmos, all of which the Bhāgavata Purāṇa describes as inhabited by living beings.

MAKARA. A multiformed aquatic-terrestrial creature, typically represented as a blend of a crocodile and an elephant, with a fish's tail.

MAṆḌALA. A circular graphic figure that facilitates meditation. In the case of the Bhāgavata Purāṇa, the narrative as a whole is meant to serve as a textual *maṇḍala*, with Book Ten as its central focus of devotion and worship.

MANTRA. A verbal formula that is spoken or sung; in the Bhāgavata Purāṇa, a mantra is typically associated with devotional acts of invocation and remembrance of Bhagavān.

MANVANTARA. The period of a Manu's life. Fourteen Manus are said to live sequentially during the span of one day in Brahmā's life.

MĀYĀ. The creative power of Bhagavān that makes the creation of the phenomenal world possible. For beings in temporal bondage, *māyā* is illusion, deluding one into forgetting devotion to Bhagavān.

MOKṢA. Liberation, which ends suffering and the cycle of rebirth and is, according to the Bhāgavata Purāṇa, achieved through knowledge of the true self and devotion to Bhagavān.

MUKTI. Liberation (returning to one's constitutional position).

NIRODHA. Circumscribing or withdrawal; while sleeping, Vishnu first manifests manifold universes by exhaling, and then, upon inhaling, the *nirodha*, or withdrawal, of the universes takes place. One of the ten themes of the Bhāgavata Purāṇa.

OṀ. In the Bhāgavata tradition, a mantra that is spoken or written in order to invoke the presence of Bhagavān.

PARAMĀṆU. Primary atoms or particles that are imbued with Bhagavān's presence, as the fundamental matter of phenomenal worlds.

POṢAṆA. Literally, "nourishing," or Vishnu's mercy toward his devotees. *Poṣaṇa* is one of the ten themes of the Bhāgavata Purāṇa.

PRAKṚTI. Primordial matter out of which the universe is manifest, constituted of three ***guṇas***.

PRAMATHAS. A variety of beings associated with Shiva—literally, "tormentors."

PRĀṆA. "Life breath" or "life force."

PŪJĀ. A ritual or set of rituals of honoring and worshipping a superior being or the supreme being.

PURUṢA. An individual atemporal living being, or (in some contexts) the supreme being; contrasted with ***prakṛti***.

PURUṢĀRTHA. One of four "human aims": (1) *artha* (wealth, aggrandizement), (2) *kāma* (desire, sense pleasure), (3) ***dharma*** (righteousness), and (4) ***mokṣa*** (liberation).

RAJAS. *See* ***guṇas***.

RASA. "Taste," "juice," "that which is aesthetically relished," or "aesthetic mood." In classical Indian aesthetics, the word usually denotes the intensified emotion born of human (or divine) relationships. *Rasa* is a term of great significance for the Bhāgavata Purāṇa's later commentarial tradition and for followers of the various sectarian devotional traditions that identify the text as canonical.

RĀSA-LĪLĀ. In its narrow sense generally refers to the nocturnal circle dance of Krishna with the *gopīs* in Vraja. More broadly, it may refer to any of Krishna's activities with his close associates.

ṚṢI. A "seer" or sage, especially one who is said to reveal a hymn of the Veda.

SĀDHU. An ascetic, typically one who wanders and whose aim is to achieve ***mokṣa***.

SĀṀKHYA. "Analysis"; a metaphysical system that identifies two irreducible ontological entities—namely, ***puruṣa*** (atemporal living beings) and ***prakṛti*** (the principle of phenomenal existence)—and which functions in terms of the three ***guṇas***.

SAṀSĀRA. The potentially endless cycle of rebirth and tribulation, brought about by one's implication in the network of ***karma*** and its reactions.

SARGA. Bhagavān's creation of the primary elements and senses. *Sarga* is one of the ten themes of the Bhāgavata Purāṇa.

SATTRA. An elaborate ritual sacrifice involving the offering and partaking of ***soma*** juice.

SATTVA. *See* ***guṇas***.

SIDDHA. A perfected being; a class of semidivine beings credited with having attained perfections or special powers as a result of rigorous observance of austerities, practice of yoga, and the like.

SMṚTI. "That which is remembered," referring to several genres of sacred texts, including the Purāṇas.

SOMA. A juice extracted from an unidentified plant, which is much praised in Vedic hymns for its exhilarating and apparently hallucinogenic effects.

ŚRUTI. "That which is heard" or revealed; the Vedic texts, contrasted with, but also complemented by, the ***Smṛti*** texts.

STHĀNA. The continuance and preservation of creation by Vishnu; one of the ten themes of the Bhāgavata Purāṇa.

TAMAS. *See* ***guṇas***.

ŪTI. The impetus of living entities' desires for action; one of the ten themes of the Bhāgavata Purāṇa.

VAIKUṆṬHA. The eternal abode of Vishnu, beyond both the earth and the heavenly realm of gods like Indra; also used as an epithet of Vishnu.

VAIRĀGYA. Renunciation, detachment.

VAIŚEṢIKA. Atomism; one of the six orthodox schools of philosophy (*darśanas*), which teaches that all things in the universe are reducible to a finite number of indivisible atoms (*paramāṇu*).

VARṆA. Social categories indicating an individual's ***dharma*** and social standing. The four *varṇas* are the ***brāhmaṇas*** (priests, teachers), ***kṣatriyas*** (rulers, administrators), *vaiśyas* (farmers, merchants), and *śūdras* (workers, artisans).

VIRAHA. Love in absence, an emotion felt by a devotee for Bhagavān.

VISARGA. The secondary creation of a variety of beings by Brahmā; one of the ten defining characteristics of the Bhāgavata Purāṇa.

YAKṢAS. Semidivine beings associated with trees and fertility.

YOGA. Literally, "yoke," a set of processes or disciplines by which a practitioner, or yogi, seeks to control the senses and mind, ultimately to attain ***mokṣa***. The Bhāgavata Purāṇa particularly champions the practice of devotional, or bhakti, yoga, aimed at pleasing Bhagavān.

YOJANA. A measure of distance, variously estimated at 2.5 to 18 miles.

REFERENCES

Bedekar, V. M. 1967. "The Legend of the Churning of the Ocean in the Epics and the Purāṇas: A Comparative Study." *Purāṇa* 9, no. 1:7–61.

Bell, Catherine M. 2001. *Who Owns Tradition? Religion and the Messiness of History*. Santa Clara Lectures, vol. 7, no. 2. Santa Clara, Calif.: Santa Clara University, Bannan Institute for Jesuit Education and Christian Values. http://www.scu.edu/ic/publications/upload/scl-0102-bell.pdf.

Bhāgavata Purāṇa. 1965. *Śrīmad Bhāgavata Mahāpurāṇam*. Ed. Kṛṣṇaśaṅkara Śāstrī. Ahmadabad: Śrībhāgavatavidyāpīṭh. Contains the Sanskrit commentaries of Śrīdhara Svāmin's *Bhāvārthadīpikā*, Śrī Vaṃśīdhara's *Bhāvārthadīpikāprakāśa*, Śrī Rādhāramaṇadāsa Gosāmin's *Dīpinī*, Śrīmad Vīrarāghava's *Bhāgavatacandrikā*, Śrīmad Vijayadhvaja Tīrtha's *Padaratnāvalī*, Śrīmad Jīva Gosvāmin's *Kramasaṃdarbha*, Śrīmad Viśvanātha Cakravartin's *Sārārthadarśinī*, Śrīmad Śukadeva's *Siddhāntapradīpa*, Śrīmad Vallabhācarya's *Subodhinī*, Śrī Puruṣottamacaraṇa Gosvāmin's *Subodhinīprakāśaḥ*, Śrī Giridharalāla's *Bālaprabodhinī*.

Bhāgavata Purāṇa. 1976. *Śrīmad Bhāgavatam*. Trans. A. C. Bhaktivedanta Swami Prabhupāda. Los Angeles: Bhaktivedanta Book Trust.

Bhāgavata Purāṇa. 1983. *Bhāgavata Purāṇa of Kṛṣṇa Dvaipāyana Vyāsa*. Trans. G. V. Tagare. Ed. J. L. Shastri. Delhi: Motilal Banarsidass.

Bhāgavata Purāṇa. 1983. *Śrīmadbhāgavatapurāṇam of Vyāsa, Śrīdharasvāmin*. Ed. J. L. Shastri. Delhi: Motilal Banarsidass.

Bhāgavata Purāṇa. 1996–1998. *The Bhāgavata*. Vols. 1–4. Critically edited by H. G. Shastri, Bharati Shelat, and K. K. Shastree. Ahmadabad: B.J. Institute of Learning and Research.

Bhāgavata Purāṇa. 2003. *Bhāgavata Mahapurāṇa, with Sanskrit Text and English Translation*. 2 vols. Trans. C. L. Goswami. Gorakhpur: Gita Press.

Bhaktivedanta Swami Prabhupāda, A. C. 2008. *Kṛṣṇa: The Supreme Personality of Godhead*. Los Angeles: Bhaktivedanta Book Trust.

Bhaktivedanta Swami Prabhupāda, A. C., and Hridayananda Das Goswami, trans. 1993. *Śrīmad Bhāgavatam*. Cantos 1–12 in 18 vols. Los Angeles: Bhaktivedanta Book Trust.

Includes Sanskrit text, translation, and commentary. Cantos 1–10, part 1, by Bhaktivedanta, canto 10, part 2, to canto 12, by Goswami.

Biardeau, Madeleine. 1975. "Narasiṁha, mythe et culte." *Puruṣārtha: Recherches des sciences sociales sur d'Asie du Sud* 1:31–49.

——. 1993. "Kāmadhenu: The Religious Cow, Symbol of Prosperity." In *Asian Mythologies*, ed. Yves Bonnefoy, 99. Chicago: University of Chicago Press.

——. 1999. *Hinduism: The Anthropology of a Civilization*. New Delhi: Oxford University Press.

Biswas, Ashutosh Sarma. 1968. *Bhāgavata Purāṇa: A Linguistic Study, Particularly from the Vedic Background*. Dibrugarh, Assam: Vishveshvaranand Book Agency.

Black, Brian. 2007. *The Character of the Self in Ancient India: Priests, Kings, and Women in the Early Upaniṣads*. Albany: SUNY Press.

Brown, C. Mackenzie. 1990. *The Triumph of the Goddess: The Canonical Models and Theological Visions of the Devī-Bhāgavata Purāṇa*. Albany: SUNY Press.

Bryant, Edwin F. 2002. "The Date and Provenance of the *Bhāgavata Purāṇa* and the Vaikuṇṭha Perumal Temple." *Journal of Vaishnava Studies* 11, no. 1:51–80.

——. 2004. *Krishna: The Beautiful Legend of God*. London: Penguin.

Colas, Gérard. 2003. "History of Vaiṣṇava Traditions: An Esquisse." In *The Blackwell Companion to Hinduism*, ed. Gavin Flood. London: Blackwell.

Dāsa, Gopīpāraṇadhana, trans. 2013. *Śrī Tattva-sandarbha by Śrīla Jīva Gosvāmī*. Vrindavan: Girirāja.

Doniger, Wendy. 1993. "Echoes of the *Mahabharata*: Why Is a Parrot the Narrator of the *Bhagavata Purana* and the *Devibhagavata Purana*?" In *Purana Perennis*, ed. Wendy Doniger, 31–57. Albany: SUNY Press.

Eck, Diana L. 1998. *Darśan: Seeing the Divine Image in India*. 3rd ed. New York: Columbia University Press.

Goldman, Robert, trans. 1990. *The Rāmāyaṇa of Vālmīki*. 6 vols. Princeton: Princeton University Press.

Goodall, Dominic. 1996. *Hindu Scriptures*. Berkeley: University of California Press.

Griffiths, Paul J. 1999. *Religious Reading: The Place of Reading in the Practice of Religion*. New York: Oxford University Press.

Gupta, Ravi M. 2007. *The Caitanya Vaiṣṇava Vedānta of Jīva Gosvāmī: When Knowledge Meets Devotion*. London: Routledge.

Gupta, Ravi M., and Kenneth R. Valpey, eds. 2013. *The Bhāgavata Purāṇa: Sacred Text and Living Tradition*. New York: Columbia University Press.

Haberman, David L. 1994. *Journey Through the Twelve Forests of Vrindavan*. Oxford: Oxford University Press.

——. 2002. *The Bhaktirasāmṛtasindhu of Rūpa Gosvāmin*. Delhi: Motilal Banarsidass.

Hacker, Paul. 1959. *Prahlāda: Werden und Wandlungen einer Idealgestalt*. Wiesbaden: Akademie der Wissenschaften und der Literatur.

Hamilton, Sue. 2001. *Indian Philosophy: A Very Short Introduction*. Oxford: Oxford University Press.

Hawley, John Stratton. 1983. *Krishna, the Butter Thief*. Princeton: Princeton University Press.

Heim, Maria. 2004. *Theories of the Gift in South Asia: Hindu, Buddhist, and Jain Reflections on Dāna*. New York: Routledge.

——. 2010. "Gift and Gift Giving." In *Brill's Encyclopedia of Hinduism*, ed. Knut A. Jacobsen et al., 2:747–52. Leiden: Brill.

Hirst, J. G. Suthren. 2005. *Śaṁkara's Advaita Vedānta: A Way of Teaching*. London: RoutledgeCurzon.

Holdrege, Barbara A. 2006. "From Purāṇa-Veda to Kārṣṇa-Veda: The Bhāgavata Purāṇa as Consummate Smṛti and Śruti Incarnate." *Journal of Vaishnava Studies* 15, no. 1 (fall): 31–70.

Hospital, Clifford. 1995. "*Līlā* in Early Vaiṣṇava Thought." In *The Gods at Play:* Līlā *in South Asia*, ed. William S. Sax, 21–34. New York: Oxford University Press.

Hudson, D. Dennis. 2008. *The Body of God: An Emperor's Palace for Krishna in Eighth-Century Kanchipuram*. New York: Oxford University Press.

Jarow, E. H. Rick. 2003. *Tales for the Dying: The Death Narrative of the "Bhāgavata-Purāṇa."* Albany: SUNY Press.

Jha, Ganganath. 1999. *Manusmrti, with the "Manubhāṣya" of Medhātithi*. 1920–1939. Reprint, Delhi: Motilal Banarsidass.

Joshi, Rasik Vihari. 1974. "*Catuḥślokī* or *Saptaślokī Bhāgavata*: A Critical Study." *Purāṇa* 16, no. 1:26–46.

Keith, Arthur Berriedale. 1969. *Aitareya Āraṇyaka*. Oxford: Clarendon Press.

Khandelwal, Meena. 2009. "Research on Hindu Women's Renunciation Today: State of the Field." *Religion Compass* 3, no. 6:1003–14.

Kinsley, David. 1988. *Hindu Goddesses: Visions of the Divine Feminine in the Hindu Religious Tradition*. Berkeley: University of California Press.

Kloetzli, Randy, and Alf Hiltebeitel. 2004. "Kāla." In *The Hindu World*, ed. Sushil Mittal and Gene Thursby, 553–86. London: Routledge.

Klostermeier, Klaus K. 1994. "Calling God Names: Reflections on the Divine Names in Hindu and Biblical Traditions." *Journal of Vaiṣṇava Studies* 2, no. 2:59–69.

——. 2007. *A Survey of Hinduism*. 3rd ed. Albany: SUNY Press.

Larson, Gerald James. 1979. *Classical Sāṁkhya: An Interpretation of Its History and Meaning*. 2nd ed. Delhi: Motilal Banarsidass.

Mason, David. 2009. *Theatre and Religion on Krishna's Stage: Performing in Vrindavan*. New York: Palgrave Macmillan.

Meister, Michael W. 1996. "Man and Man-Lion: The Philadelphia Narasiṁha." *Artibus Asiae* 56, no. 3/4:291–301.

Meulenbeld, Gerrit Jan. 1999. *A History of Indian Medical Literature*. 5 vols. Groningen, Neth.: Forsten.

Minkowski, Christopher. 2001. "The Paṇḍit as Public Intellectual: The Controversy over Virodha or Inconsistency in the Astronomical Sciences." In *The Pandit: Traditional Scholarship in India*, ed. Axel Michaels, 79–96. New Delhi: Manohar.

——. 2005. "Nīlakaṇṭha's Vedic Readings in the Harivaṁśa Commentary." In *Epics, Khilas, and Purāṇas: Continuities and Ruptures; Proceedings of the Third Dubrovnik International Conference on the Sanskrit Epics and Purāṇas*, ed. Petteri Koskikallio, 411–33. Zagreb: Croatian Academy of Sciences and Art.

Monier-Williams, M. 2015. *A Sanskrit English Dictionary Etymologically and Philologically Arranged*. Springfield, Va.: Nataraj Books.

O'Flaherty, Wendy Doniger. 1980. *The Origins of Evil in Hindu Mythology*. 2nd ed. Berkeley: University of California Press.

——. 1984. *Dreams, Illusion, and Other Realities*. Chicago: University of Chicago Press.
Richman, Paula, ed. 1991. *Many Rāmāyaṇas: The Diversity of a Narrative Tradition in South Asia*. Berkeley: University of California Press.
Rocher, Ludo. 1986. "The Purāṇas." In *A History of Indian Literature*, vol. 2, fasc. 3, ed. Jan Gonda. Wiesbaden: Harrassowitz.
Sardella, Ferdinando, and Abhishek Ghosh. 2013. "Modern Reception and Text Migration of the Bhāgavata Purāṇa." In *The Bhāgavata Purāṇa: Sacred Text and Living Tradition*, ed. Ravi M. Gupta and Kenneth R. Valpey, 221–47. New York: Columbia University Press.
Schweig, Graham M. 2005. *Dance of Divine Love: India's Classic Sacred Love Story; The Rāsa Līlā of Krishna*. Princeton: Princeton University Press.
Sheridan, Daniel P. 1994. "Śrīdhara and His Commentary on the Bhāgavata Purāṇa." *Journal of Vaiṣṇava Studies* 2, no. 3:45–66.
Sheth, Noel. 1984. *The Divinity of Krishna*. Delhi: Manoharlal, 1984.
Smith, Frederick M. 2006. *The Self Possessed: Deity and Spirit Possession in South Asian Literature and Civilization*. New York: Columbia University Press.
Soifer, Deborah A. 1991. *The Myths of Narasiṁha and Vāmana: Two Avatars in Cosmological Perspective*. Albany: SUNY Press.
Theodor, Ithamar. 2010. *Exploring the "Bhagavad Gītā": Philosophy, Structure and Meaning*. Farnham, Surrey, U.K.: Ashgate.
Thielemann, Selina. 2000. *Singing the Praises Divine: Music in the Hindu Tradition*. New Delhi: A.P.H. Publishing.
Thompson, Richard L. 1996. *Vedic Cosmography and Astronomy*. Los Angeles: Bhaktivedanta Book Trust.
Tracy, David. 1994. *Plurality and Ambiguity: Hermeneutics, Religion, Hope*. Chicago: University of Chicago Press.
Tull, Herman W. 2004. "Karma." In *The Hindu World*, ed. Sushil Mittal and Gene Thursby, 309–31. London: Routledge.
Valpey, Kenneth Russell. 2006. *Attending Kṛṣṇa's Image: Caitanya Vaiṣṇava Mūrti-sevā as Devotional Truth*. London: Routledge.
——. 2009. "The *Bhagavata Purana* as a *Mahabharata* Reflection." In *Parallels and Comparisons: Proceedings of the Fourth Dubrovnik International Conference on the Sanskrit Epics and Puranas, September 2005*, ed. Petteri Koskikallio, 257–78. Zagreb: Croatian Academy of Sciences and Arts.
van Buitenen, J. A. B., trans. and ed. 1973. *The Mahābhārata: 1. The Book of the Beginning*. Chicago: University of Chicago Press.
Vaudeville, Charlotte. 1980. "The Govardhan Myth in North India." *Indo-Iranian Journal* 22:1–45.
Vemsani, Lavanya. 2009. "Narasiṁha, the Supreme Deity of Andhra Pradesh: Tradition and Innovation in Hinduism—an Examination of the Temple Myths, Folk Stories, and Popular Culture." *Journal of Contemporary Religion* 24, no. 1:35–52.
Venkatakrishnan, Anand. 2013. "A Tale of Two *Smṛtis*: Scholastic Challenges to the Sanskrit Scriptural Canon." University of Toronto 2013 Graduate Student Conference. Unpublished manuscript.
Waghorne, Joanne Punzo, and Norman Cutler, eds. 1996. *Gods of Flesh, Gods of Stone: The Embodiment of Divinity in India*. New York: Columbia University Press.

INDEX

bees: in garlands worn by the Lord, 63, 72, 73, 140, 147; gatekeepers and, 62, 64; Hari, singing the stories of, 61, 249n68; honey bee, occupied with sweetness, 250n75; messenger bee, addressed by *gopī*, 175, 176–77, 219–22, 223–24, 274nn74–75; Mohinī, drawn to, 141; sages, compared to, 183–84, 275n9
Bhagavad Gītā, 19, 186, 246n46, 252n13, 258n9, 258n11
Bhagavān. *See* Krishna; Vishnu
Bhāgavata Purāṇa: Bhagavān as import of entire Purāṇa, 279n5; bhakti, main message of, 1, 16, 27, 67; Book Ten, importance of, 3, 7–8, 24, 52–53, 160; Brahmasūtra, comparisons to, 199–200; central themes and concerns, 9–13, 14, 21, 28, 53, 78, 155; commentators, background, 5–6; cosmogony and time, 55; defining characteristics of, 52–53; devotional theology of, 179; dharma, transcended by bhakti, 11, 13, 155, 211, 218, 228n10; first verse, commentary on, 18–19, 199–204, 229n2; gatekeepers' story, emphasis on, 205–10; Krishna, life of as main attraction, 2, 3; *maṇḍala* as key to structure of text, 3, 7–8, 228n8, 273n69; *phala-śruti* as expected result of reading the text, 20–21; as portable, 19–20; Puṁsāvana vow, mentioned, 117; Rāmāyaṇa, retelling of, 155–56, 227n1; *rasa* in, 9, 29, 228n9, 229n4, 260n32; *rāsa-līlā* as the central passage of, 171; service to hearing, 230n11; Śuka, reciting text to Parīkṣit, 8, 15, 36, 42, 43, 50–51, 90, 155, 192, 197, 279n6; superiority of, 196–97; theistic Sāṁkhya, teaching, 67, 77, 230n14; translation challenges, 16–18, 21–23, 24, 25–26; Upaniṣads connection, 18–19; Veda, as authenticating, 4, 43; Vishnu, revealing essential verses of, 51–52; Vyāsa, composed by, 28, 31
bhāgavatas (worshippers): Ambarīṣa, praise for, 151; becoming a *bhāgavata*, 2; Bharata as a perfect *bhāgavata*, 93; Citraketu as a heroic *bhāgavata*, 116; exalted *bhāgavatas*, 112, 135, 154, 260n32, 260n39; Manus, as descendants of, 8; Prahlāda, protected by Nṛsiṁha, 119; Vishnu, never wishing for oneness with, 67
bhakti (devotion): Bhāgavata, as central theme of, 1, 16, 27, 67; bhakti path, kings receiving corrections on, 77–78; bhakti yoga, 29, 30, 31, 186, 190, 218, 259n24, 267n20; cultivation of, 15; dharma and, 13, 21, 30–31, 107, 155, 211, 218, 228n10; exalted bhakti, lesson in, 219; foot dust in bhakti tradition, 253n15; impurities, destroying, 103, 109–10; Kapila, delineating practice of, 75; Krishna and, 21, 30, 103, 194; Kumāra brothers, lacking in, 207, 245n38; of Prahlāda, 15, 126, 228n10; reversing power of, 9–13. *See also gopīs*
Bhaktivedanta (commentator): on *aṅga-saṁśrayā* as the Lord's better half, 266n11; on *ātmābhicāraḥ* as a transgression against oneself, 264n5; Caitanya tradition, belonging to, 5; on the child-sages, 208, 245n39, 245n41; on the devotees of the Lord, 232n24, 244n34, 246n46, 263n9, 264n2; on the gatekeepers, 209, 246nn44–45; on gems, emerging from the ocean, 262n4; on the *gopīs*, 272n60, 272n63; on Hiraṇyakaśipu, 261n3, 261n6; on meditation on the personal form of Nārāyaṇa, 247n51; on messengers of Yama, confusion of the, 258n18; on partiality in reception of the Lord's mercy, 231n21; on Vaikuṇṭha, time having no influence in, 245n38; Western audiences, commentary geared toward, 6
Bharata (sage-king): deer, transformation into, 94–97, 256n10, 256n16; fawn and, 95–97, 256nn11–12; Rāma, as brother of, 155, 156–57; retreat to hermitage,

Ṛṣabha (king), 46, 90, 91–94, 255n1, 255n5, 256n9
Rudra (form of Shiva), 60, 82, 115, 116, 140, 260n38

Śaṁkara (teacher), 19, 21, 153
Sāṁkhya tradition, 186, 268n31; *guṇas* in the Sāṁkhya thought system, 257n4, 258n17, 268n32, 270n48; Kapila as speaker of Sāṁkhya philosophy, 67, 77; *prakṛti*, analysis of, 258n8; *puruṣa* in Sāṁkhya dualism, 248n57; Sāṁkhya school, represented in Bhāgavata, 3–4; theistic Sāṁkhya, 67, 230n14; Vedāntic Sāṁkhya, 248n58. *See also prakṛti*; *puruṣa*
Sanātana (commentator): on the beauty of Yaśodā, 266n6; on bowing for obeisance, 267n16; on Brahmā as the guru of *bhaktas*, 266n11; on the clouds of final destruction, 269n37; on devotees, covering of, 269n44; on divine activities as inexpressible, 267n19; on fulfillment of devotees' desires, 267n20; on the *gopīs*, 220–21, 271n59; on Krishna, 266n8, 266n14, 270n47, 271nn54–56; on Mount Govardhana, lifting of, 270n50, 271n52; on Parīkṣit, addressed by Śuka, 271n58; on *puruṣārthas*, 268n27; on Rādhā and the messenger bee, 220
Śāstrī, Kṛṣṇaśaṇkara, 4, 25, 279n3
Satī (daughter/wife), 138, 251n3; as Bhavānī, 81, 99, 138–39, 252n11, 257n22; Dakṣa and, 78–79, 81–83, 252n10, 252n12, 253n18, 253n20, 254n23, 254n25; Dharmaśāstras, alluding to injunctions in, 253n19; yogic practice of, 254n24
Śaunaka (sage), 23, 37; as a leader of sages, 192, 233n38; Sūta, interactions with, 28, 45, 55; Ugraśravas and recitation of Bhāgavata, 1–2, 18, 29
Schweig, Graham, 272n61, 272n64, 273n72
Shiva, 101, 254n23; anger of, 49, 84, 236n13; auspiciousness and, 72, 79, 82, 251n5, 253n16, 262n6; Brahmā and, 82, 84, 92, 139, 253n18; Citraketu, friendship with, 116, 260nn39–40; Dakṣa, receiving animosity from, 78–80, 82, 83, 88, 251–52n5, 253n18, 254n26; as destructive, 238n27; Durvāsā, seeking refuge with, 153; ghosts and spirits, associated with, 80, 82, 251n2; Indra as Shiva personified, 255n31; Kumara brothers, approaching, 253n17; Mārkaṇḍeya, blessing with long life, 192, 195; Mohinī, chasing after, 142; poison, drinking, 138–39, 253n20; as Rudra, 60, 82, 115, 116, 140, 260n38; Satī, as spouse of, 78, 81–84, 251n3, 252nn10–11; travel in the mind, 253n21; Vishnu, as a devotee of, 254n26
Śiṣupāla (demon king), 23, 119–20, 177, 178, 206, 246n43
Sītā, 47, 155–56, 156–57, 255n32
Soifer, Deborah, 11, 228n10
Śrī. *See* Lakṣmī
Śrīdhara (commentator), 197, 229n5, 230n11, 235n7, 257n19, 260n39, 273nn72–73; on Ajāmila, 211, 257n2, 259n25; on *ātma-bhāva*, 278n1; on the atomic parts of objects, 242n14; on *avatāras*, Brahmā's reference to, 238n30; on bhakti, 240n43; on Bharata and fall from yogic practice, 256n14; on Bhīṣma, epithet for, 232n30; on the body and what is related to it, 235n5; on the bondage of *saṁsāra*, 275n13; on Book Ten of Bhāgavata, 53; on *brahman*, constructing forms of, 248n61; commentary of, 5, 17, 19; on desirelessness, 276n24; on devotees and no desire to live in heaven, 264n3; on dissolution, causes of, 241n9; on divine names, invocation of, 215, 216; on eightfold yogic path, 244n37, 247n51; on fault